749863   £15·00

Monetary Theory and the Demand for Money

Monetary Theory and the Demand for Money

Douglas Fisher

Mathematical Appendices by
Jeffrey I. Bernstein

Martin Robertson

First published in 1978 by Martin Robertson & Co. Ltd.,
17 Quick Street, London N1 8HL

ISBN 0 85520 142 8

Filmset in 'Monophoto' Times 10 on 12 pt. by
Richard Clay (The Chaucer Press), Ltd., Bungay, Suffolk
and printed in Great Britain by
Fletcher & Son Ltd., Norwich

Contents

Preface

This is a study of the modern literature on the demand for money as it has been developed in theory and tested empirically. While occasionally we will consider the influence of different formulations of the demand for money on various macroeconomic models, the principal questions concern the appropriate formulation of the demand-for-money function (and the empirical record). The methods employed are both microeconomic and macroeconomic and range in mathematical complexity from the simple-intuitive to dynamic consumption and investment; indeed, a considerable amount of consumer and producer theory is scattered about, although the most difficult parts are in the last three chapters and in the mathematical appendices. This alone suggests that advanced and graduate students or specialists in the area of monetary studies will be the principal users of this study.

While this is a survey, and sticks pretty close to the literature, there are some original contributions as well. Some of these are scattered about (notably in Chapter 2, on the definition of money), but both Chapter 6 (on the term structure) and the mathematical appendices contain new results. The former uses formal term-structure theory – in the mean-variance and dynamic consumption models – to consider the question of which interest rate belongs in the demand for money. The answer given is that either a long or a short rate could work best, but that a general preference (in the theory) for the long-term rate is provable, at least in the context of the two models just mentioned. Indeed, these are exact results which are intended to supplement the vast amount of seemingly contradictory empirical results one presently finds in the literature. The mathematical appendices, as well, provide results in two areas.

1. In Appendix A there is developed, in addition to a survey of the microeconomic (consumer) theory of the demand for money, a general utility function (providing all of the Neoclassical restrictions) to deal with the dual budget constraint formulation of the consumer's demand for money.

2. In Appendix B there is developed a model of producer behaviour – properly constrained – which generates a business demand for money that avoids placing money in the production function.

The mathematical appendices are the work of Jeffrey I. Bernstein.

In preparing this summary of a complex literature I have aimed at presenting things in a non-controversial manner, emphasising similarities rather than differences and eschewing doctrinal disputes. Furthermore, I have followed the literature pretty closely, even allowing the originators of some ideas space in these pages, in the form of generous quotations. Notation has been a bit of a problem, though, and I am afraid that in several cases I had to switch (being careful, I hope, to define everything) when it seemed inadvisable to alter the original severely. Thus, I generally employed lower-case letters for 'real' and upper-case letters for 'nominal' variables; but at several points, when consumption and investment functions were flying about, I felt I had to abandon the practice. I also defined the nominal interest rate as i and the real rate as r, but in Chapter 6 (on the term structure), where there were no real rates, I cheerfully abandoned the practice so that R could define a yield and r a one-period interest rate. But for the rest I hope I was consistent.

A considerable number of graduate students in monetary and macro-economics at Claremont Graduate School and Concordia University have looked at and commented on my material as it evolved, and I am very grateful for their assistance. Most helpful, as I recall, were May-Lin Clutterbuck, David Glyer, Jacques Garon, Amy Haasz, Rasik Hathi, Ki-Jung Joeng, Kotaro Norizoe, Carlo Tucci, Stylianos Vournas and Jose Vriljczak. Jon Breslaw and Donald Ebberler also made useful comments. But my principal debt is to my colleague at Concordia University, Jeffrey I. Bernstein, who has read through all of the recent drafts of the book and made numerous suggestions for improvement, some of them backed by hard work. Indeed, our joint efforts are identified at certain points in this study, and Jeffrey has contributed the two appendices.

But, of course, I am responsible for all remaining errors.

Douglas Fisher
North Carolina State University, Raleigh
November 1977

To My Wife

CHAPTER 1

Introduction and Summary

1.1 Introduction

The subject of monetary economics has expanded so considerably in recent years that a major research effort is required to keep abreast of developments. While the main literature is generated around policy issues, particularly in these inflationary days, considerable interest is still expressed in some of the traditional topics. Perhaps the traditional topic with the longest pedigree is that of the demand for money. That the subject is alive and well and (for those who care) relevant is a fact of much interest to economists, for the demand-for-money literature considers a number of topics that are common to many other areas. Furthermore, many of the tools we are now comfortable with were actually fashioned to deal with monetary problems. Indeed, there is a sense of familiarity we all feel when we approach the monetary debate; unfortunately, however, the familiarity is not also a relaxed one, as any reader of the classic modern studies by Keynes, Hicks, Patinkin, Pesek and Saving, and Leijonhufvud will testify.

This project on the demand for money, by taking a very broad swing through the literature, is designed to underscore the unity of purpose and result of a truly remarkable literature. It will cover both the theoretical and the empirical work and will seek to establish important generalisations. It almost goes without saying that, while the theory will often be examined in its own light, the principal uses of the theoretical discussion will lie in three areas:

1. to generate testable hypotheses (in some sense);
2. to provide an interpretation of certain well-established empirical results; and
3. to suggest *a priori* restrictions of use in empirical work.

There will be many examples of each of these three uses.

The book will be divided into six main chapters, each a survey of a particular topic as it bears on the demand for money. The topics covered will be:

1. the definition of money;
2. the wealth and real balance effects;

3. the macroeconomic (and empirical) demand for money;
4. portfolio and inventory-theoretic analysis;
5. the term structure of interest rates; and
6. inflation and growth.

The rationale for this selection and arrangement of topics is as follows. To begin with the arrangement, the principal argument for this division is that it corresponds to the actual compartmentalisation in the literature; thus, less repetition of reference occurs when one follows the topics as they are actually presented. With regard to the selection of topics, one can only remark that this set of topics covers the entire literature on the subject of the demand for money except for that on 'international money'. This latter is a rapidly developing area which has had considerable success in explaining recent inflation (via supply effects) but has produced only minimal results on the demand for money. I suspect that this situation will change rapidly. The principal weakness one encounters in following the literature (too closely) is that one is in danger of accepting the division of labour common in the area and may miss important generalities. We will, consequently, attempt as broad a survey as possible, keeping in mind the problem described by Leijonhufvud as follows:

> The increasing amount of empirical findings accumulated and organized within the given conceptual framework requires an increased effort on the part of the individual who would learn the 'state' of the field. It also creates more questions than in settles and tends, therefore, to lead to increasing specialization. When this happens, it becomes more and more difficult for the individual to avoid scientific myopia, and to keep the subject in perspective and maintain a dispassionate overview of the entire field. In particular, it becomes difficult to keep in mind that alternative, latent Visions, capable of organizing the same collections of 'facts', must always exist – or to imagine what these alternatives would be.[1]

Nevertheless, no latent Vision will emerge in this study, although it is hoped that the existing areas of consensus will be made clear.

1.2   A summary of the argument

Throughout this study the various chapters will contain both microeconomic and macroeconomic sections, and in some cases both types of material will be blended, pretty much as the literature is often presented. Thus, the task undertaken in Chapter 2 is to make as clear as possible what is involved in defining the role of money (microeconomics) and in defining money for empirical studies (macroeconomics); the survey of the literature here is generally broader than in the other chapters of the study. A microeconomic definition may concentrate on the properties of the medium of exchange (Debreu) or it may concentrate on the characteristics (Lancaster); furthermore, among the properties/characteristics, one must sort out the arguments concerning the role of the unit of account, the store of value, the medium of exchange and even the means of payment (Clower). A macroeconomic definition, on the other hand, is an aggregation. Here, what one looks for is either a comparatively successful result with the aggregate (Friedman) or, formally, satisfaction of the composite goods theorem (or the condition of substitutability). Finally in Chapter 2, a brief survey of the empirical evidence is presented, as it pertains to the various aggregations of the data (e.g., broad versus narrow money or business versus private demand, to take product and demand function aggregations separately).

The most perplexing debate in the monetary literature, and possibly in economics, is over the Pigou-real balance–wealth effects and their respective roles in the adjustment process in the various microeconomic and macroeconomic models; this broad topic is developed in Chapter 3. There is an interesting micro-foundation literature here (Patinkin, Lloyd, Clower) as well as what one might provisionally term a micro-based macro-foundation literature (Patinkin; Pesek and Saving). We are not directly interested in the various effects here except in so far as they imply restrictions, etc., in our demand for money functions, but we will nevertheless take a fairly broad turn through the literature in Chapter 3 in order to try to establish important generalisations about both static and dynamic aspects of the theory with particular reference to which variables one might expect to influence the demand for money. This leads us deep into formal consumer theory and into the development of homogeneity and other properties of demand and even utility functions (for ultimate use, possibly, in empirical work). Finally, the microeconomic discussion initiated in this chapter is continued and the various strands of consumer theory (from Samuelson to Kalman and Dusansky) are drawn together in the first mathematical appendix at the end of the book.

In Chapter 3, as well, we develop an approach to the broad topic of wealth effects which is adhered to throughout much of the book. That is, after presenting the basic results – usually in a static model – extensions into dynamics, particularly using the apparatus of adjustment to equilibrium (as in Patinkin), are presented. The principal conclusions of the disequilibrium analysis, as is well known, concerns the fact that in such a case the structure of the model is directly relevant, since demands (for example) will normally be frustrated; this implies that the typical 'reduced forms' of this literature may very well be seriously mis-specified (at least in the cases when disequilibrium is prolonged). As well, in this chapter, a running commentary on the empirical work is attached, often in the footnotes.

The literature most widely read on the demand for money is surveyed in Chapter 4; this subject is the (empirical) macroeconomic demand for money. The typical study here is of a single-equation model, and in practically every case there are empirical results purporting to illustrate the researcher's particular hypothesis. This literature is relatively simply grouped into Keynesian and Monetarist streams; but, it is pointed out, this grouping is mainly the result of an *a priori* vision rather than of one's model choice or, especially, results. It is shown here that the polar theories cannot in general be distinguished on the basis of theoretical predictions, and in particular that what we know – that the demand for money is (probably) a stable function of a few variables (an income or wealth variable and an interest rate) – is consistent with both Keynesian and Monetarist formulations. Nevertheless, considerable ingenuity has been exercised in this vast literature – particularly in the efforts to locate precautionary and speculative demands and, of course, in the effort to find a liquidity trap – and there are some firm results to show for this work. Also in Chapter 4, we consider the rapidly growing literature on the stability of the macroeconomic demand for money; for some time now this has been accepted, but studies using recent observations have begun to bring in findings that the current monetary disturbances have led to shifts in the demand function. Finally, some results for the lag specification of the demand for money are discussed, and some results for the business demand are given; both sets of findings establish further worries about the aggregations commonly employed in the literature.

Both Chapter 5 and Chapter 6 are more technical in their nature but on no account are they peripheral to the discussion. The first part of Chapter 5 is devoted to the presentation of the standard portfolio model – presented as if it were a problem in consumer theory – on the grounds that it provides asset demand functions that one could estimate; one of these assets, that is to say, could be money (especially if a suitable explicit rate of return on money could be found). The main point, though, is to show how the theoretical restrictions carry through to the empirical work (little of which has been used, unfortunately, on the demand for money). Following a section summarising Tobin's generalisation of Keynes's liquidity preference function, using the portfolio model, and some discussion of the limitations of mean-variance analysis (as well as some recent developments on the demand for money), we turn to the second part of the chapter, and the inventory-theoretic model. This approach, it turns out, provides some significant differences to ponder.

1. It generally provides lower *a priori* income elasticities (at least in some versions).
2. It is solved via cost minimisation rather than (expected) utility maximisation.

3. It seems to fit the business demand rather better than the private demand for money.

Interesting recent work exists on this approach and in particular we seem to be moving towards an effective reconciliation of the 'utility theory' with the 'transactions costs' approach. Then, the relevant theoretical and empirical material on the business demand for money is gathered into a long section of its own, at the end of Chapter 5. This latter is justifiable since:

1. there is considerable empirical evidence that the demand functions (as functions of the same variables) differ; and
2. the models employed on the business demand are usually of the transactions costs variety, of which the inventory-theoretic is a case in point.

In addition, there is a second mathematical appendix at the end of the book, which presents a reworking of producer theory and the firm's demand for money, considering how money might legitimately be entered into the production function (S. Fischer) and how, more generally, it might not.

Chapter 6 works towards a resolution of which interest rate – a long rate or a short rate – is most appropriate for the demand for money. To set the stage, firstly, the formal literature on the term structure of interest rates – beginning with Hicks and running up to the recent work of Modigliani and Sutch – is carefully scoured for a rather skimpy collection of propositions of relevance to the demand for money. A few results are obtained, in Monetarist and Keynesian frameworks, but the various *ad hoc* propositions do not generalise easily; furthermore, the empirical tests are hopelessly disparate, with long-term rates working best in some cases and short-term rates in others. Part of the answer lies in the facts: *if* short rates are strongly influenced by the government, and *if* long rates are left free to expectational factors, then 'model specification' (as to its ability to comprehend these facts) is related to the results one gets. Furthermore, there are some *a priori* arrangements of a particular stringent nature (not necessarily satisfied by the results), such as Keynes's preference for a long-term rate based on an aggregation, itself adopted for convenience.

The second major part of Chapter 6 introduces two recent and general models of the term structure in the context of money holding. The first of these is a dynamic consumption model, which follows some suggestive work by Stiglitz and Green. In this case, when money is added into a three-period model, and made part of the general equilibrium, it is possible to deduce that

1. the appropriate interest rate for the demand for intermediate balances (first- and second-period balances) is a long-term rate, on account of an aggregation requirement; and

    2. the appropriate interest rate for the demand for final balances (third-period balances) is either a long-term or a short-term rate depending on the relative weight of long- and short-term securities in the portfolio.

The second model used in Chapter 6 is, quite naturally, the mean-variance model, following in this case an early paper by Bierwag and Grove (who did not put money into the problem). It turns out that in this case the short-term rate does not affect the demand for money (first- and second-period balances) in a determinate way, while the long-term rate does (in all but one case). Furthermore, the demand for final balances (third-period balances) has the same characteristics, but in this case one must first specify the slope of the actual yield curve. Only when the yield curve is down-sloping (long rates less than short rates) is the negative relationship obtained. Finally, some explicit results for an 'expected interest rate', unique in the literature on the demand for money, are obtained. The conclusion, inevitably, is that the disparate empirical results may be correct, although a further investigation (with the implied restrictions from this discussion) is necessary to prove this.

    Chapter 7 continues the discussion of dynamics from Chapter 3. Firstly, the vast and growing literature on inflation and hyperinflation is investigated for its bearing on questions of the demand for money. The earliest literature here is grouped around the Gibson Paradox, but the chapter starts with the simplest case – the hyperinflation debate – because the methods fit neatly into earlier discussions and because this is a case in which

    1. inflation rates seem clearly to affect the demand for money; and
    2. there is a distinct possibility that the demand for money is unstable in this case.

The Gibson Paradox – that prices and interest rates are positively related in both the short and the long run (a paradox because various models are unable to explain it) – has been discussed actively since the nineteenth century, and the leading explanations are those of Keynes–Wicksell and I. Fisher. By and large, the Fisher explanation (in terms of nominal and real interest rates) is the one that survives recent empirical tests; in a demand-for-money model this implies that both types of interest rate should enter if the relation is variable, as it seems to be.

    But Chapter 7 is also a bit of a catch-all, and here the demand for money question is turned around to consider the role of different formulations of the function itself in three popular literatures – the models of nominal income determination (Friedman), the Phillips Curve (Lipsey), and the literature on money growth. Various suggestive results are produced here – such as Friedman's claim that the demand for money is not in dispute in the Keynes–Classics debate – but in no way are these discussions intended to be complete with regard to the models discussed. Thus, only one derivation of the Phillips Curve is considered – that of Lipsey – and the interest is only in the rather sketchy dynamic formulation he proposes (leaving out disequilibrium in the money market, in particular). The last topic in the chapter, then, is the money-growth literature, particularly as it is presented by Stein and by Fischer. The following points seem to stand out, again in a survey that is only intended to be suggestive (considering that it is somewhat peripheral).

1. The polar positions – Keynes versus the Neoclassics in this case – provide exactly the same demand for money functions.

2. This explicit demand for money functions, of the nature of a 'reduced form', has all the standard variables in it, including the rate of inflation, with the standard signs. This provides a firm theoretical rationale for all of the *ad hoc* material of earlier chapters.

3. As with the disequilibrium analysis of the static case in Chapter 3, it is demonstrated that the parameters of the demand for money (and the supply, for that matter) are relevant when one is considering points off the dynamic equilibrium path.

Footnotes

1. A. Leijonhufvud, *On Keynesian Economics and the Economics of Keynes*, pp. 5–6.

CHAPTER 2

The Definition of Money

2.1 Introduction

The first problem one must tackle when considering the demand for a product (money) is the question of the definition of the product and of its price. In the case of an agricultural product such as no. 2 red wheat, this does not seem to be a particularly perplexing problem; but for some good reasons, when economists turn to money, the debate over definition is a furious one. The survey that follows, while sometimes peripheral to the demand for money problem, pursues two related streams – one micro and one macro – through the recent literature on the subject of the definition of money. The purpose is primarily to remove definitional problems from demand problems, or at least to focus attention on underlying differences in conception which produce, on occasion, important differences in conclusions.

When one 'defines' something, basically he has two choices: he can attach labels to real-world objects, in which case he is a nominalist, or he can attach labels to bundles of concepts and then search for the real-world entity that best satisfies these criteria, in which case we can call him an empiricist (on the definition of money). The nominalist has an efficient arrangement for empirical work on economic problems: he begins with a real-world entity (currency plus demand deposits), gives it a name (money), and then gets on with his work (on the demand for money). The empiricist might introduce a list of economic characteristics and then search among all of the possible types of (or aggregates of) financial instruments to find those that fit. A considerable empirical effort is required here, for invariably there will be more than one characteristic and more than one candidate for the honours.

The problem of the definition of money is also tied up with the problem of aggregation, as we shall see in the later part of this chapter. That is, since it is impossible (in practice) to think of a single service product, one must, in choosing a particular entity, suppress some factors in the data, factors that one must judge to be of lesser importance, explicitly or implicitly, than those retained. No matter which approach we take – nominalist or empiricist – so long as we have any aggregate at all, we must have this suppression (even currency consists of various denominations). Thus, by emphasising a certain

8

set of characteristics (or functions) that money must have – for example, medium of exchange, store of value and unit of account – we open the door to a host of problems of this sort. When we adopt the empirical approach we are facing the problem directly, but even when we simply attach a name to a collection the problem is there, although we are not proposing to do anything about it.

2.2 Money as a medium of exchange

In pre-Keynesian times one found both 'institutional' and 'functional' definitions of money, often, indeed, from the same pen. What seems, for example, to be a clear example of the institutional view was written by Irving Fisher, as follows.

> Any property right which is generally acceptable in exchange may be called 'money'. Its printed evidence is also called money. Hence there arise three meanings of the term money, viz. its meaning in the sense of wealth; its meaning in the sense of property; and its meaning in the sense of written evidence. From the standpoint of economic analysis the property sense is the most important.[1]

In commenting on this scheme, which clearly emphasises the institution of property, Fisher put considerable emphasis on the concept of 'general acceptability in exchange'. He was even willing to consider demand deposits as non-money, since

1. as wealth, or as the evidence of wealth, they are clearly not generally acceptable;[2] and
2. only with the institutional buttressing of legal tender status, or with the institutional force of custom, could they become generally acceptable.

Notwithstanding this preference, however, Fisher, along with a lot of economists of his time (and earlier and later), has to be put on record as favouring a definition of money at least as broad as 'narrow money' (currency plus demand deposits).[3]

The functional approach – usually listing the functions of medium of exchange, store of value and unit of account – recurs throughout the nineteenth and twentieth centuries, and will be with us for a long time to come. The most serious general problem with the functional scheme is that a technique of 'implicit definition' is also generally employed. That is, we often define an economic entity in terms of there being a market (i.e., a demand and supply) for its services (functions); this, at least, is how price theory is often worked. More particularly, we will construct a set of axioms from which a unique theoretical definition of money will emerge, *implicitly*; the empirical problem, then, becomes that of finding a real-world counterpart to the abstraction, a task that will be frustrated if the theory is worked in terms of functions jointly possessed by a large number of real-world concepts, as it is with the functions mentioned here. Consider, for example, the real-world counterpart of the Walrasian auctioneer. We will return to these problems, and to the Walrasian auctioneer, at several points in our discussion.

2.2.1   *The medium of exchange*

The medium of exchange function has the best pedigree of all the functions, but ambiguities abound. One should, of course, link this idea with the 'generally acceptable in exchange' notion of I. Fisher; indeed, this is by far the most widely employed description of what 'medium of exchange' means. But there are still some conceptual problems. One of these is that there are alternative descriptions of how to define 'medium of exchange' itself. This can even involve one in tongue-twisters, like the following from P. Wicksteed:

> As soon as this custom begins to be well established it will automatically extend and confirm itself, and the commodity in question will become a 'currency' or 'medium of exchange', the special characteristic of a medium of exchange being, that it is acceptable by a man who does not want it, or does not want it as much as what he gives for it, in order that he may exchange it for something he wants more.[4]

More conventionally, but also in somewhat the same manner, consider L. Yeager's offering:

> Nothing is more ultimate than money. Instead of going out of existence, unwanted money gets passed around until it ceases to be unwanted.[5]

That is, the special attribute of nominal money balances as a medium of exchange is that they are indestructible (unless the inflation rate reaches infinity) in this role, so long as they are 'acceptable'.

Another problem with these schemes is that one still has to deal with the complications brought about by the 'jointness' that arises because money is also wealth to its holder and is consequently a personal store of value.[6] Finally, there is the problem that what one really wants to do to preserve the best of this Classical tradition is to describe more carefully the process of exchange so that the role of money as an 'exchange intermediary' can be laid out.[7] These three elements are interwoven in the following, partly historical, paradigm.

When one defines the word 'economy' a state of economic organisation is implied. Among the reasons for forming a monetary organisation of an economy that was previously barter (or primitive), quite possibly the political dominates. That is, in order to exercise power more effectively, and/or to make the tax system more efficient, the use of money might be promoted so that all values will have a common (taxable) denominator. One of the important features of such a scheme will be the designation of what is 'legal tender'; historically, such a device might even be used to ward off competitors to the government money-creating machinery. But it is essential to note that the private sector will also develop its own monetary organisations. Since markets are often separated geographically, causing buyers to confront sellers indirectly and tending to widen the gap between bid and ask prices, a non-governmental money-creating industry will tend to emerge anyway. One thinks immediately of private bank notes and of organisational devices such as organised regional (or commodity-based) markets. One also thinks of improvements in communications and in the transport of people and goods (and gold bricks). These devices will have several uses, of course, but for our purposes here it is essential to note that each form will cost resources (which are taken from the spread between bid and ask prices in the various markets) to organise and operate; later we will want to emphasise that money creation also requires such resources.[8] One might as well note that the technology of market organisation should be analysed in a dynamic context here, in anticipation of some points we will make below; this occurs both because a stock of the 'medium' is formed and because the industry benefits from technological change. But let us state the whole argument sequentially.

Organising markets is of use to the economy and gets its fair reward in a competitive world; so too will the introduction of certain commodities – immutable, recognisable and portable – as means of payment and as stores of value. These commodities will, of course, serve as commodities as well; even so, without legal restrictions only one price will control their use. At that price, the various utilities and services of the commodity will conform to the production of those utilities and services; these services will include the monetary services. The analytical problem of 'jointness' which arises here is no more perplexing than the jointness associated with the different functions served by any commodity; that is, it is equally intractable.

To continue with the pseudo-history, we might suppose that particular traders of great reputation begin to offer promissory notes, or to issue and accept bills of exchange, based on commodities or even on commodity money, with the notes themselves serving as media of exchange. In comparison with commodity money, the paper money thus introduced represents a quantum improvement in the technique of exchange. The issuers of this form of money will profit in some way (possibly in connection with the money-lending function), and the issue of this money will continue so long as profits can be made. Again, real resources are involved in the production of the 'money'. There seems to be no particular reason not to push an analogy with a typical product market here, and, indeed, to refer to a tendency towards the equality of marginal cost and marginal revenue. Again, one can visualise the product as being manufactured by means of a production function, and one can think of the effects of technical progress in this industry. Of course the issuer of money, like the modern banker, seems to be making his money as an intermediary in some sense; indeed, it would be appropriate for him to judge his contribution in terms of the spread between two interest rates. Further, he is clearly making two markets more efficient; that is, the commodity market and the market for loans are hereby improved.

Pseudo-history marches on, and the authorities may now issue a money of their own and designate it as 'legal tender', the reasons for this improvement, as noted above, depending on the circumstances. The legal tender can still exist comfortably with other financial forms of money, although one supposes that the authorities, with the taxing system at their disposal, will quickly succumb to the temptation to drive out their competitors, either by subsidising their own money-producing operation or by explicitly increasing the cost of production of their rivals, perhaps through a tax. Both the paper money and deposit money of the government's rivals could be eliminated in this way, but if the development of a modern economy was achieved with a good measure of private initiative, it is likely that a credit network, itself useful to the government, would exist, and bank deposits would normally be preserved, possibly through a fractional reserve banking system in which the government retains the right of determining the total quantity of circulating media in the economy. This part of the paradigm, as it stands, follows Western experience pretty closely.[9]

One thing that happens when the government gets into the act is that costs and returns in the money industry can cease to reflect what might be termed their 'scarcity equivalents'. When money was commodity money – a product offering joint services – as the value of money in exchange increased its price tended to increase; further, as its usefulness in exchange increased, so too did the possibility of preserving its bulk by issuing notes based on 100 per cent cash reserves. But if the government is the sole producer of a part of the money stock, and if the government has policy objectives of its own and operates on a large scale in the money market to achieve these objectives, the actual money stock could be unequal to the money stock desired at the prevailing price level and interest rate. Of course, the system as a whole is constantly adjusting to such realities (e.g., real money balances can be destroyed in the process of spending them and driving up the price level), but it is clear that, since such adjustments take time, the authorities can consistently oppose market forces in pursuit of their own (short-run) objectives.

When a commodity market like the market for money is out of equilibrium, there are in effect two prices (or two quantities) for the product operating at the same time. Without knowing the value of the government's (partially) achieving its objectives, it is impossible to assert that a movement towards equilibrium will increase values in general; economic theory contains no such insights. This being the case, it is also impossible to assert, unequivocally, that an increase in the money stock increases welfare in all cases, although it may be shown in certain frameworks. But modern economies are generally growing, and in a growing economy the growth of the money industry may easily dominate the chance (or systematic) deviations of the monetary totals from their short-run equilibrium values; in this case economic development may be hampered by too rapid or too slow a growth of the money industry. Furthermore, the growth of this industry, like the growth of any other, is partial evidence that someone is receiving rewards, in a systematic fashion, for producing a product that is probably of (growing) use to the community; that 'somebody' will normally be both the government and the financial community.

While one is operating on the level of generality of the preceding paragraphs, and is not required to deal with actual models, one can be as generous as he wants with the specification. The Walrasian model, as one popular Classical prop, permits no such informality, and it is at this point that we touch down again on the surface of the modern debate. In particular, the adjustment mechanism that appears to best describe the Walrasian system is one in which:

> The *tatonnement* process implies that no transactions occur until equilibrium is attained (i.e., recontracting is essential); hence, anyone holding money either during the auction or till the next period is irrational. Why hold money if it is really not needed for transactions, since in equilibrium goods trade for goods ..?.. As Hahn has recently admitted 'the Walrasian economy that we have been considering, although one where the auctioneer regulates the terms at which goods shall exchange, is essentially one of barter'.[10]

But, as J. R. Hicks points out, there are several ways one might get around this restriction.[11] In a commodity or fiat money economy, a transactions cost, proportional to the volume of transactions, could exist. This cost would then be reduced by finding a commodity (or fiat money) acceptable in all markets and hence capable of reducing the volume of transactions; in this event the details of the Walrasian equilibrium are intact (net of the transactions cost). In the case of the auctioneer referred to here, one might argue that intermediate deals are in titles to property (money, then, is one such title), and only the final deals are in the property itself. Thus the role of money is again well defined as improving the intermediate exchange of titles. This we could describe as an 'institutional' definition of the role of money; of course, some rule would have to be devised for those who got stuck with the money balances at the end (the fiat money system has this feature as well).

The auctioneer, incidentally, returns in a dynamic context in Chapter 7, below.

P. Davidson argues the same point as Hicks in the following words (they follow a quotation from the same Hicks paper):

> The desire on the part of rational economic men to minimize all costs – including transactions costs, leads to the discovery that, while the introduction of a medium of exchange reduces transactions costs over a barter system, the process of clearing titles to money rather than taking delivery of the intermediary commodity itself can lower transactions costs even further.[12]

Thus, unless an efficient and general market for titles exists, certain forms of private debt will not be money:

> What prevents other kinds of private debt (e.g., trade credit; commercial paper) from becoming part of the medium of exchange is either the absence of a specific clearing institution ... or if such an institution exists its facilities are not available for most of the transactors in the community.[13]

We will argue below, however, that, if one adopts a 'means of payment' instead of a 'medium of exchange' criterion, then trade credit could be included in the definition of money. Recall, as well, that at the start of this chapter we called attention to the fact that I. Fisher also considered the exchange of titles important in the concept of money.

The struggle to define the transactions role of money has been a mighty one, and will be pursued throughout this book. In the static framework we are now considering, in addition to the institutional approaches, one finds frequent reference in recent years to uncertainty, the lack of synchronisation of receipts and payments, and the reduction of the cost of acquiring information.[14] We will discuss uncertainty and information here, returning to the other matters at other points in the study. Uncertainty, we will argue below, is the rationale for the holding of speculative and, quite possibly, precautionary balances, but not necessarily transactions balances.[15] There are, though, some writers who go further, for example, C. Goodhart:

> the need for money as a means of payment is caused by the existence of uncertainty.

and

> So the main function of money, defined as a specialized means of payment, is to meet and alleviate problems of exchange under conditions of uncertainty.

and

> transactions costs mainly, if not entirely, reflect the cost of obtaining information (i.e., of reducing uncertainty).

and even

> In a world of uncertainty there is neither the information nor the (marketing) mechanisms (e.g., a Walrasian auctioneer) available to allow equilibrium to be achieved.[16]

P. Davidson has also written on this problem, noting that

> It is the synchronous existence of money and money contracts over an uncertain future which is the basis of a monetary system whose maxim is '*money buys goods and goods buy money; but goods do not buy goods*'.[17]

The latter is a quotation from R. Clower, who is not discussing the case of uncertainty at all, but rather the expenditure constraint for his analysis of money-holding in a monetary economy.[18] Davidson's uncertainty, incidentally, does not permit itself to be expressed as a probability distribution; in this respect he is deliberately following G. L. S. Shackle, rather than J. Tobin.[19] What really matters, though, is how individuals actually act – i.e., whether in Shackle's sense or in Tobin's – and for that we are more in need of empirical work than of opinion.[20] We might conclude with a rather remarkable statement from P. Davidson:

> Thus the main characteristics of a real world monetary economy are Uncertainty, Fallibility, Covenants, Institutions, Commerce, Finance, and Trust. These are the Seven Wonders on which the Modern World is based. Simultaneously, these are the sources of the outstanding faults of a modern, monetary free market economy. . . .[21]

We should enter a strong warning here – made explicit in the works of Brunner and Meltzer – that each of the rationales just mentioned assumes that money (the 'transactions-dominating' asset) already exists:

> Uncertainty about the price-level clearly presupposes money, otherwise there would be no price-level to be uncertain about. . . . Similarly, uncertainty about the timing of payments and the non-synchronous nature of payments schedules only imply the existence of an inventory problem but do not explain the concentration of these inventories on a small subset of assets.[22]

The answer that Brunner and Meltzer give is to base the case for the existence of money on its special ability to provide information to transactors; thus,

> it is the uneven distribution of information and not the existence of an undifferentiated uncertainty that induces individuals to search for, and social groups to accept, alternatives to barter,[23]

Thus we are led to a 'unit of account' definition of money which emphasises that calculating in money terms reduces the 'matrix of prices' one needs to know to be fully informed about relative values:

> The gain from the use of a unit of account is analogous to the gain that comes from introducing a common unit of measure such as height, weight, or temperature.[24]

But the case for the 'information approach' does not rest on the existence question alone; Brunner and Meltzer also point out that the 'medium of exchange' function can be explained in their framework. Thus, an economic agent normally uses resources to obtain information ('invests in information') and to produce market exchanges. Since he includes this calculation in his own optimising decisions, under certain conditions,

> the production of information is optimized when the loss in welfare due to the use of endowed resources in the production of information is matched by the gain in welfare associated with more information.[25]

The latter are associated with the marginal utility of an improved trading position and with reduced uncertainty. This extension of the analysis, though, appears to presuppose the existence of money (the unit of account did not, since it could be imposed); on net,

> There are many stages of development between barter and a fully monetary economy. At some stage, a few assets are used with dominant frequency in transactions.... Thus, money as a medium of exchange, as a transaction-dominating asset, results from the opportunities offered by the distribution of incomplete information and the search by potential transactors to develop transactions chains that save resources.[26]

In any event, the Brunner and Meltzer model seems particularly useful in describing the transactions demand for money in a flexible way however much it helps in dealing with the frustrating issue of how to describe formally how money has come to exist.

We will return to the Brunner and Meltzer approach in Chapters 4 and 5, but for now let us consider a contribution to the discussion of transactions costs by J. Niehans, who discusses some of the technicalities involved. He notes, especially, that transaction costs include those of

> communications,
> information,
> the drawing up of accounts,
> the keeping of records, and
> the inspection, weighing and measuring of the items exchanged,

to which one might add the insurance against losses. Thus, he warns, while 'some may argue that all transactions costs are really costs of gathering information ... it may be better not to be dogmatic about this'.[27] He cites Brunner and Meltzer. It is worth noting that in his own paper Niehans assumes that transactions costs are paid out of an imaginary central fund, rather than from production and consumption flows, precluding 'consideration of some of the most fundamental problems'. J. Ostroy constructs a transactions theory of money which also does not depend on uncertainty – 'price uncertainty is neither necessary nor sufficient to explain the presence of a medium of exchange'[28] – but on money's information-providing capacity. Then, in contrast to Brunner and Meltzer, Ostroy does not rely on any unique properties of the monetary commodity but on 'the record keeping function of money' and its superiority in this respect in a cost-minimising framework. In this case *any* 'money' – without reference to any 'transactions-dominating' characteristic – will provide the necessary cost-reducing information to establish a case for its existence.

2.2.2 *Some further microeconomic aspects of medium of exchange theory*

The mainstream argument on the microeconomic definition of money can be found in Patinkin.[29] Money, usually, does not reward the holder with any cash return, and, while it deteriorates at the rate of inflation, so do all other assets denominated in money terms; only for very rapid inflation will this aspect dominate. This has led to the notion of a 'non-pecuniary' (and, unfortunately, unobservable) return to money which occurs as a direct service to consumers or provides the rationale for money's use as an input in the firm's production function.[30] In Patinkin, for example, money is entered as an argument in the utility function, not because of any direct utility or because of any utility associated with *spending* money, but because of the utility associated with holding money. This utility is explained as the result of what happens when an individual runs out of cash:

> Assume also that an individual who runs out of cash during the week can meet the situation in one of two ways. Either he can default temporarily on any payment that he is called upon to make – a course of action that is assumed to generate some embarrassment for him; or he can replenish his balances by achieving an intraweek redemption (at their maturity value) of the bonds he holds – an action which is assumed to necessitate some extra bother on his part.[31]

The debate here is between putting nominal money into both the utility function (along with the price level) and the budget constraint, or putting it only into the budget constraint. In the latter case, some further function should be stated for money if the solution is not to be uninteresting. In the case of the former, the reluctance of economists to swallow *ad hoc* models has to be overcome. There is considerable discussion of these problems in Chapter 3 and especially in Appendix A.

By analogy, if nothing else, one can also put money into the investment function of firms using, as a prior step, money in the firm's financial budget constraint (for availability of cash flow or other reasons) and/or money in the production function. Patinkin considers the role of money as a producer's good, but here, instead of considering money as a direct factor of production, he makes use of the inventory theories of Baumol and of Tobin.[32] Again, it is inconvenience that dominates (along with different firm efficiency in cash management and differences in brokerage fees paid), with this time an objective (rather than a subjective) penalty cost attached to the running out of money during the payments period.

In recent years a literature has developed around the proposition that money is best conceived of as a 'means of payment', or even as a 'means of final payment', rather than as a medium of exchange; we have not made any distinct use of this concept to this point. Briefly, as a 'means of payment' we wish to emphasise what actually transpires when a commodity changes hands (for money). Thus, while a medium of exchange is anything that helps mediate exchanges (e.g., a stock exchange facility), a means of payment concentrates, as noted, on the actual payment process; in this event, payment by credit card is (roughly) equivalent to payment by cash and ought to be so appreciated in the literature. This distinction is not much debated in the literature (Friedman and Schwartz, for example, totally ignore it),[33] but, even so, there are some variations on the theme. One of those, as already suggested above, is that of C. Goodhart, who prefers the 'means of *final* payment'. Thus, in his view, payment by cheque is not final (it must be cleared), and 'it is ... the provision of adequate transmission facilities, as well as the fixed price ratio, that makes demand deposits a substitute means of payment alongside currency'.[34] Furthermore, a credit arrangement is involved (and one does not want to confuse money and credit!).[35] Credit cards (a form of trade credit, then), which do not involve the individual's credit as such, are also not a means of final payment. The final payment to the seller occurs when the credit card company pays up (or, rather, when its cheque is cleared); the final payment by the buyer occurs when his cheque to the credit card company is cleared. These are 'media of exchange' but not means of final payment, even though, usually, the buyer cannot reverse the arrangement.[36] Any warranty arrangement is beside the point, either here, with the credit card, or above, with the cheque drawn on the demand deposit account.

2.2.3   *Some macroeconomic aspects of medium of exchange theory*

Much macroeconomic work, as we shall see below, takes an essentially empirical and thus eclectic approach to the problem of the definition of money, but there is a body of literature that attempts an *a priori* approach based on the medium of exchange concept. By far the most comprehensive of the works in that literature is that of B. Pesek and T. Saving, who, as well, argue that money, including demand deposits in its total, is net wealth to society. Money, indeed, is contrasted with debt; the contrast is clearly defined in that debt pays interest while money does not. Debt, in its turn, because it is an asset for some and a liability for others, is not itself net wealth. We are not interested here in their other conclusions, but rather in the attempt to set up *a priori* conditions that will produce a usable definition of money. This consists of three conditions, following Friedman and Schwartz's summary of their argument.[37]

For the first, they argue that 'commodity money and fiat money are assets to their holders and liabilities to no one', a position that is clearly admissible, although the problems do not stop here. W. Smith, for example,[38] points out that, if government debt, which is interest-bearing, is also not regarded as one of their liabilities by private wealth-holders, then an open market operation (e.g., a purchase of debt for fiat money) results merely in an exchange of one asset for another and not in any obvious conclusions about the change in net wealth as the consequence of monetary policy (without some further discussion of interest rate effects). At the other extreme, if we make both fiat money and government debt liabilities, that is if we argue that individuals expect the government to 'pay back' its loan of money by means of tax revenues, we also get a neat cancelling out. Only to the extent that government debt is considered a private liability, while fiat money is not, will a clear case for a net 'wealth effect' from open market operations emerge. This line of attack also leads one towards a distinction between 'inside' and 'outside' money; the latter is the fiat money issued by the government and the former is money based on private debt (e.g., the demand deposit). Indeed, this distinction was the basis of the Gurley and Shaw proposals, and would seem to lead to the conclusion that only high-powered money or the monetary base could satisfy Pesek and Saving's first criterion here, at least on an *a priori* basis.[39]

Pesek and Saving also argue, for their second condition, that, if the charters for commercial banks are rationed by the government, then the charter, as evidence of a limited monopoly in the production of money, is itself valuable. Thirdly, if money production by banks is costless and no interest payments can be made on deposits, then the quantity of bank money, the value of the equity of the bank or the net wealth of the bank will reveal the value of the monopoly. The last result, of course, is the case in which the liability of the bank is ignored, an essentially technical question here. It is, of course, the charter that is valuable, and an economic analysis of that is required. Pesek and Saving, then, go on to attempt a distinction between money and debt that is based on the interest rate (their third condition). In the words of Friedman and Schwartz, Pesek and Saving are saying that

> The payment of interest on deposits transferable by check converts them into money-debt, which has the property of losing its money-ness (its capacity to serve as a medium of exchange) as the interest rate paid tends to approach the market interest rate. At the limit, it is entirely debt – in no part money. ... Hence, theory provides a sharp line of demarcation between 'money' and 'debt', money consisting of items used as a medium of exchange which are best regarded as assets to their holders but liabilities to no one.[40]

This reintroduces the medium of exchange function which must then be defined in some way, possibly as a non-pecuniary return to be included in the utility function.[41]

There is a related point, argued by W. Newlyn, that, if the asset in question can be employed in exchange for commodities or factors of production, without affecting the market for loans, it is money.[42] This criterion of *neutrality*, to use Newlyn's term, is most obvious when it applies to a non-interest-bearing asset, and it is here that Newlyn and Pesek and Saving converge. The argument is not that no ultimate changes occur, for obviously portfolio adjustments will follow, but that the *impact* is neutral. There is also a literature on the distinction between financial intermediaries and banks which asserts that the uniqueness of money (in this case, demand deposits) depends on how money enters the system; the general idea is that currency and demand deposits are unique because their total can be changed only at the will of the central government (the central government also offsets any undesired changes in the currency : deposit or reserve : deposit ratios). This is not an especially useful way of stating this distinction, for now one's definition depends not only on the existence and success of a particular government policy, but even on the government's perception of its role in the economy. This sort of neutrality is explicitly not part of Newlyn's framework, as he comments elsewhere.[43] But Newlyn, it would seem, is a medium of exchange man.

At this point we might consider the answers given by Friedman and Schwartz to the 'net wealth' argument, as just described. Their main line of attack is that all the relevant assets have joint properties in common and that, most especially, these properties cannot be separated by any hard-and-fast rule. They underscore the point that if for some reason demand deposits paid interest exactly equal to the interest rate, people would then acquire transactions services as a free (but joint) good. The paying of interest as such, say Friedman and Schwartz, doesn't make a demand deposit any less acceptable in exchange. This is true, but possibly beside the point. It is precisely because the owner of the deposit refuses to agree to surrender (tacitly) his claim to liquidity that he gets no interest payments; that is, we can argue that Pesek and Saving are talking about an *ex ante* arrangement which, given the cost of adjustment, is negotiated for a definite period of time. So far as Newlyn's version of neutrality is concerned, Friedman and

Schwartz argue that neutrality is achieved only because the person who acquired (or departed with) funds acted in a non-rational way. Newlyn requires that a person who acquires a demand deposit be satisfied with it; but, as they point out, if he decides to convert it to currency, another kind of money by Newlyn's criterion, bank reserves will fall (in a fractional reserve system), and as banks sell securities to replenish the loss, interest rates will rise. This is essentially an immediate effect. So one's ability to define money by this scheme depends on adventitious institutional details or, worse, on deliberately neutralising governmental policy, after all.

2.3 Money as a store of value

As a store of value, money is of special interest to the economist. While it is obviously its long history as a medium of exchange that is at the root of its store of value function, it is also true that to store one's wealth in this form normally does not require the wealth-holder to have any special information about how financial markets work; this is in contrast to the problems of storing one's wealth in stocks or bonds, for example.[44] Of course, one surrenders something in the form of interest payments if his wealth is held as non-interest-bearing money; and this, indeed, is why the financial markets are driven to produce close money substitutes such as the interest-bearing time deposit. Actually, 'substitute' is not a good word to apply to time deposits here, for although it is true that instant translation from time deposits into currency and demand deposits is usually possible, it would seem that whether or not there are frequent *actual* shifts between time and demand deposits in response to changes in the price ratio between them has not been verified. Below we will discuss studies that suggest that the substitution 'in practice' may be quite weak.

The first question that arises is essentially a tactical one: is money best studied as a stock or a flow? Normally we measure economic entities either as stocks (at an instant of time) or as flows (per period of time). This is not necessarily a question of fact, as it might seem at first – after all, money is a stock in common with all capital, physical or non-physical – but it depends on which aspects of the entity one wishes to bring out most effectively. For example, in the macroeconomic formulation of the 'equation of exchange' associated with the Cambridge School, two stocks are related,

$$M = kY \tag{2.1}$$

whereas in the Neoclassical model, V (for velocity) serves the function of converting the money stock into a flow, so that the equation is dimensionally valid:

$$MV = Y. \tag{2.2}$$

Specific uses follow immediately. Equation (2.1), for example, would most naturally fit into a portfolio problem, while equation (2.2) presents a flow explanation, for example of the relation between national income (Y) and the stock of money. Nor, in practice, are the two approaches perfectly reciprocal, since M for equation (2.1) would be measured at a moment in time (Y would be the rate of flow of income centred as near to that point of time as possible), while in equation (2.2) Y would be the rate of flow over a period of time (say a quarter of a year), while M might naturally be measured as the average stock of money over the comparable period. Nor can the two be made to match precisely, because changes in stocks can never, except in the limit, be described as rates of activity.

So money is clearly a stock. Money, however, is also an economic good in so far as it provides services and is in scarce supply relative to its demand. One of the services it performs is to mediate in exchanges. Exchanges necessarily take time, and at a moment in time, no exchange can occur; in fact, having money around enables one to save time in exchanges. Thus this service of money is more naturally described in the flow dimension. To push the point a little further, we can argue that, at any moment in time, all money is held as assets in private and public portfolios; a moment later some of it has changed hands, and we can now observe a new distribution of assets and commodities. We can invoke revealed preference to argue that an economic gain of some sort must have occurred between the two points in time and that the use of money to facilitate the exchange was directly responsible for some of the gain, but this does not lead to any obvious test of the value of these services, since the trade itself can be presumed to have provided some gain as well.[45]

There is another difference between equations (2.1) and (2.2) which is frequently mentioned. If our framework is equation (2.1), the stock version, we will be pushed in the direction of analysing the motives for holding money. Thus the function just described – that of speeding up exchanges – would be presented as the transactions motive – holding for future exchanges – whether that future exchange be tomorrow or next week. An implicit return is presumably foregone so long as money is held – a return which takes the dimension of an interest rate, and which can be compared with the explicit rates of return on other assets in the portfolio. On the other hand, if we adopt the framework of equation (2.2), we find a more natural explanation of the 'flow of services' aspect of money: over a period of time, money 'services' national income; indeed, its velocity describes how many times, on average, it was turned over in performing this function during the period. On the other hand, in the context of equation (2.2), it becomes more difficult to show how the interest rate regulates the quantity of money, since the interest rate, as the rate of return on some other financial entity, is defined (that is, measured) at a point in time.

But all this seeming clarity is confounded by the one essential problem that, as an asset (store of value), money is drawn into the close range of other financial assets. As. H. Johnson puts it:

> While the treatment of money as an asset distinguished from other assets by its superior liquidity is common ground among contemporary theorists, the transition from the conception of money as a medium of exchange to money as a store of value has raised new problems ... these problems result from recognition of the substitutability between money ... and the wide range of alternative financial assets provided by government debt and the obligations of financial institutions.[46]

There is a vast literature here, very little of which is solely on problems of definition, but the central issues seem to have concerned the concept of liquidity. The view associated with Gurley and Shaw, a version of which is contained in the *Radcliffe Report,* is that money is not especially unique in being a liquid asset and, consequently, if its supply is restricted, wealth-holders will be almost as happy with 'near-money' such as Treasury (or other) bills.[47] There are two major issues here, one empirical and one theoretical.

The theoretical problem is that of the definition of the term 'liquidity', and there are three main approaches employed, the first two of which dovetail somewhat with the medium of exchange concept. The high ground here belongs to the notion of liquidity as suggesting the 'ready availability of the asset at a well-defined market price'.[48] Furthermore, this idea can be tested by the difference between 'bid' and 'ask' prices, and when this is done there are few anomalies: 'money' is perfectly liquid (begging the question of how to define money), Treasury bills are highly liquid, and, not surprisingly (when you consider the lowvelocity figures), time deposits are fairly illiquid. The last are judged by the high interest penalty one suffers when he converts a time deposit to cash. The second *a priori* definition of liquidity is the 'ability to sell an asset on demand ... for a nominal sum fixed in advance'. By this scheme, 'money' is again perfectly liquid, but so are time deposits and Treasury bills, with the former, by modern practices at least, available on demand as well.

The last-mentioned scheme was two-dimensional and therefore of less use in that some formula for dealing with trade-offs needs to be established. That is, the fee for surrender of time deposits is high, but it can be done on demand, while the fee on Treasury bills is relatively low, but one has a fairly long potential wait for his request to be filled. This last consideration brings up a third scheme, the 'term-to-maturity', which Friedman and Schwartz actually prefer.[49] The general idea is that, the longer the maturity of the instrument, the more 'capital risk' there is, a point that is both indisputable (under certain conditions) and empirically approachable. Thus, currency, demand, and time deposits, and savings and loan shares or building society shares (for example) are equally liquid and, by this criterion, equally money. This is a technical scheme, and is very precise in that a line between money and non-money can be drawn quite distinctly in most cases,[50] but it fails to deal directly with the fact that whether or not there is capital risk depends on the 'holding period' of the wealth-holder. Thus, for insurance companies with long-dated horizons, there may be no asset short of a perpetuity that offers it any risk in that the company plans (with reasonable certainty) to hold all of its assets to their maturity.[51] Thus, demand creeps back into the problem and so does 'portfolio balance', leaving us, after all, with a severe empirical problem in some cases.

The empirical literature that is relevant to the liquidity debate is that on the 'substitutability along the demand curve for liquid assets'. This substitutability, of course, covers more ground than either the liquidity question or the broader definition of money question requires; furthermore, this literature is inconclusive:

> In regard to substitutability, all of the studies show that various assets are substitutes for one another to some degree, as is to be expected. Estimates of the degree of substitutability differ, but the major differences among authors is less in the numerical size of the elasticities they find, than in the adjectives they use to describe the size. The same numerical elasticity is described by one author as showing that the assets are 'close' substitutes, by another that they are 'weak' or 'distant' substitutes.
> This ambiguity reflects the absence of any clear purpose in terms of which to judge the size of the elasticity.[52]

Be this as it may, there are some interesting questions raised in this literature, particularly as to the sensitivity of the tests both to the models and to the definitions of the data employed. Perhaps the first such study was E. Feige's, in which cross-elasticities of the demand for demand deposits suggested that demand deposits might even be the *complements* of savings and loan deposits; his data were cross-section.[53] In a later study of the demand for demand deposits, Feige extended his study by use of both a covariance model and a random coefficients model; the latter is also employed in a second paper with Swamy.[54] The conclusions of these separate studies are:

1. that, for the United States, a geographical aggregation may be unwise (i.e., that the demand for some assets is unstable geographically);
2. that commercial bank time deposits are a weak substitute for demand deposits;
3. that mutual savings bank deposits are a weak substitute for demand deposits; and
4. that savings and loan deposits are either a weak substitute or a weak complement for demand deposits.

Thus, Feige's position has not changed appreciably over the course of his studies.

This analysis has not gone unchallenged, of course, and Feige's acknowledged inability to eliminate temporal instability has been, perhaps, the most serious problem in his work. Thus, T. Lee noted that pre-1951 data on savings and loan deposits should be omitted (Feige's original test went over the period 1949–59) on the grounds that these institutions first received deposit protection similar to FDIC (Federal Deposit Insurance Corporation) after 1950); indeed, some effect is clear in Feige's original tables.[55] As noted, Feige is unrepentant. All of this work, though, is called into question by J. Moroney and B. Wilbratte, who point out that the multiple interest rates necessarily included in such studies (Feige even used an estimate for the rate of interest on demand deposits) are highly colinear, producing inefficient estimates.[56] Their approach might be considered here briefly. Building on a suggestion of V. K. Chetty,[57] who set up a model in which consumers maximise a utility function with money and assets in it – subject to an asset budget constraint – they instead rely on a property of duality:

> if identical variables are entered in a utility function or a transactions constraint having the same parametric form, the alternative behavioral models yield identical derived asset demand equations.[58]

Thus, Moroney and Wilbratte propose to study a problem in which the aggregate household maximises wealth subject to a technological transactions constraint; then, they find no significant difference between the substitutability of time deposits and that of either short- or long-term government bonds for demand deposits – or, for that matter, aggregates of demand deposits and mutual savings bank deposits and savings and loan deposits. This suggestion of a much broader measure of money than that found by any other of the empirical studies will certainly be challenged in due course. Perhaps, finally, one might be tempted to take J. Tobin's advice to 'reflect on the characteristic properties of assets', although we may well find it hard to make 'reflective distinctions' when in practice the market may frequently change the 'definitions' of the relevant concepts.[59] This is a reminder, if one is needed, that the substitution we are discussing is a demand phenomenon. Some further aspects of this subject are continued below, where we discuss the results of the Monetarist empirical work on the definition problem.

2.3.1 *The store of value as a microeconomic problem*

In Debreu's *Theory of Value* a commodity is defined as follows:

> A commodity is characterized by its physical properties, the date at which it will be available and the location at which it will be available.[60]

Obviously, the more precise one is about the physical properties, the better the definition; further, this definition obviously makes us think about the economic value associated with time and distance. If we hold properties and place constant, then at two different points in time a given commodity is still two different things. Putting aside all thought of deterioration of the commodity at these different points in time, one can measure an interest rate by looking at the differences in value of the commodity. Indeed, paper money and deposits do not suffer physical deterioration, at least not in the sense of commodities, so a comparison here reflects 'the' interest rate, although, it should be added, this is not one of the unique properties of money. Holding properties and time constant and allowing location to vary, one then gets an exchange rate between commodities; if it is between national currencies, it will be 'the' exchange rate.

But Debreu sidesteps questions of how to define money other than in terms of its physical properties, an evasion that is partly responsible for the development of a promising literature on 'sequence economies'.[61] A sequence economy is distinguished from a Debreu economy in that, in the former, 'the relative prices of goods faced by agents are independent of the transactions dates and households do not have to balance their books at each transaction date but only over all dates taken together'.[62] That is, while both economies might be assumed to have the same preferences, endowments and technologies, the sequence economy imposes the condition that the books must be balanced in every sub-period because of, for example, the lack of information that traders have about the solvency of each other. When it comes time to define money, Hahn, confessing no interest in the theoretical problem posed by his artificial way of motivating money holdings, works his problem in terms of the following scheme:

> In this section money will perform only as a store of value. I assume (a) that money does not enter the utility function, (b) that spot transactions in money are costless so that there is no difference between the spot buying and selling of money, (c) that each household has a positive initial endowment of money and (d) that each household at t returns (to the 'government') whatever money it has been endowed with.[63]

Of course it is (d) that is bothersome here, although, as we have seen, there is some link-up possible with the opponents of the 'net wealth' position, as described above.

D. Starrett proposes that transactions costs of purchasing future commodities exist. If this is the case, then the sequence economy of early-Hahn becomes generally inefficient.[64] Starrett then argues that

> we showed that we could introduce an asset into the model in such a way that equilibrium would exist and always be efficient. Any time the economy would have otherwise been inefficient, this new

equilibrium must surely generate positive demands for these assets. Since the assets involved are essentially privately created interest-bearing money, we are provided with a rationale for the introduction of a certain kind of 'paper money' into the 'real' world.[65]

Thus, while this money is costlessly produced and does not involve any new transactions costs (in financial markets), a 'transactions' alternative to Hahn's 'store of value' paradigm is established. The difference, in Debreu's terminology, is that Hahn's prices differ at each point in time, containing implicitly the interest rate which is itself formally part of the Starrett analysis.

An important problem that emerges from the Debreu scheme of operation arises because of the joint economic properties that money and all economic goods possess. Currency, for example, is jointly a medium of exchange and a store of value; consider, for example, what happens to the 'utility' of currency as a store of value if its exchange value is deteriorating rapidly because of overproduction (as in a hyperinflation). To put the matter formally, it is conceivable that it is the characteristics of money that ought to go into individual utility functions, rather than money itself. Debreu's presentation isn't exactly hostile to this point of view, since he urges us to specify our properties carefully, but there is available an alternative method of analysis – that of K. Lancaster – which is basically more sympathetic to the problem of jointness we are facing here.[66]

Of course we must be as precise about characteristics as we are about physical properties if we are to do any empirical work, and this precision is not easily achieved; but for the present, let us consider an example that proceeds as if we have found a reasonable measurement scheme. Suppose we have three money commodities, each imparting the qualities we are interested in, as follows in Table (2.1).[67] Let us further suppose that the con-

Table 2.1 The Characteristics of Money.

Commodities	Characteristics			
	Acceptability	Pays interest	Bid–ask	Price ($)
Currency	0.3	0.1	0.3	1.00
Time deposits	0.2	0.2	0.1	1.00
Treasury bills	0.1	0.2	0.2	1.00

sumption at time t was 50–30–20 units of the three commodities, respectively. If one does the arithmetic, this means that the consumption of the three characteristics, if we interpret the table entries as 'utils', is 23–15–22, respectively. Suppose, then, that the price of currency rises to $2.00 per unit and that the consumption figures change to 30–35–5. This is not an unusual result, and the consumption of the time deposit is now larger than the consumption of cash, also not an unusual result. But underlying this is a 'peculiar' result for characteristics, for the consumption of characteristics is now 18.5–11–13.5; which is to say, the use of characteristics declined uniformly. The examination of the goods themselves may have led us to suppose that the acceptability function was relatively less desirable in the new equilibrium when, in fact, it was slightly more desirable (relatively). It is clear that the examination of 'characteristic space' for the money problem is at least as important as it is for any commodity, and perhaps even more so, in view of the policy implications of mistakes in this area.

2.4   The problem of definition as an aggregation problem

Let us consider firstly some of the general aspects of the aggregation problem itself. The first point of principle is that one's purpose in aggregating is generally to attain simplicity, and to employ microeconomic perceptions in a macroeconomic context; the successful achievement of the simplicity makes the subsequent theory or empirical work easier to manipulate and less costly. The saving in cost or effort is balanced by the fact that every aggregation suppresses some information and it is a question of judgement, with an empirical aspect as well,[68] as to which aggregation is best under the particular circumstances of any given problem. In aggregating one is necessarily *defining* an economic entity for purposes of analysis; an aggregate, that is to say, is treated as a single product. It is this linking of the aggregation and the definitional problem that has motivated much of the existing empirical work on the definitional problem, although empirical work seems at first glance to be hostile to the essentially arbitrary process of definition. The empirics enter, to repeat the point, because there is information (of potential damage) suppressed, which ought in some way to be compared with the simplicity achieved.

Aggregation itself normally is generally over transactors (i.e., over individual demand or supply functions), over goods, or over assets (like time and demand deposits). The other side of the aggregation chosen, if it is over goods, is the definition of a price index; and the task the economist faces in this context is the proof that the aggregation and its price behave like economic entities in theory and, when we wish to become empirical, in practice. To deal with the goods problem on a general level, we have Hicks's Composite Goods Theorem; a particularly clear explanation of this is given by Patinkin. The theorem states that

> when, for a defined group of commodities, all price changes are proportional, such a group can be treated as a single commodity in demand analysis.

The cost of this assumption is that, if the actual price changes in a particular situation are not proportional, then damage will result, possibly even to the extent of the disproportionality. It is worth remarking on this point now, because we will later look at empirical tests for which this proportionality is not tested. Thus, as we aggregate over commodities, we must look to the lack of synchronisation of price changes as the principal empirical problem. We may also show 'perfect substitution'. In this event,

> The condition, in the simplest two-goods case, is that the two goods be perfect substitutes in consumption at some given rate of substitution. ... Here it is the indifference curves ... which show up as straight lines. ...[69]

It is the latter fact that guarantees satisfaction of the composite goods theorem at equilibrium. Thus, in practice, we may look at price proportionality or at the degree of substitution to establish an empirical case.

When we turn to assets, says Leijonhufvud, we need not concern ourselves about the characteristics of assets (assuming that we do not intend to put the assets into the utility function) but only about the problem of substitutability. Furthermore, it is the substitution of the expected streams of returns that matters, and not the substitution of the assets themselves (the 'sources' of the streams). Since we are aggregating over future returns, we can reduce the aggregation problem in this case to that of the problem of risk, by assuming that all assets mature at the same date. Then, if there are differences in risk among assets, an aggregation problem still exists. To put it another way, if all assets are alike in maturity and all 'risks' are perceived to be the same, we can aggregate as we wish, assuming the assets are perfect substitutes in their streams of returns. Further, if all assets (in the proposed bundle) are alike in expected risk and return, and unalike in maturity, the aggregation problem is one of maturity. Thus, one may argue, currency and non-interest-bearing demand deposits are perceived of as equally risky (these days) and can be safely aggregated, since their term-to-maturity is alike, while Treasury bills, with a term-to-maturity of ninety days (for example), present an empirical aggregation problem which can be solved in their favour if Treasury bills are particularly close substitutes for demand deposits and currency, their maturity notwithstanding. The question of time deposits is more difficult (although it can be resolved in the same way) only because for time deposits one must deal with an 'implied maturity' in some way.

2.4.1 *The Keynesian approach*

Leijonhufvud has argued that there is a fundamental difference between the aggregation employed by Keynes and that employed by his lineal descendants, the Keynesians. If one accepts the argument to this point, then one should also agree that this is a difference of definition; and, with such a difference, all sorts of differences in the results of conceptual experiments should follow. Leijonhufvud notes that standard macro-theory deals with five aggregates – consumer goods, producer goods, labour services, money and bonds – but that, at the same time, only three relative prices are solved for – the price level, the wage rate and the interest rate. With an overall constraint on the solution, this implies that one of the goods must be absorbed into one of the others (or eliminated in some way); Leijonhufvud argues that:

> We then come to a rather interesting question: In the three-price models belonging to the Keynesian tradition, is the fifth good always eliminated, by aggregation, in the same way? This, as we shall see, is where Keynes and the Keynesians part company.[70]

The difference, in particular, is that Keynes aggregates capital goods (or their financial manifestations, equities) with bonds, to produce

consumer goods
non-money assets
labour services and
money

as his four goods, while Keynesians combine consumer goods and investment goods to produce

commodities
labour services
bonds
money

for theirs. Further, in selecting a representative yield, a choice that follows logically from the specification of the problem to this point, Keynes chooses a long-term rate to stand for the yield on non-money assets, while the Keynesians prefer a short-term rate.

The reason Keynes would select a long-term rate is that it represents, directly, the yield on the conglomerate long-term asset; thus, it should be emphasised, Keynes would prefer a very broad definition of money and possibly one broader than that used by the Keynesians. The latter would gather all bonds together (as the natural antithesis of money) and represent the conglomerate by the yield on the shortest asset in the collection, the Treasury bill yield.[71] We are not interested in the documentation of Leijonhufvud's propositions, but we can note that they do seem to apply to a broad part of the work of both Keynes and the Keynesians; we should also carefully take the point that different conclusions should follow immediately from these different perceptions of the real world. In some ways the aggregation in Keynes is more ambitious, but in either case we eliminate equities;

this is certainly not always desirable, especially when there is a variable rate of inflation to be dealt with (see Chapter 7 below). Finally, we should note that it is not the relation between money and short or long debt that matters (in the choice of definition), because Keynes can always pick another representative rate; that is, essentially, each of his aggregates stands or falls on the basis of the substitutability within the aggregate, not on the basis of its relation to any particular price chosen to represent the aggregate's rate of return.

2.4.2 The Monetarist view

Where, then, do the Monetarists fit into this picture? The answer, essentially, is that a pragmatic approach is taken; two direct quotations from Friedman and Schwartz, indeed, seem to lead one towards specific tests of the appropriate definition of money:

> Strictly speaking, the 'best' way to define money depends on the conclusions that we reach about how various monetary assets are related to one another and to other economic variables; yet we need to define 'money' to proceed with our research. The solution, also common in scientific work, is successive approximations.

> The selection is to be regarded as an empirical hypothesis asserting that a particular definition will be most convenient for a particular purpose because the magnitude based on that definition bears a more consistent and regular relation to other variables relevant for this purpose than do alternative magnitudes of the same general class.[72]

Let us look to a paper by G. S. Laumas for some clarification here. Laumas, employing a technique now widely used,[73] proposes that we find out what is money on the basis of a regression of

$$\Delta Y = f(\Delta M, \Delta S) = \alpha + \beta_1 \Delta M + \beta_2 \Delta S + \gamma \qquad (2.3)$$

where M is currency and demand deposits, and the 'moneyness' of an asset is measured by the ratio β_2/β_1, that is by the relative amount of the variation in income (Y) that is explained by changes in the assets in question. S, then, is broadened from regression to regression and some arbitrary line is drawn; the empirical results, for

$S_1 = $ time deposits
$S_2 = S_1 + $ mutual savings bank (MSB) deposits + post office savings
$S_3 = S_2 + $ savings and loan (S and L) deposits

show that the relative moneyness declines in the order $S_1 > S_2 > S_3$. Immediately, one wonders why S and L deposits are broader than MSB deposits, even granting that the regression coefficients are significantly different from each other (which they are not).

But there are some serious technical questions one might raise here, as well. Aside from not being the sort of test envisaged by an application of the Composite Goods Theorem (or of the substitutability condition), it also seems clear that this is an attempt to kill two monetary birds with one stone. That is, this test is getting a lot of mileage out of the mutually dependent relation between changes in some items of wealth and income. Another problem concerns the form of the test behind equation (2.3); here, the assumptions of ordinary least squares require that the independent variables be non-stochastic (fixed in repeated samples). If they are non-stochastic, then there remains no empirical problem to solve about them; the remaining empirical problem concerns their relative efficiency in predicting Y; in that sense each of Laumas's formulations is equivalent, as judged by the multiple correlation coefficients he obtained (0.43, 0.42, 0.42, respectively) in his tests. Put another way, the reader of these results has no way of directly comparing the variables because there is no sampling distribution attached to them; the variables are already 'defined' when they enter each equation. The consequence is that the appeal to some other perception must be made or we might discover that automobiles are money on the basis of equation (2.3).[74]

There is other empirical work of the same type, and, to say the least, the results cannot be considered convincing. In one line of attack, a distributed lag form of regression is substituted for the non-lagged version used by Laumas; here Kaufman finds that broader definitions have longer lags,[75] in a method that makes it perfectly clear that this form of the Monetarist definition of money test is identical to the 'monetary indicators' tests and to the 'monetary multipliers' tests of another generation.[76] This, of course, is another way of saying that, to a hard-core Monetarist (of this particular persuasion), there is no separate issue of the definition of money: 'The selection of a specific empirical counterpart of the theoretical concept to the term money seems to us to be a matter of convenience for a particular purpose, not a matter of principle.'[77] D. Hulett brings these issues out even more clearly when he comments that:

> The empirical method used to define money should correspond to the form of the money demand function in the underlying model. . . . If money is held mainly to facilitate transactions, the appropriate scale variable to use should include financial and inter-industry transactions. . . . If money demand is related to wealth in a portfolio balance model, wealth or permanent income would reflect the underlying assumptions more accurately than would current GNP.[78]

Thus the results one gets on the definition problem would depend on the model chosen, the accuracy of its specification, and even on changes in the institutional structure of financial markets. There are, clearly, severe empirical problems here, although one could argue that they are not really problems of definition.

But the Monetarist case for empirical work does not rest on these simple precepts alone. Friedman and Schwartz have also noted that:

> It is an empirical generalization that this is not the case: there is a subtotal, labeled 'money' for convenience, which it is useful to distinguish because it is related to other economic magnitudes in a fairly regular and stable way, though its particular content may be different from place to place or time to time. This empirical generalization underlies the distinction between price theory and monetary theory – a distinction that has been central in economic analysis for centuries.[79]

The broad gauge of the shells fired here should not distract one from noting a particularly interesting point about the 'stability question'. An explanation of this is provided by Laidler, who comments as follows:

> Now one can only define what is meant by a 'sufficiently close substitute' if he will specify the problem with which he wishes to deal, and as far as the definition of money is concerned the most important issue has been the identification and measurement of a stable aggregate demand for money function. ... A 'more stable demand function' is precisely one that permits the consequences of shifting the supply of money to be more easily and accurately predicted.[80]

The purpose, that is to say, is to have an effective monetary policy, and the empirical definitional issue is the stability of the demand for money function, when we test alternative aggregates. We don't do as much work as we should on stability in monetary economics, and the testing of the stability of the demand for money function is only peripherally a matter of definition; but there is some common ground here with our earlier discussion. Until recently, at least, we tested stability in two main ways: we looked to see if the coefficients of an estimated relationship differ markedly from time period to time period, or we compared R^2 from alternative regressions, usually for different (non-overlapping) time periods. From the latter point of view, Laidler's comment on Laumas's results might very well have been that the results are equally stable for the alternative definitions tested, since the R^2s are the same; in consequence, so far as we can tell from this work, this implies that the definitions (S_1, S_2, S_3) are the same.

Another version of the Monetarist approach is supplied by L. Yeager. Laidler seems to be talking about definitions in a way that would lead us to pick a definition based on the definition of a function; indeed, Friedman and Schwartz seem to applaud this approach. Yeager, in his turn, in the following passage, seems to be pursuing the idea in Laidler (whose work came later) of the identification of the function in question:

To recognize how nonmonetary liquidity affects total demands for money and for goods and services, we need not blur the definition of money so badly as to subvert measurement and control of its quantity. We need not blur the distinctions between supplies of and demands for assets and between influences on supply and influences on demand. We can define the supply of money narrowly, as a measurable quantity, and see it confronted by a demand for cash balances – a demand influenced, to be sure, by the availability and attractiveness of other assets.[81]

The reason this approach – which actually seems almost to say that 'money' is defined by supply and demand – provides essentially a definition of the demand for money function, is simply that in 'defining' the supply of money (as, for example, a distinct function) we can *identify* (a mathematical property) the demand function, after the confrontation.

When we get down to actually enumerating what the demand for money literature has told us about the definition of money, we are clearly engaging in a substantial overlap with the former topic, much of which is treated in Chapters 4, 5 and 6 below. Briefly, we can list the following as some of the most relevant findings of this literature – relevant to the definitional debate.

1. The aggregation of currency and demand (current account) deposits is a safe one, except in times of very unusual monetary strain.

2. The aggregations of individual and business demand functions is a poor one, since the evidence suggests that:

(a) businesses have different types of monetary assets, for example more Treasury bills (as a percentage of the total);
(b) businesses respond more quickly to financial influences; and
(c) businesses respond to different financial variables, in particular to short-term interest rates rather than to long (but see the term structure discussion in Chapter 6).

3. The aggregation of narrow money and time deposits, while sometimes producing an effective indicator of monetary influences on the economy, has the problem derived from point 2 that businesses do not hold their fair percentage of time deposits, as well as the problem that time deposits appear to be a depository for funds held to purchase consumer durables later (or even for the permanent storage of wealth).[82]

4. There is, finally, some evidence that in recent years the broader measures (M_2, M_3), which include savings, outperform M_1, at least if the 'stable demand function' is one's criterion. This evidence is far from complete, however.[83]

One might generalise that, so far as the definition of money is concerned, the empirical frontier seems to be between time deposits and demand deposits rather than between time deposits and some broader measure. Two major qualifications are in order, though: one arises because this statement is made independently of any formal model, the structure of which might tend to dictate a different (or broader) aggregation of short-term assets; and the other arises because no formal analysis of the components of narrow money itself is undertaken here.[84]

Footnotes

1. I. Fisher, *The Purchasing Power of Money*, p. 5. This institutional discussion is continued later in this chapter.
2. ibid., p. 11.
3. ibid., pp. 97–101.
4. P. Wicksteed, *The Common Sense of Political Economy*, Vol. 1, p. 136.
5. L. B. Yeager, 'Essential Properties of the Medium of Exchange', p. 50. G. Tullock ('Competing Monies') has another version:

> Money, in and of itself, is an almost perfect expression of a large externality. The reason I want money is because I realize that many other people want it, and hence it is readily exchangeable for other things I want. Its wide acceptability, paradoxically, depends on its wide acceptability. [p. 491]

Money, that is to say, is judged by Tullock to be a 'public good'.
6. For the moment we evade the problem of whether (or which) money is net wealth to society as a whole.
7. See especially R. Clower, 'A Reconsideration of the Microfoundations of Monetary Theory'.
8. See especially B. Pesek and T. Saving, *Money, Wealth, and Economic Theory*; J. Hicks, in 'The Two Triads, Lecture 1' in *Critical Essays in Monetary Theory*, has a partly historical paradigm with a similar drift to the rest of this section.
9. M. Friedman and A. J. Schwartz, *A Monetary History of the United States*; and B. Hammond, *Money and Politics in America*. K. Brunner ('A Survey of Selected Issues in Monetary Theory') notes, as also described in some detail below, that the movement from a barter to an advanced monetary economy is accompanied by a reduction of the cost of information by means of the growth of the use of money in this capacity:

> The legislation of the 1860's which replaced private banknotes by US notes appears thus as a device which lowered substantially the public's information costs bearing on private money. [p. 17]

The event was, to be sure, a dramatic one, but it took a change in the enabling legislation permitting the new money to be 'legal tender' and a tax on 'competing monies' to persuade bankers of the advantages of the new system. In the old system, bill brokers (e.g., Jay Cooke) provided (at a cost) information on the market values of the numerous bank notes then in circulation. Not only did the old notes continue in circulation, but it is surely an exaggeration to argue that the new system replaced one without effective information-generating mechanisms. Indeed, calculations might show the reduction in the cost of information to be quite trivial.
10. P. Davidson, 'Money and the Real World', p. 101; F. H. Hahn, 'Equilibrium With Transactions Costs', p. 3.
11. J. Hicks, 'The Two Triads: Lecture I' in *Critical Essays in Monetary Theory*.
12. P. Davidson, *Money and the Real World*, p. 151.
13. ibid., p. 152.
14. The main references are: K. Brunner and A. H. Meltzer. 'The Uses of Money'; J. M. Ostroy, 'The Informational Efficiency of Monetary Exchange'; D. Starrett, 'Inefficiency and the

Demand for "Money" in a Sequence Economy'; and C. Goodhart, *Money, Information and Uncertainty.*

15. See J. R. Hicks, 'The Two Triads: Lecture I' in *Critical Essays in Monetary Theory.*

16. C. Goodhart, *Money, Information and Uncertainty*, quotations from Chapters 1 and 2.

17. P. Davidson, *Money and the Real World*, p. 142.

18. We will discuss Clower's model briefly in Chapter 3; a much more detailed analysis is carried in Appendix A.

19. The J. Tobin model is the mean-variance formulation of the demand for money ('Liquidity Preference as Behaviour Towards Risk'); it is discussed in Chapter 5 below. Shackle's book, *Uncertainty in Economics*, contains his basic position on these issues.

20. This opinion was expressed to Davidson by M. Friedman ('Comments on the Critics'). A similar argument appears in H. Johnson ('Keynes' General Theory: Revolution or War of Independence').

21. P. Davidson, *Money and the Real World*, p. 147.

22. K. Brunner, 'A Survey of Selected Issues in Monetary Theory', p. 6.

23. K. Brunner and A. Meltzer, 'The Uses of Money', p. 786.

24. ibid., p. 787.

25. K. Brunner, 'A Survey of Selected Issues in Monetary Theory', p. 9.

26. ibid., p. 19.

27. J. Niehans, 'Money in a Static Theory of Optimal Payment Arrangements', p. 709.

28. J. Ostroy, 'The Informational Efficiency of Monetary Exchange', p. 609.

29. D. Patinkin, *Money, Interest and Prices.*

30. This discussion is continued in Chapter 4, with respect to the production function.

31. D. Patinkin, 'Money and Wealth: A Review Article', pp. 79–80.

32. W. J. Baumol, 'The Transactions Demand for Cash'; J. Tobin, 'The Interest Elasticity of the Transactions Demand for Cash'.

33. M. Friedman and A. J. Schwartz, 'The Definition of Money', in *Monetary Statistics of the United States.*

34. C. Goodhart, *Money, Information and Uncertainty*, p. 14.

35. Clower favours a broader definition of money than 'narrow' money. This view is shared by A. Laffer in 'Trade Credit and the Money Market'. Indeed, both argue that trade credit should be included. Recall the argument above (attributed to P. Davidson) that trade credit is not part of the medium of exchange since the claims for it are not traded in a market, nor are they generally traded.

36. In the case of the cheque, the main legal recourse the buyer has is to 'stop payment'. In this case the cheque is returned to the sender (it is his property), who is still free to regard the original sale as final (i.e., consummated) and press the buyer legally (the buyer would, normally, lose, since the cheque was accepted as payment).

37. M. Friedman and A. J. Schwartz, *Monetary Statistics of the United States*; the main work is B. Pesek and T. Saving, *Money, Wealth, and Economic Theory.*

38. W. L. Smith, 'On Some Current Issues in Monetary Economics'.

39. D. Patinkin, 'Money and Wealth: A Review Article'; J. G. Gurley and E. S. Shaw, *Money in a Theory of Finance.*

40. M. Friedman and A. Schwartz, *Monetary Statistics of the United States*, p. 111.

41. T. Saving, in a later paper ('Outside Money, Inside Money, and the Real Balance Effect'), reiterates his concern with the interest rate issue, and presents a model of the role of money in a dynamic consumption model in which the use of money saves time in consumption activities. The time saved is then available for work or leisure; it is the latter that provides the non-pecuniary return in the utility function. He shows that under these conditions the inside–outside distinction is not important so long as no interest is paid on deposits; in particular, even if there are positive production costs, there is a real balance effect – the result, to be sure, of the role money has been given as a reducer of the time spent in making transactions. This discussion is continued in Chapter 3.

One might also note that Friedman and Schwartz really go too far here in saying that Pesek and Saving are arguing that money has lost its capacity to serve as money. That is, a gun that is converted into a flower pot is still a gun – still has the capacity to serve as a gun – but as a flower pot, in fact, the relevant price for it is that of other flower pots, in the first instance.

42. W. T. Newlyn, *Theory of Money*. Yeager ('The Essential Properties of the Medium of Exchange') also has this neutrality argument. He argues that normally a glut or shortage in a commodity or asset market is largely eliminated in its own market. Money, not having a market of its own (always trading at par), must spill over to eliminate an excess or shortage of money itself. Newlyn, in further elaboration, notes that, when there is an imbalance in a commodity market and the medium of exchange is employed to eliminate this imbalance, there is no appreciable excess or shortage of money since

1. its total is not changed; and
2. the imbalance having been eliminated, only money and goods have changed hands, to everyone's satisfaction.

As noted in the text, this is an impact neutrality. Even so, (1) will not hold if, when (e.g.) deposit money changes hands, it is redeposited in a bank with a different reserve ratio. See the discussion on this and related points in D. Pierce and D. Shaw, *Monetary Economics*, Chapter 2.

43. W. T. Newlyn, 'The Essential Qualities of Money: A Note'. This is part of a dialogue between Newlyn and E. V. Morgan ('The Essential Qualities of Money'): 'Perfect acceptability and fixity of value in terms of the unit of account are together necessary and sufficient conditions for an asset to qualify as money.' (p. 242). This applies to legal tender (currency), clearly, but excludes deposits. Morgan, however, includes bank deposits under the same 'neutralising policy' rule as was attributed to Newlyn. See the discussion in D. Pierce and D. Shaw, *Monetary Economics*, pp. 47–51.

44. One also hears of money described as a unit of account, but this is not really an accurate usage; rather, it is important for its role that money be fixed in terms of the unit of account. It is not unique in this respect; neither, accordingly, is it unique in providing the basis for a standard of value, since all other items fixed in terms of the unit of account could also serve equally well in this capacity. Our standard of value, of course, is the price level, compared with some basis, and our unit of account is the dollar, the pound, etc., a fact that enables us to name the money prices of things in some accounting equivalent; money, that is to say, has an accounting price, but the money price of money (its rate of exchange with money) is, of course, zero. We will return to these problems in Chapter 3. Resources are involved in the creation of the unit of account, and they are certainly involved in changing the unit of account, as recent British experience confirms.

45. The literature on Clower's expenditure function is much more precise on these problems. See R. Clower, 'A Reconsideration of the Microfoundations of Monetary Theory'; C. Lloyd, 'The Microfoundations of Monetary Theory: Comment'; and Appendix A below.

46. H. Johnson, 'Monetary Theory and Policy', p. 351.

47. J. Gurley and E. Shaw, *Money in a Theory of Finance* (Report of the Committee on the Workings of the Monetary System).

48. M. Friedman and A. J. Schwartz, *Monetary Statistics of the United States*, p. 129. J. Hicks ('The Two Triads, Lecture III', in *Critical Essays in Monetary Theory*) distinguishes between 'running assets' (for running the business, whether the business be a firm or a household), 'reserve assets' (which are used for emergencies) and 'investment assets' (which are held for future yield). Much of the money stock is held as a running asset (not 'demanded', since it is more of a technical consideration) but the interesting points of monetary theory (says Hicks) relate to the reserve asset (speculative and precautionary demands) holdings of money. Then,

> It is essential, if a financial asset is to function as a reserve asset, that it should possess some degree of liquidity. . . . It need not be fully liquid, but it must possess liquidity in that looser *Treatise* sense of being 'realisable at short notice without loss'; it must, at the least, be readily marketable. [p. 41]

This description of liquidity – and the link with the demand for money – is pretty much the same view as that argued by P. Davidson and C. Goodhart in works already cited. Note that we are referring to the speculative and (mainly) the precautionary demands and that, apparently, transactions balances are to be thought of as not 'demanded' but merely as 'used'.

49. M. Friedman and A. J. Schwartz, *Monetary Statistics of the United States*, pp. 132–7. Friedman is on record, as well, as favouring a definition of money that emphasises its role as a 'temporary abode of purchasing power'. Friedman says that a temporary abode enables one to

separate the act of purchase from the act of sale. All assets could be employed in this role, but, presumably, longer-term assets would be more likely to be depositories of 'permanent wealth' than of purchasing power (itself an item of wealth, of course). See especially, M. Friedman, 'Post-War Trends in Monetary Theory and Policy'. Friedman and Schwartz also prefer the 'temporary abode' to the medium of exchange concept, but there are some conceptual problems, as described by K. Brunner ('A Survey of Selected Issues in Monetary Theory'). Most importantly, it would seem, money serves along with durable consumer goods as a temporary abode; thus a further characteristic – medium of exchange – seems necessary to restore clarity. The 'term-to-maturity' is also not much help unless, of course, one's analysis is arbitrarily restricted just to financial assets. This would leave no solution to the 'existence of money' problem, a point of much concern to Brunner. See also the literature cited by R. Clower in 'The Anatomy of Monetary Theory'.

50.   A. Leijonhufvud presents an explanation of Keynes's scheme for the definition of money which sounds very much like Friedman's:

> In Keynes' thinking, the dichotomy of 'short' vs 'long' overrode in importance all other distinctions between stores of value. . . . Apart from *ad hoc* observations of a less than systematic nature, his theory of relative asset prices was basically a theory of the term structure of interest rates. . . . With only 'money' representing the short end of the maturity continuum, and 'non-money assets' representing the long end, the term structure of rates becomes indistinguishable from 'the' level of the money rate of interest.

(*On Keynesian Economics and the Economics of Keynes*, pp. 149–50.) The dividing line, incidentally, is set at ninety days: the Treasury bill is money to Keynes. This scheme, as noted, compares favourably with Friedman's insistence that whether an asset pays interest or not is irrelevant, and with his preference for the broad money definition.

51.   J. M. Culbertson, 'The Term Structure of Interest Rates'; L. Wehrle, 'Life Insurance Investment. the Experience of Four Companies'. See Chapter 6 below, as well.

52.   M. Friedman and A. Schwartz, *Monetary Statistics of the United States*, p. 128.

53.   E. Feige, *The Demand for Liquid Assets*; in another study, of British commercial banks by M. Parkin, *et al.* ('The Portfolio Behaviour of Commercial Banks'), Treasury bills and private bills were actually estimated as complements, in bank portfolios. That study used the mean-variance model described in Chapter 5 below.

54.   E. L. Feige, 'Alternative Temporal Cross-Section Specifications of the Demand for Demand Deposits', and E. Feige and P. Swamy, 'A Random Coefficient Model of the Demand for Liquid Assets'.

55.   T. Lee, 'Substitutability of Non-Bank Intermediary Liabilities for Money: The Empirical Evidence'. Lee argues that a close substitution between demand and S and L deposits can be observed after this correction.

56.   J. Moroney and B. Wilbratte, 'Money and Money Substitutes'.

57.   V. K. Chetty, 'On Measuring the Nearness of Near Money'. Chetty basically agreed with Feige, but his study came under fire from T. Lee, for the same reason, with the same result (T. Lee, 'On Measuring the Nearness of Near Money: Comment').

58.   J. Moroney and B. Wilbratte, 'Money and Money Substitutes', p. 183.

59.   J. Tobin, 'Money, Capital, and Other Stores of Value'.

60.   G. Debreu, *Theory of Value*, p. 28.

61.   F. Hahn, 'On Transactions Costs, Inessential Sequence Economies and Money'; F. Hahn, 'Equilibrium With Transactions Costs'; D. Starrett, 'Inefficiency and the Demand for "Money".' See also the discussion of disequilibrium in Chapter 3 below.

62.   F. Hahn, 'On Transactions Costs, Inessential Sequence Economies and Money', p. 451. Furthermore, transactions activities require no resources here. See A. Ulph and D. Ulph, 'Transactions Costs in General Equilibrium Theory – A Survey'. These authors present a detailed survey of this literature to bring it up to date.

63.   F. Hahn, 'On Transactions Costs, Inessential Sequence Economies and Money', p. 456.

64.   F. Hahn, 'Equilibrium With Transactions Costs', is 'early-Hahn'.

65.   D. Starrett, 'Inefficiency and the Demand for "Money",' p. 447.

66.   K. Lancaster, 'A New Approach to Consumer Theory'.

67. One could also add the characteristic 'term-to-maturity' and the demand deposit, but three assets and three characteristics are sufficient to make the point here.

68. A. Leijonhufvud, *On Keynesian Economics and the Economics of Keynes*; and H. Green, *Aggregation in Economic Analysis.*

69. A. Leijonhufvud, *On Keynesian Economics and the Economics of Keynes*, p. 120.

70. ibid., p. 131.

71. This discussion is not complete and will be continued below, in two places. The Keynesian aggregation is discussed in Chapter 5, where it is pointed out that the choice of the short rate can be justified if the short asset 'dominates' longer assets in the decision of the wealth-holder. The question of Keynes's aggregation – and a more careful theoretical justification for it – occurs in Chapter 6, where it is shown that, without an explicit role for money (such as an insertion into the utility function), money must be aggregated with its neighbouring assets if one is to solve a dynamic consumption problem with money, a long-term bond, a short-term bond, and consumption in two future periods.

72. M. Friedman and A. Schwartz, *Monetary Statistics of the United States*, p. 91.

73. G. Laumas, 'The Degree of Moneyness of Savings Deposits'. In a later paper with P. Laumas, G. Laumas gets roughly the same results ('The Definition of Money and the Relative Importance of Autonomous Expenditures and Money'). See also J. Conlisk, 'Cross Country Inflation Evidence on the Moneyness of Time Deposits'; and R. Timberlake and J. Fortson, 'Time Deposits in the Definition of Money'.

74. The use of the *t*-test for β_1 and β_2 implies the assumption of normality of the distributions of the βs. But the distribution of the ratio of two normal variables, β_1/β_2, is not itself normal as is the presumption of the test. What we want to know is the sampling variance of the ratio of the two coefficients, and there is little for one to go on there.

75. We should note that customarily a temporal aggregation is effected in such models, and this, too, presents problems of interpretation. Following Goldfeld ('The Demand for Money Revisited'), we may write

$$M^d = a + bY^e + ci^e$$

Then if

$$Y^e_t - Y^e_{t-1} = \lambda(Y_t - Y^e_{t-1})$$

and

$$i^e_t - i^e_{t-1} = \lambda(i_t - i^e_{t-1})$$

we can deduce the standard 'short-run' demand for money as

$$M^d_t = a + b\lambda Y_t + c\lambda i_t + (1 - \lambda)M_{t-1}$$

in which case the lags on the two variables are constrained to be the same: λ, that is to say, is an aggregate speed of adjustment. In this context the Almon procedure, which is widely used, is an attempt to find the appropriate length of lag (by trying various aggregations of the lag) when λ is not the same for each variable in the equation, or when a more complex weighting scheme is desired. See the discussion in Chapter 4.

76. M. Friedman and D. Meiselman, 'The Relative Stability of Monetary Velocity and the Investment Multiplier in the United States'; M. Keran, 'Selecting a Monetary Indicator – Evidence from the United States and Other Developed Countries'; and J. Tanner, 'Indicators of Monetary Policy: An Evaluation of Five'.

77. M. Friedman and A. Schwartz, *Monetary Statistics of the United States*, p. 91.

78. D. Hulett, 'More on an Empirical Definition of Money: Note', pp. 465–6.

79. M. Friedman and A. Schwartz, *Monetary Statistics of the United States*, p. 90.

80. D. Laidler, 'The Definition of Money: Theoretical and Empirical Problems', p. 515.

81. L. B. Yeager, 'Essential Properties of the Medium of Exchange', p. 47.

82. S. Goldfeld ('The Demand for Money Revisited') finds, for the postwar quarterly United States data, that M_1 behaves well in a simple demand for money function, but that M_2 is slower to react (5–20 per cent), has a higher income elasticity (2.3 to 0.7) *and is unstable*. Laidler's summary of the literature gave quite a different impression. Goldfeld did not find the difference in interest rate effects generally found by other researchers.

83. See, for example, L. Meyer, 'Alternative Definitions of the Money Stock and the Demand for Money'. Meyer's technique is to look at prediction errors, assuming a short-run demand for money function (as in Goldfeld). The prediction errors are calculated in two ways: that of K. Brunner and A. Meltzer ('Predicting Velocity: Implications for Theory and Policy') and that of S. Goldfeld ('The Demand for Money Revisited').

84. S. Goldfeld disaggregates in this way. He finds M_1^d stable, but, while C^d and D^d estimated separately are still stable, he gets better results from a dynamic simulation in the disaggregated form. In general this topic is not taken up in this book, although it is of growing interest. We have discussed E. Feige's contribution ('Alternative Temporal Cross-Section Specifications of the Demand for Demand Deposits') in terms of 'cross interest rate effects'; see also an earlier study by G. Kaufman ('The Demand for Currency'). A second line of attack is typified by W. E. Becker ('Determinants of the United States Currency–Demand Deposit Ratio'), who argues that, since (in his tests) time deposits and demand deposits are *strong* substitutes, *three* rates of return influence the demand for currency relative to demand deposits:

1. the time deposit rate (a positive relation);
2. the rate of return on demand deposits (a negative relation); and
3. the opportunity cost of holding all three assets (a positive relation).

He obtained some empirical support for his proposition, although he had some difficulty with 2, of course. Finally, another approach to this problem is provided by A. Santomero ('On the Role of Transactions Costs and the Rates of Return on the Demand Deposit Decision'), who uses a variant of the Baumol–Tobin model – described in Chapter 5 – and attributed to E. Feige and M. Parkin ('The Optimal Quantity of Money, Bonds, Commodity Inventories, and Capital') and A. Santomero ('A Model of the Demand for Money by Households'). After some discussion of the measurement of the rate of return on demand deposits, he presents empirical results which emphasise the importance of opportunity costs (including inflation) and transactions costs variables. The latter is justified by reference to the T. Saving paper (e.g., 'Transactions Costs and the Demand for Money') and in this respect this paper is the most comprehensive work in the literature.

Let us recall that we have assumed that $P_n \equiv 1$; we can now move directly to a statement of the total demand and supply situation and to a formal statement of Walras's Law. Total demand, for all commodities, consists of the demand for money (equation 3.5) plus the demand for all commodities summed (equation 3.4). This global sum produces equation (3.6):

$$\sum_{i=1}^{n} P_i D_i \equiv \sum_{j=1}^{n-1} P_j D_j + D_n \equiv S_n + D_n. \tag{3.6}$$

Similarly, total supply, taken from the same relations, is given by equation (3.7):

$$\sum_{i=1}^{n} P_i S_i \equiv \sum_{j=1}^{n-1} P_j S_j + S_n \equiv D_n + S_n. \tag{3.7}$$

Since things that are identical to the same thing are identical to each other, we may deduce equation (3.8):

$$\sum_{i=1}^{n} P_i D_i \equiv \sum_{i=1}^{n} P_i S_i. \tag{3.8}$$

We will refer to this equation as Walras's Law; as it appears here, it is the direct result of the statement that all planned or actual spending of funds (in or out of equilibrium) must equal all expected or actual receipts.[15] Thus, we are restricting our analysis to points along the budget hyperplane, where this identity holds; further, since no mechanisms were stated, the assumption of Walras's Law implies that only points of equilibrium (which are, of course, on the budget hyperplane by assumption) are of interest to us. Later we will look at some problems of disequilibrium (in a macroeconomic context).

The n equilibrium equations described as equation (3.3), along with the Walrasian condition that all things must add up (equation 3.8), produces a solution for (at most) the $n - 1$ money prices in the system; these, it should be recalled, are the only unknowns in the system, the quantities of the goods being given. There are, as well, $n - 1$ independent equations, the application of Walras's Law removing, in effect, one of the relations specified in equation (3.3). This solution for the $n - 1$ money prices makes it possible for us to calculate an equilibrium price level, consisting of the unique values of the money prices weighted by the original quantities available:

$$P = P(P_1, \ldots, P_{n-1}).$$
$$\partial P / \partial P_j > 0 (j = 1, \ldots, n - 1). \tag{3.9}$$

Here, the weighting scheme is not specified and only the property that an increase in a single price will increase the price level is considered. The price level is, of course, the opportunity cost of money in this problem; the existence of this price is guaranteed by the fact that it is composed of the variable money prices, themselves determinate in this framework; its temporal

stability is another matter. Thus we have defined a system of general equilibrium, with money in the budget constraint but not in the utility function,
which provides us with an equilibrium quantity and price (*P*) of money. This
is a sufficient framework for us to deduce a demand function for money (as it
would be for all other goods); however, this demand function is not an
interesting one unless further restrictions are imposed on the system, and it
contains no empirical implications, as we shall see. It is also a non-
dichotomised system.

3.2.3 Three Classical propositions and the demand for money

The principal Classical propositions of interest to monetary economists of
the Patinkin generation are the conditions under which a doubled price level
will follow on the heels of a doubled money stock. This is the theoretical
problem of 'neutrality' tackled by Patinkin, and it boils down to the enum-
eration of the minimum set of assumptions that are necessary to generate
this result in the general equilibrium system, accepting its stability. There are
several ways to proceed:

1. we may state a quantity relation;
2. we may assume the 'homogeneity postulate'; or
3. we may assume Say's Law.

Consider the quantity approach. Let us define the market excess demand
for each of the $n - 1$ commodities as in equation (3.10).

$$D_j(P_1, \ldots, P_{n-1}) - S_j \equiv X_j(P_1, \ldots, P_{n-1}). \ (j = 1, \ldots, n - 1) \quad (3.10)$$

Then, leaving the excess demand for money undefined for the moment, the
$n - 1$ independent equilibrium conditions for the excess demand problem are
given by equation (3.11) and Walras's Law by equation (3.12):

$$X_j(P_1, \ldots, P_{n-1}) = 0 \qquad\qquad (j = 1, \ldots, n - 1) \quad (3.11)$$

$$X_n(P_1, \ldots, P_{n-1}) + \sum_{j=1}^{n-1} P_j X_j(P_1, \ldots, P_{n-1}) \equiv 0. \quad (3.12)$$

X_n here is the excess demand for money. To generate a specific result for X_n,
then, we may follow any of the three routes just mentioned above. To pursue
1, we must define equation (3.13) or its equivalent, for the aggregate
case:[16]

$$D_n \equiv \alpha \sum_{j=1}^{n-1} P_j S_j. \quad (3.13)$$

This relation states that consumers desire to hold a proportion of the money
value of their initial balances in the form of money balances (because,

presumably, this money balance is expected to facilitate transactions). Since

$$X_n \equiv D_n - S_n$$

we may write equation (3.14), the excess demand for money:

$$X_n \equiv \alpha \sum_{j=1}^{n-1} P_j S_j - S_n \equiv X_n(P_1, \ldots, P_{n-1}; \alpha, S_i). \ (i = 1, \ldots, n) \quad (3.14)$$

This is, as noted, a function of the $n - 1$ money prices, the n initial quantities and the parameter α.

Equation (3.14) is the excess demand for money function we are after, and it provides us with the essential Classical result. That is, if we double all money prices in equation (3.14) we get a *positive* excess demand for money.[17] On the other hand, if we *also* double initial money balances, we get an excess demand for money function that is homogeneous of degree 0 in money prices and initial money balances, as the first part of equation (3.14) makes transparently clear. Other Classical results, such as that a doubling of the quantity of money is consistent with unchanged holdings of commodities so long as money prices also double, also hold in this system.

Let us, then, consider case 2, the 'homogeneity postulate'. The condition we require to get the Classical result, again employing equations (3.10), (3.11) and (3.12), is to assume that the $n - 1$ commodity excess demand functions are homogeneous of degree 0 in money prices.[18] This property of the commodity excess demand functions can be visualised as equation (3.15):[19]

$$X_j(\lambda P_1, \ldots, \lambda P_{n-1}) = X_j(P_1, \ldots, P_{n-1}). \ (j = 1, \ldots, n - 1) \quad (3.15)$$

That is, increasing prices by a factor λ does not affect excess demand, for each product. Then, returning to the basic model embodied in equation (3.12), we can conceive of all money prices being doubled ($\lambda = 2$), which produces equation (3.16):

$$X_n(\lambda P_1, \ldots, \lambda P_{n-1}) + \sum_{j=1}^{n-1} \lambda P_j X_j(\lambda P_1, \ldots, \lambda P_{n-1}) \equiv 0. \quad (3.16)$$

We can now apply equation (3.15) directly to the right-hand term in equation (3.16); the λ vanishes there, so that equation (3.17) results:

$$X_n(\lambda P_1, \ldots, \lambda P_{n-1}) + \sum_{j=1}^{n-1} \lambda P_j X_j(P_1, \ldots, P_{n-1}) \equiv 0. \quad (3.17)$$

Recalling that equation (3.12) contains another version of the second term in equation (3.17), we may substitute that directly into equation (3.17); the result is equation (3.18), in which the excess demand for money is shown to be homogeneous of degree 1 in money prices as a result of the assumptions made (Walras's Law, the homogeneity postulate, and all other miscellaneous assumptions):

$$X_n(\lambda P_1, \ldots, \lambda P_{n-1}) \equiv \lambda X_n(P_1, \ldots, P_{n-1}). \tag{3.18}$$

What we have established is, however, essentially trivial – even though a proposition about the demand for money resulted – because none of the restrictions of consumer demand theory can be shown to apply. To be sure, we can establish that doubling M and doubling all money prices leaves the equilibrium undisturbed. To see this, we need merely look at equation (3.10), the definition of the excess demand functions. It is clear there that a doubling of initial real balances (S_n), accompanied by a doubling of money prices, necessarily implies a doubling of demand if the equilibrium condition expressed in equation (3.11) is to hold. Thus, we have established the Classical conditions for a general equilibrium system, under which the doubling of the quantity of money can be *linked* with a doubling of the price level. Note, in particular, that we assumed overall equilibrium and that we did not state how, if they do, things come about in this way; notice, as well, that we are indifferent to how the change in money balances comes about – we merely wished to state a logical possibility. Thus, as Patinkin notes, we have not provided a mechanism for determining money prices and what we have, essentially, is a barter economy ($n - 2$ independent relations, by virtue of the application of *both* the homogeneity postulate and Walras's Law).

Let us, then, apply Say's Law (case 3). In terms of the model employed here, this is usually considered to be the assumption embodied in equation (3.19) that the excess demand for *commodities* is identically equal to zero:

$$\sum_{j=1}^{n-1} P_j X_j \equiv 0. \tag{3.19}$$

If money were not in the budget constraint, then it would not be in the problem as an economic entity and equation (3.19) would be a correct picture of the situation; this is a trivial case, as discussed by Henderson and Quandt:

> The crucial point in considering Say's Law and money is whether or not money is in the consumers' budget constraints. If it is, [3.19] is an equilibrium condition. If it is not, [3.19] is an identity.[20]

That is, if

$$\sum_{j=1}^{n-1} P_j X_j \equiv 0 \quad \text{(Say's Law)}$$

and

$$\sum_{i=1}^{n} P_i X_i \equiv 0 \quad \text{(Walras's Law)}$$

we have

$$\sum_{j=1}^{n-1} P_j X_j + P_n X_n - \sum_{j=1}^{n-1} P_j X_j \equiv 0$$

which implies equation (3.20):

$$X_n \equiv 0. \qquad (3.20)$$

This is more than one would desire of neutrality, since it is a condition that presumably holds at all points in budget space, leaving us with no room whatsoever for an interesting monetary theory. Since we feel we cannot release Walras's Law, this implies that we must relax Say's Law to the force of an equality.[21] This leaves us with $X_n = 0$ and we can proceed, as before, to employ equation (3.13) to achieve a solution with a non-homogeneous demand for money function.

That is, assuming equation (3.19) is an equilibrium condition, along with Walras's Law, implies that there are at most $n - 2$ independent equations, and, correspondingly, only $n - 2$ variables for which values can be found, at equilibrium. This leaves us with no solution to the doubling of prices/money problem, since the latter requires determinate money prices to make sense. We have neutral money, to be sure, because doubling prices or M or both has no effect on our barter commodity markets; but we have no solution to our money demand problem as it stands, and consequently the solution holds no interest for the monetary economist. We may, then, construct the excess demand for money function which we employed above, with the constant α, as

$$X_n(P_1, \ldots, P_{n-1}) = \alpha \sum_{j=1}^{n-1} P_j S_j - S_n$$

and, at equilibrium, for $X_n = 0$, we would have equation (3.21):

$$S_n = \alpha \sum_{j=1}^{n-1} P_j S_j. \qquad (3.21)$$

This is recognisable as the equation of exchange once again, but here it is not interpreted as an identity but as an equilibrium condition. This case is, in effect, that of case 1, consequently.

3.2.4 *Some refinements: money in the utility function and the expenditure constraint*

At this point it is useful to go backwards analytically and consider the properties of the utility functions and the budget constraints that underlie demand functions such as those we have just considered; in this respect, the argument of this section is a short verbalisation of the material presented in Appendix A, which also contains the relevant proofs. In particular, then, the Patinkin model has been shown to have two major features that inhibit its usefulness; it contains essentially no useful empirical implications, and it relies on the insertion of money (and the price level) in the utility function. To deal with both of these problems, R. Clower has suggested that, if consumers are *required* to make all transactions by means of the medium of exchange – using a second constraint – then one can arrive at a useful formulation.[22] Firstly, assume consumers maximise equation (3.22) for $n - 1$ commodities,

$$u = U(S_1, \ldots, S_{n-1}) \tag{3.22}$$

subject to a budget constraint

$$\sum_{i=1}^{n-1} S_i P_i + S_n = M + Y \tag{3.23}$$

and a constraint imposing a proportionality on money holding (as in equation 3.13):

$$S_n = k \sum_{i=1}^{n-1} S_i P_i. \tag{3.24}$$

Here S_n is the final money balance and M is the initial balance. Collapsing these constraints together (consumers do not choose S_n but only S_i in this individual maximising problem) produces

$$(1 + k) \sum_{i=1}^{n-1} S_i P_i = M + Y. \tag{3.25}$$

The first-order conditions for this system are given by equations (3.26).

$$U_i = \lambda(1 + k)P_i \qquad i = 1, \ldots, n - 1$$
$$(1 + k) \sum_{i=1}^{n-1} S_i P_i = M + Y. \tag{3.26}$$

To produce a 'demand-for-money' function, though, we need merely manipulate equations (3.23) and (3.24) – ignoring the first-order conditions – to obtain

$$S_n = \frac{k}{1 + k}(M + Y). \tag{3.27}$$

Thus, $\partial S_n / \partial Y > 0$ (for $k > 0$) and $\partial S_n / \partial P_r = 0$ exhaust the characteristics of the demand for money in this 'Lloyd Classical model' system.

Lloyd proposes, then, that what is essential for the Classical case – and thus provides a useful point of departure – is that the consumer's demand function for money be homogeneous of degree 1 in prices, income and money holdings. Thus, he suggests that the dual constraint problem can be set up with equations (3.22) and (3.23) and with equation (3.28), the demand for money assumed to have the homogeneity property just mentioned:

$$S_n = f(P_1, \ldots, P_n, Y, M). \qquad (3.28)$$

Then, the consumer will be assumed to maximise (3.22) subject to (3.23) *and* (3.28). As Lloyd then explains, the model has all of the Neoclassical properties as well as an (assumed) demand for money function which is less restrictive (being homogeneous of degree 1 in all of its arguments, rather than rigidly proportional to expenditures).

Basically, then, we are asked to consider two choices for the role of money in our Classical monetary economy. The first of these is the Lloyd Classical model, which uses equation (3.22) as its utility function, and the second is equation (3.29), the Samuelson–Patinkin utility function:

$$u = U(S_1, \ldots, S_{n-1}, M, P_1, \ldots, P_n). \qquad (3.29)$$

In equation (3.29) then, both the nominal quantity of money and the list of money prices (the latter to represent the idea that money is demanded not for itself, but only for what it will buy) are in the domain, while in the former, only real commodities enter. In particular, we should note, in place of $P_1, \ldots, P_n$, we could use equation (3.9) to calculate P; this is Patinkin's version.

The Lloyd Classical model has the limiting feature that the role of money is entirely arbitrary, while the Patinkin–Samuelson model, as based on equation (3.29), treats money just like all other goods.[23] That is, in the latter system, even with the explicit role given to money by equation (3.29), we must impose further conditions to ensure that money has a unique role to play. In particular, equation (3.29) treats all of its arguments with an even hand – the consumer reacts directly to changes in any of the demands and prices in the domain of U according to his preferences. Moreover, this reaction initiates changes in the quantities of every commodity demanded, which in turn alters the absolute and relative contribution of the various variables to the level of preference satisfaction. This sweeping adjustment is an extremely unrealistic mode of behaviour, and it is more realistic to argue that consumers do not react in such a complete manner but actually lump together commodities exhibiting similar characteristics; this, one might argue, can be effected by means of the assumption of a weakly separable utility function. Furthermore, the Samuelson–Patinkin model is normally taken along with the assumption that equation (3.29) is homogeneous of degree 0 in all of the monetary variables; this, too, is somewhat restrictive. Finally, the Samuelson model does not possess the full list of Neoclassical restrictions; in particular, it is lacking in the symmetry of the substitution effects, the negativity of the 'own substitution' effects and the negative semi-definiteness of the matrix of substitution effects.

A promising addition to this literature has been generated variously by P. Kalman, R. Dusansky and B. Wickström, who have at different times used the utility functions listed as equations (3.20) and (3.21).[24] The first of these is consistent with the Samuelson–Patinkin framework, while the second introduces the distinction between the reservation demand (M) and the transaction demand (m) for money, as in Clower.

$$u = \alpha\left(\sum_{i=1}^{n-1} P_i S_i + M\right) + \beta(S_1, \ldots, S_{n-1}, M) + \delta(P_1, \ldots, P_n) \quad (3.30)$$

$$u = \alpha\left(\sum_{i=1}^{n-1} P_i S_i + M + m\right) + \beta\,(S_1, \ldots, S_{n-1}, M, m) + \delta\,(p_1, \ldots, p_n). \quad (3.31)$$

Here α is a positive constant, and β and δ are functions. These functions do, indeed, permit the relevant Neoclassical restrictions; further, the second, coupled with the dual budget constraint of the Clower model, provides a useful model of the choice problem in the monetary context. But, although the authors claim the contrary, this is not the most general formulation possible – being in the additively separable form – and can be improved upon.

It can be shown then – and is shown, in Appendix A – that, in the context of the dual budget constraint formulation, the weakly separable utility function exhibited here as equation (3.32) possesses all of the Neoclassical restrictions:

$$u = U[\varphi(S_1, \ldots, S_{n-1}), M, m, P_1, \ldots, P_n]. \quad (3.32)$$

Here, as in equation (3.31), m represents the demand for transactions balances, M the demand for reservation balances, S_i the demand for the ith real commodity, and $\varphi\,(S_1, \ldots, S_{n-1})$ is called the 'branch' or proper utility function. In the appendix then it is proved that this function, with its property of *weak* separability, retains all of the familiar Neoclassical restrictions and empirical implications, including, especially, the symmetry property for the commodities that are either demanded or supplied. Furthermore, it is demonstrated there that if the marginal utilities of the transaction and reservation demands are equal (at the optimum), then the substitution effects are symmetrical across *all* commodities. We will leave these matters, however, and turn to some macroeconomic aspects of this literature.

3.3   Patinkin's macroeconomics: statics and dynamics

3.3.1   *The demand for money in the basic Patinkin model*

A lot of the richness of detail of what has gone before in this chapter is lost when we turn to a macroeconomic consideration of the real-balance and wealth effects, but there is a proportionate gain in generality and in the policy implications one can draw; also, one can begin the long trek to the empirical studies of the demand for money. We intend to study the Patinkin macro-system and then to use the framework generated, in a dynamic version, to consider the analysis of Pesek and Saving. This work will be essentially theoretical, only occasionally involving the demand for money itself, but will provide the essential background to Chapter 4, where a considerable variety of explicit models will be discussed as if they come from some part of this analytical tradition.

The labour market. In the Patinkin system there are four markets, those for commodities, labour, bonds and money. The labour market is the standard macroeconomic version, with a production function and a supply function for labour. The production function assumes a fixed capital stock ($\bar{K}$) and is exhibited as equation (3.33); y, here, is real GNP:

$$y = \varphi(L,\bar{K}). \tag{3.33}$$

We should note, for later reference, that real money balances are not included in (3.33) although it is certainly consistent with Patinkin's argument for the consumer that they could be treated as a factor of production. A. Sinai and H. Stokes have discussed this question in a paper which also produces some empirical estimates for the US manufacturing sector. They advance the argument that money improves the efficiency of factor markets (or saves time in the hiring of inputs), which is reasonable, although quite possibly hard to capture empirically.[25] Earlier, M. Nadiri, in a paper discussed below, also argued for such an effect.[26] S. Fisher considers these views and argues that one can set up a model in which money is legitimately a factor of production, if one 'introduces an interaction between production and financial decisions', for example by permitting money to economise on labour costs (on labour used in transactions). In particular, in the aggregate,

> Real balances are not described as a factor because increases in real balances directly increase physical production, but rather because increases in real balances free resources which would otherwise be tied up in transactions.[27]

Such a result also holds if the firm employs cash in connection with its output (e.g., a vending machine business). This is relevant depending on the degree of aggregation across goods – i.e., it seems less relevant when the US manufacturing industry is considered and more relevant for a production function of GNP (in which retail sales are included). Fisher concludes with some kindly words to those who wish to put money in the utility function.

The labour supply function, then, is a simple function of real wages only, as equation (3.34) argues:[28]

$$L^s = R\left(\frac{W}{P}\right) \tag{3.34}$$

If we assume a perfect labour market, then we can argue that the real wage is equal to the marginal product of labour, as in equation (3.35):

$$\frac{W}{P} = \varphi_L(L,\bar{K}). \tag{3.35}$$

The labour demand function that results from competitive hiring and the assumed production function is then given by equation (3.36); this results directly from the inversion of equation (3.35):

$$L^d = Q\left(\frac{W}{P}, \bar{K}\right). \tag{3.36}$$

This gives us five distinct equations (with $L^d = L^s = L$) in six unknowns (y, P, W, L^s, L^d and L); under the assumptions stated, we can determine the real wage, real income and the quantity of labour in this sector. We may, then, refer to this determined value of real income as y_f, full employment real income, in the sections which follow.[29]

The commodity market. The consumption function that Patinkin assumes is a standard one, except for the presence of household holdings of real money balances (M_0^h/P); C is measured in real terms here.

$$C = C\left(y_f, i, \frac{M_0^h}{P}\right). \tag{3.37}$$

The presence of the real money balances here, where the 0 represents initial balances and the h represents households, can be justified intuitively from what went earlier in this chapter; that is, money is an item of wealth which performs services to the consumer. Changes in wealth, like changes in income, will affect consumption.[30] This has implications for the demand for money, at least if one is performing single-equation estimates of this function. Thus, assume the following linear consumption function:

$$C_t = \beta Y_t^e + \alpha(M_{t-1} - M_t^d) + \eta i_t \tag{3.38}$$

where Y_t^e is permanent income and α represents the adjustment during time period t of desired balances (M_t^d) to actual balances at the end of the previous period (M_{t-1}); i_t is an interest rate. With a long-run demand for money function like equation (3.39), an adjustment equation for money (equation 3.40) and a Koyck lag (λ) for permanent income, equation (3.41) represents a reduced form for the demand for money that could be estimated ($S_t = Y_t - C_t$):

$$M_t^d = \gamma Y_t^e - \delta i_t \tag{3.39}$$

$$M_t - M_{t-1} = c(M_t^d - M_{t-1}) + dS_t \tag{3.40}$$

$$M_t = (1 - c - d\alpha - \lambda)M_{t-1} - \lambda(1 - c - d\alpha)M_{t-2} + [(1 - \lambda)(c\gamma - d\beta + \alpha\delta\gamma) + d]Y_t -$$
$$(d\eta + c\delta + d\alpha\delta)i_t + \lambda(d\eta + c\delta + d\alpha\delta)i_{t-1} + \text{error}_t - \lambda\,\text{error}_{t-1}. \tag{3.41}$$

Aside from the mess in the error term, this equation suggests some problems with single-equation estimates of the demand for money.[31] Firstly, the influence of the interest rate on the demand for money will be incorrectly estimated on account of the wealth adjustment parameter (α), with the effect being underestimated if such a wealth effect occurs.[32] Secondly, the income term is complicated by a negative term (which is, though, small).[33]

The investment function, depending on the same arguments as the consumption function, appears as equation (3.42); again, I is measured in real terms:

$$I = I\left(y_f, i, \frac{M_0^f}{P}\right). \tag{3.42}$$

Following Jorgenson, we might derive this function from a formal maximisation (over time) of the profit function of business firms. We can conceive of a firm's net profits as given by a function of the time paths of input prices and quantities, output prices and quantities, the interest rate and various tax variables.[34] Business firms, in the Jorgenson framework, are conceived of as being constrained by a production function (free of real money balances as in Patinkin) and the need to maintain their capital equipment. If we do not actually enter real money balances as a factor of production, and Patinkin allows that we have this choice, then we must introduce real money balances as a part of a budget constraint if it is going to come through to equation (3.42). The Jorgenson model does not do this, although there is no technical difficulty involved, but it is necessary, if we are to think of the Jorgenson model as underlying Patinkin's aggregate investment function, to think of the firm as subject to a financial constraint in which the various sources of capital funds (bonds, retained earnings and money, in our case) appear. By entering this constraint into the formal model underlying equation (3.42) we would, for example, give the firm the opportunity of investing in plant and equipment from the proceeds of changes in the value of its money balances (not to mention paying dividends). We could also generate an interesting business demand for money function in this manner.

As noted above, we are analysing four markets, one of which is this, the commodity, market. We are not, at the moment, interested in the system of

Keynes, so we proceed to effect an aggregation. If we assume the absence of distribution effects and the composite goods theorem on the behaviour of the prices of both consumer and investment goods, we obtain equation (3.43):

$$F\left(y_f, i, \frac{M_0}{P}\right) = C\left(y_f, i, \frac{M_0^h}{P}\right) + I\left(y_f, i, \frac{M_0^f}{P}\right) + G_0. \qquad (3.43)$$

Here a fixed level of government expenditures (G_0), hereafter to be ignored, is introduced for purposes of consistency. Note, as well, that an aggregation of money is also assumed:

$$\frac{M_0}{P} = \frac{M_0^h}{P} + \frac{M_0^f}{P}.$$

We may refer to equation (3.43) as the aggregate demand function for commodities.

The aggregate supply of commodities function is given by equation (3.33) above, under the assumptions we have made concerning the labour market. Thus, we may express equilibrium in the commodity market by equation (3.44):

$$F\left(y_f, i, \frac{M_0}{P}\right) = y_f. \qquad (3.44)$$

This is an *IS* curve in the familiar (i, P) dimension; it is one equation in two unknowns (i, P), and it contains one parameter (M_0); y_f, here, is essentially predetermined, to make a useful distinction.

The bond market. In order to justify a market rate of interest, there ought to be a bond market in the problem. The bond traded here is a private one and will be conceived of as paying a coupon of \$1, with a term-to-maturity of infinity (i.e., it is a perpetuity). Its price, therefore, will be \$1/i, and its quantity, in real terms, will be given by B/P. Bonds are produced by firms and taken up by final wealth-holders. Thus the following three equations, in four unknowns (i, B^d, B^s, P) describe this sector; there is again one parameter (M_0).

$$B^d = iPH\left(y_f, \frac{1}{i}, \frac{M_0^h}{P}\right) \qquad (3.45)$$

$$B^s = iPJ\left(y_f, \frac{1}{i}, \frac{M_0^f}{P}\right) \qquad (3.46)$$

$$B^s = B^d \qquad (3.47)$$

Note that the demand for bonds is by lenders (households), and that H and J are functions, while i and P are variables.

We can move to the (i, P) dimension by considering the effect on the equilibrium of a change in the price level, holding the interest rate constant. While one normally expects that the absence of money illusion would mean that the nominal demand and supply of bonds would simply double if prices doubled, in the Patinkin model the shift in the demand curve is assumed not equal to that in the supply curve; this is sufficient to establish that the bond equilibrium curve equivalent to the *IS* and *LM* curves has a definite slope. When there is a price rise, both the demand and supply functions for bonds (in the $(1/i, B)$ dimension) shift to the right equally. But the reaction to the fall in the real value of money holdings is different for demanders than for suppliers; that is, while both suffer a loss of wealth and reduce their total portfolios, business firms (who are the bond suppliers) will require some additional funds 'to replenish their real balances', the total of which has deteriorated. To do this, they will tend to issue bonds. Thus a higher interest rate is associated with a higher price level in the bond market and the bond equilibrium curve is up-sloping. This, of course, is an *ad hoc* formulation which 'gets the job done'.

To complete the bond market we will impose an equilibrium condition similar to that for the *IS* curve. In this case, since the bond is an inside bond (i.e., a bond not issued by the government), the equilibrium can be given by equation (3.48):

$$B\left(y_f, \frac{1}{i}, \frac{M_0}{P}\right) = 0. \tag{3.48}$$

The demand for money (the market for money). Actually, if we apply Walras's Law, the fourth market has already been fully described, even to the properties of the functions; this is especially convenient, since it is the demand for money we wish to examine in this study, and if the supply is fixed, at M_0, we will then have several derived properties of some interest. Let us, then, specify the *LM* curve as in equation (3.49); here we have one equation in the two unknowns (i, P):

$$\frac{M_0}{P} = L\left(y_f, i, \frac{M_0}{P}\right). \tag{3.49}$$

It should be obvious that the three equilibrium conditions remaining after the application of the Classical assumptions to the labour market, equations (3.44), (3.48) and (3.49), are more than enough to determine the remaining two variables in the system (i, P). The reason for this overdetermination, clearly, is that we have a system in which Walras's Law holds (or can be assumed to hold) and we have not yet applied it. Thus, equation (3.50), representing the fact that the excess demand for money is equivalent to the excess demand for commodities plus the net bond demand, completes the system at this point.[35]

$$\frac{M_0}{P} - L\left(y_f, i, \frac{M_0}{P}\right) \equiv \left[F\left(y_f, i, \frac{M_0}{P}\right) - y_f\right] + B\left(y_f, \frac{1}{i}, \frac{M_0}{P}\right). \quad (3.50)$$

By rearranging the above equation, we see that our assumptions have been strong enough to *define* the demand for money, as in equation (3.51); this applies to both the interest rate and price arguments.

$$L\left(y_f, i, \frac{M_0}{P}\right) \equiv \left[y_f - F\left(y_f, i, \frac{M_0}{P}\right)\right] - B\left(y_f, \frac{1}{i}, \frac{M_0}{P}\right) + \frac{M_0}{P}. \quad (3.51)$$

We may calculate the sign of the interest rate effect on the demand for money as composed of the sum of the effects on the commodity demand and bond demand functions:

$$\frac{\partial L}{\partial i} \equiv - \frac{\partial F}{\partial i} - \frac{\partial B}{\partial i}.$$

Since $\partial F/\partial i < 0$ and $\partial B/\partial i > 0$, we see that this effect is an ambiguous one. To put it another way, we would expect $\partial L/\partial i$ to be negative (from the bond market influence alone), modified by the effect of the interest rate on spending. To Keynes (it can be argued), the latter effect would be zero, and thus the liquidity preference function is defined as a negative relation deriving from the bond market.

Instead of directly obtaining $\partial L/\partial P$, whose properties are possibly not very interesting anyway, let us rewrite equation (3.51) as (3.52):

$$\frac{M_0}{P} \equiv \left[F\left(y_f, i, \frac{M_0}{P}\right) - y_f\right] + B\left(y_f, \frac{1}{i}, \frac{M_0}{P}\right) + L\left(y_f, i, \frac{M_0}{P}\right) \quad (3.52)$$

Then, when we differentiate by M_0/P, we obtain the following interesting result, where (e.g.) F_3 represents the partial derivative of the aggregate demand function with respect to its third argument:

$$1 \equiv F_3 + B_3 + L_3. \quad (3.53)$$

This result argues that the sum of the propensities to spend out of real balances (themselves functions of the variables in the system, of course) must be unity in a system in which Walras's Law holds. The derived property of the demand for money, of course, is

$$L_3 \equiv 1 - F_3 - B_3.$$

One may also directly test equation (3.52), preferably subject to the constraint given as equation (3.53).[36]

The foregoing Patinkin model is certainly a useful one, but it nevertheless has a number of prominent defects which are central to its efficient operation. Following Brunner and Meltzer, we can list the problem areas as follows.[37]

1. Bonds and real capital are (in effect) aggregated and their price is represented by the interest rate.
2. Indeed, there is only one relative price in the model – the interest rate – so that an effective analysis of substitution effects necessary to understand the adjustment mechanisms in the economy is impossible.
3. The assumption of full employment prevents the analysis of some interesting cases.
4. The empirical record is poor.

The details of the Brunner and Meltzer analysis, which includes the specification of a credit market alongside a money market, need not detain us here. On the other hand, to capture the flavour of their position, we can briefly examine their money market. This consists of an equilibrium condition,

$$mB = M \qquad (3.54)$$

(where B is the monetary base and M the desired stock of nominal balances), an equation that determines m (the banking multiplier) and a demand-for-money function (equation 3.56):

$$m = m(i, e, i_t, P_k, W_n, W_h) \qquad m_1, m_2 > 0; m_3, \ldots, m_6 < 0 \qquad (3.55)$$

$$M = M(i, e, P_k, W_n, W_h, P) \qquad M_1, M_2 < 0; M_3, \ldots, M_6 > 0 \qquad (3.56)$$

where i here is a nominal interest rate (or an average market rate), e is the expected rate of return on real capital, P_k is the price of existing real capital, W_n is non-human wealth, W_h is human wealth and P is the price level. The model thus has three relative prices (i, e and P) and, curiously, has the feature that P_k – the price of existing real capital – is determined in the money market.[38] From the point of view of this chapter, what is essential here are Brunner and Meltzer's conclusions that in such a climate:

1. the real-balance effect is neither a necessary nor a sufficient condition for a positive response of output to changes in money or the monetary base; and
2. The dominant wealth effect induced by monetary (and some fiscal) policies is a change in the price of existing real assets (P_k) relative to the price level (P).

These occur because changes in the quantity of money (or the price level) or changes in the stock of debt (whether from a deficit or via an open-market operation) cause changes in asset prices. The changes in the asset prices, then, react on equation (3.55) *directly* – as well as on the expenditure curves

– inducing shifts (in the *i*, *P* dimension of Patinkin). Thus the adoption of a broader asset spectrum for wealth-holders, because it implies the possibility of substitution (not to mention complementarity) between money and other assets, raises the possibility that the actual real-balance effect could be negative.

3.3.2 *Disequilibrium results for the demand for money*

In the microeconomic analysis of Patinkin and his critics we considered the role of the real-balance effect in comparative statics; here, instead, we will study a new problem, the adjustment around equilibrium, assuming that the equilibrium exists. The macroeconomic model just laid out is especially suitable for this purpose. What we now want to know is whether (or rather under what conditions) a system with a real-balance effect in it will converge to equilibrium if, for any reason, it starts from a position away from equilibrium. In what follows, we will form adjustment equations in prices and the interest rate, assuming for the moment that the labour market is in equilibrium, and ask if the motion is towards or away from equilibrium in these two remaining variables. There will be various intermediate results as well, some involving the demand for money.

We may begin with a simple Keynesian model of the adjustment process, although with the un-Keynesian assumption that the labour market is in equilibrium; then, the assumption of Walras's Law enables us to dispense with the money market disequilibrium. This leaves us the product and the bond market to analyse; that is, the comparative dynamics of the system can be described completely in terms of the adjustment in these two markets, with the assumptions that we have made to this point. A Keynesian version of the adjustment process might be that prices adjust only in response to excess demand in the product market and that the interest rate responds only to excess demand in the bond market. Equations (3.57) and 3.58) represent this situation:

$$\frac{dP}{dt} = K_1\left[F\left(y_f, i, \frac{M_0}{P}\right) - y_f \right] \qquad K_1 > 0 \quad (3.57)$$

$$\frac{di}{dt} = -K_2 B\left(y_f, \frac{1}{i}, \frac{M_0}{P}\right) \qquad K_2 > 0 \quad (3.58)$$

In equation (3.57), where y_f represents full-employment real income, the argument is that dP/dt is proportional (K_1) to the difference between aggregate demand and aggregate supply (y_f). The sign for K_1 is obtained by arguing that, if there is excess demand in the commodity market, then a rise of prices will eliminate that excess demand; excess demand is also a cause of price rises generally, but that is not how we are using it here, just yet. If the excess demand for bonds is positive, that is, if the demand for bonds exceeds the supply at the current interest rate, then bond prices will rise (or, rather, a bond price rise will restore equilibrium). This, of course, implies a fall in interest rates and explains the negative sign on K_2. Again, we are asserting that the fall in the interest rate will clear the market, not that it will actually happen that way, necessarily.

But equations (3.57) and (3.58) also completely explain the determination of prices and interest rates in this Keynesian-type model. That is, not only does equation (3.57) present the assumption of stabilising price behaviour; but also, as a model of the economy, it is a complete explanation of the determination of prices. This is, therefore, a dichotomous system, and it is, as we shall see below, a stable system as well. It might be thought that in this way – in a system in which excess demand in the commodity markets does not affect interest rates and excess demand in the bond market does not affect prices – a change in the quantity of money (as in the liquidity trap) could not affect the system in any way; but this is actually not so because of the need to satisfy equation (3.52). Certainly it is true that under our assumptions there are only two adjustment parameters needed (K_1 and K_2) to explain the dynamics fully, but, as an inspection of equation (3.59) makes clear, if we are to keep to Walras's Law, a disequilibrium in the money market will in general affect both prices and interest rates:

$$\frac{1}{K_1}\frac{dP}{dt} - \frac{1}{K_2}\frac{di}{dt} \equiv \frac{M_0}{P} - L\left(y_f, i, \frac{M_0}{P}\right). \qquad (3.59)$$

That is, the fact that equations (3.57) and (3.58) describe completely the parameters of adjustment does not also imply that there is no influence of money on the system. Even in the extreme case of the liquidity trap, in which case $di/dt = 0$, there is still adjustment left in equation (3.59), of the kind that will restore equilibrium.

But special cases are of less interest than general cases, at least if one wishes to concentrate on the stability properties of the system. Consider, in place of equations (3.57) and (3.58), the following *ad hoc* adjustment equations, in which the more general multiple causation is assumed:

$$\frac{di}{dt} = -K_1 B\left(y_f, \frac{1}{i}, \frac{M_0}{P}\right) - K_2\left[F\left(y_f, i, \frac{M_0}{P}\right) - y_f\right] \qquad K_1, K_2 > 0 \quad (3.60)$$

$$\frac{dP}{dt} = K_3 B\left(y_f, \frac{1}{i}, \frac{M_0}{P}\right) + K_4\left[F\left(y_f, i, \frac{M_0}{P}\right) - y_f\right] \qquad K_3, K_4 > 0. \quad (3.61)$$

In this set of equations, K_1 and K_4 bear the signs of K_2 and K_1 in equations (3.57) and (3.58) for the same reasons given there. The other two 'off-diagonal' signs can be established as follows.

If spending is greater than full employment income, then the situation is as pictured in Figure 3.1. Given the position of the F schedule (i.e., given the interest rate), we may imagine that the private economy 'desires' to be at an income of y_a. At that income there is excess savings, of the amount $E_1 - E_2$;

Fig. 3.1. Disequilibrium in the product market.

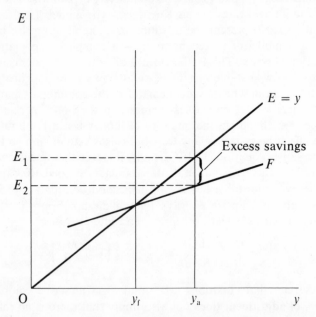

this excess can be removed by an interest rate adjustment. That is, a fall in the interest rate, as if the F schedule were to shift upward, will discourage saving; this comment explains the negative sign in front of the K_2 coefficient. With regard to the relation between the bond market and the price level, the sign established here depends on the asymmetry of the real-balance effect between the bond demand and the bond supply. The result, it can be recalled, was that the demand curve shifted more than the supply curve so that, for example, a rise in the interest rate resulted from a rise in the price level. If we have a situation of excess demand for real bonds, as shown in Figure 3.2 at point a, then this position (for a given interest rate) is equivalent to one taken up by a fall in prices; a rise in prices, by shifting the demand curve back faster than the supply curve, will eliminate this discrepancy and restore equilibrium at the stated interest rate. This establishes that the sign for K_3 is positive.

Equations (3.60) and (3.61) contain sufficient parameters to give us a meaningful appraisal of the likelihood of the stability of overall equilibrium in the broader model. The parameters we would use would be the slopes, whose *a priori* values have already been given, and the adjustment parameters, each of which has been signed under 'stabilising' assumptions. The conceptual

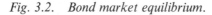

Fig. 3.2. Bond market equilibrium.

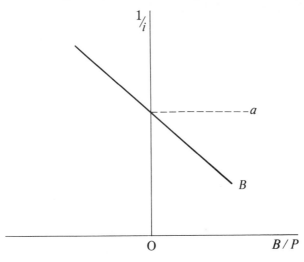

experiment performed here is that of taking up a position off equilibrium and observing the mechanics of the adjustment. In particular, we form the following linear approximation around the equilibrium values (P_0, i_0) of our dependent variables:

$$\frac{di}{dt} = \left(\frac{K_1 B_2}{i_0^2} - K_2 F_2\right)(i - i_0) + \left(\frac{K_1 B_3 M}{P_0^2} + \frac{K_2 F_3 M}{P_0^2}\right)(P - P_0) \qquad (3.62)$$

$$\frac{dP}{dt} = \left(-\frac{K_3 B_2}{i_0^2} + K_4 F_2\right)(i - i_0) +$$
$$\left(-\frac{K_3 B_3 M}{P_0^2} - \frac{K_4 F_3 M}{P_0^2}\right)(P - P_0). \qquad (3.63)$$

Note, in these results, that the notation B_2, for example, means the partial derivative of the bond equilibrium function with respect to its second argument $(1/i)$, and that the terms in larger brackets are simply the partial derivatives of each equation with respect to, alternately, the interest rate and the price level. The chain rule was employed on the troublesome derivatives. This procedure is clearly analogous to taking the total derivative of the system for each of the two dependent variables.

The results just obtained can be simplified into the following two equations:

$$\frac{di}{dt} = (-K_1 a - K_2 b)(i - i_0) - (K_1 c + K_2 d)(P - P_0) \qquad (3.64)$$

$$\frac{dP}{dt} = (K_3 a + K_4 b)(i - i_0) - (K_3 c + K_4 d)(P - P_0). \qquad (3.65)$$

The values of the parameters are:

$$a = -\frac{B_2}{i_0^2} > 0; \, b = F_2 < 0; \, c = -\frac{B_3 M}{P_0^2} < 0; \, d = -\frac{F_3 M}{P_0^2} < 0$$

It is this system whose properties we shall discuss.

Any non-zero column vector $\tilde{x}$ is said to be a characteristic vector of the matrix $\mathbf{A}$ if there exists a number λ such that

$$\mathbf{A}\tilde{x} = \lambda\tilde{x}. \tag{3.66}$$

The number λ is called a characteristic root of $\mathbf{A}$ corresponding to the characteristic vector $\tilde{x}$, and vice versa; an examination of the characteristic roots of our equation system will tell us of its stability properties. $\mathbf{A}$, the matrix in equation (3.66), is the coefficient matrix of the system expressed by equations (3.64) and (3.65) as noted in the following:

$$\mathbf{A} = \begin{bmatrix} -K_1 a - K_2 b & -K_1 c - K_2 d \\ K_3 a + K_4 b & K_3 c + K_4 d \end{bmatrix}. \tag{3.67}$$

To solve for the roots of this system, we solve the following quadratic equation, expressed in terms of the original parameters and λ.[39]

$$\begin{vmatrix} -K_1 a - K_2 b - \lambda & -K_1 c - K_2 d \\ K_3 a + K_4 b & K_3 c + K_4 d - \lambda \end{vmatrix} = 0. \tag{3.68}$$

When we do that we get a quadratic which is exhibited as equation (3.69); the parameters of our problem are then defined in the bracketed expressions to the right:

$$\lambda^2 + g\lambda + h = 0 \begin{cases} g = K_1 a + K_2 b - K_3 c - K_4 d \\ h = -K_1 K_4 ad - K_2 K_3 bc + K_1 K_4 bc + K_2 K_3 ad \end{cases}$$

$$\tag{3.69}$$

The solution of this equation is available in a standard form; adapted to our problem, the stability properties of this system can be derived from an examination of equation (3.70). In particular, if this function has negative real parts (a situation that doesn't always hold), we will have stability.[40]

$$\lambda_1, \lambda_2 = \frac{-g \pm \sqrt{(g^2 - 4h)}}{2}. \tag{3.70}$$

We see then that explicit assumptions in the various theoretical models produce generalisations about the stability of this system, as well as some interesting comparisons. For example, if the interest elasticity of the aggregate spending function is zero, so that b is zero, then, since all of the remaining parameters in g are positive, stability is insured (if K_2 and K_3 are small); this comes from a Keynesian assumption, although it is not, quite possibly, a result Keynes himself would have applauded. Another condition we might find interesting here occurs when direct effects on market dominate indirect (off-diagonal) – or when K_2 and K_3 are zero. In that case, as well, both g and h are positive and stability can be guaranteed. This is the case when causation is 'simple-Keynesian' as described above.

A third case we might find interesting occurs when real-balance effects are zero, so that both B_3 and F_3 are zero. This, of course, is also a Keynesian system, at least in the sense of downgrading the real-balance effect, and is one in which c and d are therefore zero. In this event equations (3.64) and (3.65) collapse into two simpler equations in $(i - i_0)$, and the sign on K_3, which depended on a difference between the real-balance effect on bond-demanders from that on bond-suppliers, cannot be stated *a priori*. Both equations (3.64) and (3.65) would then depend on the interest rate disequilibrium, which would put the idea of the liquidity trap into its strongest light (if the equilibrium interest rate is less than the liquidity trap rate). Further, as long as the trap prevailed, equilibrium is unattainable. In this case we see the importance of the real-balance effect in undermining the Keynesian 'general disequilibrium'. Note that if $F_3 = 0$ only, we still have stability here.

There are a lot of reasons why one might be interested in disequilibrium models, but the principal reason we are interested in them *here* involves the correct estimation of econometric models of the demand for money. D. Tucker notes (pessimistically) that, since macro-markets are only accidentally in equilibrium, and never all at the same time, we inevitably have severe econometric problems:

1. whenever any single market switches from excess demand to excess supply the structure of the whole system changes; and
2. the estimation of a model that assumes a market is cleared when in fact it is not produces inconsistent estimates.

Thus,

> in the presence of significant and shifting market disequilibrium the demand for money is an ambiguous and arbitrary (and hence treacherous) concept and this limits its usefulness for studying *short-run* phenomena.[41]

In particular, monetary policy would be difficult to operate successfully if such structural 'shifts' occurred to any significant extent.

Turning to a more formal use of the disequilibrium properties of the demand-for-money function, it is necessary first to put down a system that contains the kind of disequilibrium envisaged in the Keynesian literature. Retaining equations (3.43), (3.48) and (3.49), let us introduce a new labour supply function in nominal rather than in real wages:

$$L^s = R^*(W). \tag{3.71}$$

We will retain equation (3.36) for the labour demand and the market will still clear for $L^s = L^d$, but now the possibility exists that the labour market will generate a quantity of employment that is not equivalent to the full-employment total. Needless to say, the quantity achieved (L) will be less than the full-employment total except in equilibrium.

We may, in these circumstances, rewrite the aggregate production function of equation (3.33) as the following:

$$y = \begin{cases} \left[Q\left(\frac{W}{P}, \bar{K}\right), \bar{K} \right] \text{ if } W/P \geqslant (W/P)_0 \\ \left[R\left(\frac{W}{P}\right), \bar{K} \right] \quad \text{ if } W/P \leqslant (W/P)_0 \end{cases} \qquad (3.72)$$

That is, the actual output of commodities (y) – or rather, its equivalent in income actually produced – will now be determined by the actual quantity of labour employed. This actual quantity will depend on whether we are above or below the equilibrium real wage ($(W/P)_0$). If we are above, then the quantity of labour actually employed is read off the demand curve; if below, it is read off the supply curve. Thus, as Tucker notes, the value of y carried forward to other markets is itself dependent on different structural parameters (R versus Q). Even if the structure itself is constant, we will have structural shifts of reduced-form functions which use real income, as the demand for money does, if we are examining anything but long-run equilibrium.

Other markets could be put into disequilibrium, of course, but this is enough for our purpose here, which is to demonstrate the problems that arise.[42] The implication, at any rate, is that (with labour market disequilibrium), in other markets, *effective* demands will be less than equilibrium demand (in the bond market and in the commodities market). That is, whether the R or Q function dominates in equation (3.72), the quantity of employment will be less than the equilibrium (full-employment) total and aggregate demands will exceed aggregate supplies. We may also suppose that these markets fail to clear for reasons of their own, in which case the demand for money function – itself deduced by application of Walras's Law – would have the general form of equation (3.73), since actual demands for funds to purchase labour services, commodities and bonds will reflect the actual activity in these sectors:

$$M^d = f\left(i, \frac{M_0}{P}, y; Q^* - Q, L^* - L, B^* - B \right). \qquad (3.73)$$

We note that, in each case, whether we are on the demand or supply schedule (and hence which structural parameter is relevant) will depend on whether we are above or below equilibrium. Tucker's paper considers some of the estimation problems that arise.[43, 44]

3.4   Pesek and Saving [45]

We have already, in Chapter 2, taken up the main definitional foundations of the Pesek and Saving argument, which has now grown into the 'net wealth' controversy. The present chapter is involved primarily with wealth and real-balance concepts and the implications for the demand of money, but we should emphasise that if Pesek and Saving are right – that is, if the best way to conceive of inside money is as net wealth to the economy – then the theorems of the Neoclassical Monetarists so aptly described by Patinkin apply to a much wider range of assets (e.g., narrow money) in a fractional reserve system based on outside money, than explicitly discussed by Patinkin, whose money is of the outside variety. There are immediate policy implications as well, and it is clear that under these conditions an important part of the transmission mechanism carrying monetary policy through to the final variables could be the result of direct wealth effects of a monetary origin.

Monetary economists have found it difficult to swallow much of the Pesek and Saving analysis. Some of this seems to have been the result of those authors' ability to ruffle the feathers of their contemporaries by such passages as:

> The history of the wealth effect is one of the most ironic ones in economics. Keynes stated both parts of the wealth effect, emphasized their importance, and then let wealth slip through his fingers by his failure to build it into his analysis.[46]

The effects mentioned here are:

1. the price-induced wealth effect attributed to Patinkin (and others, before); and
2. the interest-induced wealth effect best explained by Metzler.[47]

The latter is the concept that Pesek and Saving wish to add to standard analysis, and it involves the revaluing of a flow of services (more particularly the services of money) expected to be received in perpetuity as a result of a change in the appropriate interest rate. The effect itself is on consumption (and investment) and it could be caused initially by an open market operation; it operates independently of a price level effect, by which we mean that, even if prices cannot change for institutional reasons, a wealth effect by means of interest rate changes could operate as the result of, say, an expansionary open-market operation.

The argument over the Pesek and Saving position, that inside money is net wealth, has gone on for some time now. Their main views, that the liability of the bank is essentially dissolved upon the issue of demand deposits and that the interest payment foregone in holding money is a good measure of the services that money provides, are surprising, perhaps, only because of the extremity to which they are pushed. For example, Pesek and Saving argue that, once demand deposits start paying interest,

1. demand deposits will continue serving as money only if interest payments cease; or
2. interest payments will continue but then demand deposits will cease serving as money; or
3. some intermediate position will be found.[48]

Friedman and Schwartz challenge these views, and note that

a zero *price* for the transactions services of demand deposits does not mean that the quantity of money in the form of demand deposits is zero,[49]

and later, on the ability of money to retain its liquidity and yet pay an interest rate,

We have seen that the view and shelter are two economic dimensions of the house that cannot be added directly together, though the values attributed to them can be. Likewise, the 'dollar' of moneyness and the 'dollar' of interest-payingness can be two dimensions of the 'dollar' of deposits that cannot be added directly together, though the values attributed to them can be.[50]

Indeed, Friedman and Schwartz conclude that the logic of the Pesek and Saving position is that money (as net wealth) ought to be high-powered money, a concept more in line with the Patinkin approach, after all, and one explicitly rejected by Pesek and Saving as too narrow. Patinkin, as noted in Chapter 2, agrees with Friedman and Schwartz here.[51]

As might be expected, Pesek and Saving also provoked Patinkin, both by their style and by their content. Patinkin argues that we should take the point of view of the banking system and examine its 'net wealth'. Pesek and Saving had been rather harsh on traditional methods of accounting here, noting that

economists may accept the balance sheets prepared by the banking industry only if they are willing to abdicate their own responsibility for making analytical decisions. . . .[52]

Patinkin, however, concludes that

the essential point . . . is that the origin of the net worth of the banking sector is not in the production of bank money *per se*, but in the monopoly rights which this sector has received.[53]

This view also appears in Friedman and Schwartz and in Laidler.[54] Clearly, it is correct to argue that, if money is costless to produce and if 'overproduction' is prevented by the need to obtain a monopoly right, then the market value of the monopoly rights (or, equivalently, the market value of the firms that obtain them) will correctly measure the value of the services of money. But the essence of an inside-money economy is surely that it uses private resources to 'manufacture' money. More fundamentally, perhaps, the critics of Pesek and Saving, some of them accepting many of the policy implications, are involved in an argument that sounds as if an exchange of money for non-money, in a perfectly competitive economy including, of course, the banking system, would be effected without a gain in welfare. As Buchanan warns,

> If pushed to their extreme limits, accounting conventions 'prove' that gains from exchange are impossible ... broadly speaking, this procedure is acceptable so long as all transactions are assumed to be made in full equilibrium where there are offsetting transfers of expected present values between contracting parties. The unique feature of the call-loan is that no such offsetting transfer takes place.[55]

Then, one replaces the hard-line, exact dollar 'liability' of the commercial bank with the expected value of the call-loan (demand deposit, in this case) to the bank. The expected value would then be expected to fluctuate with the probability of recall (or 'repurchase', to use the terminology of Pesek and Saving) of the 'loan'; the value of the bank would suffer, for example, in times of bank runs, when the probability of a recall would tend to go up. This seems to get at the fundamental nature of the problem of 'liquidity' that appears to underlie the Pesek and Saving distinction.

K. Brunner has commented in some detail on this issue. He notes that the debate is not so much about whether or not inside money is net wealth but about the analysis of bank liabilities:

> The present value of deposit liabilities appears thus as a function of the costs associated with operation and maintenance of deposit accounts, the probability distribution governing realization of the repurchase clause and the rate of time discount.[56]

This is clearly an acceptance of the Pesek and Saving approach, modified by Buchanan as just discussed. Furthermore, says Brunner, there are two cases to consider: the monopoly bank and the perfectly competitive bank. If the monopoly right (for which the quantity of inside money approximates net wealth) is eroded by free entry,

> There remains, however, a contribution to the public's net wealth which is made by the banking sector. This magnitude is determined by the market value of the real capital K_b invested in the banking sector. An open competitive equilibrium only removes the 'wealth contribution of inside money', i.e., the value of the operational position of a bank.[57]

It still, that is to say, provides optimal information. This leaves the empirical issue about which little can be said. W. Smith, who indulges in casual rejection of the possibility of important wealth effects,[58] comes in for some timely (but harsh) treatment here; Brunner, in his turn, suggests that

> a combination of monopoly positions and persistent disequilibria are sufficient to maintain ... a wealth-contribution of inside money. Both conditions seem to prevail for most banking systems.[59]

Which, in my opinion, leaves us with an interesting empirical problem.

Footnotes

1. M. Friedman, *A Program for Monetary Stability*.
2. M. Friedman, 'The Demand for Money: Some Theoretical and Empirical Results'; A. Meltzer, 'The Demand for Money: The Evidence from the Time Series', D. Laidler, 'Some Evidence on the Demand for Money'; and D. Laidler, 'The Rate of Interest and the Demand for Money'.
3. A. C. Pigou, *The Veil of Money*, and A. C. Pigou, 'Economic Progress in a Stable Environment'.
4. As identified by A. Leijonhufvud in *On Keynesian Economics and the Economics of Keynes*.
5. D. Patinkin, *Money, Interest and Prices*, pp. 18–19.
6. J. Gurley and E. Shaw, *Money in a Theory of Finance*.
7. In a pure inside money economy, whether or not there are financial intermediaries, there is only a substitution effect, but one is still able to obtain classical neutrality (H. G. Johnson, 'Monetary Theory and Policy').
8. B. Pesek and T. Saving, *Money, Wealth, and Economic Theory*.
9. T. Saving, 'Outside Money, Inside Money, and the Real Balance Effect'.
10. A great deal of stir was created by A. Lerner, who is supposed to have remarked, roughly, that a great deal of this sort of monetary economics would go out of the window if the nth good were peanuts. Of course the designation here really means that one (any one) of the goods is money, and no more than that. But later in this section we will argue that, if money is 'just another good' without its economic properties explicitly specified, then there is a danger that nothing interesting can be said about it. This might have been Lerner's meaning.
11. J. Henderson and R. Quandt, *Microeconomic Theory*, p. 174. We are here following the approach of Hicks ('The Two Triads: Lecture 1' in *Critical Essays in Monetary Theory*) in thinking of money as aiding exchange without actually imparting direct utility. This approach was discussed in Chapter 2. Patinkin, who enters the discussion later, puts money (and money prices) into the utility function.
12. J. Henderson and R. Quandt, *Microeconomic Theory*, pp. 176–7.
13. In the analysis of Henderson and Quandt something called an 'absolute price' appears. That is, Henderson and Quandt consider a system with a budget constraint of

$$\bar{Y}_j \equiv \sum_{i=1}^{n} P_i S_{ij}$$

for the jth consumer. With money as one of the n goods, the P_i ($i = 1, \ldots, n$) clearly have no economic interpretation. That is, the money prices we are used to are only $n - 1$ in number and are written as P_j/P_n ($j = 1, \ldots, n - 1$) if the nth good is money, in *their* system. Henderson and Quandt carry the n absolute prices along until they disappear in solution (in much the same way λ disappears). This creates a notational complexity at a later point, when Say's Law is introduced, so the convention is adopted here that the P_j are money prices (and are referred to as absolute prices).

14. See, in particular, the papers by T. Saving on the demand for money ('Transactions Costs and the Demand for Money', and 'Transactions Costs and the Firm's Demand for Money') and the literature cited by R. Clower in 'The Anatomy of Monetary Theory'.

15. Essentially, the role of money here is as a 'unit of account', as it is in the model of Walras, as described by Hicks (*Critical Essays in Monetary Theory*, p. 3):

> For although Walras does not take one of his *n* commodities as numeraire (or unit of account) it is an essential part of his theory that the numeraire does not enter into the exchange in any different way from any other of the commodities.

This, as well, is a characteristic of the Samuelson–Patinkin models – in which money and money prices are entered into the utility function – as discussed in Appendix A. Hicks regards the Patinkin approach as 'cutting the knot' rather than untying it.

16. We assume that $\alpha_k = \alpha$ for all consumers ($k = l, \ldots, K$) whose individual functions we are not interested in.

17. Let $\lambda = 2$ for the doubling experiment. Then

$$X_n = \alpha \sum_{j=1}^{n-1} \lambda P_j S_j - S_n$$

and when we calculate $\partial X_n / \partial \lambda$ we get $\alpha \sum_{j=1}^{n-1} P_j S_j$, which is strictly positive.

18. Homogeneity, in general, is the condition that, if when each argument of a function is multiplied by a constant the constant can be factored out, with or without an exponent, the function is homogeneous. The degree of homogeneity is expressed by the value of the exponent. In terms of equation (3.15), this function would be homogeneous of degree r if the following were true, where λ is the constant in question and r the degree:

$$X_j(\lambda P_1, \ldots, \lambda P_{n-1}) = \lambda^r X_j(P_1, \ldots, P_{n-1}).$$

19. Walras's Law in this system is the relation

$$\sum_{i=1}^{n} X_i \equiv 0$$

as noted in equation (3.12). It is not correct to write equation (3.12) as an equality rather than an identity, for the statement that we are on the budget constraint implies that the excess demand for money is also identical to the excess supply of commodities. While equation (3.12) always holds, equation (3.11) only holds at equilibrium. We are not writing out X_n explicitly here because, as we shall see, its properties are implied by the system we are building.

20. J. Henderson and R. Quandt, *Microeconomic Theory*, pp. 177–8. It is hard to rationalise a situation in which money is not in the budget constraint, and Henderson and Quandt do not provide such a rationale. Nevertheless, here we use their argument.

21. K. Lancaster (*Mathematical Economics*) notes that Walras's Law is neither necessary nor sufficient for the purpose for which it has been used, and that this implication has been used to generate many fruitless arguments, especially in monetary theory. We are, thus, engaging in fruitless arguments. Note, also, that relaxing either of these rules permits us some flexibility of approach here.

22. The early Clower paper ('Classical Monetary Theory Revisited') is presented here as explained by C. Lloyd ('Two Classical Monetary Models').

23. This material draws heavily on the paper, 'Weak Separability and Household Behavior in a Monetary Economy' by J. Bernstein and D. Fisher.

24. These references are provided in Appendix A, where the proofs of these propositions are contained.

25. A. Sinai and H. Stokes, 'Real Money Balances: An Omitted Variable From the Production Function?' They obtain results for a Cobb–Douglas model, with two different specifications, as follows:

(a) $Y_t = AK_t^\alpha L_t^\beta M_{t-1}^\gamma e^{ut}$

(b) $Y_t = AK_t^\alpha L_t^\beta M_{t-1}^\gamma e^{\gamma t} e^{ut}$

These are compared with some British estimates (D. Fisher, 'Wealth Adjustment Effects in a Macroeconomic Model', p. 71) in the following table:

| | British results, quarterly, 1955–68; | | American results, annual 1929–67* | |
Coefficient	Trend	No trend	Trend	No trend
Constant	−27.111	−0.625	−2.273	−3.022
α	2.562 (7.28)	0.433 (11.23)	0.428 (3.69)	0.585 (10.09)
β	0.491 (3.04)	0.216 (1.07)	0.966 (7.85)	0.945 (7.68)
γ	0.700 (5.26)	0.306 (2.02)	0.127 (2.50)	0.172 (3.82)
λ	−0.029 (6.07)		0.006 (1.50)	
Σ coefficients	3.753	0.955	1.527	1.702
$\bar{R}^2$	0.942	0.902	0.995	0.993
DW	1.603	0.741	1.45	1.43

* Adjusted for first-order serial correlation.

These coefficients are implausible in either case, and the effect of the trend variable (representing omitted variables?) is pronounced. If real balances are an argument in the aggregate production function, then they ought also to appear in an aggregate investment function. In the British case they do, but only marginally (0.029 or 0.038 – see the study just cited for the details) and not significantly. Of course, real balances do belong in the firm's constraints, and this could be what such a result implies, but it is not encouraging for the Sinai and Stokes result. There are some econometric problems as well as discussed by Z. Prais ('Real Money Balances as a Variable in the Production Function: Comment').

26. M. Nadiri, 'The Determinants of Real Cash Balances in the U.S. Total Manufacturing Sector'.

27. S. Fisher, 'Money and the Production Function', p. 525. See also J. Moroney, 'The Current State of Money and Production Theory' and E.-M. Claasen, 'On the Indirect Productivity of Money'. Fisher's demonstration is in terms of the Baumol–Tobin model described in Chapter 5 below.

28. If the consumption function has real balances in it, then so should the labour supply function. That is, if an unanticipated change in real balances makes consumers wealthier, they will, *ceteris paribus*, offer less of their services on the labour market. In more commonsense terms, if one makes enough in stock and bond speculation, one can stop working.

29. If equation (3.34) is written in nominal terms (as $L^s = R'(W)$), reflecting money illusion in the supply of labour, then the possibility arises that the solution for this sector will be inconsistent both with full employment (in some sense) and (thereby) with full employment income. Individuals will spend what they actually earn, and if the incomes generated in the labour market are inadequate on account of the effect of money illusion (or whatever) then the spending functions will not be written in terms of full-employment income. We may reflect this possibility by substituting $Q(W/P,\bar{K})$ into (3.33) and $\varphi[Q(W/P,\bar{K}),\bar{K}]$ into the spending and demand for money and bond functions, instead of y_f. This, one could reasonably argue, is Keynesian in spirit.

30. We should at this point note that consumers are assumed to hold two kinds of financial assets, money and bonds. We have not said, yet, what sort of a bond we have, but as we shall see below, it is a private bond, issued by business firms; the government only provides money and does not run a deficit (other than that financed by money creation, which it gives back to the private sector). Money enters the system directly and not by open market operations as that would involve the government in the holding of private debt. Presumably, individuals voluntarily surrender real goods and/or property to enjoy the benefits provided by money.

31. Equations (3.39) and (3.40) come from the G. Chow model of the demand for money ('On the Long-run and Short-run Demand for Money'); it is discussed in Chapter 4 below. The model used here, as well as some empirical work, are in D. Fisher, 'Real Balances and the Demand for Money'.

32. In the paper from which these conclusions are drawn it is estimated that the true interest rate coefficient might be as much as three times higher if the estimated values of α are

correct (D. Fisher, 'Real Balances and the Demand for Money'). The parameters are drawn from both the consumption function and the demand for money function, both of which are estimated there. Thus, we can use the interest rate coefficient from an estimated consumption function and one from equation (3.41) as two equations in two unknowns (η and δ, the two interest rate parameters):

(a) $- (d\eta + c\delta + d\alpha\delta)$ = interest coefficient of demand for money;
(b) $\eta + \alpha\delta$ = interest coefficient of consumption function.

Since the real-balance effect parameter (α) represents a shift between the money and commodities markets, the terms containing α drop out of the solution. Thus, in the following table an arbitrary value for α, as noted, is used, and the 'true' value of η is calculated. As noted, it is much larger than the original estimate (in two different specifications).

Money	d	c	α	Original interest rate coefficient	$-d\alpha\delta$	Final interest rate coefficient
Broad	0.592	0.480	0.142	−21.896	−5.558	−66.113
Narrow	0.442	0.384	0.143	−55.690	−10.487	−165.916

33.   There is a lot more to the real-balance and wealth literature than is contained in these pages. The reader interested in the complicated development of the concept would do well to read the various surveys by H. Johnson, listed in the bibliography. See also the general discussion in L. Meyer ('Wealth Effects and the Effectiveness of Monetary and Fiscal Policy') and J. Hynes ('On the Theory of Real Balance Effects').

34.   The tax variables in Jorgenson concern the 'double taxation' of corporate profits, the possibility of the deduction of interest payments from gross income, the difference between marginal tax rates on income and capital gains, and the tax write-offs possible for depreciation.

35.   If we had retained the idea that $L^s = R'(W)$, then another variable would appear here (e.g., actual y) and another equilibrium condition:

$$[Q(W/P), \bar{K}) - R'(W) = 0].$$

Walras's Law, then, would eliminate one of the four markets. Keynes's dislike of the assumption of Walras's Law could also be interpreted here as the substitution of an equality for an identity in equation (3.51). Out of equilibrium, that is to say, excess demands need not sum to zero.

36.   I have published estimates of the real-balance effects described here, obtained in single and two-stage forms ('Wealth Adjustment Effects in a Macroeconomic Model'). In this test, Walras's Law was applied to eliminate the bond market (which was thereby calculated in the residual) and the F function was disaggregated to the C and I functions; the constraint in equation (3.53) was used to calculate the bond coefficient rather than applied at the estimation stage. The results were:

Function	2SLS	OLS
	(t-values in parentheses)	
Consumption	0.238 (6.52)	0.249 (6.32)
Investment	0.038 (1.33)	0.029 (1.15)
Money demand	0.216 (2.53)	0.236 (2.78)
Bonds (residual)	0.508	0.486
Sum	1.000	1.000

These results are suggestive, but one would want equities in the problem, quite possibly; one would want to try different lag specifications; one would desire to get closer to Patinkin's specification; and, most particularly, one would want to estimate a constrained system, since the theory does provide some constraints, particularly in the form of equation (3.53).

37. K. Brunner and A. Meltzer, 'Money, Debt, and Economic Activity'.

38. This model is evidently adapted from the Friedman model which is described in Chapter 4.

39. The reader unfamiliar with this approach could consult J. Van Doorn, *Disequilibrium Economics*, for this and later results in this section.

40. This discussion is based on D. Patinkin, *Money, Interest and Prices*, pp. 484–6.

41. D. Tucker, 'Macroeconomic Models and the Demand for Money under Market Disequilibrium'.

42. See R. Barro and H. Grossman, 'A General Disequilibrium Model of Income and Employment', for a more general treatment, including feedback on the labour market.

43. Tucker notes that in normal practice we use actual M for M^d and that this implies that the money market is in equilibrium – somewhat of a *non sequitur* under the circumstances of this section. Tucker suggests that we should impose another constraint, as follows:

$$M - M^* = P(Q^* - Q) + \frac{(B^* - B)}{P} + w(N^* - N)$$

which argues that actual balances deviate from desired balances because of the inability to spend in other markets. Then, one can formally derive an estimating equation in M rather than in M^d – in the form of equation (3.73). Of course, we are simplifying considerably here, in particular in the sense of H. Grossman ('The Nature of Quantities in Market Disequilibrium'), who distinguishes between:

1. the quantities demanded and supplied;
2. the quantities ordered and offered;
3. the quantities bought and sold;
4. the quantities produced and consumed.

44. The foregoing discussion is macroeconomic. Recently, a literature has developed in a general equilibrium context which addresses many of the same issues. In particular, following the ideas of R. Clower ('The Keynesian Counter Revolution'), A. Leijonhufvud (*On Keynesian Economics and the Economics of Keynes*) and H. Grossman ('Money, Interest and Prices in Market Disequilibrium'), and following the line of attack used in the 'Sequence Economy' as described in Chapter 2 (an additional paper here is by J. Green, 'Temporary General Equilibrium in a Sequential Trading Model with Spot and Futures Transactions'), one notes especially papers by J. Benassey, 'Neo-Keynesian Disequilibrium Theory in a Monetary Economy' and J.-M. Grandmont and G. Laroque, 'On Temporary Keynesian Equilibria'. The latter give a 'monopolistic competition' framework to Keynesian disequilibrium.

45. B. Pesek and T. Saving, *Money, Wealth, and Economic Theory*; and T. Saving, 'Outside Money, Inside Money, and the Real Balance Effect'.

46. B. Pesek and T. Saving, *Money, Wealth, and Economic Theory*, p. 21.

47. L. Metzler, 'Wealth, Saving, and the Rate of Interest'.

48. B. Pesek and T. Saving, *Money, Wealth, and Economic Theory*, p. 109.

49. M. Friedman and A. Schwartz, *Monetary Statistics of the United States*, p. 114.

50. ibid., p. 116.

51. D. Patinkin, 'Money and Wealth: A Review Article'. See also W. Smith, 'On Some Current Issues in Monetary Economics: An Interpretation' and H. Johnson, 'Recent Developments in Monetary Theory – A Commentary'. These authors are quite critical of the Pesek and Saving analysis.

52. B. Pesek and T. Saving, *Money, Wealth and Economic Theory*, p. 139.

53. D. Patinkin, 'Money and Wealth: A Review Article', p. 1143.

54. M. Friedman and A. Schwartz, *Monetary Statistics of the United States*; and D. Laidler, 'The Definition of Money'.

55. J. Buchanan, 'An Outside Economist's Defense of Pesek and Saving', p. 814.

56. K. Brunner, 'A Survey of Selected Issues in Monetary Theory', p. 38.

57. ibid., p. 38.

58. W. Smith, 'On Some Current Issues in Monetary Economics: An Interpretation'.

59. K. Brunner, 'A Survey of Selected Issues in Monetary Theory', p. 42.

CHAPTER 4

The Macroeconomic Demand for Money: A Survey of Empirical Work

4.1 Introduction

In this chapter we will survey the empirical literature on the macroeconomic demand for money.[1] The principal problems in this literature concern the appropriate variables, functional form, aggregation and lag structure of the demand for money and, concomitantly, the stability of the various representations over time (and even geographically). We will divide our discussion into three parts, roughly:

1. the Keynesian literature;
2. the Monetarist literature; and
3. other matters: temporal stability, lags and the business demand for money.

Most concern at this stage will be with the measure of income used – especially with regard to the usefulness of a measure of permanent income – and with the influence of the interest rate. We will argue that, while the polar theories here are distinct enough in an *a priori* sense, it is hard in practice to find any evidence that supports one or the other, except with regard to details. Even so, the evidence assembled in this chapter suggests:

1. that permanent income offers a marginal improvement over the level of income;
2. that tests performed on narrow money are generally better than (and almost always different from) tests on broad money;
3. that there is some evidence in favour of a speculative demand in general and a liquidity trap in particular;
4. that the lags in the money market are possibly more rapid than early studies have indicated;
5. that the demand for money has been stable except, possibly, in the post-1971 period;

6. that the aggregation of business and private money holdings is attended with some risk; and

7. that problems of temporal aggregation may have led to the unreasonably long estimates of the lag in the demand for money common in this literature.

But most of these are provisional conclusions in view of the state of this rapidly growing literature.

4.2 Keynes, some Keynesians, and the demand for money [2]

4.2.1 *Some theoretical problems*

Perhaps the most interesting aspect of the literature on Keynes concerns the textual difference between Keynes and those who have interpreted his results, both friends and foes. Keynes, it will be recalled, emphasised three 'motives' for holding money: transactions, precautionary and speculative. The main problem seems to stem from an equation in Keynes which was used by Hicks in his original formulation of the *IS–LM* analysis,[3] and which has come to represent the model of Keynes in much of the textbook literature on the subject; one version of this is given by equation (4.1), which is an additively separable demand for money function (containing, implicitly, an aggregation of precautionary and transactions balances):

$$M = M_1 + M_2 = L_1(Y) + L_2(i). \qquad (4.1)$$

While there is no doubt that Keynes used such a device – which strongly suggests that the actual money stock (or, at least, the demand for money) could be divided into a transactions or active component (M_1) and a speculative or idle component (M_2) – he also used words very similar to those of Friedman and Schwartz, as cited in Chapter 2, to explain his formulation:

> Money held for each of the three purposes forms, nevertheless, a single pool, which the holder is under no necessity to segregate into three watertight components; for they need not be sharply divided even in his own mind, and the same sum can be held primarily for one purpose and secondarily for another.[4]

But it is very clear in the current literature that in a proper interpretation of Keynes, no matter what the motive for holding money – transactions, precautionary or speculative – the interest rate represents the foregone returns and income represents the wealth of the money-holding unit.[5]

Hicks, somewhat apologetically, offers the following interpretation:

> I think that Keynes was absolutely right in the distinction which he drew between M_1 and M_2; more exactly right than some of his

followers (including myself) have been, when we have formulated the 'Demand for Money' in ways that blurred the distinction. But I rather doubt that he described the distinction in quite the right way.[6]

The right way, says Hicks, is to emphasise that M_1 is money that is *needed* (rather than demanded) to circulate commodities while M_2 is voluntarily held, for 'motives'. M_1, perforce, is large relative to M_2, but it is M_2 that is important (in Hicks's words, 'live and exciting') for policy and for the demand for money. Curiously, Hicks says, it is often referred to as 'idle' balances. Thus, all motives, but especially the 'precautionary' and the 'speculative', are involved in M_2. Hicks, clearly, is writing as a Keynesian (in Leijonhufvud's sense). In fact, Hicks prefers the precautionary motive as an explanation of M_2, although a substantial number of Keynesians put the precautionary balance in M_1. Note, further, that the 'additive separability' much criticised in the literature is (apparently) accepted by Hicks. Indeed, as a research strategy leading to effective empirical work, this may well be useful.

Thus, attempts to separate money into components have continued, and an empirical literature, mostly predating the period studied in this chapter (which is generally post-1959), has arisen to deal with this problem. Keynes, himself lumping precautionary balances in with transactions balances, hoped that 'it is a safe first approximation to regard the amounts of these two sets of cash-holdings as being largely independent of one another',[7] a view that led directly to tests of equation (4.1). In one such test, demand deposits were thought to be 'active' and time deposits 'passive' (idle),[8] but this is clearly an unusual way of proceeding in that, not only is 'jointness' a problem for each component, but even casual observation suggests that time deposits are, for many holders, either used actively (e.g., for the purchase of consumer durables), or used for precautionary purposes. A more sensible approach, but one not pursued very far in the literature, was that of J. Tobin, used later by Bronfenbrenner and Mayer in a modification.[9] Approximately, the idea was to estimate maximum active balances and then to subtract them from total money balances to obtain idle balances. The procedure of Bronfenbrenner and Mayer was to calculate

$$m_1 = \frac{GNP_t}{V^*} \qquad (4.2)$$

where V^* is the highest recorded annual velocity of real (narrow) money balances in the series. This procedure is built on the Cambridge equation, since m is total money balances and V is calculated as a residual after all the other information is obtained; thus, if the current value of velocity is used, there would be no idle balances. V^* is taken to be the highest recorded velocity. What we really want here is the *fluctuating* transactions velocity, a number that is probably higher, even, than $V*$.[10] We will briefly discuss the results in the next section of this chapter.

As already noted, the Keynesian interpretation of the *General Theory* provides motives for holding money under three headings – transactions, precautionary and speculative. If this is a complete classification, as is obviously the intention in an analysis of the long-run demand for money, then an 'adding up' theorem can be invoked as follows: analysis of any two of the three motives will yield predictions about the form of the third so long as overall equilibrium in portfolios can be assumed.[11] There are separate issues, to be sure, as we shall see, but so long as our framework is not disequilibrium (so that the demand and supply schedules in each of the categories are relevant), not all three need to be included. Even so, there is still an issue, which we will discuss shortly, as to which motive should be eliminated and whether (if it *is* the precautionary demand – which is the usual case) the precautionary demand should best be conceived of as added to the transactions or as added to the speculative demand.

The logic of the Bronfenbrenner and Mayer approach just considered suggests that income (or wealth) will bear a positive relation with the demand for money for transactions purposes, and this view can be found in Keynes, as well. Further, a richer person will be able to hold larger precautionary and speculative balances, although whether or not he will depends on whether, as he gets richer, he changes the form of his precautionary and speculative activities. For example, an individual at a low income may hold his transactions balances in his current account and his precautionary balances in a savings account, but at a larger income he may begin to hold speculative balances and to hold both speculative and precautionary balances in an essentially immeasurable form – as, for example, an unused margin at his stockbroker's, or an accumulated excess balance in an instalment purchase such as a car or a house. Money, like potatoes, quite possibly is an inferior good in precautionary and speculative terms, although probably not in transactions terms (at least for the ordinary consumer?).

The main line of inquiry with regard to the effect of the interest rate on the demand for money has concerned the speculative demand. If one visualises the interest rate as moving reciprocally to bond prices, then a steady rise in interest rates (indicating a fall in bond prices) will (under stabilising assumptions) produce a fall in the quantity of money demanded – or a rise in the quantity demanded of bonds (in anticipation of a rise in bond prices). Causes matter as well, and Keynes emphasised that the effects are different in terms of two causes behind the change in interest rates, one that affects the supply of money schedule (given the demand function) and one that affects both the supply and demand schedules:

> Open-market operations may, indeed, influence the rate of interest through both channels; since they may not only change the volume

of money, but may also give rise to changed expectations concerning the future policy of the Central Bank or of the Government.[12]

Fixed ('inelastic') expectations themselves – when the news is differently interpreted by individuals – provide the main reason for the negative slope of the demand for money as a function of the (long-term) interest rate. This is the well-known 'differences of opinion' formulation with regard to what is a 'normal' rate of interest; the result, though, is not a clear relationship, since:

> a given M_2 will not have a definite quantitative relation to a given rate of interest of r; – what matters is not the absolute level of r but the degree of its divergence from what is considered a fairly *safe* level of r, having regard to those calculations of probability which are being relied on.[13]

A safe level of r is, clearly, a 'normal' r, so that what is implied here is that, since individuals will have different views as to what is normal, an observable negative relation between money demanded and the interest rate will develop. That is, as more and more opinion swings to the view that there is going to be a rise in interest rates in the future (as it falls), the further below the safe level one is, and the more likely one is to be in money rather than in bonds. The aggregation, here, is across individual portfolios in the sense that individuals hold either bonds or money, but not both; the negative relationship emerges in the market as more and more switch.[14] Indeed, it may come to pass that no one expects the interest rate to fall any further, so that speculative money balances absorb all future increases in the quantity of money available for speculative purposes (the liquidity trap). We will continue this discussion in the next section.

Life here is not as simple as all this, however, and the effect of the interest rate on transactions and precautionary balances has also to be considered. The most obvious consideration here is contained in the 'opportunity cost' principle, whereby the effect of a rise in short-term rates increases the income foregone by holding non-interest-bearing (or fixed-interest-bearing) assets, whatever one's motive for holding them. In the dynamic consumption models of Chapter 3, for example, both present and future money balances become more expensive as interest rates rise, the latter, presumably, if the rise is expected to hold on the date of future planned holding. There is, further, an interest-induced wealth effect here, with the same negative sign on the actual balances held (see Chapter 3). With regard to precautionary balances alone, other considerations become involved, although, once again, the principal expectation is for a negative relationship. In a paper by M. Weinrobe, because the interest effect seems even more obvious here, the author suggests that the following aggregation is the more obvious:

> One might wish to conclude that the precautionary demand should join with the transactions demand for money to replace the

speculative demand . . . as the primary source of the interest elasticity of the demand for money.[15]

In particular, if we argue that the precautionary demand arises from uncertainty (or from 'uninsurable risk') over future income and spending, and that, the more one holds of liquid assets, the better protected he is against the costs of running out,[16] then it is clear that some trade-off will exist between the expected disutility of the penalty cost and the expected utility attached to the interest income. Clearly, the required negative relation can be derived. One might add that the speculative demand is not so obvious, perhaps, because (1) the difference of opinion is a weak formulation, (2) expectations change frequently, and (3) individual speculators may often ignore the interest cost of speculation. The latter is, by implication, argued by Weinrobe, and is clearly debatable; (2) and (1), on the other hand, do provide the concern that they are difficult to capture econometrically.

Finally, we should note that Keynes also suggested that there was a 'finance' motive, most easily justified for business firms but applying to consumers as well; this is a function not of actual activity, but of expected activity.[17] To capture this, we might enter expected income (along with actual income) into equation (4.1). P. Davidson pursues this line of thought and suggests that the demand for money could have the following form, reflecting his judgement that the two components of GNP (reflecting the consumer and the corporate sectors) will have radically different expected cash uses (and, presumably, will respond differently over time):[18]

$$M^* = \alpha C^* + \beta I^*. \tag{4.2}$$

Thus, if $\alpha = \beta$ we could aggregate and obtain the traditional function. The 'finance motive' is an appealing idea, clearly; and there is, indeed, some evidence to suggest that the business demand for money is different from the personal, as we have seen at several points in this book (see below, as well). Davidson, though, goes on to substitute the following consumption and investment functions into equation (4.2):

$$C^* = a_1 + a_2 Y - a_3 i \tag{4.3}$$

$$I^* = b_1 - b_2 i. \tag{4.4}$$

In his words, 'Combining Equations [4.3] and [4.4] into [4.2] we get the demand for transactions balances function as'[19]

$$M^* = (\alpha a_1 + \beta b_1) + \alpha a_2 Y - (\alpha a_3 + \beta b_2)i. \tag{4.5}$$

Actually, this equation is not a 'pure' demand for money function; and, further, it contains three endogenous variables (as, for that matter, did equation 4.2). It explains not a transactions demand (as such) but the net effect of the two other sectors as they operate through the demand for money. To see this clearly, think of equation (4.5) as a regression equation, with the stock of money substituted for the desired transactions balance on the left-hand side. It is clear, then, that there will be a positive influence of income and a negative influence from the interest rate on the demand for money, even though no such relation has been postulated, operating through the effect of these variables on consumption and investment. Indeed, equation (4.5) has seven parameters in it, while only three can be estimated, as things stand. Thus Davidson is not correct when he asserts that

> The demand for money function is not independent of changes in the real sector. . . . Whenever there is a shift in the aggregate demand function, there will be a concomitant shift in the demand for money schedule.[20]

He is incorrect because equation (4.2) is the demand-for-money schedule, not equation (4.5). The former recognises shifts in the underlying investment and consumption schedules as changes in its arguments, C^* and I^*; it does not itself shift in his experiment. What is true, and Davidson has a discussion of this later, is that one cannot successfully dichotomise the real and the monetary sectors along the lines of the traditional *IS–LM* apparatus in this event, since these curves will not be independent of each other. Thus Davidson's analysis does provide a warning that single-equation tests of the demand for money may run into complications because of omissions (e.g.) of Keynes's finance motive – as well as because of problems of a simultaneous-equations nature.

P. Meyer and J. Neri also consider the finance motive important and turn to Friedman's question, 'Are transactions variables or asset variables most important in determining the demand for money?'[21] In this case the transactions variables (e.g., permanent income) represent the finance motive. Meyer and Neri estimate a measure, λ, of this effect from

$$Y_t^e - Y_t = \lambda(Y_t^n - Y_t) \qquad (4.6)$$

where

$$Y_t^n = \sum_{i=0}^{\infty} (1 - \beta)\beta^i \, Y_{t-i}$$

is the Friedman–Cagan measure of permanent income (see below). The results, for the annual US data much used in this literature, show that the transactions motive dominates the asset motive and that this dominance increases, the narrower the measure of money. This last result is not unexpected, of course.

4.2.2 *A generation of empirical work on the Keynesian demand function for money*

In what follows, three main lines of inquiry will be pursued, all intended to stand as direct tests of equation (4.1) or its variants. The total evidence will be amassed in this chapter and the next, but the main issues just raised can be illustrated with regard to the single-equation tests of Bronfenbrenner and Mayer, the simultaneous-equations tests of Teigen and the speculative-demand tests of Starleaf and Reimer, and of Pifer.[22] This literature and the critical pieces built around it will be treated here, somewhat unjustly, as emanating from the perceptions of Keynes as laid out and modified in the preceding section.

The first set of results is that of Bronfenbrenner and Mayer. The general purpose of their study was to calculate 'liquidity functions', and they were most interested in the determinants of their measure of 'idle' balances, as described above; the conception was deliberately Keynesian:

> The Keynesian system of aggregation economics rests, in its empirical aspects, on three major statistical foundations ... the third is the liquidity function, or liquidity preference, relating money holdings to interest rates.[23]

The questions they raise, and the principal questions considered by the empirical literature described here, are as follows.

1. Is there a definite observable liquidity function, i.e., a relation between money holdings and interest rates?
2. Assuming the function exists, what is its interest elasticity?
3. Assuming the function exists, what is its stability over time?
4. If shifts are observed, what are their causes?
5. Does the liquidity function appear to impose an observable floor to interest rates?

In the next section we will consider all of these topics again, where the 'liquidity function' will include (at the least) income and an interest rate as arguments, in the context of the search for the liquidity trap; here, instead, we continue with the broader topic of the existence of the speculative demand for money – or, for that matter, of a significant interest elasticity to the demand for money.

As noted above, the definition of the Bronfenbrenner and Mayer dependent variable is based on the Tobin method; the independent variables used were the short-term interest rate,[24] total national wealth, private GNP and, when used, the lagged value of the dependent variable. The functions estimated were in log form, so, although no theoretical equation was provided by Bronfenbrenner and Mayer, it might have been equation (4.7), where all variables except the interest rate are deflated:

$$m_t^d = \beta_1 i_t^{\beta_2} y_t^{\beta_3} w_t^{\beta_4} m_{t-1}^{\beta_5} e^{u_t}. \tag{4.7}$$

While we have no particular quarrel with this model, no reason was advanced for setting it up in this way, although it has certainly become fashionable. The results on the annual US data can be classified as follows.

1. The interest elasticity was negative and significant and, for idle balances, was between -0.3 and -0.5.
2. Real income dominated real wealth, and when both appeared real wealth had an unexpected (but insignificant) sign.

Needless to say, the fits were good and the Von Neumann test for autocorrelation satisfied, in view of the presence of the lagged dependent variable. Bronfenbrenner and Mayer also studied the temporal and product aggregation, but the method employed, being either graphical or the simple comparison of means, does not seem to meet the requirements of a more rigorous test; similarly, the claim of lack of stability on the same data put forward by R. Eisner in his comment seems premature. Finally, their rejection of the liquidity trap, based, essentially, on graphical relationships dominated by serial correlation, seems unfounded.[25]

The next important study in this tradition is that of R. Teigen, who obtained estimates of both demand and supply functions for the United States, employing quarterly data covering the period from 1946-IV to 1959-IV; these he represents as tests of (over-identified) structural equations. The supply function is unusual, and was subject to later criticism, and so appears here as equation (4.8):

$$\frac{M}{M^*} = \beta_1(i - i_d). \tag{4.8}$$

The denominator of the dependent variable is the maximum money stock that could be obtained on the basis of actual reserves, and the independent variable is the difference between a short-term rate and the rediscount rate (i_d) of the Federal Reserve. The model was completed with (of course) the demand function and an equation for national income. The test employed was two-stage least squares, a technique which removes rather than explains the troublesome endogeneity in such a model. By running a number of variations on his theme, Teigen concludes that:

1. a demand lag exists;
2. the supply of money function ought to be made endogenous;[26]
3. income elasticities were generally around unity, on the lower side.

Teigen's work has been challenged, in what seems to be a never-ending debate, by W. Gibson. There are problems with the data and, more importantly, there are problems with the structure of the model. As Gibson notes,

> Most importantly, the equation he presents as an estimate of the supply function of money is not a supply function but rather a function determining the volume of free reserves held by the banking system, a function which is not identical with an overall supply function of money.[27]

Thus equation (4.8), in Teigen's tests, shows that:

> free reserves are positively related to the discount rate and negatively related to market interest rates. These results square nicely with the theory of bank behaviour, but should not be taken alone to constitute a money supply function.[28]

The appropriate function, Gibson argues, would be one like equation (4.9):

$$M^s = f(R, i, i_d) \tag{4.9}$$

where R is total reserves adjusted for reserve requirement changes. The result of Gibson's re-estimations is a tighter fit (up to 90 per cent from 80 per cent), a greater response of income and the interest rate in the demand for money and, significantly, evidence of a very speedy adjustment in the money market (Teigen's first conclusion) – within one quarter. The latter is a somewhat unusual result – attributed by Gibson to a different measurement of the data[29] – although there is no *a priori* reason to reject Gibson's finding. This debate has been continued in recent years with Teigen accusing Gibson of measurement errors and standing firm by his supply function and his result of a longer lag.[30] Support for Teigen's simultaneous-equations framework is also provided in a recent paper by B. Klein, who argues, as well, that the traditional studies provide downward-biased estimates of the interest elasticity of the demand for money.[31]

More provocatively, there are also direct tests of the Keynesian speculative demand, the best known of which is that of Starleaf and Reimer.[32] The elements of Keynes's theory that we emphasised above were income, the rate of interest and a measure of the 'normal' rate of interest, the latter (quite possibly) able to capture the influence of the 'differences of opinion' that Keynes used to motivate the negative slope of the liquidity function. Starleaf and Reimer argue that Keynes should have written equation (4.1) as equation (4.10) here:

$$M = M_1 + M_2 = L_1(Y) + L_2^*(i - i_e) \tag{4.10}$$

where i_e is an expected normal rate of interest, referring to Keynes's 'state of expectations'. Thus,

> We maintain that these empirical investigations are not tests of the Keynesian demand function; they are tests of a neo-Keynesian

speculative demand tests

demand function for money, for the interest rate which was used as an independent variable in each of these tests was an *absolute* level of interest not its divergence from the expected normal rate of interest.[33]

i_e, then, is estimated as a 'permanent' interest rate, using Freidman's weights (see the next section in this chapter); expecting a negative sign on the $(i - i_e)$ term, they occasionally get a positive sign that is even significant (three out of twelve cases); with apparently little determination for the formulation, Keynes was pronounced dead.

Actually, it is unlikely that Keynes would have condoned equation (4.10) as a valid correction of equation (4.1). The major problem is that equation (4.10) is intended to represent an equilibrium relationship, and in equilibrium – in Keynes – the long-term interest rate is determined by expectations. That is, $i = i_e$ in equilibrium. Keynes seems to be saying this when he comments that

> Nevertheless, there are two reasons for expecting that, in any given state of expectations, a fall in *r* will be associated with an increase in M_2.[34]

Since expectations are not constant, in fact, no *a priori* sign can be established for $(i - i_e)$ if one is still following Keynes. Indeed, Keynes does suggest a method for dealing with the problem that is, essentially, disequilibrium; thus, if we assume that

> The short-term rate of interest is easily controlled by the monetary authorities...[35] [but that the] monetary authority often tends in practice to leave the price of long-term debts to be influenced by belated and imperfect reactions from the price of short-term debts[36]

then the appropriate model is a 'short-run' model (such as the Chow model), which appears here as equation (4.11).

$$m_t = f(y_t, i_{st}, i_{Lt} - i_{st}, m_{t-1}). \tag{4.11}$$

Such an equation has been tested, in ordinary and two-stage least squares formats, with the 'error in prediction of the one-year rate' also substituted for $i_L - i_s$, with some success;[37] this topic will be continued in Chapter 6, since the tests involve the term structure of interest rates. At any rate, this way of proceeding, in which a specific hypothesis is borrowed from term structure theory, makes it clear that, without putting an explicit theory of the formation of expectations on the line, it is not possible to test the hypothesis that a particular variable is determined by expectations. To put the matter another way, an unsuccessful test – such as the Starleaf and Reimer one – because it is an unsuccessful test of a joint hypothesis cannot lead to a rejection of the general hypothesis that expectations affect the demand for money, but only to the total package of hypotheses. A successful test –

assuming there are no other problems – can be interpreted as support for Keynes, at least if one agrees that Keynes was (relatively) agnostic as to how expectations are actually formed.

Then, there is some interesting – but heavily criticised – work by H. Pifer, who estimates liquidity traps by the use of 'non-linear maximum likelihood estimates'.[38] If the basic model to be tested is given as equation (4.12), then it is a four-parameter model (b_1, b_2, b_3, i_{min}) that contains only three estimable parameters when transformed into logarithmic form, as it is in equation (4.13), and tested by ordinary least squares:

$$M_t = b_1(i_t - i_{min})^{b_2} \ Y^{b_3} e^{u_t} \tag{4.12}$$

$$\text{Log } M_t = \log b_1 + b_2 \log (i_t - i_{min}) + b_3 \log Y_t + u_t. \tag{4.13}$$

By maximum likelihood procedures, one can perform iterations over various values of i_{min} (selected to be less than the lowest observed interest rate to avoid taking the logarithm of a negative number). When the dependent variable is the money stock, then, in Pifer's test, the i_{min} that produces the lowest variance of the residuals (for the same annual data employed by Meltzer, as discussed below) for the 1900–58 period lies between 2.04 and 2.20 for four different specifications of the demand-for-money function. But, as Pifer notes, these estimates are not significantly different from zero.

The critical literature here consists of papers by R. Eisner and K. White, as amended by J. Spitzer.[39] In the case of tests of equation (4.12), Eisner obtains significant results using the same data as Pifer; this he attributes to a better regression programme. With regard to the test of Pifer which has $i - i_{min}$ as the dependent variable (on the grounds that the money stock is exogenous in the aggregate) – an idea proposed by Eisner in his criticism of Bronfenbrenner and Mayer (and discussed above) – Eisner proposes a different test. He notes that if the dependent variable is ($i - i_{min}$) it does not have a constant variance from test to test (since we are varying i_{min} from test to test) and proposes a 'Box and Cox' procedure. This works and produces a significant i_{min} in the same general range as that obtained by Pifer for equation (4.13).

White's objections are more fundamental in some ways. He notes the failure of the literature generally to distinguish between the absolute trap (Bronfenbrenner and Mayer) and the asymptotic trap (Pifer). The former, it can be argued (following Brunner and Meltzer),[40] is exceedingly unlikely to rule; the latter, however, does have some scope, again according to the same authors, and Pifer's test is thus the more relevant. But the problem with Pifer's procedure – in common, for that matter, with all of the empirical tests of the Starleaf and Reimer variety – aside from the probability that his residuals are not normally distributed, is that the Pifer model is in a very specific form – the logarithmic. Indeed, White finds that 'The liquidity trap, which was significant in the Pifer formulation, is not significant when a more general functional form is permitted.'[41] Indeed, both the value and the significance of the value of i_{min} seem sensitive to the choice of functional form.

This literature has also considered the sensitivity of the analysis to the choice of functional form in a more general way.[42] Equation (4.14) thus exhibits a generalised Box-and-Cox function for the problem at hand:

$$\frac{M_t^{\gamma_0} - 1}{\gamma_0} = \alpha_0 + \frac{\alpha_1(Y_t^{\gamma_1} - 1)}{\gamma_1} + \frac{\alpha_2[(i_t - i_{min})]^{\gamma_2} - 1}{\gamma_2} + u_t. \quad (4.14)$$

Pifer's equation assumes that $\gamma_0 = \gamma_1 = \gamma_2 = 0$ – i.e., that

$$\lim_{\gamma \to 0} \frac{X^\gamma - 1}{\gamma} \to \log X.$$

Furthermore, White's test of the equation has $\gamma_0 = \gamma_1 = \gamma_2$; the more general equation, then, is equation (4.14).[43] J. Spitzer, whose work this is, using a maximum likelihood approach, claims the following:

1. there is a significant i_{min} but it increases as the generality of the model increases;
2. the most general model does best in terms of the likelihood test statistic; and
3. the generalised form is only marginally superior to the Pifer formulation, which is thereby supported by this test.

Furthermore, on the important question of the connection between the functional form and the parameter estimates, Spitzer finds that the variable elasticity form he has chosen produces an income elasticity of the demand for money that is greater than unity for a substantial period (1943–65). The earlier studies either found an estimate of 0.90 (White, Pifer), assuming it was constant, or assumed that it was less than unity (Konstas and Khouja). Spitzer, thus, claims that his more flexible approach is superior in this respect.[44]

4.3 The Monetarist stream of work on the demand for money

One is tempted to shirk the task of establishing a precise definition of the term 'Monetarist' and let the story tell itself; but because the story is a long and complicated one, that is not a good idea here. Briefly, one can distinguish between avowed Monetarists – those who, like Friedman, emphasise the pivotal role of monetary policy for good or, more usually, bad – and a stream of 'pro-Monetarist' results, which tend to define the role of money in such a way that it has some scope for significantly affecting the economy. Consider some specific cases. Friedman is a Monetarist and Tobin is not. Laidler, who is a Monetarist, employs both Keynesian and Monetarist for- mulations and finds in favour of the former. Goldfeld, who may well be neither, gets results that Monetarists would applaud. The central result in common with all of these writers is: if the demand for money is a stable function of a few key variables, then, lags aside, monetary policy may well have a large and even predictable impact. We turn, then, to the bread-and- butter issues of the macroeconomic demand for money; these issues concern which variables (other than long-term interest rates versus short-term in- terest rates, which we reserve for Chapter 6) enter the function, and whether or not the function is stable.

4.3.1   *Friedman's formulation of the demand for money*

M. Friedman's interest in the empirical demand for money seems to have been more in connection with his 'permanent income' hypothesis than with some of the other issues raised to this point. Noting the empirical fact that 'Income velocity therefore rises during cyclical expansions as real income rises and falls during cyclical contractions as real income falls,' [45] and that, in contrast, during secular expansion velocity falls and during secular (long- run) contractions it rises, Friedman suggested that the permanent income hypothesis (about consumption) would be of some special use here. As a first approximation, he argues that:

> it seems useful to regard the nominal quantity of money as de- termined primarily by conditions of supply, and the real quantity of money and the income velocity of money as determined primarily by conditions of demand. [46]

This separates questions of nominal from real and suggests that the demand for money is homogeneous of degree 1 in the price level; the demand for money is further explicitly assumed to be stable and the money market in full equilibrium.

Dismissing the interest rate as of no particular use for the secular–cyclical problem just raised, Friedman suggests that the obvious explanation – that consumers allow their money balances to build up during cyclical upturns because they are unable to allocate their windfall gains quickly enough – implies that *measured* income velocity will fall rather than rise (as noted in the preceding paragraph). Thus,

> This interpretation may be valid for very short time periods. However, if it were valid for periods as long as a business cycle, it would produce a cyclical behavior of velocity precisely the op- posite of the observed behavior. [47]

Instead, if money is regarded as a durable good whose quantity is related to permanent income rather than to measured income, then, since permanent income rises less than measured income at cyclical peaks, one might expect the *measured* income velocity to rise whatever was happening to the permanent income velocity. The secular results, then, show the true picture, for here an average income is used to measure velocity; this average is, indeed, akin to Friedman's idea of how to measure permanent income.

The specific equation for the demand-for-money function recommended by Friedman is given by equation (4.15):

$$m = \frac{M}{P} = \frac{P_p}{P}\gamma N^{1-\delta}Y_p^{\delta} \tag{4.15}$$

where the p subscript indicates a permanent variable estimated by a relation such as

$$Y_p(T) = \beta \int_{-\infty}^{T} e^{(\beta-\alpha)(t-T)}\, Y(t)dt \tag{4.16}$$

γ and δ in equation (4.15), then, are demand parameters, and the Cobb–Douglas form is chosen, as usual, for simplicity 'and because it gives a satisfactory fit'. N is population.[48] The result, then, is an estimate (M^*), converted into nominal terms, of

$$M^* = (0.00323)\left(\frac{Y_p}{N}\right)^{1.81} NP_p$$

from which it appears that the *per capita* demand for nominal money balances suggests that money is a luxury good (the elasticity is 1.81). It also suggested to Friedman that interest rates were a determinant neither of the demand for money nor of velocity. This last conclusion, based on a systematic empirical study, has not been widely repeated in either the Monetarist or Keynesian literature that has followed.[49]

But Friedman's actual tests of the demand for money do not look much like his well-known equation from his 'restatement' paper;[50] indeed, only Y/i, here representing wealth (calculated net of the reproduction cost of human capital), and P, representing the transactions motive, are carried through to that later test just described in equation (4.15). The earlier theoretical model appears here as equation (4.17):

$$M^d = f\left(P, i_b - \frac{1}{i_b}\frac{di_b}{dt}, i_e + \frac{1}{P}\frac{dP}{dt} - \frac{1}{i_e}\frac{di_e}{dt}, \frac{1}{P}\frac{dP}{dt}; w; \frac{Y}{i}; u\right). \tag{4.17}$$

This equation has long been thought to be an important point of evidence showing that Friedman is, at heart, a Keynesian. Indeed, a case can be made for this, for this is a 'stock' equation, as in Keynes, and it treats money as one of the five principal forms of holding wealth. These are defined to be represented by:

money $\left(P \text{ and } \dfrac{1}{P}\dfrac{dP}{dt} \right)$

bonds (i_b)
equities (i_e)
physical non-human goods (Y/i)
human capital (W)

There is, in this literature, a considerable concern with 'confronting the theory with data', and this has given a direction to empirical studies of the demand for money which has often overlooked a central point in the last two paragraphs: both theories share a common core which may, indeed, cover the demand for money.[51] To highlight this similarity, consider the following derivation by A. Meltzer of Bronfenbrenner and Mayer's Keynesian-inspired liquidity function from Friedman's collapsed version of equation (4.17). The collapsed equation appears here as equation (4.18), to start things off:

$$M = f(i,q,d,W_n). \tag{4.18}$$

Here W_n is the money value of non-human wealth, d is the yield on human wealth, i is a financial yield and q is the yield on equities; these are taken in the gross sense defined in equation (4.17).

If we assume that equation (4.18) is homogeneous of degree 1 in the money value of non-human wealth, we may write (4.18) as (4.19):

$$M = f^*(i,q,d)W_n. \tag{4.19}$$

Then, define

$$d = \frac{\text{human income}}{\text{human wealth}}$$

and multiply it by

$$\frac{\text{expected human income}}{\text{expected human income}} \ (= 1).$$

The result, upon rearrangement, is

$$d = \left(\frac{\text{human income}}{\text{expected human income}} \right)\left(\frac{\text{expected human income}}{\text{human wealth}} \right). \tag{4.20}$$

In the short run, then, human income may well differ from expected human income, but not in the long run (the context to be studied); therefore, let the first term in equation (4.20) be a constant ($= b$). The rate of return expected on human wealth may well also be a constant ($= a$); thus

$$d = ab \qquad (4.21)$$

a constant. Finally, assume that all the interest rates are equal, and equal to the rate of interest on bonds; in this case equation (4.19) would look like equation (4.22):

$$M^d = g(i)W_n. \qquad (4.22)$$

Then, if we define the unspecified function $g(i)$ to be equal to the exponential i^b, we obtain, in logarithmic form, equation (4.23).

$$\log M = b \log i + c \log W_n \qquad (4.23)$$

where c is expected to be equal to 1. This, of course, is one of the equations tested by Bronfenbrenner and Mayer, as promised.

Such an exercise is a little unnerving to one brought up on the conflict between Keynes and the Classics, but it is useful none the less. For one thing, it reminds us of a central problem in macroeconomics: the simple (equilibrium) equations we actually test on the data can generally be derived from the different polar positions under fairly reasonable (although dissimilar) assumptions. For another thing, the list of assumptions used will differ and, while we normally do not test assumptions directly, we can compare them (in certain cases) as to their 'strength'. Finally, one can imbed the complete theory, along with its restrictions (if any are implied by the theory) in a full-scale model and compare the predictive content of the various possible models. As recent work has demonstrated, this is not particularly impressive for the simple models of either the Keynesians or the Monetarists; they do, however, turn out to be evenly matched, if that is any consolation.[52]

Meltzer's results showed generally higher interest elasticities (-0.40 to -1.04) with high t-values and even, in one case, a significant interest elasticity of -1.77; his income elasticity was generally less than unity and, when wealth was in the equation, tended to be dominated by wealth. Bronfenbrenner and Mayer, it will be recalled, obtained an opposite result for income/wealth. Meltzer noted that:

> a comparison of estimates for various measures of wealth and various definitions of money strongly suggests that the demand function developed here is stable for several alternative definitions of money.[53]

Meltzer also notes that

> The results ... strongly suggest that the demand function for money constructed here, based on a theory of asset preference, is stable.[54]

Such an observation, from an inadequate test of stability, promoted T. Courchene and H. Shapiro to calculate the Durbin–Watson statistics, to correct the data by 'generalised least squares', and to apply the Chow test to determine rigorously the stability properties of the model.[55] They, in turn, concluded that

1. the presence of serial correlation seriously overstated the fit of the equations; when corrected, many distinctions, such as a different wealth elasticity between broad and narrow money, could not be maintained; further,
2. the Chow test for the two periods chosen (1900–29, 1930–58), for both the broad and narrow definitions of money, indicated a significant difference between the two periods.

But the Courchene and Shapiro results, while destructive of Meltzer's conclusions, do not deal with other time periods or other specifications, and the search for a stable demand function for money went on.

4.3.2   *Measures of income and the demand for money: later results*

The literature mentioned to this point has made little use of the distinction raised in the Friedman papers concerning whether to use permanent income or the level of income in the demand for money. While it is very obvious that, by the usual measures of permanent income (geometrically declining weights, for example), one is smoothing (a statistical property) the income series – and is especially likely to get a better fit on trend-dominated data – there has been some attempt in the literature to state a theoretical case for one or the other, as we have seen with Friedman's discussion. Laidler, for example, proposes four demand-for-money functions which could bracket the differences of opinion on this subject. These are:

$$M^d = f\left[Y_p, \int_{-\infty}^{t} (Y_T - C_T), i \right] \tag{4.24a}$$

$$M^d = F\left[\int_{-\infty}^{t} (1 - k)Y_p, \int_{-\infty}^{t} (Y_T - C_T), i \right] \tag{4.24b}$$

$$M^d = g(Y_p, i) \tag{4.24c}$$

$$M^d = G(Y, i). \tag{4.24d}$$

Thus, equation (4.24c) is a Friedman-type function, while equation (4.24d) is often referred to as Keynesian, and is described by Laidler as 'textbook'. The subscript T in the first two equations indicates a transitory component, so the term in the brackets is 'transitory savings'; Laidler argues that

transitory income and negative transitory consumption are added to money balances, so their levels at any time will depend upon all past levels of these transitory components.[56]

But there is a problem here. While we will also argue below that one might construct a model around the idea that unanticipated or transitory (not the same thing) savings must be held as money balances – see the discussion of the Chow model – one would expect the sum of these errors over time to be zero. That is, if we are following Friedman, at any rate, the average value of transitory income (and hence of transitory consumption) will be expected to be zero; consequently the average savings of a transitory nature will also be zero. Statistically, of course, we might get a number in this integral, particularly with trend-dominated data; even so, what we really want to do here is to look at a short-run model, as described below. Finally, Laidler argues that the 'permanent savings' in equation (4.24b) should be dominated by the 'transitory savings' in the same equation, since the former will not normally be held in the form of money.

The results Laidler reported were obtained from regressions using first differences (for convenience). Equation (4.24a), as one might have suspected, did badly for broad money, narrow money and time deposits (all that was calculated) and was rejected. Equation (4.24b) showed significance for all variables and some reasonable stability (in terms of the values and significance of the coefficients for various time periods), but the R^2 was low and very variable – one suspects that a Chow test might have been failed here. Laidler couldn't use logs here because the transitory series sometimes showed negative values, so while the absolute coefficients showed a stronger effect from the transitory component of savings, I would hazard a guess that the elasticities, calculated at the mean, would show a dominance from the permanent savings variable. Equations (4.24c) and (4.24d) are also compared and the former, representing the permanent income hypothesis, dominates. This is a standard result – for long-run formulations – and can be accepted. One must note, however, that the serial correlation obviously present was not measured in these tests.

Actually, tests like the ones just reported do not deal with an important aspect of the permanent income hypothesis, implicit in Friedman's distinction between the cyclical and secular behaviour of velocity and underscored by Meltzer in his conclusions to the earlier paper. In Meltzer's words,

> The model and the evidence presented here together with recent developments in money supply theory ... suggest that changes in the policy variables that are exogenous determinants of the supply of money give rise to desired money holdings that differ from actual money holdings.[57]

This aspect was further elucidated by G. Chow,[58] who more or less returns the argument full-circle by offering a distinction between the long-run and the short-run demand for money. If the long-run demand is given by equation (4.25), then equation (4.26) could represent the short-run adjustment of money balances:

$$M_t^d = b_0 + b_1 Y_{pt} + b_2 i_t \qquad (4.25)$$

$$M_t - M_{t-1} = c(M_t^d - M_{t-1}) + d(A_t - A_{t-1}). \qquad (4.26)$$

The former equation has the desired money stock as the dependent variable. In the latter equation, actual changes in the money stock $(M_t - M_{t-1})$ are divided into

1. desired changes $(M_t^d - M_{t-1})$ modified by an adjustment parameter (c), and
2. residual changes equal to some percentage (d) of the change in total assets (A) over the same time period.

The first of these is referred to as a long-run component and the second as a short-run component of the actual change in the money stock.[59]

Equation (4.25) can be estimated in the usual ways, but to achieve an estimating equation for the short-run demand for money, further manipulations are necessary. Thus, $(A_t - A_{t-1})$, the change in assets, is equal to S_t, the flow of savings, if A_{t-1} is assets at the beginning of the period and A_t is assets at the end. Thus equation (4.26), which is a 'stock-adjustment' equation, acquires a flow term which is itself equal to $(Y_t - C_t)$. At this point Chow invokes Friedman's permanent income hypothesis about the consumption function to complete the system; this appears as equation (4.27):

$$C_t = \theta Y_{pt}. \qquad (4.27)$$

When we combine the three equations in the model and rearrange the terms somewhat, we arrive at the 'short-run' demand-for-money function frequently tested in the literature (although it is rarely derived in so explicit a fashion), which appears here as equation (4.28):

$$M_t = cb_0 + cb_1 Y_{pt} + cb_2 i_t + (1 - c)M_{t-1} + dY_t - d\theta Y_{pt}. \qquad (4.28)$$

This equation still contains one unobservable variable (Y_{pt}), but Koyck or other transformations can then be applied to get an equation in present and past values of the other variables. What is interesting here, though, is that the coefficient on Y_{pt} in this equation is $(cb - d\theta)$ and consists of influences that offset each other in so far as they contribute to the short-run demand for money. Thus, in the short-run models, permanent income (or its proxies) would be expected to be out-performed by the level of income. Chow's tests, of both long- and short-run functions for the US data, confirm that this is so.[60]

We next turn to a discussion of stability and temporal aggregation, in so far as this has not already been discussed; we leave the subject of which interest rate to employ to Chapter 6, where it is introduced in the context of the theory of the term structure of interest rates.

4.4 Stability and temporal aggregation of the macroeconomic demand for money

Preceding sections have dealt partly with the topic of this section, so by way of introduction we might summarise what has been said so far on these two interrelated subjects. With regard to stability, we wish to know whether or not the demand function for money (as a function of whatever variables it is a function of) has shifted frequently; furthermore, if it has shifted, we wish to know if there is something systematic about the shifts (so that we can search for a unique cause which can then be added to the list of variables) or whether they have been random (or unexplainable). Policy reasons are usually mentioned here as the reason for taking a special interest in this problem, but it is sufficient to invoke a theoretical reason: a relevant empirical test of a theoretical proposition (presumed to apply generally) is the stability of the relationship, when it is parameterised and tested. With regard to the temporal aggregation, the concern is with the attempt to measure the lagged influence of the independent variables on the dependent variable under study. Here we aggregate, generally, because a series of lagged values of the independent variables will often (usually) exhibit multicollinearity; a second reason is that the techniques of aggregation (e.g., the Almon procedure) are flexible enough to permit us to assume that the peak of the influence of the independent variable is not the present or the immediate past. This advantage has produced clear gains in the study of the investment and consumption functions, but as we shall see seems less important in the more rapidly adjusting money market. The two are interrelated because, for example, an incorrect temporal specification could produce evidence of instability that is, essentially, unjustified, or vice versa. But we are hampered here because we have no idea what the appropriate division of time might be and, for that matter, no ideas as to what length and what degree of lag are appropriate, *a priori*. We will elaborate on these themes.

In the studies mentioned in the body of the text so far the temporal aggregation has been quite simple and generally limited to the use of explicit measures of permanent income or to the use of the Koyck transformation. Both of these produce estimates of the independent variables (income, prices, interest rates) with monotonically declining weights assigned to the past values of the variables. The (temporally) aggregate income then achieved (e.g.) is a defensible concept, of course; and, in view of the lack of a theory, is about as far as one can go if he believes that the past either influences or guides the present decision-maker, but is nevertheless completely hazy about the exact form of that influence. With regard to the stability of the models discussed up to now, the most important generalisation probably is that the strongest evidence of instability occurs with annual data and with broader measures of money.

But the policy-maker does not require that the demand for money be stable over the entire period from 1860 to 1960, but only that recent versions of the function be stable over recent data – data very much like that which he has available to guide him in his policy formulations. In this spirit the significant studies of Goldfeld on the postwar US (quarterly) data and of Price and Haache on the British data provide a very convincing (for the moment) demonstration that the demand for narrow money has been stable in these two different contexts, and that the demand for broad money (or M_3, as well) has not.[61] These studies have in common that they employ a short-run model, as follows:

$$M_t^d = f(i, Y, P) \tag{4.29}$$

$$M_t - M_{t-1} = \beta(M_t^d - M_{t-1}) \tag{4.30}$$

so that they are readily comparable. The estimating equation, after assuming the absence of money illusion, which deals with the price variable, contains much the same variables as equation (4.28), although the coefficients are different, since that model was derived from a model that had equation (4.26) instead of (4.30). This affects primarily the income terms (after Y_{pt} is dealt with by some form of transformation).

There is a problem here, of course, since the Chow model, containing two more parameters, is obviously richer in its implications – if it can be accepted. If we assume that $Y_{pt} = Y_t$, then the coefficient on the income variable in the former case is

$$(cb_1 + d - d\theta)$$

while the latter provides

$$(1 - \gamma)b_1$$

where $\beta = (1 - \gamma)$. Looking at Haache's numbers, for example, a reasonable number for γ is 0.5 – the range he produces is 0.38 to 0.64 – which is convenient, since it implies that c is also 0.5. Thus, if the true income elasticity (b_1) is 1.0, the Bank of England (BOE) version of the model predicts a coefficient value for Y_t of 0.5, while the Chow form, when the propensity to consume (or, rather, the elasticity) is near unity, predicts a slightly larger value. The BOE model, then, if the coefficient on income turns out to be low (as it does in their studies) must (given γ) attribute this result to a low income elasticity; the Chow model, on the other hand, could get the same result in that way *or* from a high propensity to consume. Furthermore, if the income elasticity of consumption is greater than 1, as it very well may be for Y_t as opposed to Y_{pt}, we could get a value on this coefficient, using the Chow model, that is negative. Indeed, several studies have produced low or negative results here, results that the BOE model is not flexible enough to comprehend.

Neither Goldfeld nor the BOE authors comment on the difference between their formulation and that of Chow, but the difference, clearly, is that the latter contains the assumption that there is a short-run component to money accumulation. That is, Chow assumes that there are some money balances piled up which have not yet been converted to other forms of wealth. The assumption in the other models, apparently, is that these adjustments are completed within the quarter or are random. This, clearly, is an empirical question; some support for this view can be obtained with reference to the paper by Gibson, and by simple adjustment parameters obtained under the Koyck transformation in the British and American studies just described. On the other hand, the results for the Almon specification (Price; Goldfeld) imply a longer adjustment, particularly for income. And there the matter rests, so far as I can tell.

With regard to the stability of the simple model, now that its position in the literature has been elucidated, consider the following quotations:

> [Goldfeld [62]]: On the whole, the money demand function does not exhibit marked short-run instability [p. 590]; [With reference to the long-run model,] On balance, then, the evidence does not seem to suggest any need to estimate the money demand equation over separate subsamples of the postwar period. [p. 592]. [On the other hand,] both of these are significant at the 1 percent level, allowing one easily to reject the hypothesis that the equation for M_2 is stable over the sample period. [p. 594]

> [Haache [63]] It shows that the demand for money narrowly-defined (M_1) has in only a few quarters been significantly out of line with expectation, and that holdings of broadly defined money (M_3) by the personal sector were also much as predicted until 1973.

Price, earlier, felt that the stability was more obvious, and extended even to the business sector (a finding not corroborated by Haache); we will return to these issues.

There are other studies of the US data, although the evidence still seems generally to run in favour of the stability of the demand-for-money function. M. Khan, for one,[64] has put the Laidler paper through a Brown and Durbin test, and found very much in favour of a stable demand for money. In his words:

> Laidler's (1971) view that the evidence of the existence of a stable relationship between the demand for real balances and a few

variables is 'overwhelming' is supported by the results in this paper for the United States for the period 1901–65. This is especially true if the 'few' variables include a long-term rate of interest rather than a short-term rate. It does not appear to matter whether current real per capita income or the longer-run concept of permanent real per capita income is used as the other explanatory variable.[65]

Goldfeld, it might be noted, would disagree only on the choice of the rate of interest, but, it will be recalled, both the data period and the form of the model are different in his case.

Then, there is a study of the stability of the demand for money during one of the most troubled times in American history, the 1929–33 period, by A. Gandolfi. The model employed was a cross-sectional test of the US data by state, and estimates of the demand function were compared for each of the five years in the sample by comparing the errors from a pooled estimate with the sum of the errors from each of the regressions. Gandolfi concludes that, not only is the overall function stable, but also the constant term is (somewhat unexpectedly) stable. His demand-for-money function was of the Friedman type, with the addition of a long-term interest rate and a term to capture the effect of expected bank failures on the value of deposits.[66] On the other hand, M. Slovin and M. Sushka have argued that, in a standard demand-for-money model, the substantial rise in Regulation Q ceilings in 1962, which improved the attractiveness of interest-bearing deposits, did cause a structural shift in the demand for money.[67] In particular, the time deposit rate affects the demand for money after (but not before) the change, and the speed of adjustment is dramatically faster in the later period. These results are obtained on both the demand for demand deposits and the demand for currency (see Chapter 2); quite possibly a broad measure of money (M_2 or M_3) would not show this instability, though.

There are now also some further British results on this question. To begin with, there was the view of A. Walters, achieved on annual data for a comparably long period as the major American studies; this was for an unstable if not chaotic money market.[68] But Walters has since revised his views, although he is far from convinced, I would surmise, and offers us some timely warnings:

> The first point to be made is that the velocity of circulation is relatively unstable. Although the coefficient of variation is between 6 and 22 per cent according to the period chosen, this is much too large to be useful for policy purposes.[69]

He did, as noted, accept that the demand-for-money function itself might well be stable; nevertheless, his concern in the above quotation was the problem of the 'chaotic' money market; indeed, he notes that 'The existence of such a stable demand function does not necessarily imply that there exist also stable monetary multipliers.' [70] While this carries us beyond the brief of this study, in that it raises the question of the policy uses to which we might put the (stable) demand for money, it is worth remarking on, since many Monetarists seem happy with just the bare minimum here. Friedman, I would submit, agrees with Walters completely now.[71]

As mentioned, G. Haache noted some instability in the recent data, and this result has inspired a certain amount of follow-up work on the most recent British data. Thus M. Artis and M. Lewis argue that traditional demand-for-money functions do legitimately show some instability in recent years, but when reformulated to make the money supply exogenous, and with the assumption that money markets are slow to adjust, this instability disappears.[72] Finally, in an important working paper, T. Mills considers the stability of the standard demand function when the structure of the model is variable (as in the Pifer literature). He finds evidence of structural instability, particularly centred round the policy of 'competition and credit control' in 1971,[73] but no evidence of functional instability. But these are provisional results.

With regard to the temporal aggregation of the demand for money, there again exist roughly parallel results for Britain and the United States. The problem ultimately concerns the length of the lag between the causes and effects in the demand function; and, it should be recalled, estimates of this lag vary considerably in the papers referred to so far, with Gibson's being the shortest and some results quoted by Goodhart being the longest.[74] There is a policy problem here, as well, for a long lag implies an important slippage in monetary policy; if the lag is unstable as well, we have further policy problems. The normal method of estimating this lag, by using the least squares estimate of the coefficient on the lagged value of the dependent variable, tends to produce an overstated lag if there is positive serial correlation in the underlying model.[75] If one first removes the serial correlation from the data (for example by utilising a technique such as the 'generalised least squares' described by J. Johnston [76]), as Courchene and Shapiro did for the Meltzer test, then some resolution can be achieved. F. deLeeuw did this, but found that the adjustment actually slowed down.[77] Actually, a prior problem – discussed by J. Thomas and implicit in the debate between Teigen and Gibson [78] – is that the use of quarterly or annual data (viewed as an aggregation over monthly data), when the correct aggregation is monthly, produces an upward bias in the estimate of the length of the lag, which is, of course, most severe for annual data.

At this point a number of researchers have brought in the flexible Almon lag technique, first employed on the investment function.[79] The general problem here is to estimate an equation of the general form of equation (4.31):

$$M_t = \alpha + \sum_{i=1}^{T} \beta_i X_{t-i} + \gamma_t. \tag{4.31}$$

Here the β_i are not necessarily restricted to be declining weights as in the Friedman or Koyck weighting schemes described above. The approach, instead, is to expand the X variable(s) to an r-degree polynomial of length T, to maximise the $\bar{R}^2$ of the expanded relation (as a function of the M_t) and, finally, to interpolate for the lag coefficients (and their standard errors) from the best-fitting polynomial equation (and its dispersion matrix). When this was done by Dickson and Starleaf on quarterly US data (1952–69), the total lag was found to be much shorter than was the result for the annual data studies (for narrow money); time deposits, further, were found to have a longer lag than narrow money, and to respond to different variables, casting doubt on the usefulness of the broad definition of money.[80] Goldfeld, later, reported similar results. Shapiro, in a parallel study also using the US quarterly data (1950–70), fitted an equation in first differences. He comments that:

> The first point to be noted is the rather rapid response of the demand for money to all independent variables, regardless of the definition of money employed.[81]

In comparison, for example, to deLeeuw, Shapiro finds a lag of money to income which is 75 per cent complete after eighteen months; deLeeuw's results took three years to reach the 75 per cent point. Of course, eighteen months is a long time, and Friedman's concern with a total lag of six to eighteen months in the conduct of monetary policy still seems valid, Shapiro's conclusions (stated later) to the contrary notwithstanding.

Goldfeld's work on the postwar US quarterly data again provides a benchmark here because of his thoroughness. First of all, Goldfeld underscores a point, already mentioned in Chapter 2 above, that the lag on interest rates would not be expected to be the same as that on income (or wealth); the simple Koyck procedure treats both alike. He proposes a rationale for lagged adjustment which is different from the usual lag of actual to desired balances:

> the adjustment can be conceived as a slow response of desired stock itself to actual current values of income and interest rates, rather than a gradual shift in money holdings to meet a promptly adopted new level of desired holdings.[82]

This produces an equation of the same general form as the short-run models described above, but in his case the adjustment parameter comes from an equation showing how expectations are revised, such as equations (4.32) or (4.33):

$$y_t^e - y_{t-1}^e = \gamma(y_t - y_{t-1}^e) \tag{4.32}$$

$$i_t^e - i_{t-1}^e = \delta(i_t - i_{t-1}^e). \tag{4.33}$$

Thus, rather than

$$M_t - M_{t-1} = (1 - \lambda)(M_t^d - M_{t-1}) \qquad (4.34)$$

the estimating equation we would derive from his case is in the form of equation (4.35), after substitution of $M_t = a + bi^e + cy^e$, with a Koyck model for the lags.

$$M_t =$$
$$a_0 + a_1 y_t + a_2 y_{t-1} + a_3 i_t + a_4 i_{t-1} + a_5 M_{t-1} + a_6 M_{t-2} + e_t. \qquad (4.35)$$

The form of this equation is just like that used in empirical tests reported above (e.g., Chow's), but here the coefficients have different interpretations (i.e., they represent a different structure); the adjustment coefficients are interpreted differently (as rates of revisions of expectations rather than as actual adjustments); and the error terms will also have a different form. One could as well use equation (4.34), in which case a further lag in the variables would result (and the coefficients would become even more complicated).

Direct estimates of equation (4.35) are inhibited by multicollinearity, so Goldfeld produces some results using Almon lags. He expects the weights on income to decline monotonically, but the weights on the interest rate might well have a humped pattern, in his view. But rather than searching over all degrees and lag lengths, as his agnosticism might suggest, Goldfeld only allows the lag to vary without limit (he picks a third-degree polynomial). In any event, the results show longer lags for income, but that Koyck and (the sum of) Almon coefficients are equal (although the Almon lag shows longer lags); the interest rate does exhibit the humped pattern. Thus, in this test at least, some advantages are shown to occur to techniques more flexible than the Koyck, although the differences are, perhaps, marginal.

The British results appear in a paper by L. Price.[83] Price finds a rather quicker adjustment than in the American case, but with the individual (as opposed to the business) demand for money very slow in response to interest rates. Since British monetary policy during the period in question was often aimed at interest rates, this was considered disconcerting. Price noted that the aggregation of business and private demand appeared to be both at the cost of 'speed of adjustment', which was faster for business firms, and 'argument'; with regard to the latter, firms responded to the short-term interest rate, while individuals responded to the long-term interest rate. We will pursue the topic of the business demand in the next section; the question of which interest rate is appropriate is postponed until Chapter 6, where some theoretical results are derived.

4.5 The business demand for money: some single-equation results

The results for the business demand for money are scattered about in this study mainly because this study is organised around the method of approach – and generally all methods of approach have been tried on the business demand. We have already discussed the generation of a business demand for money from a Jorgenson-style model, in Chapter 3, and we will consider in some detail the business demand from the Baumol–Tobin framework in Chapter 5. Here, instead, we will consider work that has much in common with the (generally) single-equation macroeconomic formulations that form the basis of this chapter.

The motive for studying the business firm as a separate entity goes back at least to Keynes,[84] and we have already expressed interest in the questions that arise if the aggregation of business and private demands is an unwise one (in Chapter 2). The basic recent study here, aside from a great deal of work on the inventory-theoretic model (discussed in Chapter 5), is that of A. Meltzer, who was interested in the different estimates of the income elasticity of the demand for money in the Baumol–Tobin (low) versus Friedman (high) studies.[85] Meltzer's model builds on the quantity theory model, which was developed above as equation (4.22), itself derived from the Friedman equation (4.17). With W_{fj} the non-human wealth of the fth firm in the jth industry, then the internal rate of return for the industry (following the line of Modigliani–Miller)[86] is given as

$$\rho_j = \frac{S_{fj}}{W_{fj}}$$

where S_{fj} is the gross income of the firm (= value of sales).

Since the relation between S_{fj} and W_{fj} will vary over time if there is substitution of capital for labour or if there is excess capacity, we must introduce the parameter K_{fj} to modify the internal rate of return:

$$K_{fj}\rho_j = \frac{S_{fj}}{W_{fj}}. \qquad (4.36)$$

The model employed earlier by Meltzer is then written as equation (4.37):

$$M = ki^\alpha W^\beta \qquad (4.37)$$

Thus, the substitution of (4.36) into (4.37) produces equation (4.38), a demand-for-money function for the firm:

$$M_{fj} = \frac{ki^\alpha}{K_{fj}\rho_j} S_{fj}^\beta \qquad (4.38)$$

There are, then, qualitative results from this marriage of the business firm with Meltzer's version of the quantity theory of money.

1. A rise of the interest rate (i) along with an increase of sales will (since $\alpha < 0$) produce a less-than-proportionate increase in money holding – whether β is unity or not.[87]

2. A rise in ρ or in K (the proportion of assets used in production) will also contribute to a lower sales elasticity than examination of the β alone would indicate.

3. Since prosperity usually brings both a rise in the interest rate and a rise in K (and even ρ), we would expect business velocity to rise over the business cycle (which it does).

4. We expect inter-firm differences in the use of cash balances.

The question of economies of scale is obviously a complicated one.

G. Maddala and R. Vogel went over the Meltzer study, which when tested produced mild economies of scale in business cash balances, and are quite critical.[88] In particular, they criticise some comparisons Meltzer made between results from time series (his own) and cross-section studies, and the use of sales rather than a wealth variable; they are also dubious about the role of the interest rate in the model. With regard to the wealth variable, Maddala and Vogel ran tests using total assets and found *firmer* evidence of the existence of (still mild) economies of scale for business firms. Meltzer, then, returned to battle, aided by K. Brunner,[89] in a study discussed in Chapter 5; in this paper they argue (after accepting much of the Maddala–Vogel criticism) that the Baumol–Tobin models themselves, when completed properly, do not necessarily provide a theoretical case for the less-than-unit income (or wealth) elasticity.

Finally, we may turn again to the study by L. Price for the Bank of England,[90] a paper we have mentioned several times, mostly in passing; here the Almon lag technique was employed on the short-run, single-equation model featured in much of this chapter. The results for a very broad measure of money (M_3) – because no narrow money figures were available for business holdings – showed remarkable differences for the two types of deposit owners:

1. companies adjusted their actual balances (to changes in the arguments of the functions) much more rapidly than did individuals;

2. companies responded more to a short-term interest rate (the local authority borrowing rate) and individuals more to a long-term rate (the Consol rate);

3. companies showed a much greater volatility of their cash balances;

4. the income elasticity of personal demand was around 2, while for businesses it was less than unity;

5. the fit of the equations for businesses was generally much less satisfactory than it was for persons.

By any account, should they survive other studies (and data), these are good reasons for regarding the aggregation of business and private demand functions as potentially troublesome; the only hopes arise under item number 5, and for the result, noted earlier, that many researchers have found the demand for broader measures of money unstable.

Footnotes

1. In this chapter we will not take up the results of work on the demand for liquid assets in the context of portfolio or inventory-theoretic models. These topics will, instead, be discussed in Chapter 5, after the properties of the models themselves are described. Goldfeld ('The Demand for Money Revisited') is one of the latest to consider the question of the breadth of the definition of money (he opts for M_1); a few years ago there were many studies that compared the demand for the various aggregations, but the practice seems to have largely disappeared, along with the journal space to publish what must appear to editors as mere variations on a theme.

2. J. M. Keynes, *The General Theory*, Chapter 15; *A Treatise on Money*, Vol. 1, Chapter 3.

3. J. R. Hicks, 'Mr Keynes and the "Classics"; A Suggested Interpretation'. Hicks has it as $L(i, y)$.

4. J. M. Keynes, *The General Theory*, p. 195.

5. Laidler writes equation (4.1) as $M^d/P = ky + \lambda(i)W$ in his survey of the demand for money (*The Demand for Money: Theories and Evidence*). The reason for λ (i), a function, is that one expects a nonlinear relation; the reason for W is that Keynes's argument for a liquidity preference function is stated in terms of the proportion of assets held in the form of money and the λ function needs to be scaled by total wealth to get all the terms in the equation into conformity, dimensionwise. Patinkin (*Money, Interest and Prices*, p. 278) notes that Keynes had $PL_1(y) + L_2(i) = M$, where M is in nominal terms and y is real income. Thus, he says, the function exhibits money illusion, whether intended or not, arising from the second term. In the text, above, we write it without money illusion.

6. J. R. Hicks, *Critical Essays in Monetary Theory*, p. 15.

7. J. M. Keynes, *The General Theory*, p. 199.

8. L. R. Klein, *Economic Fluctuations in the United States*.

9. J. Tobin, 'Liquidity Preference and Monetary Policy', and M. Bronfenbrenner and T. Mayer, 'Liquidity Functions in the American Economy'. Early British studies which employed similar methodology are by A. J. Brown, 'Interest, Prices and the Demand Schedule for Idle Money', and A. Khusro, 'An Investigation of Liquidity Preference'.

10. We are, of course, discussing income velocity, although using the term 'transactions' velocity. In a well-known paper now somewhat neglected, R. Selden discusses the distinction between the two concepts ('Monetary Velocity in the United States'). Selden notes that the two concepts will not be equal, of course, and may not even be proportional to each other (a) if the prices of the goods implied in each measure ('income goods' or 'transactions goods') move differently or (b) if the volume of transactions as a percentage of the volume of income changes. The latter would result from the differing behaviour of financial institutions, from a change in the structure of industry towards or away from specialisation, or from a change in the percentage of transactions in the form of barter. These are Selden's reasons, to which we might add the use of trade credit and of credit cards and electronic funds transfers. He provides others as well.

11. At the end of this section we discuss a fourth Keynesian motive, the 'finance motive'.

12. J. M. Keynes, *The General Theory*, p. 198.

13. ibid., p. 201.

14. J. Tobin, an important paper ('Liquidity Preference as Behaviour Towards Risk'), employs mean-variance analysis to get rid of the awkward 'differences of opinion' motivation of Keynes. It will be discussed in the next chapter. A variation of the earlier theme resurfaced in the *Radcliffe Report* in England in 1959:

> we frequently came upon a 'three-gears' view of the level of interest rates. At any given time people consider the current level as 'high', 'low', or 'middle' ('normal'), and how

they behave seems to be governed not so much by the precise percentage but by whether that percentage fits into the high, low or normal bracket . . . if they are to be shaken into some change, of course, the gear must be changed. [§442]

Specifically, 5 per cent was considered to be the upper end of the normal range and, variously, 3 or 4 per cent was put as the lower bound.

15. M. R. Weinrobe, 'A Simple Model of the Precautionary Demand for Money', p. 11.

16. In Chapter 5 we will discuss these questions in terms of the inventory-theoretic model. There we will look at models with specific costs – such as a per unit penalty cost, or the need to rediscount at the Central Bank – and at models that distinguish between the 'cash flow' problems of individuals, banks, business firms and financial institutions.

17. J. M. Keynes, 'The Ex-Ante Theory of the Rate of Interest'.

18. P. Davidson, *Money and the Real World*.

19. ibid., p. 168; the consumption function here has an interest effect not in Davidson's formulation.

20. ibid. p. 169. He also says:

The inevitable conclusion is that even this Neoclassical-Bastard Keynesian system cannot be dichotomized into independent real and monetary subsets; consequently, it is not correct to separate monetary economics as has often been done.

One should note that only this particular formulation is shown to have an 'invalid dichotomy' by Davidson, and only as he has set it up.

21. P. A. Meyer and J. A. Neri, 'A Keynes–Friedman Money Demand Function', p. 610.

22. M. Bronfenbrenner and T. Mayer, 'Liquidity Functions in the American Economy'; R. Teigen, 'Demand and Supply Functions in the United States: Some Structural Estimates'; D. Starleaf and R. Reimer, 'The Keynesian Demand Function for Money: Some Statistical Tests'; and H. Pifer, 'A Non-linear Maximum Likelihood Estimate of the Liquidity Trap'.

23. M. Bronfenbrenner and T. Mayer, 'Liquidity Functions in the American Economy', p. 810.

24. In the scheme explained by A. Leijonhufvud this makes the test Keynesian rather than 'of Keynes' – see the discussion in Chapter 2. Bronfenbrenner and Mayer note this, but apparently attach no importance to it. R. Eisner ('Another Look at Liquidity Preference') finds this unsound, if one is following Keynes, but A. Meltzer ('Yet Another Look at the Low Level Liquidity Trap') also attaches no importance to it, claiming that one is merely looking for a trap between relevant variables, not doggedly following Keynes.

25. As already noted, R. Eisner ('Another Look at Liquidity Preference') found Bronfenbrenner and Mayer's use of the short-term rate inconsistent with Keynes. He also noted that

1. the use of equation (4.7) implies a trap in theory since for $i = 0$, $M^d = \infty$ (β_2 is negative);
2. their definition of idle balances is arbitrary and, in particular, produces nonsense in one year (1926), when the logarithm of zero had to be computed. He suggested adding a constant to the relation;
3. the assumption of a stable supply function for money seemed to him unwise, since before 1934 the Federal Reserve's monetary policy was passive, while afterwards it was in favour of easy money. I would add the caveat that after the Accord of 1951 it was also different. In fact, there were probably many switches of policy over the period (see M. Friedman and A. Schwartz, *A Monetary History of the United States*).

Meltzer, in commenting on Eisner, also noted the point made in the text here, that the Bronfenbrenner and Mayer procedure for calculating transactions balances made most of total M belong to M_1.

26. Teigen argues that this is because of the good fit for the $(i - i_d)$ term in his regressions. In fact, if that term were purified of exogenous influences by the two-stage procedure, it would be the low R^2 (at most 0.80), which might justify this conclusion. I was not able to judge, in reading the paper, which of these views is best justified, but I am inclined to the latter. It should be noted here, as well, that there is a literature – generally ignored for some reason – which argues that if individuals are price-takers, then, in the aggregate (especially in single-equation models where $M_s = \bar{M}$), the 'chain of causation' is reversed, and the interest rate should be taken as the dependent variable. Eisner discusses this issue in his comment on Bronfenbrenner and Mayer ('Another Look at the Liquidity Trap') and includes some estimates that show

higher interest elasticities. H. Pifer, in his paper discussed below, also employed this formulation, and A. Walters and N. J. Kavanagh, on the UK data, made much of it ('Demand for Money in the UK, 1877–1961: Some Preliminary Findings'). Aside from the higher interest elasticity generally found, the fit of the model is often worse (especially for Pifer – but see Eisner's comment, also discussed below); this provides two reasons why the approach might have been rejected in the literature.

27. W. Gibson, 'Demand and Supply Functions for Money in the United States: Theory and Measurement', p. 361.

28. ibid., p. 364.

29. Gibson measures the stock data as averages over the quarter rather than as point estimates (as in Teigen and many others). This would tend to eliminate the lag, but it also kills Gibson's re-estimate of equation (4.8) which falls to an R^2 of around 0.3. Gibson's argument that Teigen's procedure is incorrect for the demand for money is only marginally interesting since Teigen's 'mean lag' of two quarters just makes it on a t-test of its difference from a one-quarter lag. The latter is built into Gibson's measurement. Whichever way we proceed to relate a stock to a flow we are dealing in approximations, so as long as we appreciate that Teigen has to show a lag longer than one-quarter (which he does), we can accept his procedure as correct.

30. R. Teigen, 'Demand and Supply Functions for Money: Another Look at Theory and Measurement'. Teigen expresses his confidence in a 'free reserves' supply function and cites, among others, D. I. Fand, 'Some Implications of Money Supply Analysis'; A. J. Meigs, *Free Reserves and the Money Supply*. Gibson's short reply is somewhat of a capitulation ('Demand and Supply Functions for Money: A Comment').

31. B. Klein, 'Competitive Interest Payments on Bank Deposits and the Long-run Demand for Money'. Klein, as well, finds that the assumption that the interest payment (on demand deposits) restriction is totally ineffective provides (when applied) a better fit than the converse. That is, he estimates an 'own' interest rate on cash and employs it successfully on the demand for money.

32. D. R. Starleaf and R. Reimer, 'The Keynesian Demand Function for Money'.

33. ibid., p. 72. In several of their tests, i_L was included as an additional variable.

34. J. M. Keynes, *The General Theory*, pp. 201–2.

35. ibid., pp. 202–3.

36. ibid., p. 206.

37. D. Fisher, 'The Speculative Demand for Money: An Empirical Test'.

38. H. Pifer, 'A Non-Linear Maximum Likelihood Estimate of the Liquidity Trap'; in all of these tests but Spitzer's, below, the value of assets (A) rather than income (Y) was the most generally employed 'wealth' proxy. Actually, there is not a good microeconomic case for the existence of an actual liquidity trap, but, as described by J.-M. Grandmont and G. Laroque ('The Liquidity Trap'),

> we shall prove a general property of the trade-off between the short run equilibrium rate of interest on long term bonds and the short run equilibrium money stock, in an economy where a central bank intervenes by open market operations. Specifically, *equilibrium* interest rates on long term bonds which tend to zero are associated with *equilibrium* money stocks which tend to infinity, once the assumption of inelastic price expectations is made. [p. 129]

This paper, consequently, provides an existence proof in a climate much like that in Keynes's *General Theory*, although the trap is at zero.

39. R. Eisner, 'Non-Linear Estimates of the Liquidity Trap'; K. White, 'Estimation of the Liquidity Trap with a Generalized Functional Form'; J. Spitzer, 'The Demand for Money, the Liquidity Trap, and Functional Form'.

40. K. Brunner and A. H. Meltzer, 'Liquidity Traps for Money, Bank Credit, and Interest Rates'.

41. K. White, 'Estimation of the Liquidity Trap with a Generalized Functional Form', p. 196. What happens, as noted above in a different context, is that the form chosen by Pifer assumes that the interest elasticity of the demand for money function will somewhere be ∞ so long as i_{min} is greater than 0. The more general case used by White does not do this.

42. This paragraph closely follows the survey of this material in J. Spitzer, 'The Demand for

Money, the Liquidity Trap, and Functional Form'. Spitzer, as noted earlier, employs income in lieu of total wealth.

43. In an earlier paper, P. Konstas and M. Khouja ('The Keynesian Demand-for-Money Function') test an equation that is equivalent to (4.14) with $\gamma_0 = \gamma_1 = 1$ and $\gamma_2 = -1$.

44. Much of the same ground is gone over in a recent paper by J. Breslaw and D. Fisher ('The Non-Linear Estimate of the Liquidity Trap: British Estimates of a Reformulated Model'). In this case, in which the ratio of money to the national debt is the dependent variable, a highly significant liquidity trap on recent quarterly British data is found around an interest rate of 4.30 per cent. Various forms, including the additively separable Keynesian function (equation 4.1) are found here to produce comparable results; as well, an unsuccessful attempt is made to locate an i_{max}. This is frustrated, quite possibly, because the upper limit on expectations is totally unbounded, while the lower limit is packed in between the lowest observed rates and zero. We will return to this study, which also contains results relevant to the term structure debate, in Chapter 6.

45. M. Friedman, 'The Demand for Money: Some Theoretical and Empirical Results', pp. 111–12.

46. ibid., p. 117.

47. ibid., p. 119.

48. If we assume an (individual) household demand function is given by

$$M_{it} = \beta_{0i} + \beta_{1i}Y_{it} + u_{it} \tag{a}$$

then the aggregate for N_t households is given by

$$\sum M_{it} = \sum \beta_{0i} + \sum \beta_{1i}Y_{it} + \sum u_{it}. \tag{b}$$

We may assume that $\beta_{0i} = \beta_{0j} = \beta_0$ and $\beta_{1i} = \beta_{1j} = \beta_1$, in which case (b) is written as

$$\sum M_{it} = \beta_0 N_t + \beta_1 \sum Y_{it} + \sum u_{it}. \tag{c}$$

Then, by calculating on a *per capita* basis, we will remove the collinearity between $\beta_0 N_t$ and $\beta_1 \sum Y_{it}$; the regression will then be correct so long as the u_{it} are uncorrelated. If not, we could take the logs of the variables in (c) to restore the balance, although when we do we should be careful to run our *t*-tests (etc.) from the log-normal distribution. Friedman, of course, works from the Cobb–Douglas form into a logarithmic regression, and it is clear that his error term is multiplicative as in equation (4.7) above. Presumably, the independence of individual errors is assumed, producing, if they are actually positively correlated, an understatement of the true variance. See the discussion in J. Cramer, *Empirical Econometrics*, Chapter 8.

49. It should be noted here that this is a somewhat sensitive issue – Friedman's reasons for omitting the interest rate – as any reader of the long first footnote in his paper on 'Interest Rates and the Demand for Money' will see for himself. Taking Friedman's writings as a whole, there is a very poor case for the accusations that have been made on this account. With regard to this particular article (on the demand for money), Friedman points out that in his view the interest elasticity is low (e.g., -0.15) and the contribution of the term to the demand for money is also low, compared with real *per capita* income; these he regards as sufficient reasons to ignore the interest rate. We can also note that, since Friedman uses broad money as his measure of 'cash balances', a small interest rate effect is possibly to be expected on account of the aggregation itself – or because of the instability of this particular aggregate. While Friedman might not be happy with this line of attack, it is clear that a number of recent studies find the demand for broad money to be unstable (see below).

50. M. Friedman, 'The Quantity Theory of Money – A Restatement'.

51. See Chapter 7 below for a discussion of Friedman's version of the 'common model'.

52. The recent study is by W. Poole and E. Kornbluth, 'The Friedman–Meiselman CMC Paper: New Evidence on an Old Controversy', the old controversy started with the paper by Friedman and D. Meiselman, 'The Relative Stability of Monetary Velocity and the Investment Multiplier in the United States'; the early critics were A. Ando and F. Modigliani, 'The Relative Stability of Monetary Velocity and the Investment Multiplier', and M. DePrano and T. Mayer, 'Tests of the Relative Importance of Autonomous Expenditure and Money'.

53. A. H. Meltzer, 'The Demand for Money: the Evidence from the Time Series', p. 244.

54. ibid., p. 241.

55. T. Courchene and H. Shapiro, 'The Demand for Money: A Note From the Time Series'. The Chow test is described in G. Chow, 'Tests of Equality Between Sets of Coefficients in Two Linear Regressions'.

56. D. Laidler, 'Some Evidence on the Demand for Money', p. 56.

57. A. H. Meltzer, 'The Demand for Money; the Evidence from the Time Series', p. 245.

58. G. Chow, 'On the Long-run and Short-run Demand for Money'.

59. One can obtain this result from standard portfolio theory, following Meltzer's lead, as described above. If we assume that savings can be held in three forms – bonds (B), money (M) and real properties plus equities (R), then, for given period, net savings will be constrained as follows:

$$S_t = \Delta B_t + \Delta M_t + \Delta R_t$$

where ΔM_t is the actual change in money holdings. If we assume that $\Delta R_t = 0$ for convenience, that is if we assume that new savings are held in the form of either money or bonds, then we need to construct a simple portfolio theory to get to the Chow equation. We may assume that in the long run individuals desire to add bonds and money into their portfolios in the ratio c_1, i.e.,

$$\Delta B_t^* = c_1 \Delta M_t^*$$

where $\Delta M_t^* = M_t^* - M_{t-1}$. This implies that long-run savings will be held as in

$$S_t^* = (1 - c)\Delta M_t^*.$$

But in the short run, individuals will have excess savings, held as money balances as Meltzer suggests; the weights b_1 and $(1 - b_1)$ suggest how these actual savings are apportioned between the two categories in the Chow model:

$$S_t = b_1[(1 - c_1)\Delta M_t^*] + (1 - b_1)(M_t - M_{t-1}).$$

We may, then, rearrange this expression to get

$$M_t - M_{t-1} = \frac{b_1(1 + c_1)}{(1 - b_1)}(M_t^* - M_{t-1}) + \frac{1}{(1 - b_1)}S_t$$

which, as claimed, is the Chow adjustment equation, more fully developed. The weights in the original Chow equation are thus seen not to sum to unity, by this interpretation, at least.

60. In two of my own British tests, using post-war quarterly data, this conclusion was upheld (D. Fisher, 'The Demand for Money in Britain: Quarterly Results', and 'Real Balances and the Demand for Money'). Work by D. Laidler and M. Parkin, 'The Demand for Money in the United Kingdom, 1956–1967: Preliminary Results', suggested that my use of Friedman's weighting scheme on quarterly data when the scheme was estimated originally on annual data, and the failure to deflate by population, may have introduced a spurious stability and firmness of fit. But the former hypothesis was not tested by Laidler and Parkin, and later work has not been particularly sanguine on this distinction (see below). Many studies have found shorter lags in general, and a recent paper by R. L. Jacobs ('Estimating the Long-run Demand for Money from Time-Series Data') argues that:

> Our theoretical model indicated that three common methods of defining the aggregate money demand function – deflating the aggregate data by population and prices, deflating by prices only, or using nominal data undeflated by population or prices – are mathematically equivalent when the data are dominated by a time trend. [p. 1235]

Since the deflation by population and prices implies the demand is homogeneous in these items, there ought to be some investigation of these assumptions, then.

With regard to the choice of weights to measure permanent income, the general argument can be advanced that the results from the annual data seriously overstate the length of the lag (see the papers by Gibson, already discussed and J. Thomas, discussed below), and that by speeding up the adjustment, for example by using annually derived weights on quarterly data, one might actually get a better fit. Some of these issues are considered in a paper by C. Clark ('The Demand for Money and the Choice of a Permanent Income Estimate'), who investigates the assumption that the consumption horizon and the asset demand horizon are different, as well. Of course this argument is close to asserting that two wrongs make a right, so perhaps we can leave it that more work needs to be done on this problem.

61.   S. Goldfeld, 'The Demand for Money Revisited'; L. Price, 'The Demand for Money in the United Kingdom: A Further Investigation'; G. Haache, 'The Demand for Money in the United Kingdom: Experience Since 1971'. A study by K. Clinton, 'The Demand for Money in Canada, 1955–1970', also finds the demand for narrow money stable and that for broad money unstable.

62.   S. Goldfeld, 'The Demand for Money Revisited', pp. 590, 592, 594.

63.   G. Haache, 'The Demand for Money in the United Kingdom: Experience Since 1971', p. 284.

64.   M. Khan, 'The Stability of the Demand-for-Money Function in the United States, 1901–1965'.

65.   ibid., p. 1217.

66.   A. E. Gandolfi, 'Stability of the Demand for Money During the Great Contraction – 1929–1933'. In a later study, A. E. Gandolfi and J. R. Lothian ('The Demand for Money from the Great Depression to the Present') argue that, not only have the slope coefficients of the demand for money (a double-log function of permanent income and 'a measure of the opportunity cost of holding money') been stable over the period 1929–68, but also the interest elasticity of the demand for money tended to *decrease* during the Great Depression. The intercepts of the model, however, were unstable (but it was a secular rather than a cyclical instability).

67.   M. Slovin and M. Sushka, 'The Structural Shift in the Demand for Money'.

68.   A. Walters and N. J. Kavanagh, 'The Demand for Money in the United Kingdom, 1877–1961: Some Preliminary Findings'; A. Walters, 'Monetary Multipliers in the U.K.'; A. Walters, 'The Radcliffe Report – Ten Years After. A Survey of Empirical Evidence'; and C. Barrett and A. Walters, 'The Stability of Keynesian and Monetary Multipliers in the United Kingdom'.

69.   A. Walters, 'The Radcliffe Report – Ten Years After', p. 47.

70.   ibid., p. 50.

71.   See, for example, M. Friedman, 'The Monetary Studies of the National Bureau', and M. Friedman and W. Heller, *Monetary Versus Fiscal Policy*.

72.   M. Artis and M. Lewis, 'The Demand for Money in the United Kingdom, 1963–1973'. The traditional demand for money is, in logarithmic form,

$$M_t = \alpha_0 + \alpha_1 Y_t + \alpha_2 (i - i_m)_t + \alpha_3 q_t + \alpha_4 M_{t-1} + w_t$$

where i_m is the 'own rate of interest on money balances' and q is an index of the quality of alternative assets. The latter was measured by a standard deviation, justified with reference to the portfolio literature.

73.   T. Mills, 'Sensitivity and Stability of the U.K. Demand for Money Function: 1963–1974'. The policy of 'competition and credit control' is described in Bank of England, 'Competition and Credit Control'.

74.   C. Goodhart and A. Crockett, 'The Importance of Money'.

75.   Z. Griliches, 'A Note on Serial Correlation Bias in Estimates of Distributed Lags'.

76.   J. Johnston, *Econometric Methods* (2nd edn).

77.   F. deLeeuw, 'The Demand for Money – Speed of Adjustment, Interest Rates, and Wealth'.

78.   J. J. Thomas, 'Some Aggregation Problems in the Estimation of Partial Adjustment Models of the Demand for Money'.

79.   S. Almon, 'The Distributed Lag Between Capital Appropriations and Expenditures'.

80.   H. Dickson and D. R. Starleaf, 'Polynomial Distributed Lag Structures in the Demand Function for Money'.

81.   A. A. Shapiro, 'Inflation, Lags and the Demand for Money', p. 89.

82.   S. Goldfeld, 'The Demand for Money Revisited', p. 599.

83.   L. Price, 'The Demand for Money in the United Kingdom: A Further Investigation'.

84.   J. M. Keynes, *A Treatise on Money*.

85.   A. H. Meltzer, 'The Demand for Money; A Cross-Section Study of Business Firms'.

86.   F. Modigliani and M. Miller, 'The Cost of Capital, Corporation Finance, and the Theory of Investment'.

87.   This connection between the measured income elasticity and the interest rate (if the latter changes) is also underscored in Whalen's study, to be discussed in Chapter 5.

CHAPTER 5

The Demand for Money and the Mean-Variance and Inventory-Theoretic Models

5.1 Introduction

One of the more recent developments in monetary economics has been the introduction of portfolio models into a variety of contexts in which capital asset pricing – or portfolio selection – has been studied. The general portfolio problem has been well understood since the 1950s,[1] and, roughly, there are two main streams of work to follow: the mean-variance and the inventory-theoretic. In the former – sometimes subtitled the 'capital asset pricing model' – securities are described by their expected average yield and expected variance of yield, and two main problems are studied:

1. what lies behind the actual portfolio choices of individuals, banks, life insurance companies, etc.; and,
2. given that wealth holders fit the assumptions of the model reasonably well, what determines the actual market prices of certain (or all) capital assets (e.g., stocks, bonds, etc.).

The research on 1 is the line of activity pursued in this chapter, and we will express particular interest in the quantity of money that a particular (and an aggregate) wealth-holder decides to include in his portfolio. As we will see, this method provides us with a formal context for dealing with the problem of the substitution (or complementarity) that exists between various assets. We will then, in the next chapter, consider the application of the mean-variance model in the more general context of the entire spectrum of maturities.

The inventory-theoretic model is not a portfolio model, as such (although, as we will see, it can be used to solve a portfolio problem) and is actually an outgrowth of some earlier work on inventory cycles. In the material discussed in the second major part of this chapter, however, little of this cyclical context is preserved. Instead, we will look at an individual (or business)

111

wealth-holder as if he were subject to some stochastic drain on his resources, a drain that produces penalty costs of some sort if some fundamental balance sheet constraint is violated. Again, an optimising model will produce a testable reduced form used, most often, for business firms, although some suggestive work for the general demand for money also exists. We will also discuss, throughout the chapter, some of the empirical work, and we will include slightly more general transactions costs models in the discussion.

5.2   Mean-variance methods in financial analysis [2]

5.2.1   *Basic definitions*

Let us define the mean of a series of yields as the following sum:

$$\bar{r} = \sum_{i=1}^{n} \frac{r_i}{n} \tag{5.1}$$

and the variance of the yields as

$$V(r) = \frac{\sum_{i=1}^{n} (r_i - \bar{r})^2}{n}. \tag{5.2}$$

For any security traded rather generally, there exist data on the past behaviour of the yields of the security, such that the average yield and the variance of the yield are matters of historical record. While these numbers will not necessarily be expected to be repeated in the future, quite often one's best guess is that they will be; if this is the case, then the yield will be used as the expected return on the security, and the variance of the yield will be used as the best measure of the expected risk. It is the expected risk because it is a measure of the expected variation in the yield (which itself combines price movements and interest rate movements) of the security.

What matters in the selection of a security is not the past behaviour of the yield of the security, but the behaviour that is expected to occur. In the previous paragraph the use of the past behaviour was employed to measure the expectations only because no other good measure of expectations was (assumed to be) available. The mean that we calculated there was constructed, in fact, on the assumption that each of the past outcomes was equally likely to occur; hence we divided by n. It might be the case, on the other hand, that certain outcomes are more likely than others, or at least that the outcomes are not expected to be equally likely. Thus, while equation (5.1) can be interpreted as an expected return, a more general formulation appears as equation (5.3), where the returns are weighted by their probability of occurring; the probabilities (p_i) themselves sum to unity, of course:

$$E(r) = \sum_{i=1}^{n} p_i r_i. \tag{5.3}$$

The probabilities in any particular portfolio problem are not, in fact, matters of record; indeed, individual investors will have their own (essentially) subjective probability distributions for any set of outcomes, and aggregate probabilities can only emerge in practice, as people act on their beliefs. If, in particular, investors are especially agnostic about a certain situation, and if investors are equally well-armed with financial resources and are particularly numerous, then it might be argued that the market as a whole 'expects' returns to be normally distributed. If so, we can assume – with some confidence – the normal distribution with its simple and well-known properties. At a later point in this chapter, we will see that much of the existing empirical work in financial markets is based on this perception.

Each of the securities in a particular constellation bears an expected return and a variance of expected return; in a perfect capital market, since variance could represent risk, these securities would come to be balanced with each other such that more return was associated with more risk, assuming that market behaviour exhibits no risk preference (etc.) as such. This would seem to dispose of the problem, except that the returns on the various securities in most portfolios have various positive and negative correlations with each other. Indeed, it is the presence of interactions between securities (all oil stocks tend to move together, for example) that essentially justifies the use of portfolio analysis, as it turns out.

Individual investors can be thought of as defining their investment problem in terms of portfolios. A portfolio is itself defined to be any set of holdings of assets; the holdings could be defined in terms of the number of shares of each asset, the percentage of one's total assets involved in each asset or the value of each asset bundle, where in any case ten shares of General Motors is viewed as one asset. However one conceives of the problem, it is clear that an expected earnings and an expected variance can be constructed for the portfolio as a whole; with such a set of numbers, various potential portfolios can be considered, and a best one selected. Thus, the expected earnings of a portfolio could consist of the individual expected returns for each of the assets proposed, weighted by the percentage invested in each of the assets; equation (5.4) represents this idea. The weights sum to unity:

$$E(S) = \sum_{i=1}^{n} W_i E(r_i). \tag{5.4}$$

A particular portfolio, in this view, is really a set of weights chosen by the economic agent.

The variance defined in equation (5.2) can also be viewed as an expectation; in particular, it can be conceived of as the expectation of the squared difference between each event and the expected value (mean) of the events:

$$V(r) = E\{[r_i - E(r_i)]^2\} = E[(r_i - \bar{r}_i)^2]. \tag{5.5}$$

Equation (5.5) provides the variance for a single security. When there is more than one security in a portfolio, then a more general formulation is needed, one that includes the covariation between the securities. An equivalent expression, for two securities, is given by equation (5.6):

$$V(S) = V(r_1) + V(r_2) + 2\,\text{cov}(r_1 r_2) \tag{5.6}$$

This form, though, is unweighted; the weights are the choice variables in the problem before us, so the more general weighted form, here described as equation (5.7), is the expression employed for further analysis in this chapter:

$$V\left(\sum_{i=1}^{n} W_i r_i\right) = W_1^2 V(r_1) + \ldots + W_n^2 V(r_n) + 2W_1 W_2\,\text{cov}(r_1 r_2) + \ldots$$
$$+ 2W_{n-1} W_n \text{cov}(r_{n-1} r_n).$$
$$\tag{5.7}$$

The result of equation (5.7) emphasises that for each portfolio there is a unique variance, but that the variance depends on the values of the covariances as well as on the sum of variances of the individual components. It is also important to notice that, while each new stock itself adds only one variance to the computation, it adds a covariance with every other stock already in the portfolio; this complexity causes a severe limitation on the applicability of these methods in certain contexts and provides one compelling reason why consumer units might prefer relatively uncomplicated portfolios, or even to operate by non-maximising rules of thumb.[3] The covariances of equation (5.7) are either positive or negative numbers, so it should be obvious that any particular stock, when considered as an addition to the portfolio, may raise or lower the 'risk' (i.e., variance) of the entire portfolio, holding its contribution to the average return constant.

5.2.2   *Efficient portfolios*

So far we have not established any rationale for picking one portfolio over another, or any rationale for applying the methods to particular sectors or subsectors of the economy; we will proceed, in this section, to develop the former. What we will show is that certain portfolios, while possible, can be ruled out by the rational investor as a matter of arithmetic; the set left will be referred to as 'efficient portfolios', and the choice problem will be restricted to them. To anticipate, all portfolios that are not feasible, given a

budget constraint, and all portfolios that can be shown to be worse than one
in the 'efficient' set, will be eliminated. What will remain will be a set of
portfolios for which more return costs more risk. We will however express
some concern, at a later point in this discussion, about the extent to which
investors are actually cognisant of risk.

Each individual investor, in what follows, will be assumed to have a specific budget constraint, in the sense of a total amount of wealth available.
Furthermore, we will assume that each investor has a finite (and possibly
small) number of assets that he is considering. In money terms, the investor
will have a budget constraint like equation (5.8):

$$\bar{Y} = \sum_{i=1}^{n} P_i X_i \tag{5.8}$$

where $\bar{Y}$ is the asset-holder's given wealth. We may divide both sides of
equation (5.8) by $\bar{Y}$, in which case the budget constraint would look like
equation (5.9), although perhaps it would be better not to refer to this expression as a budget constraint, since it expresses a sum of proportions:[4]

$$1 = \frac{\sum_{i=1}^{n} P_i X_i}{\bar{Y}}. \tag{5.9}$$

In this form, the weighting function is clearly implied, as the weights there
were simply the relative amounts spent $(P_i X_i / \bar{Y})$ on each of the i securities.
Thus, the expected return of a portfolio was given by equation (5.4), and
equation (5.9) provides the weights; we may use the fact that the weights in
this problem sum to unity to eliminate one of them. This gives us the 'equal
earnings hyperplanes' of equation (5.10):

$$E(S) = r_n + \sum_{j=1}^{n-1} W_j(r_j - r_n) \tag{5.10}$$

where r_n is the yield on the security whose weight was eliminated by use of
the fact that all funds must be spent. In equation (5.10), for each rate of
return $E(S)$ there is an infinite number of combinations of weights of the
stocks possible to give that average return. These 'iso-earnings' planes will
fill the portfolio (or weight) space and be non-intersecting, as illustrated in
figure 5.1 for the three security case. So much for earnings.

The variance of a portfolio, as described by equation (5.7), is a quadratic;
we will rewrite that formula as equation (5.11):

$$V\left(\sum_{i=1}^{n} W_i r_i\right) = \sum_{i=1}^{n} W_i^2 V(r_i) + 2\sum_{i=1}^{n}\sum_{j=1}^{n-1} W_i W_j \text{cov}(r_i r_j). \qquad i \neq j \tag{5.11}$$

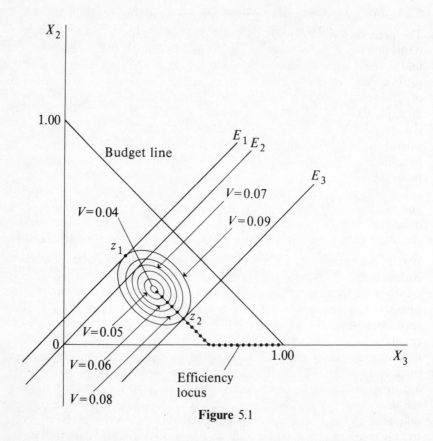

Figure 5.1

In a three-stock space, the largest problem that can be visualised in two dimensions, this formula would produce a series of equal-risk ellipses which would also fill the asset space. Each of these ellipses would be tangent to two of the parallel equal earnings lines. Since one of those lines would show a higher return than the other, the other would be eliminated; the locus of the surviving points, for various degrees of risk, is termed the 'efficiency locus', and it is along this locus that the individual will make his choice, depending on his subjective trade-off between risk and return. Along the locus more return can be bought only for more risk; this result clearly has some intuitive appeal. Figure 5.1 illustrates one such arbitrary example. Point z_1 is shown there to be inferior to point z_2, although both offer equal risk, since z_1 offers lower earnings; the earnings lines in this illustration are here arranged so that $E_3 > E_2 > E_1$. The efficiency locus, along which choices will be made under our assumptions, is marked as well.

5.2.3   *From portfolio space to mean-variance space* [5]

The preceding discussion has provided a description of each portfolio in terms of a mean and a variance; the choice of portfolio that an asset-holding unit actually makes will now be described. It would have been possible to provide other moments (than the mean and the variance) of the distribution of returns and capital gains from securities, but we have enough to provide an explanation of why actual portfolios are diversified, and we can model risk-aversive, risk-neutral and risk-preferring situations; this offers us considerable flexibility in interpreting the problem of asset choice in uncertain circumstances, as we shall see. It also leads directly to the demand for money.

Let us begin by formulating, rather vaguely, a utility function in both risk and return, with the properties that return provides utility and risk provides disutility:

$$u = U(E, \sigma^2) \qquad U_1 > 0 \quad U_2 < 0. \qquad (5.12)$$

It is a straightforward exercise, if investors can be described in terms of equation (5.12), to derive indifference curves in mean-variance space, particularly if we set down a specific form of this function – as we would do if our objective was empirical work. We are not interested in generating indifference curves here (in mean-variance space), but the idea of obtaining exact results is an attractive one, and will be pursued in this section. Furthermore, following Tobin, if we restrict ourselves to the two-parameter functions (such as equation 5.12), then, whether we use particular forms of the utility function (especially the quadratic), or particular probability distributions of the distribution of outcomes (especially the normal), we will find that 'indifference curves – loci of combinations of equal expected utility – derived by this second route must have the same properties as those derived by the first route. . . .' [6] The properties, for the risk-averse individual, are a positive slope in the risk-return dimension, and a curve that is convex towards the risk axis.

Because we are here interested in a model with empirical predictions (and restrictions), we will, essentially, follow the second route and go for a statistical approach. Thus, the expected utility referred to in the preceding quotation is the result of weighting each of the events in a particular situation by the probability of each event occurring. We must begin somewhere, so let us assume the following function generates utilities:

$$U = a - ce^{-b\pi} \qquad (5.13)$$

where π, the earnings of a portfolio, provides utility (as it should), and a, b and c are positive constants. [7] We can take expectations of equation (5.13); this produces equation (5.14):

$$E(u) = a - cE(e^{-b\pi}) = a - ce^{-E(b\pi)}. \qquad (5.14)$$

Our basic result comes not so much from the form chosen for equation (5.13) but from, following Tobin, the choice of the normal distribution to represent the expectation about earnings. That is, we may replace the expectation on the right-hand side of equation (5.14) with the probability derived from the normal distribution. This is how equation (5.15) was obtained:

$$E(u) = a - ce^{-(b/2)(u_\pi - \frac{b}{2}\sigma_\pi^2)} \qquad (5.15)$$

To find the maximum of this function, we note that anything that maximises the spread between the return (π) and risk (σ^2) will make the term ce as small as possible. For any positive a, this amounts to maximising the expected utility. Thus we may work with the function given as equation (5.16) as our objective function in what follows:

$$W = \mu_\pi - \frac{b}{2}\sigma_\pi^2 \qquad (5.16)$$

Finally, we note that for equation (5.15) the conditions that $\partial E(u)/\partial \mu_\pi > 0$ and that $\partial E(u)/\partial \sigma_\pi^2 < 0$ are upheld, as required for actual rather than expected utility in equation (5.12). The following exercise takes up the task of constructing demand functions for assets, beginning with the definition of more general formulas for the arguments of the objective function defined by equation (5.16).

5.2.4   *The derivation of demand functions for assets*

Now let us switch to matrix notation for ease of exposition. Let **v** be a vector ($n \times 1$) of sums invested in assets including money, and **m** be an associated vector of actual yields. Thus the actual yield of the portfolio (π) is given by the following inner product:

$$\pi = \mathbf{m}'\mathbf{v}. \qquad (5.17)$$

When one constructs a portfolio, he naturally does so not with the actual yields of equation (5.17) but with expected yields. To work in this direction, we can write actual yields in stochastic form as the sum of expected returns (**m***) plus an error term (ξ), where the error term represents a vector of forecasting errors; this results in equation (5.18), in which, to anticipate, the mean of the forecasting errors will be assumed to be zero:

$$\mathbf{m} = \mathbf{m}^* + \xi. \qquad (5.18)$$

We may now combine (5.17) and (5.18) to get equation (5.19):

$$\pi = (\mathbf{m}^* + \xi)'\mathbf{v} = \mathbf{m}'\mathbf{v} + \xi'\mathbf{v}. \qquad (5.19)$$

This expression relates the actual return of the portfolio to the expected return plus the forecasting error. Since $E(\pi)$ defines expected returns, we can also write equation (5.20), which makes use of the already stated assumption that the mean forecasting error is zero:

$$\mu_\pi = E(\pi) = \mathbf{m}^{*\prime}\mathbf{v}. \tag{5.20}$$

This gives us μ_π for use in equation (5.16). Needless to say, of course, $\mathbf{m}^{*\prime}$ is a vector of expected yields and will not be directly observable; we will comment further on that problem.

The variance of the yield (σ_π^2) is the other parameter that we require for equation (5.16). One of the definitions employed above was that

$$\sigma_\pi^2 = E\{[\pi - E(\pi)]^2\}. \tag{5.21}$$

We may directly rewrite the term within the braces here in terms of equations (5.19) and (5.20), to get equation (5.22):

$$\sigma_\pi^2 = E\{[(\mathbf{m}^{*\prime}\mathbf{v} + \xi'\mathbf{v}) - \mathbf{m}^{*\prime}\mathbf{v}]^2\} = E[(\xi'\mathbf{v})^2]. \tag{5.22}$$

We are thus seen to be asserting the reasonable proposition that actual variations in earnings come from forecasting errors entirely. Note now that $\mathbf{v}$ is $(n \times 1)$; ξ' is $(1 \times n)$ since ξ is $(n \times 1)$, with the consequence that $\xi'\mathbf{v}$ is a scalar (or, rather, an inner product); thus we can write $(\xi'\mathbf{v}) = (\xi'\mathbf{v})'$. Since this is so, we may write out the square in equation (5.22) as another equivalent scalar: $\mathbf{v}'\xi\xi'\mathbf{v}$. When we take the expectations, we get another form for equation (5.22) which is more convenient:

$$\sigma_\pi^2 = \mathbf{v}'E(\xi\xi')\mathbf{v} = \mathbf{v}'\mathbf{S}\mathbf{v}. \tag{5.23}$$

Here we find the variance in our problem really consists of a weighted expression – with the amounts invested ($\tilde{\mathbf{v}}$) providing the weights – in the variance–covariance matrix of forecasting errors ($\mathbf{S}$). From our earlier discussion on portfolio space we concluded that the covariances – off-diagonal terms in S – were relevant to the choice problem, so this result should have some intuitive appeal at this point.

The model just formulated is short-period and is restricted to a given total size of portfolio (call this the 'equality constraint'). Normally, also, one assumes that all assets are held in positive or zero amounts (call this the 'non-negativity constraint'). The fact that our formulation is single-period raises the possibility that a further assumption, concerning the stability of the solution over time, will be required if the model is applied to an economic time series of (historical) data, but we will continue to ignore that sort of problem for now, since no actual estimation is attempted in this chapter. Another problem of a related nature is that formulations requiring a long time horizon – for example, certain models of the term structure of interest rates – will not be easily adaptable to this formulation; but we will return to this topic in Chapter 6, where some solutions are found. The non-negativity constraint enables one to look at equilibrium (i.e., actual) holdings of assets, but leaves one without any effective hold on the almost infinite number of potential assets one *might* hold. This problem becomes worse as the portfolio considered becomes more disaggregated; but on the level of typical macroeconomic studies, this method is still a powerful device for many problems, such as the demand for money, as we shall see.

Let us assume in what follows that the asset-holding unit in question is restricted to holding only a certain set of types of assets, and holds positive quantities of each. For example, we might be looking at final wealth-holders' collection of cash, bonds and equities, or at the aggregation of commercial banks' holdings of the various assets that they are permitted to hold. The result is a budget constraint of the following form:

$$\mathbf{v'i} + F = 0 \tag{5.24}$$

where F consists of any non-relevant assets and all balancing items in the portfolio (e.g., capital assets) and $\mathbf{i}$ is the unit vector of suitable length, introduced here merely to effect the sum required. The combination of equations (5.16), (5.20) and (5.23) yields a new statement for the objective function as in equation (5.25):

$$\theta = \mathbf{m^{*'}v} - \frac{b}{2}\mathbf{v'Sv}. \tag{5.25}$$

It is this specific function that the wealth-holding unit will be assumed to maximise in what follows.

The maximising problem we have set ourselves is: given $\mathbf{m^*}$, $\mathbf{S}$ and F, choose $\mathbf{v}$ such that equation (5.25) is maximised subject to (5.24). To solve the problem we form the Lagrangean expression (noting that it is a stochastic formulation) as follows:

$$L = \mathbf{m^{*'}v} - \frac{b}{2}\mathbf{v'Sv} + \lambda(\mathbf{v'i} + F) \tag{5.26}$$

where λ is the Lagrangean multiplier. We can then state the first-order conditions for a maximum as in equations (5.27):

$$\frac{\partial L}{\partial \mathbf{v}} = \mathbf{m^*} - b\mathbf{Sv} + \lambda\mathbf{i} = 0$$

$$\frac{\partial L}{\partial \lambda} = \mathbf{v'i} + F = 0. \tag{5.27}$$

Assuming that the second-order conditions are also met, we can write our stable solution vector for $\mathbf{v}$ and λ as equation (5.28):

$$\begin{bmatrix} \mathbf{v} \\ \lambda \end{bmatrix} = \begin{bmatrix} b\mathbf{S} & -\mathbf{i} \\ -\mathbf{i'} & 0 \end{bmatrix}^{-1} \begin{bmatrix} \mathbf{m^*} \\ F \end{bmatrix}. \tag{5.28}$$

The inverse needed for equation (5.28) is particularly easy to obtain directly, following the rules for obtaining the inverse of partitioned matrices. After finding the inverse, we can construct a series of demand functions for each of the assets in the portfolio; equation (5.29) describes these functions:

$$\mathbf{v} = \frac{1}{b}\left(S^{-1} - \frac{S^{-1}\mathbf{i}\mathbf{i}'S^{-1}}{\mathbf{i}'S^{-1}\mathbf{i}}\right)\mathbf{m}^* - \left(\frac{S^{-1}\mathbf{i}}{\mathbf{i}'S^{-1}\mathbf{i}}\right)F. \qquad (5.29)$$

Note, before considering the properties of these functions, that, provided we have solved the problem of finding a rate of return, one of the assets could be money. The properties, then, are derivative facts about the solution vector in equations (5.29), which are of direct use in the actual empirical work one might undertake. They represent restrictions that ought to be applied across equations since they are implications of the theory. The restrictions apply because the problem has certain additive, etc., features; the properties follow:

1. S is a symmetric matrix, clearly, and so is S^{-1}; this being the case, since $(S^{-1}\mathbf{i}\mathbf{i}'S^{-1})/(\mathbf{i}'S^{-1}\mathbf{i})$ is symmetric, so is the entire first matrix in the brackets in equation (5.29). This result is similar to the condition in consumer demand theory which requires that the matrix of substitution effects among commodities be symmetric.

2. The row sums of this matrix are zero. To calculate a row sum, we simply post-multiply a matrix by the unit vector; this gives us

$$S^{-1}\mathbf{i} - \frac{S^{-1}\mathbf{i}\mathbf{i}'S^{-1}\mathbf{i}}{\mathbf{i}'S^{-1}\mathbf{i}} = S^{-1}\mathbf{i} - S^{-1}\mathbf{i}\left(\frac{\mathbf{i}'S^{-1}\mathbf{i}}{\mathbf{i}'S^{-1}\mathbf{i}}\right) = 0$$

3. The first matrix has non-negative diagonal terms, again a result that corresponds with one in consumer demand theory.

4. The column sums of the second matrix in equation (5.29) are unity. This property, which corresponds to 'Engle aggregation' in consumer demand theory, is easily established by pre-multiplying that term by $\mathbf{i}'$.

In addition to the study by M. Parkin of the London discount houses, as noted above, there is an excellent application of this methodology in the Southampton volume on the econometric model of the United Kingdom.[8] The demand functions just described are fit for the London clearing banks, with the suggested restrictions applied. The assets included are call loans, Treasury bills, commercial bills and bonds, and the results are reasonably satisfying, although commercial bills and Treasury bills turn out to be complements rather than substitutes, as a study of the technical features of these two instruments might suggest. The literature is full of this sort of thing,[9] and one has to accept it, for the absence of *a priori* signs on the off-diagonal terms of the substitution matrix in equation (5.29) is essential if it is to retain its full economic meaning. To repeat, banks must be permitted (in the analysis) to think of their portfolios in any reasonable way they want; that is, the result is not irrational and, if we have faith in the model, suggests that banks do this in practice. We turn, then, to applications of these methods to some problems of the demand for money.

5.3   Mean-variance analysis and the demand for money [10]

Actually, the preceding analysis generalises perfectly to the demand-for-money problem, provided one is able to obtain a satisfactory rate of return for money. For example, the Friedman demand for money described in Chapter 4 presents an analysis of the problem of choice facing a private wealth-holder who must find the optimum portfolio among five items of wealth – money, bonds, equities, non-financial wealth and human capital. That is, equation (5.29) is an exact specification of the Friedman model – or of a Keynesian model, for that matter – which can be exposed to the data, for a representative (or aggregate) wealth-holder. All this holds, and suggests a course of action, if a rate of return on money – other than the short-term interest rate (foregone) – can be found. The wage rate, as suggested in Chapters 3 and 4, may be the answer, although the work described there, and in the next section, only loosely relates to the model of this chapter.

There is, to be sure, an additional literature on the demand for money out of the mean-variance model, and it is that of J. Tobin who, at the same time, provides a more general and acceptable version of Keynes's theory of liquidity preference. In Keynes, it will be recalled, this relationship was a negative one; further, he employed a long-term interest rate while, as we will emphasise, Tobin employs a short-term one. Further, Keynes is responsible for the 'differences of opinion' – which is not an uncertainty analysis – while Tobin opts for the mean-variance approach. Nevertheless, to begin the discussion of Tobin's work, the same *general* perception seems to have motivated both Keynes and Tobin, as a comparison of the following quotations should suggest.[11]

> Why should anyone outside a lunatic asylum wish to hold money as a store of wealth.
> Because, partly on reasonable and partly on instinctive grounds, our desire to hold money as a store of wealth is a barometer of the degree of distrust of our own calculations and conventions concerning the future. ... The possession of actual money lulls our disquietude; and the premium which we require to make us part with money is the measure of the degree of our disquietude.[12]

Nearly two decades of drawing downward-sloping liquidity preference curves in text books and on classroom blackboards should not blind us to the basic implausibility of the behaviour they describe. Why should anyone hold the non-interest bearing obligations of the government instead of its interest bearing obligations? ... We shall distinguish two possible sources of liquidity preference, while recognizing that they are not mutually exclusive. The first is inelasticity of expectations of future interest rates. The second is uncertainty about the future of interest rates.[13]

Tobin, after describing how Keynes obtains his demand function (which is, of course, the inelastic expectations case), argues that this is Keynes's theory, in effect:

But the explanation to which Keynes gave the greatest emphasis is the notion of a 'normal' long term rate, to which investors expect the rate of interest to return. When he refers to uncertainty in the market, he appears to mean disagreement among investors concerning the future of the rate rather than subjective doubt in the mind of the individual investor.[14]

The reconciliation we can offer is that Keynes's comments on 'differences of opinion' were meant to provide a specific (and therefore potentially testable) model which has implications that can be observed. Tobin does this as well, so that once again we find a similarity of approach between the two. That Keynes's investors are plungers while Tobin's diversify is, presumably, a testable difference, however simple-minded we might find this test to be.

The essential derivation in Tobin is a mean-standard deviation model which is exactly like that already discussed except, of course, for the specific results. Tobin shows that a risk-averter, who requires a premium of some sort to compensate him for any risk he bears, will operate a diversified portfolio, in this case one with consols and cash in it. In Tobin's words:

The theory of risk-avoiding behaviour has been shown to provide a basis for liquidity preference and for an inverse relationship between the demand for cash and the rate of interest. ... In this respect, it is a logically more satisfactory foundation for liquidity preference than the Keynesian theory described. ... Moreover, it has the empirical advantage of explaining diversification while the Keynesian theory implies that each investor will hold only one asset.[15]

On the important question of whether money and Treasury bills are substitutes or not, Tobin essentially offers us two results. If there are only two securities in the problem (as there are in Leijonhufvud's description of both the Keynesian and Keynes's analysis), then, somewhat trivially, the two securities will be substitutes. More significantly, if we broaden the context to three or more securities, and still require that riskless cash be held, then the separation theorem of Tobin applies. In B. Näslund's words:

The theorem states ... that (for risk averters in purely competitive markets) the proportionate composition of the noncash assets is independent of their share of the total asset holdings when utility functions are quadratic, or the rates of return are normally distributed.

This means that in the event that some of the riskless asset is held, the proportions in which the risky assets are held in an optimum portfolio are independent of wealth $[\bar{Y}]$, the minimum return level $[\pi]$ and the risk level $[\sigma^2]$.[16]

Thus one may concentrate on the relation between cash and a broad category of non-cash assets, represented by (e.g.) a short-term interest rate. This is a considerable simplification, and is possibly a testable implication of the theory; it offers, in addition, a theoretical insight into why such strong substitution is actually observed – it is a matter of portfolio strategy, which is simpler, for one thing.[17]

Tobin, further, notes an ambiguity in the relation between cash holdings and the interest rate, looked at with this model. In particular, the sign of the relation between the interest rate and the demand for money is not uniquely negative. Indeed, while at

low interest rates the theory implies a negative elasticity of demand for cash with regard to the interest rate ... for high interest rates, and especially for individuals whose estimates σ_g of the risk of capital gain or loss on 'consols' are low, the demand for cash may be an increasing, rather than a decreasing, function of the interest rate.[18]

The problem, in a nutshell, is that there are both income and substitution effects; it is thus possible that an increase in the yield on consols can provide income in such a sufficiency that the individual – not perceiving much difference in total portfolio risk – will add cash at the expense of the consols in his portfolio.[19]

These kinds of worries have not weakened the profession's enthusiasm for mean-variance methods, and even the thorough lambasting of the approach by as eminent a collection of economists as has ever worked on a problem has not dried up the well. The basic problem is that the portfolio model turns out to be *only* (exactly) applicable for a two-parameter statistical model or for the quadratic utility function – just the cases that Tobin described.

In only a limited number of cases will the central limit law be applicable so that an approximation to normality of distribution becomes tenable; and it is well known that quadratic utility has anomalous properties in the large – such as reduced absolute and relative risk-taking as wealth increases, to say nothing of ultimate satiation.[20]

Consider the quadratic

$$U(Y) = a + bY + cY^2. \tag{5.30}$$

Arrow, then, shows the following.[21] Let risk aversion be measured as:

$$R_A(Y) = -\frac{U''(Y)}{U'(Y)} = \text{absolute risk aversion}$$

$$R_B(Y) = -\frac{YU''(Y)}{U'(Y)} = \text{relative risk aversion} \qquad (5.31)$$

where, e.g., $U' = dU(Y)/dY$. The computation of the former measure, for the general quadratic just given, is

$$R_A(Y) = \frac{1}{-\dfrac{b}{2c} - Y}.$$

Absolute risk aversion, intuition says, should diminish as one grows wealthier, but for $c < 0$ (diminishing marginal utility of income) and for $-(b/2c) > Y$, as Y grows large, absolute risk aversion also grows large, since $-(b/2c) - Y \to 0$. This, consequently, goes against our intuition. But Samuelson also shows that, in cases when riskiness is relatively small, the quadratic solution approximates the true general solution. It is a case of the relevant higher moments of the distribution conveniently disappearing. Whether or not this is very encouraging for the analysis of common stock-holding – where risk may not be perceived to be small – it leaves some room for the study of relatively conservative financial institutions and, of course, for aggregate wealth-holders, who may, indeed, not perceive risk to be very high in their portfolios. On the other hand, Tobin's concern that the negative relation between the quantity of money demanded and the interest rate might not seem realistic since it was just this case – when the perceived risk was relatively low – that Tobin thought could occur at high interest rates.

Results for the relation between income and the demand for money have not been frequent in this literature, as the generalisation of the Keynesian liquidity preference theorem has captured most of the intellectual interest. In the mean-variance model described above, we showed that an Engel aggregation held across all assets in the problem. Furthermore, we have already demonstrated that a quadratic utility function shows increasing absolute risk aversion which increases in income; it is thus a short step, given any particular risk aversion, to the proposition that riskless cash will become more desirable as one grows richer. This, in turn, could lead to the expectation – from mean-variance thinking – that the *income* elasticity of the demand for cash is greater than unity. Arrow, who demonstrates this proposition formally, also notes that

> The conclusion is in striking accord with statistical studies of United States time series. Studies of the movements of cash balance holdings, wealth and income (taken as a measure of wealth

... by different methods and under different assumptions, agree
in finding a wealth elasticity of demand for cash balances of at least
1 (Friedman's estimate, the highest, is actually 1.8).[22]

It is also true that, if relative risk aversion increases with wealth, then the
wealth elasticity of the demand for money (a riskless asset) will be $\geqslant 1$.[23] In
either case, as we have seen in Chapter 4, there is more disagreeable evidence
in this area than Arrow was aware of. Further, none of the tests reported
there – or cited by Arrow – imposes the restrictions implied by the mean-
variance model, so they cannot really lend much support *or* contradiction to
the theoretical deduction just described. Indeed, inventory-theoretic models,
to be described in the next section, produce a theoretical expectation of an
elasticity less than unity for income – and applaud the other half of the
empirical literature, equally irrelevantly.

Much of the precision of these results goes away when one considers the
case of many risky securities, as Cass and Stiglitz and others have demonstrated.[24] Cass and Stiglitz point out that Arrow's main result, that the
demand for money is an increasing function of wealth (and, in certain cases,
a strongly increasing function), does not extend to the multi-risk asset case
except in the event that the utility function chosen is independent of wealth
(income) and, perforce, depends only on the probability distribution of expected returns – as, indeed, has been the case in this chapter.[25] S. C. Tsiang,
on the other hand, argues that the theory is more robust than Samuelson
implies (he emphasised the case when risk is very small), and that for risks
only *relatively* small, the method meets Arrow's conditions.[26] While continuing this argument might easily tire the reader, one might note that Tsiang
claims that

> if there is a financial asset, the expected yield of which is at least
> as large as the standard deviation of that yield, then that asset will
> surely be preferred to cash as an investment.[27]

He evidently has in mind a time deposit. The implication is that one needs to
specify some other property of cash (or give it a variable return). Rather than
go on around this particular circle, let us consider one final word by K.
Borch (commenting on Tsiang's resurrection), who puts the paradox raised
in this section in a nutshell:

> This assumption can be rejected out of hand, and so can mean-
> variance analysis. In spite of this, I shall continue to use mean-
> variance analysis in teaching, but I shall warn students that such
> analysis must not be taken seriously and applied in practice.[28]

One might note, as well, that the empirical record is somewhat better, in my
opinion, than Borch implies.[29]

5.4   The inventory-theoretic (IT) model

5.4.1   *The Baumol–Tobin models*

As it turns out, possibly because of the difficulty of finding an exact rate of return for money, more direct work on the demand-for-money problem has been cast in the inventory-theoretic (IT) than in the mean-variance (EV) model. The starting point here is to frame the problem not as that of maximising expected utility, but as that of avoiding some unpleasant result by holding an optimal quantity of each asset in one's portfolio. In the case of money, clearly, the unpleasant results follow directly from running out of money; in the case of commercial banks, the unpleasant results are obtained at the discount window of the appropriate lender of last resort, or are the results of undesired liquidation costs, in the more general case. The problem we address ourselves to in this section is that of managing an asset collection when one (or more) of the assets is subject to a stochastic drain and there is some explicit penalty cost (perhaps in the cost of disposing of the asset) associated with the running out of this asset. Provided we specify an equation for the relative penalties associated with running out of each asset, this model is just as general as the mean-variance model. But in what immediately follows we will consider only a two-asset model. The result will be a set of demand functions for assets, with properties that differ from those of the mean-variance model because our operating rules are different.

The standard result in this area is from Baumol's 1952 paper which offers the often-used 'square root' formula;[30] the motivation is inventory control. The general idea is to impose some sort of cost of running out of liquid assets (which earn an interest of i) in addition to the interest cost foregone; this is met by assuming that each withdrawal of C dollars from the bank requires the payment of a brokerage fee (b). In commonsense terms, this could be the price of making trips to the bank, or even the time used up in converting one's assets into cash in this (or other) ways.[31] If we assume that an individual pays out T dollars per unit of time, then T/C represents the velocity of cash – i.e., the number of times cash must be raised – and $b(C/T)$, the money cost of these trips. The individual's average cash holdings will be $C/2$, and the cost of these holdings is $i(C/2)$, where, as noted, i represents the interest earnings foregone by holding cash.[32] Thus, the total costs of transactions will be the sum of the two components, as given by equation (5.32):

$$\frac{bT}{C} + \frac{iC}{2} = \text{total cost}. \qquad (5.32)$$

The optimal choice here, where money provides no direct utility and where no other assets are involved, is to choose C such that equation

(5.32) is at a minimum, given T, b and i. The derivative of equation (5.32) thus is

$$\frac{dT\,\text{cost}}{dC} = -\frac{bT}{C^2} + \frac{i}{2} = 0.$$

Then, at the minimum, this equation provides the 'square root' rule for the demand for currency (or money), as described in equation (5.33).

$$C = \sqrt{\frac{2bT}{i}}. \qquad (5.33)$$

That is, the demand for cash balances is proportional ($\sqrt{(2b/i)}$) to the square root of the value of transactions (T). Baumol offers the following results.

1. Even in a static world it will generally pay to keep some cash, since one of the motives here is to avoid brokerage costs, which would not drop to zero in such a case.
2. The demand for cash rises less than in proportion to the volume of transactions, so there are, in effect, economies of scale in the use of cash.
3. The interest effect on the demand for cash is negative.
4. The effect of an injection of cash, and the Pigou effect (on spending and on employment) are stronger, since transactions more than double, if you turn equation (5.33) around (and ignore any interest rate effects).

These are, of course, results taken directly from the model; what one should do at this point is to recall the various results (empirical, that is) in Chapter 4 that bear on this formulation. In this respect, (3) holds, probably, and (1) is a desirable effect, in any event. With regard to (2,) it was found that business firms, at least, might show economies of scale in their cash accounts, but that, generally, such results were obtained without specific reference to this model.

K. Brunner and A. Meltzer have provided a more general description of the inventory-theoretic model in which a different result for the income elasticity emerges. Thus, in Baumol's model,

> It is clear from his presentation, though not always recognized, that three separate cases are considered. In the first two, firms cannot receive cash by selling output. Cash is obtained only by borrowing or by selling financial assets. In these two restricted cases, the familiar square root formula for optimal cash balances is obtained.[33]

In particular, they point out that only if the time period under study is very short will there be no receipts from sales. Baumol actually does consider a cash source in his paper, and, as it turns out, this model has an income elasticity that approaches unity as – Brunner and Meltzer and Baumol agree – the quantity theory of money implies. Thus, let R be the quantity (net) of money received from sales ($R = T - I$, where I is net investment from sales), T (as before) be the dollar value of payments, K_w be the marginal cost of withdrawing cash, and K_d be the marginal cost of depositing cash:

$$C = R - \frac{T(K_w + K_d)}{i} \tag{5.34}$$

C, then, is the residual cash required to be drawn from investment (i.e. speculative) balances. Note, in particular, that this is an optimal cash balance equation and that a prior optimisation problem has been solved by Baumol to get this result.

Brunner and Meltzer argue that during the transactions period firms will hold an average of $R/2$ in net cash from sales and $C/2$ in cash realised from investments. This sum will be weighted by the relevant lengths of the periods as in equation (5.35):

$$M = \frac{R}{2}\left(\frac{T - I}{T}\right) + \frac{C}{2}\left(\frac{I}{T}\right). \tag{5.35}$$

Thus I/T, for example, is the length of the period (implied) for which no net cash receipts from sales are available. We may, then, repeatedly substitute (5.34) into (5.35) to obtain a more general 'square root formula' (recalling, again, that $R = T - I$):

$$M = \frac{bT}{2i}\left(1 + \frac{K_w + K_d}{i}\right) + \frac{T}{2}\left(\frac{K_w + K_d}{i}\right)^2. \tag{5.36}$$

This contains a version of equation (5.33) for $K_w + K_d = 0$ (in the frictionless world). Brunner and Meltzer, then, obtain the income elasticity for this function and it turns out to be close to unity, for large values of T. This, they feel, is a quantity theory result, although, as it turns out, their formulation also implies a relative large interest elasticity.[34] This latter might be thought to be a Keynesian result, essentially.

Of the studies conducted with the Baumol model, most attention has been directed towards business firms which, it is argued, might tend to economise as they grow larger and as the average size of their transactions increases. This is certainly reasonable, but it is not easy to confirm, at the least, although it is an implication of the inventory-theoretic model. Most important seem to be data problems, but aggregation bias is also often mentioned as a problem.[35] It has also been suggested that, because larger business firms hold multiple accounts (because, as firms grow, they diversify, and because much of the actual cash held is really a compensating balance), the larger firm might want more rather than less cash.[36] With regard to non-bank financial intermediaries, a comprehensive study by M. Weinrobe combines the Baumol–Tobin model (for transactions balances) with a static inventory

model (for precautionary balances).[37] In this study, while the measurement
of the scale variable caused some problems, both interest rate and scale
variables produced the expected signs. The latter were generally less than
unity (implying economies of scale). But there was some evidence of instability in the results. At any rate, what is most notable about these studies,
including the last named, is that the results definitely seem sensitive to the
level of aggregation chosen, working better, usually, for the more disaggregated cases.

E. Karni, with U. Ben-Zion,[38] has presented a reconciliation of both the
inventory-theoretic and the 'utility of money' approaches, the latter being
that described in Chapter 3, and attributed to Patinkin. Assuming that the
individual maximises equation (5.37), a utility function with real balances in
it,

$$u = U(C,m) \tag{5.37}$$

where C is consumption and $m = M/P$, they suggest that the individual be
constrained by equation (3.38), where $im + aC/2m$ is taken from the inventory model.[39]

$$C + im + \frac{aC}{2m} = Y. \tag{5.38}$$

The Lagrangean of this model is

$$L = u(C,m) - \lambda\left(C + im + \frac{aC}{2m} - Y\right)$$

and the first-order conditions (not stated by Ben-Zion and Karni) are given
by equations (5.39):

$$\frac{\partial L}{\partial m} = U_2 - \lambda i + \lambda\frac{aC}{2m^2} = 0$$

$$\frac{\partial L}{\partial C} = U_1 - \lambda - \lambda\frac{a}{2m} = 0 \tag{5.39}$$

$$\frac{\partial L}{\partial \lambda} = C + im + \frac{aC}{2m} - Y = 0.$$

Ben-Zion and Karni do not derive the relevant demand for money from this
model, which is not particularly interesting anyway; instead, they 'cost
minimise', a procedure that seems less than completely general, at least if C
is a *vector* of consumer goods.[40]

Ben-Zion and Karni are interested in showing that their model contains
the traditional utility theory and the inventory-theoretic theory as special
cases of a more general case. Thus they note that, under the inventory-
theoretic model, without m in the utility function – and with C predeter-

mined – the demand for money is given by the cost-minimising expression in equation (5.40).

$$m^* = \left(\frac{aC}{2i}\right)^{1/2}.$$ (5.40)

This is the standard way of explaining the inventory-theoretic model, and needs no apology. But when they discuss the case in which only the utility theory holds, they say that the optimal money holding is such that (for $a = 0$):

$$U_2 = \frac{\partial U}{\partial m^{**}} = \lambda i.$$ (5.41)

This, in fact, is merely the first-order condition for m, ignoring that for C and ignoring the budget constraint. This they can do if m is not in the budget constraint (which is not really sensible), or if some (unstated) rule of dominance is imposed. Finally, Karni and Ben-Zion produce an 'optimal money holding' from the combined model which is given here as equation (5.42):

$$\frac{\partial U}{\partial m^{***}} = \lambda i\left[1 - \left(\frac{m^*}{m^{***}}\right)^2\right].$$ (5.42)

This, they claim, provides a larger money holding than either (5.40) or (5.41). This is a reasonable result, although, again, it is produced in a cost minimisation framework, rather than by using the system (5.39) directly. One can anticipate further work in the coming years on the problem of integrating the two theories in an empirically relevant manner.[41]

It is also interesting to generate, as Karni has done, a result parallel to the Pesek and Saving models described in Chapter 3, and in the next section. Karni utilises equation (5.40), where all the variables are measured in real terms. If we, then, assume that total income (Y) consists of labour income (T_wW) and other income (PI), then for T_w equal to the number of hours worked and W equal to the real wage rate, we can write

$$Y = PI + T_wW.$$ (5.43)

If the transactions ($T = C$) in equation (5.40) are assumed to be proportional to disposable income (Y), then we can write equation (5.44):

$$T = a(PI + T_wW) = aY.$$ (5.44)

Karni specifies b more precisely, as well; in particular, let b, the penalty cost of the inventory model, be composed of a series of goods and their prices ($P'X$) – where the goods are such things as transportation, documents, etc. – and the time spent in the process of liquidating one's assets (T_e). The latter will be assumed to be evaluated at the real wage, by the 'value of time' hypothesis. The result of these assumptions is equation (5.45), for the penalty cost:

$$b = P'X + T_eW.$$ (5.45)

We note, in passing, that the same objections noted in Chapter 3 about the use of the wage rate – whether real or nominal – apply here, as well. After substituting these relationships into (5.26) with $T = C$, Karni directly calculates wage, income, work time and interest elasticities of the demand for money. These are given here as equations (5.46):

$$\delta_{MW} = \frac{1}{2}\left(2 - \frac{P'X}{b} - \frac{PI}{Y}\right) = \frac{1}{2}(1 - S_X + S_W)$$

$$\delta_{MT_w} = \frac{1}{2}\left(1 - \frac{PI}{Y}\right) = \frac{1}{2}S_W$$

$$\delta_{MPI} = \frac{1}{2}\left(\frac{PI}{Y}\right) = \frac{1}{2}(1 - S_W) \qquad (5.46)$$

$$\delta_{Mi} = \frac{1}{2}(S_W - 1).$$

Here S_W is the share of the wage-earner in total income and S_X is the 'share' of total penalty costs attributed to transactions goods.

Generally, we would expect these elasticities to be between zero and one, in absolute value; further, all depend in some way on the share of wage-earners in disposable income (S_W), as the results indicate. Thus, if this share is taken to be 0.7, then we would expect:

$$\delta_{MW} = 0.35$$
$$\delta_{Mi} = -0.15$$
$$\delta_{MPI} = 0.15$$

Further, if $S_X = 0.5$ (arbitrarily), then $\delta_{MW} = 0.6$. Clearly, the argument is that the wage component of income has a much higher effect on the demand for money than does non-wage income (*PI*), *a priori*. Thus a strong case can be made for some sort of disaggregation of income in this sense.

The magnitudes just established also seem to fit the results of empirical tests of the demand for money reasonably well, but, of course, they are exact results and cannot be tested directly. That is to say, we are paying a high cost, in using the inventory-theoretic model, in terms of setting *a priori* values on the coefficients, for the simplicity thereby attained. Further, a direct test of the demand function, as a function of i, Y and W, is not logical since we already know these coefficients from the theory, if S_W and S_X are taken as fixed. If we accept the theory, then, the thing to do is to see if the demand for money depends on S_X and S_W. Something like the variable coefficients model of equation (5.47) might be estimated, where the β_i are given functions of the variables S_W and S_X.

$$M_t = \alpha + \gamma M_{t-1} + \beta_1(S_W)i_t + \beta_2(S_W)Y_t + \beta_3(S_W,S_X)W_t + e_t. \quad (5.47)$$

This has not been done, to my knowledge.[42]

5.4.2   *Some generalisations of the transactions costs models*

The foregoing model, while especially rigid in its implications, is nevertheless our most popular model of the *transactions* demand for cash. Although in the Baumol model this is decidedly a rationalisation (in the sense that the motive for holding money is not revealed – we only suppose (e.g.) that it costs us to obtain money from the bank, not that the intention is to spend it immediately), the interest rate represents the opportunity cost of holding all money balances, whatever their purpose. Thus, if one holds a bond instead of cash,

> The advantage of this procedure is of course the yield. The disadvantage is the cost, pecuniary and non-pecuniary, of such frequent and small transactions between cash and other assets. . . . The greater the individual sets his average cash holding, the lower will be both the yield of his transactions balances and the cost of his transactions.[43]

Thus, if we are willing to accept a specific (and therefore non-general) model, we can obtain further results.[44] The main alternative, as we have argued above, is putting money into the utility function (see also the discussion in the Appendix). Even so, we must first, somehow, identify a speculative and precautionary element before we can apply this model literally to a set of total money holdings.

Tobin considers the case in which an individual plans to disburse the entire stock of funds which he receives as pay ($= Y$) at $t = 0$ (the beginning of the period) by the end of the period ($t = 1$). Assuming that his 'transactions' balances (T) – i.e., all of his funds by assumption – are held either as bonds (B) or money (M), then

$$T(t) = B(t) + M(t). \qquad (5.48)$$

Average balances of each of these are given by the following expressions:

$$
\begin{aligned}
\bar{T} &= \int_0^1 Y(1 - t)dt \\
\bar{B} &= \int_0^1 B(t)dt \\
\bar{M} &= \int_0^1 M(t)dt.
\end{aligned}
\qquad (5.49)
$$

The first of these expressions is equal to $Y/2$ if the total funds are spent uniformly throughout the period, but only the value of the sum of $\bar{B}$ and $\bar{M}$ can be deduced from equation (5.48). We proceed to generate the demand for transactions balances.[45]

Let us, then, suppose that the explicit cost of each transaction is a simple linear function ($a + bX$) of the amount transferred (X) from bonds to cash. The individual needs $Y/2$ for all his transactions, and if he held only idle balances, then $i(Y/2)$ would be his cost of transactions, where i is the interest foregone. In fact, assume he deposits his money in a savings account, and then runs down that account with $n - 1$ even withdrawals over the period. This makes n transfers in all, so that the total cost of transfers to him is $n(a + bX)$. Because his average balance is not $Y/2$, but $Y/2n$, his total cost is thus

$$TC = i\frac{Y}{2n} = n(a + bX). \qquad (5.50)$$

At the beginning of the period, $1/n$ of the income will be held in cash for immediate purchase of commodities; thus expenditure is $Y - (1/n)Y$ and total costs become

$$TC = \frac{iY}{2n} + na + nb\left(Y - \frac{1}{n}Y\right). \qquad (5.51)$$

This expression would then provide the optimal number of transactions (n^*) and of money balances (M^*). In the special case when transfer costs have only a fixed component ($b = 0$), these expressions are given by equations (5.52):[46]

$$n^* = \sqrt{\frac{iY}{2b}}$$

$$M^* = \sqrt{\frac{bY}{2i}}. \qquad (5.52)$$

The latter is in the form of the Karni model, as discussed above; enough has been said, though, to establish that the Baumol model is a subset of this slightly more general (Tobin) model just described.

But wealth-holders do not hold inventories of cash only for transactions purposes; they also might have precautionary and speculative balances. We will not discuss the latter in this context, but there is a literature on the former, as it turns out. The essential difference, of course, is that the inventory models to this point have been constructed under the aegis of 'certainty'. Costs, transactions and incomes are known for certain; it is because the income comes in a lump at the beginning of the period (or in discrete lumps during the period) that a motive for money holding is therefore deemed reasonable (the actual motive was to save on transactions costs by choosing the optimal number of transactions). In the case of 'precaution', though, we might suppose, additionally, that 'disbursements may exceed receipts during a given period by an unpredictable amount'.[47]

Suppose that M_p is the average precautionary balance; then, the opportunity cost is iM_p where i is the interest charge on a relevant alternative asset. Suppose, further, that individuals are assessed a penalty cost (C) every time they run out of cash and that p is the probability of this event occurring. Thus pC is the 'expected cost of illiquidity'. Thus, the total cost of the precautionary balance is given by equation (5.53):

$$TC_p = iM_p + pC. \qquad (5.53)$$

Further results are obtained by specifying a probability density function and then minimising the resulting explicit function, where the unspecified probability (above) is represented by the moments of the distribution (as in our earlier discussion of the EV model). One can also generalise the cost function along the lines of equation (5.51). If, as Whalen does,[48] we have

$$p = \frac{S^2}{M^2}$$

where S^2 is the expected standard deviation of disbursements, then optimal precautionary balances are given by equation (5.54):

$$M_p^* = \left(\frac{2S^2C}{i}\right)^{\frac{1}{3}} \tag{5.54}$$

This equation, of course, is in the spirit of the Baumol–Tobin models, although it has no scale variable (Whalen assumed this away) and concentrates on S^2 and C. We note that the negative relationship between the interest rate and the money balance demanded is again obtained, this time for a precautionary holding.[49]

We may also, in the context of an inventory model, derive the influence of changes in wealth on the demand for money – following V. Chitre[50] – but using a combined utility–IT model. Assume, then, that money pays no interest and that W is interest-bearing wealth; in this event $i(W - M)$ represents the earnings on the total portfolio, iM being an opportunity cost. Further assume that actual excess expenditure (x) for a particular period is a random variable as in equation (5.55):

$$x = PX - i(W - M) + \gamma \tag{5.55}$$

where PX represents expected expenditure and $E(\gamma) = 0$. Defining $S = i(W - M) - PX$ and $\gamma = x + S$, we can define the gross penalty cost (of running out of cash) for the individual as $H(x - M)$; thus, his expected final wealth is given by equation (5.56):

$$E(W_f) = W + S - \int_{M+S}^{\infty} H(\gamma - M - S)g(\gamma)d\gamma. \tag{5.56}$$

That is, he expects to end up with his initial wealth plus savings less any penalty costs he paid out (they are the random part of the expression); these are incurred whenever $\gamma > M + S$ (i.e., when $x > M$).[51]

Turning to the utility side of the problem, Chitre assumes that the usual measure of absolute risk aversion – the Arrow–Pratt condition – diminishes as wealth increases. This expression is, again

$$R_A = -\frac{U''(\text{wealth})}{U'(\text{wealth})}.$$

The individual will now get utility directly from his augmented wealth when he does not run out of money – which explains the first term in equation (5.57) – as well as when he does – which explains the second.

$$E(U) = \int_{-\infty}^{M+S} U(W + S - \gamma)g(\gamma)d\gamma$$

$$+ \int_{M+S}^{\infty} U[W + S - \gamma - H(\gamma - M - S)]g(\gamma)d\gamma. \quad (5.57)$$

We may differentiate this expression with respect to M – the decision variable – in which case we obtain an expression for optimal money holdings.

$$E_M(U) = -i\int_{-\infty}^{M+S} U'(W + S - \gamma)g(\gamma)d\gamma + [H(1 - i) - i]\int_{M+S}^{\infty} U'[W + S$$

$$- \gamma - H(\gamma - M - S)]g(\gamma)d\gamma. \quad (5.58)$$

The optimal demand for money, then, occurs when $E_M(U) = 0$, and this occurs, as it turns out, when

$$H(1 - i) > i$$

since, if this condition is not met, the individual will have a zero optimal cash balance. This condition, then, gives the necessary condition for money-holding in this model: the net penalty cost must exceed the interest rate.

With regard to the wealth effect on the demand for money, we can now differentiate (5.58) by W. The resulting expression (given in Chitre's paper) then shows that, if absolute risk aversion diminishes with wealth (as assumed), an increase in wealth will actually lower the expected marginal utility of money-holding at the optimum – money is an inferior asset. On the other hand, if the absolute risk aversion increases with wealth – or if we include, as we did not, the effect of wealth on planned expenditures – then a reason for a positive wealth effect on money balances is provided. This is an exact result for the generalised demand for money model. One can, as well, find the interest rate effect (unambiguously negative) in this model.[52]

To illustrate how a diversified portfolio, including money, can be obtained in an inventory-theoretic model, consider the following by M. Gray and M. Parkin,[53] in which the context is precautionary (i.e., a stochastic instead of a deterministic model is employed). The situation is one in which a stochastic drain forces the portfolio-manager (or individual cash-holder) to dispose of one or more assets at a date earlier than the 'portfolio review date'. Recalling the portfolio model above, which was expressed in matrix algebra, we define the expected return from a portfolio as

$$\mu_\pi = \mathbf{m}'\mathbf{v} + \mathbf{c}'\mathbf{v}^* \quad (5.59)$$

where c' is a $(1 \times n)$ vector of asset disposal costs and v^* is an $(n \times 1)$ vector of expected liquidations (m, v and c are non-stochastic – in particular, the earnings are known for certain – thus the analysis of cash, time deposits, etc., seems relevant here). The asset-holder will be constrained by equation (5.60), as before:

$$i'v - F = 0. \tag{5.60}$$

Finally, assume that following a stochastic drain the assets are liquidated starting with the cheapest (lowest c_i); we must assume, further, that no two assets are equally cheap to liquidate.

Gray and Parkin go on to derive several of the properties of their system, without specifying a specific probability density function for the stochastic drain. Of most interest are their conclusions that

1. diversification is optimal and is the result of each asset having different yields and liquidation costs;
2. the demand for each asset depends only on its own yield and on the yields of the two adjacent assets (when ranked by yield);[54]
3. only the demand for the nth asset depends on the scale variable, wealth.

Thus the inventory-theoretic model is, after all, capable of explaining as general a world as the mean-variance model; although, to be sure, the differences are not merely details. There is a second paper by M. Parkin (with R. Barrett and M. Gray),[55] which performs a test of the generalised IT model just described against the EV model on the British 'personal sector'. There, where the yield on money is defined as the negative of the rate of inflation (a strict Monetarist interpretation), an unexpected complementarity develops between time deposits and narrow money.

The Pesek and Saving approach also has a transactions cost version; in this case, the approach is to deal with the dynamic consumption plan of an individual where money is not inserted directly into either the production or utility function, but is given a direct role to play; this role is that of saving time in consumption (or, in a more general framework, in production as well).[56] If we assume that individuals wish to maximise utility over a horizon running from the present to the end of their horizon (h), then equation (5.61) might represent a typical dynamic utility function:

$$u = U(C_t, L_t) \qquad (t = 0, \ldots, h). \tag{5.61}$$

Here L_t represents the percentage of total time devoted to leisure, stated as an alternative to consuming goods. The individual will have a real income constraint, given by equation (5.62); t here represents the dynamic income path, and W_t is the percentage of total time spent on earning income, whatever the source:

$$Y_t = F(W_t, t). \tag{5.62}$$

It will take time to consume, of course; let transactions time be T_t, in which case a further constraint will be necessary, to apportion the total time between the three activities. This appears as equation (5.63):

$$L_t + W_t + T_t = 1. \tag{5.63}$$

To complete the model, it is useful to model a transactions time (T_t) function. We can argue that an increase in income or in consumption will increase the frequency and the size of transactions; on the other hand, the larger one's inventory of money, the smaller will be transactions costs, in general. Equation (5.64), with the *a priori* expected signs indicated on the right, presents these hypotheses in a general way:

$$T_t = G(Y_t, C_t, M_t) \qquad G_1, G_2 > 0 \qquad G_3 < 0. \tag{5.64}$$

Finally, assume that each individual is faced with a dynamic budget constraint such as in equation (5.65). Here B_0 is initial bond holdings in real terms, and M_0 is initial money balances, again in real terms:

$$\sum_{t=0}^{h}\left(\frac{1}{1+i}\right)^t Y_t + B_0 + M_0 = \sum_{t=0}^{h}\left(\frac{1}{1+i}\right)^t\left(C_t + i\bar{M}_t + \delta_{\bar{M}_t}\bar{M}_t\right). \tag{5.65}$$

At this point Saving invokes the following assumption:

> Since the problem of interest here is the demand for money, the determinants of the optimal path of consumption and leisure (C_t and L_t respectively) may be assumed to have already been chosen; that is, they may be treated as parameters.[57]

Because Y_t is an input into equation (5.64), which is itself an input into (5.65) via (5.62) and (5.63), a mathematically complex problem emerges; this is the rationale for picking $\hat{C}_t$ and $\hat{L}_t$ and then restricting the choice problem to a set of M_t values.[58] Finally, in equation (5.65), the two additional elements on the right-hand side require further explanation: $i\bar{M}_t$ represents the income forgone by holding money balances and $\delta_{M_t}\bar{M}_t$ represents the storage costs of holding money. If we restrict our analysis here (as I am doing) to currency and demand deposits, then the only important component of δ_{M_t} that we need to consider is the expected rate of inflation.

Thus, the problem of the demand for money is to choose $\bar{M}_t$ for given $\hat{C}_t$ and $\hat{L}_t$ such that equation (5.66) is maximised subject to (5.62), (5.63) and (5.64); this transformation from the utility maximisation problem is the result of the assumption just quoted in the last paragraph. Saving explains the analytical consequences in his paper.

$$W^* = \sum_{t=0}^{h}\left(\frac{1}{1+i}\right)^t Y_t + B + M - \sum_{t=0}^{h}\left(\frac{1}{1+i}\right)^t(C_t + i\bar{M}_t + \delta_{M_t}\bar{M}_t). \tag{5.66}$$

The substitution yields equation (5.67) to maximise, subject to equation (5.68):

$$W^* = \sum_{t=0}^{h}\left(\frac{1}{1+i}\right)^t F[1 - (L + T_t), t] + B + M - \sum_{t=0}^{h}\left(\frac{1}{1+i}\right)^t (C_t + iM_t$$
$$+ \delta_{\bar{M}_t}\bar{M}_t) \quad (5.67)$$

$$T = G\{F[1 - (L_t + T_t), t], C_t, \bar{M}_t\}. \quad (5.68)$$

By differentiating (5.67) subject to (5.68), we obtain the following first-order condition:

$$\frac{\partial W}{\partial \bar{M}} = \left(\frac{\partial W}{\partial F}\right)_t\left(\frac{\partial G}{\partial \bar{M}}\right)_t - i + \delta_{\bar{M}_t} = 0. \quad (5.69)$$

This equation, plus equations (5.62), (5.63) and (5.64), comprise a system of four equations (for each t) in the four unknowns T, W, Y and M. Since (5.62), (5.63) and (5.64) are each monotonic in T_t, W_t and Y_t, we can easily deduce a reduced-form equation for $\bar{M}_t$ with the general form of equation (5.70):

$$\bar{M}_t = \gamma(C_t, L_t, i, \delta_{\bar{M}_t}, t). \quad (5.70)$$

In the complete system there would also be equations for the other endogenous variables (T_t, W_t, Y_t) and any attempt to settle on an *a priori* sign for the storage costs (δ) or the interest rate would require further investigation (which is provided by Saving in his paper). In the example here, the outcome is obvious, since no other assets and no income or consumer goods stocks are held, but even when this is not the case, results can be obtained, as Saving demonstrates.

Equation (5.70), as simple as its theoretical underpinnings are, does put the demand for money in a new light since it incorporates L_t in its specification. In a recent empirical study of the demand for money, Dutton and Gramm pursue the Saving model and employ a wage rate proxy for L_t. The argument is as follows.

> From the assumption of money's usefulness in reducing transactions time it follows that a unit of leisure may be purchased either by reducing work or by increasing money balances. Thus in equilibrium the consumer holds just that level of money balances at which the marginal cost of purchasing an extra unit of leisure via an increase in money holdings would be equal to the wage rate.[59]

Their results, if anything, are too successful for both a wage rate and an unemployment variable. Furthermore, the value of time hypothesis, while an appealing notion, has the problem that, when a wage proxy is employed to represent the value of leisure time, the implication is that a marginal decision can be made. For many of us, it would seem, the decision is 'all or none', and the hours of work are stated on a union contract. Thus the wage rate may just be a proxy for income and, accordingly, works well in place of (or multicollinearly with) that variable.

The alternative approach to an explicit dynamic demand for money comes, of course, from a formulation in which money appears in the utility function; this is not a transactions costs model, but it forms a nice contrast with the foregoing. Thus, following B. Motley,[60] we write the utility function to be maximised in a continuous form:

$$u = \int_0^\infty \gamma(t)U[X(t), X'(t), t]\,dt. \qquad (5.71)$$

In this formulation $\lambda(t)$ represents the consumer's time preference, $X(t)$ is a stock of consumer goods (assumed to be proportional to the flow of services) and $X'(t)$ is the stock of real money balances, included, as noted, in the utility function. This function is maximised subject to a resource constraint given by equation (5.72):

$$\int_0^\infty e^{-it}[y(t) - P(t)C(t) - \dot{M}(t)]\,dt = 0. \qquad (5.72)$$

Here i is the interest rate on bonds, $y(t)$ is labour income in real terms, $C(t)$ is the gross purchase of consumer goods and $\dot{M}(t)$ is the rate of change of the stock of nominal money balances. Finally, we will assume that consumer goods deteriorate at the rate δ when stored:

$$C(t) = \dot{X}(t) + \delta X(t). \qquad (5.73)$$

where $X(t)$ is the stock of consumer goods.

From equations (5.71), (5.72) and (5.73), we can form the Lagrangean given in equation (5.74); this expression will be maximised:

$$u = \int_0^\infty \lambda(t)U[X(t), X'(t), t]dt + k_0\left(\int_0^\infty e^{-it}[y(t) - P(t)C(t) - \dot{M}(t)]\,dt\right)$$
$$+ k_1[C(t) - \dot{X}(t) - \delta X(t)]. \quad (5.74)$$

The resulting first-order conditions are given by equations (5.75), (5.76) and (5.77) for the choice variables $C(t)$, $X(t)$ and $X'(t)$.

$$\frac{\partial U}{\partial C(t)} = -k_0 e^{-it}P(t) + k_1(t) = 0 \qquad (5.75)$$

$$\frac{\partial U}{\partial X(t)} = \lambda(t)U_x(t) - k_1(t)\delta + \frac{d}{dt}k_1(t) = 0 \qquad (5.76)$$

where

$$U_x(t) = \frac{\partial U[\ ]}{\partial X(t)}.$$

$$\frac{\partial U}{\partial X'(t)} = \lambda(t)\frac{U_x(t)}{P(t)} + \frac{d}{dt}k_1 e^{-it} = 0 \tag{5.77}$$

and, of course, terms for k_0 and k_1.[61] We may then eliminate $k_1(t)$ between equations (5.75) and (5.76) and carry out the differentiation by d/dt to get equation (5.78):

$$\lambda(t)U_x(t) = k_0 e^{-it}P(t)\left[\delta + i - \frac{\dot{P}(t)}{P(t)}\right]. \tag{5.78}$$

Here $\dot{P}(t) = dP(t)/dt$, as before. We may rearrange equation (5.77) and carry out the differentiation to get equation (5.79):

$$\lambda(t)U_x(t) = k_0 e^{-it}P(t)i. \tag{5.79}$$

These marginal utility conditions, along with the budget constraint, are sufficient to establish a demand function for money of the following general form:

$$M(0) = M^d[W(0), i(t), i'(t), P(t)] \tag{5.80}$$

where initial wealth, $W(0)$, is given by

$$W(0) = M(0) + P(0)X(0) + \int_0^\infty e^{-it}y(t)\,dt \tag{5.81}$$

and

$$i'(t) = P(t)\left[\delta + i(t) - \frac{\dot{P}(t)}{P(t)}\right]$$

Thus, in a dynamic consumption framework, the demand for money services, assuming they are an input into the utility function, depend on the time path of the interest rate and prices, on the time path of real income and on the rental cost of commodity services. As Motley comments,

> The permanent income hypothesis of consumption frequently is cited as a theoretical explanation of the observed instability of the relation between current income and current consumption. It is of interest to note that the analysis presented here implies that the demand for money as a function of current income may be similarly unstable and for the same reason, namely, that decisions are made with reference to longer time horizons.[62]

As we pointed out in Chapter 4, this instability is not a matter of record.

5.4.3 *The business demand for money*

The discussion of the business demand for money, obviously, follows the same general lines as the personal demand except that one finds more use of inventory models in this context. Even so, we will begin with M. Nadiri's analysis of the firm's demand for money, an analysis that follows neatly from the previous discussion of the Motley paper.[63] In the Jorgenson investment model, which the reader will recognise as the prototype for the discussion of the Motley model, the desired stock of capital is given by an expression like equation (5.82):

$$K^* = \alpha \frac{P}{C} X^* \qquad (5.82)$$

where α comes from a Cobb–Douglas production function, P is the price of the desired output (X^*) and C is the 'user cost of capital'. Nadiri produces a modified version of C, here given as equation (5.83):

$$C = \frac{q}{1 - \mu}\left(i - \delta_0 + \delta_1 s - \frac{\dot{q}}{q}\right). \qquad (5.83)$$

Here q is the price of capital goods, μ is the corporate tax rate, i is the interest rate, δ_0 is the depreciation of capital due to the passage of time, δ_1 is the depreciation of capital due to the intensive use of capital, s is the rate of utilisation of capital and $\dot{q} = dq/dt$. One should note that all of these parameters are expected to change over time; equation (5.82) is a functional.

The essence of Nadiri's contribution, suggested above in our discussion of the Patinkin model, is to include real money balances (m) in the production function. Thus, desired output would generally be given by equation (5.84); the reasons such a relationship might be desirable have already been discussed, but most relevant seems the 'saving of time in the hiring of inputs'.

$$X^* = F(L, K, m). \qquad (5.84)$$

Instead of proceeding to solve the problem in the Jorgenson framework – by maximising the net worth of the firm – Nadiri proposes to minimise the following total cost function:

$$T = wL + cK + vm. \qquad (5.85)$$

v, here, is $i + (\dot{P_b}/P_b) + (\dot{P}/P)$, where P_b is the price of securities, and P the price level. The result is a general demand for money function, when v is specified, as given in equation (5.86):

$$m^* = f\left(\frac{T}{W}, i, \dot{i}, \frac{\dot{P}}{P}, X^*\right). \qquad (5.86)$$

In addition to the by now familiar arguments $(i, \dot{i}, \dot{P}/P, X^*)$ we have the ratio of total costs to the wage rate, a result that runs parallel to the Dutton and Gramm study of the Pesek and Saving model, as cited above. Here, however, it represents the total cost constraint in equation (5.85) rather than the time constraint of the individual consumer.

After providing explicit (*ad hoc*) multiplicative forms for equation (5.86), Nadiri performs tests on the US quarterly data from 1948 to 1960 (and a check on the stability of the model to 1964). The fit was good, and Nadiri offers the following summary.

1. The long-term rate and its change work reasonably well, although no comparison with the short-term rate is shown.
2. There are substantial economies of scale in holdings of cash balances that do not depend on the choice of scale variable (among sales, assets, capacity output).
3. Cash balances are sensitive to movements of factor prices and to the price level.
4. The adjustment is rapid.
5. The model passed the stability test imposed.

These conclusions run partly parallel to some results obtained by Price on British data – and discussed in Chapter 4 – although the Price study found a short-term rate to be the relevant rate for the business demand for money.

T. Saving has also worked out his 'transactions costs' model, described above, for the business firm. Saving offers his approach as an alternative to the inventory-theoretic model; although, perhaps, it would be best to think of it as a variant, in view of its focus on transactions costs. By assuming, as above, that transactions costs exist and depend on both the number and size of transactions, Saving obtains a demand for money model of the general form described in equation (5.87) where j designates separate functions for currency (c) and demand deposits (d):

$$\bar{M}_j^* = f(P, i, \delta_{\bar{X}}, \delta_{\bar{V}}, \delta_{\bar{M}_c}, \delta_{\bar{M}_d}). \qquad (5.87)$$

Here the δ_k are the storage costs for the inventories of deposits, currency, factors and output of the firm, taken in reverse order. Under the usual strict conditions, Saving is able to derive signs for the partial derivatives of equation (5.87). He concludes that

> This paper demonstrates that a theory of the firm's transactions demand for money can be developed without making money directly an argument of the production function. Fundamental to the approach followed is the concept of transactions cost and the productivity of money balances in reducing these costs.[64]

Thus, this work stands in contrast to that of Nadiri, although the final form of the demand equation is not radically different, at least if the wage rate represents the cost of storage of labour ($\delta_{\bar{V}}$), total cost represents the cost of storage of output ($\delta_{\bar{X}}$), and the inflation rate represents the cost of storage of the monetary items. But this final similarity of disparate theoretical perceptions is not uncommon in this literature, as we demonstrated in Chapter 4.

A more explicit use of the the inventory-theoretic model on the demand for money by business firms is by M. Miller and D. Orr.[65] An important characteristic of the Baumol–Tobin models is that cash comes in when the asset holder is paid – and then steadily dribbles out until the end of the payments period, when the cash balance reaches zero. This, as we noted above in the discussion of Meltzer's extension of the Baumol model, is appropriate enough for the individual (whose receipts are highly predictable and simple, usually), but not for the business firm, whose

> cash balance fluctuates irregularly (and to some extent unpredictably) over time in both directions – building up when operating receipts exceed expenditures and falling off when the reverse is true.[66]

Assuming away uncertainty (and hence the presence of precautionary balances or, as they term them, buffer stocks), Miller and Orr concentrate on a two-asset problem, where the non-interest-bearing asset is 'cash'. Let p be the probability of the cash balance increasing by m dollars during an hour (an hour $= 1/t$) and $q = 1 - p$ the probability of decreasing by the same amount. Then, assuming a Bernoulli process, over n days the observed distribution of changes in cash balances will have a mean and variance as given by equations (5.88):

$$\mu_n = ntm(p - q)$$
$$\sigma_n^2 = 4ntpqm^2 \qquad (5.88)$$

a distribution that approaches the normal as n increases.

Miller and Orr assume that $p = q = Z/X$, in which event $\mu_n = 0$ and $\sigma_n^2 = nm^2t$. Further, they assume a cost-minimising objective for the firm, as is common in this model.[67] Then, the expected cost ($E(C)$) *per day* (t) of managing the portfolio of stocks (earning an average of π) and money is given by equation (5.89):

$$E(C) = \gamma \frac{E(N)}{T} + \pi E(M) \qquad (5.89)$$

where γ represents the cost per transfer (and $E(N)/T$ is the number of portfolio transfers per day) and $E(M)$ is the average daily cash balance. This framework does not yet contain choice variables: let the firm purchase securities in the amount $(h - z)$ whenever h, the upper limit of cash balances, is reached. Whenever the lower limit (z) is reached, let it sell z worth of securities to replenish its cash balances. The limits h and z, then, are the decision variables, and one must find expressions for the components of equation (5.89) in terms of these choice variables.

The details of the derivation are contained in the Miller and Orr paper;

suffice it to say that the cost expression to be minimised is given by equation (5.90), where $Z = h - z$:

$$E(C) = \frac{\gamma M^2 t}{zZ} + \frac{\pi(Z + 2z)}{3}. \tag{5.90}$$

This is the sort of specific result one expects in this literature. The first-order conditions are

$$\frac{\partial E(C)}{\partial z} = -\frac{\gamma M^2 t}{z^2 Z} + \frac{2\pi}{3} = 0$$

$$\frac{\partial E(C)}{\partial Z} = -\frac{\gamma M^2 t}{Z^2 z} + \frac{\pi}{3} = 0 \tag{5.91}$$

and this produces optimal values for the decision parameters of

$$z^* = \left(\frac{3\gamma M^2 t}{4\pi}\right)^{1/3}$$

$$h^* = 3z^*. \tag{5.92}$$

This solution implies that the typical firm will, under the assumed conditions, set the lower point (z) well below the mid-point of the range over which cash balances fluctuate. This implies that firms will run off assets frequently (in small lots) compared with their sales; the strict result that $h^* = 3z^*$ is a result of the simplifying assumptions on form (not discussed here).

The firm's demand for money which results from this is given by equation (5.93):

$$M^* = \frac{4}{3}\left(\frac{3\gamma}{4}\sigma^2\right)^{1/3} \tag{5.93}$$

where $\sigma^2 = M^2 t$, as noted earlier. The parameters here have the usual signs, of course, with the negative elasticity of the interest rate (π) to be noted especially. We are not able to deduce a scale elasticity directly, as the model stands, because σ^2, the variance of the cash balance, is not directly related to the volume of sales in any obvious way. This, in a sense, is reasonable, as we commented earlier when we remarked that it all depends on the type, size and typical style of transactions of the business firm. Thus Miller and Orr conclude that this elasticity could range from the case of economies of scale to diseconomies without altering any of the assumptions of their model. This clearly accords well with the variety of empirical results in the literature, as reported here and in Chapter 4.

Miller and Orr have extended their basic model but, in general, the same solutions arise.[68] On the other hand, as P. Frost has shown,[69] their assumption (not yet mentioned here) that the firm's minimum cash balance at the bank (held to compensate the bank for services rendered) is *exogenous* is critical to their result in several important cases. Assume, then, that the firm gains a yield from banking services as in equation (5.94):

$$Y(S) = aS - bS^2. \tag{5.94}$$

Assume, also, that the yield from holding deposits is

$$Y(T) = \gamma t - \frac{\gamma \sigma^2}{z(h - z)} \tag{5.95}$$

following Miller and Orr ($\sigma^2 = M^2 t$).[70] Equations (5.94) and (5.95), when summed, provide a general expression for the yield from holding cash balances. To complete the model, Frost argues that $C = \rho \bar{D}$ represents the cost of average balances ($\bar{D}$ is the average balance) where ρ, the cost of capital, is the proper opportunity cost and

$$S = S(D_L, h, z) \tag{5.96}$$

represents the supply of bank services (D_L is the minimum balance).[71]

Frost considers the influence of three distinct hypotheses about the supply function, equation (5.96), on the firm's demand for money. In the case when $D_L = 0$ or when $S = gD_L$ – i.e., when the bank provides services in direct proportion (g) to the minimum cash balance maintained – one obtains the Miller and Orr result. But when the bank looks at both the minimum and the average cash balance, or when the bank looks at the mean and the variance of the firm's cash balance, then the Miller and Orr model is not general. This occurs, of course, because the flow of services depends on customer behaviour (is endogenous) and hence enters the firm's optimising framework via equation (5.96). But this carries us rather far afield.

We may also insert money directly into the production function of a business firm – along the lines of the argument in Chapter 4 – in the inventory-theoretic model, as U. Ben-Zion has done.[72] Thus, let $S(X,M)$ be the 'production of sales function', in which the arguments are the cost of production (X) and the average amount of money held (M). Let $iM + aX/2M$ describe the cost of holding money, in which case total costs are given by

$$T(X,M) = X + iM + \frac{aX}{2M}.$$

The firm will, then, maximise profits in equation (5.97):

$$\pi(X,M) = S(X,M) - X - iM - \frac{aX}{2M}. \tag{5.97}$$

We may differentiate by X and M, in which case the first-order conditions are

$$\frac{\partial \pi}{\partial X} = \frac{\partial S(X,M)}{\partial X} - \left(1 + \frac{a}{2M}\right) = 0 \qquad (5.98)$$

$$\frac{\partial \pi}{\partial M} = \frac{\partial S(X,M)}{\partial M} - \left(i - \frac{aX}{2M^2}\right) = 0. \qquad (5.99)$$

To illustrate the characteristics of the solution we may, then, assume a Cobb–Douglas function for $S(X,M)$; this is

$$S = AM^\alpha X^{1-\alpha}. \qquad (5.100)$$

In this case equation (5.99) becomes

$$\frac{\alpha S}{M} = i - \frac{aX}{2M^2} \qquad (5.101)$$

at the optimum. This, when solved for M, yields

$$M = \frac{\alpha S}{2i} + \frac{\sqrt{(\alpha^2 S^2 + 2aXi)}}{2i}. \qquad (5.102)$$

Ben-Zion also produces some results for a cost of capital variable – and some suggestive empirical work which favours using a cost of capital formulation. But of interest here are the properties of the demand for money function in equation (5.102). Thus, when $\alpha = 0$ – i.e., when money is not in the 'sales production function' – we get

$$M = \sqrt{\left(\frac{aX}{2i}\right)}$$

and when $a = 0$ – i.e., when there are no costs of cashing in one's bonds –

$$M = \frac{\alpha S}{i}.$$

In the first case the scale elasticity is 1/2 and in the second it is unity, while in the first case the interest rate elasticity is $-(1/2)$ and in the second -1. Thus, in general, inserting money into the production function of the firm provides an alternative to the Meltzer and Miller-and-Orr paradigm (in the IT framework) to rationalising a demand for money with a scale elasticity nearer unity than 1/2. This, it will be recalled, is the sort of result one sees most often in the empirical literature.

Footnotes

1. H. Markowitz, 'Portfolio Selection'; H. Markowitz, *Portfolio Selection*; R. J. Freund, 'The Introduction of Risk into a Programming Model'.

2. H. Markowitz, *Portfolio Selection*.

3. According to a recent study (M. E. Blume and I. Friend, 'The Asset Structure of Individual Portfolios and Some Implications for Utility Functions'), United States asset-holders are very undiversified in their holdings of common stocks. But one should note that individual wealth-holding units also simultaneously hold cash, demand deposits, savings deposits, government bonds, (fractions of) houses, life insurance, pensions and even lottery tickets. This could provide much of the benefit of a diversified portfolio.

4. Note that we are employing P for price and p, earlier, for probability.

5. This section is based on the study of the discount houses by M. Parkin, 'Discount House Portfolio and Debt Selection'.

6. J. Tobin, 'The Theory of Portfolio Selection'.

7. This function can be found in W. Freund, 'The Introduction of Risk into a Programming Model'. For the function

$$U_1 = \frac{\partial U}{\partial \pi} > 0 \text{ and } U_{11} = \frac{\partial^2 U}{\partial \pi^2} < 0$$

which meets the *a priori* requirements of equation (5.12).

8. M. Parkin, M. R. Gray and R. J. Barrett, 'The Portfolio Behaviour of Commercial Banks'.

9. See, for example, E. Feige, *The Demand for Liquid Assets*; T. H. Lee, 'Substitutability of Non-Bank Intermediary Liabilities for Money: The Empirical Evidence'; and the literature discussed in Chapter 2 above.

10. This section revolves around the paper by J. Tobin, 'Liquidity Preference as Behaviour Towards Risk'.

11. Recall the earlier argument of J. Hicks, discussed in Chapter 4, that we are only referring to M_2 balance here; these are those 'voluntarily' held (and thus the proper subject for the 'demand' for money), while M_1 balances (says Hicks) are held for mechanical reasons. The literature on this point is extremely unclear and one often finds reference to the entire stock of money as held for reasons of uncertainty; one also never finds proof of, or empirical testing of, the separability theorem imposed. This is a serious omission, since income and the interest rate presumably affect both M_1 and M_2, *a priori*. Compare C. Goodhart (*Money, Information and Uncertainty*) and P. Davidson (*Money and the Real World*) with J. Hicks (*Critical Essays in Monetary Theory*).

12. J. M. Keynes, *The General Theory*, p. 216.

13. J. Tobin, 'Liquidity Preference as Behaviour Towards Risk', pp. 65, 67.

14. ibid., p. 70. Keynes's 'uncertainty' in terms of differences of opinion is generally rejected as an example of uncertainty. But there are those (P. Davidson, *Money and the Real World* and G. Shackle, *Uncertainty in Economics*, for example) who regard Tobin's reformulation as a certainty case, since a *certain* probability distribution is how Tobin defines the 'subjective doubt' in Keynes. Keynes said, quoting Davidson, 'by uncertainty he meant that there "was no scientific basis on which to form any capable probability whatever. We simply do not know." ' (pp. 142–3). The quote from Keynes is from S. Harris (ed.), *The New Economics*.

15. J. Tobin, 'Liquidity Preference as Behaviour Towards Risk', p. 85.

16. B. Näslund, 'Some Effects of Taxes on Risk-Taking', p. 298.

17. Hicks (*Critical Essays in Monetary Theory*) prefers the mean-variance model for reasons already given and because he prefers not to accept the Pesek and Saving criterion (see Chapter 3) that if an asset pays interest it is not money. Thus

> It is apparent, in a new way, on this analysis, that the crucial distinction is not the distinction between a bond that bears interest and a money that does not. The crucial characteristic of money (as it appears in this portfolio theory) is that its resultant yield is certain. [p. 27]

Uncertainty, here, concerns the rate of inflation (and the interest rate, if 'money' bears some interest). In this event, the chief motive for holding M_2 (voluntarily held money holdings) is to reduce uncertainty. M_1 it can be recalled, is not voluntarily held but is held only to effect the volume of transactions.

18. J. Tobin, 'Liquidity Preference as Behaviour Towards Risk', p. 65.

19. K. Arrow notes (*Essays in the Theory of Risk-Bearing*) that

> in the choice between perpetuities and a secure asset, if the ratio of tomorrow's price to today's is distributed independently of today's price and if the demand for risky assets increases with initial wealth, then the demand for the risky assets is an increasing function of the current rate of return on the perpetuity and therefore the demand for the secure asset is a decreasing function of that rate. [p. 107]

Which gives us some help on Tobin's problem. On the other hand, F. Steindl shows ('Money and Bonds as Giffen Goods') that in the two-asset problem if money is a Giffen good (as in Tobin) so must the bond be. When there are three assets – money, bonds and real capital – one gets the more realistic result that (1) only one asset is a Giffen good; (2) bonds and real capital, but not money, are Giffen goods; or (3) all three assets are Giffen goods.

20. P. Samuelson, 'The Fundamental Approximation Theorem of Portfolio Analysis in Terms of Means, Variances and Higher Moments', p. 537.

21. K. Arrow, *Essays in the Theory of Risk-Bearing*. Note that $U''(Y) > 0$ implies risk preference, $U''(Y) < 0$ implies risk aversion, and $U''(Y) = 0$ implies risk neutrality.

22. ibid., p. 103. See also the discussion in K. Shell, 'Selected Elementary Topics in the Theory of Economic Decision-Making Under Uncertainty'.

23. See the discussion in K. Shell, 'Selected Elementary Topics in the Theory of Economic Decision-Making Under Uncertainty'.

24. D. Cass and J. E. Stiglitz, 'Risk Aversion and Wealth Effects on Portfolios with Many Assets'.

25. O. Hart ('A Proof of the Impossibility of Obtaining General Wealth Comparative Statics Properties in Portfolio Theory') shows that this 'separability property' is both necessary and sufficient. Unless it is met, no wealth (income) effects can be studied in this context, since no *a priori* signs can be obtained – as a result of the deficiencies of the analysis.

26. S. C. Tsiang, 'The Rationale of the Mean-Standard Deviation Analysis, Skewness Preference, and the Demand for Money'.

27. ibid., p. 369.

28. K. Borch, 'The Rationale of the Mean-Standard Deviation Analysis: Comment', p. 430.

29. See, especially, the papers in M. Jensen (ed.), *Studies in the Theory of Capital Markets*.

30. W. J. Baumol, 'The Transactions Demand for Cash: An Inventory-Theoretic Approach'.

31. T. Saving, 'Transactions Costs and the Demand for Money'.

32. By using $C/2$ we are assuming that the individual is paid once per time period and plans to run out of cash. This could be a problem if, for example, typical pay periods were weekly, while annual data were being examined. We are also assuming that his cash uses are evenly spaced out over the payments period. In an extension of this part of the model, K. White ('The Effect of Bank Credit Cards on the Household Transactions Demand for Money') uses the IT model (without the interest penalty or costs of conversion) to demonstrate a case in which the use of credit cards is at the expense of average deposit holdings. This occurs because individuals may find it convenient to pay their bills all at once, just after payday, using the credit cards to fill any gaps left. His empirical results provide some support, but it should be emphasised that White has ignored transactions and interest costs.

33. K. Brunner and A. Meltzer, 'Economics of Scale in Cash Balances Reconsidered', p. 423. See below in this chapter for a further discussion of the firm's demand for money in the IT mode.

34. S. Ahmad, 'Transactions Demand for Money and the Quantity Theory'.

35. J. J. McCall ('Differences Between the Personal Demand for Money and the Business Demand for Money') suggests this, but R. T. Selden ('The Post-War Rise in the Velocity of Money – A Sectoral Analysis') found that small firms actually economised compared with large. E. L. Whalen ('A Cross-Section Study of Business Demand for Cash') suggests that all of this sort of work is beside the point on account of significant aggregation bias (big firms are not, for

example, dealing in the same product as small). He finds, using the Baumol model and his own version (a parabolic relation: $M = a + bS + c\sqrt{S}$, where S is sales) that there is considerable evidence of diseconomies of scale in a cross-section context. He also experiments with the Meltzer model ('The Demand for Money: A Cross-Section Study of Business Firms'), which seems to provide scale elasticities closer to unity.

36.   C. Sprenkle, 'The Uselessness of Transactions Demand Models', and 'On the Observed Transactions Demand for Money'. In the second of these papers, supposing that the model might work better for the UK data (no use of compensating balances there, for one thing), Sprenkle finds that it probably doesn't, in his *ad hoc* test. Sprenkle is sharply criticised by D. Orr ('A Note on the Uselessness of Transactions Demand Models') on the grounds that the data are not very good; Orr proposes use of the M. Miller and D. Orr model ('The Demand for Money by Firms: Extension of Analytic Results'), which seems to work better. On the question of whether compensating balances add to the net demand for money, Orr argues the opposite on the basis of an earlier paper by Davis and Guttentag ('Are Compensating Balances Irrational?'). Their view is that banks compete for compensating balances by offering addititional services (in lieu of forbidden interest payments). Thus, the balances are not circulating money, but a form of time deposit. But this entire question has yet to be rigorously debated. See below, in the section on the business demand for money, for some further results.

37.   M. Weinrobe, 'The Demand for Money by Six Non-Bank Financial Intermediaries'.

38.   E. Karni and U. Ben-Zion, 'The Utility of Money and the Transactions Demand for Cash'.

39.   They attribute this constraint to E. Feige and M. Parkin ('The Optimal Quantity of Money, Bonds, Commodity Inventories, and Capital'); the latter's model is dynamic consumption. In Karni and Ben-Zion, i represents the opportunity cost of holding money – a similar rationale was noted in the dynamic consumption model in Chapter 3. In Feige and Parkin the approach is taken that i is the explicit return on money. That is, money is interest-bearing in the Feige and Parkin framework. The problem with the Karni–Ben-Zion rationale is that all stocks (of commodities, etc.) should receive equal treatment in the way they propose.

40.   See the discussion below, of the Miller–Orr model.

41.   Formally, as we generalise in this way, we see that the IT model is a close alternative to the EV model. This emerges strongly in a paper by S. M. Goldman ('Flexibility and the Demand for Money'). Recalling that the typical portfolio problem starts with the assumption of a fixed consumption plan and a stochastic portfolio, Goldman works the problem with certain asset yields and an uncertain consumption plan. Thus, if we force the wealth-holder to pick his proportion of bonds and money *before* (in time) he knows what his preferences are, then, in this case, the more 'flexible' his future choice is to be, the more money he will hold. Goldman assumes that a consumer whose preference for first-period consumption is too great must sell bonds at a penalty and a consumer whose preference for first-period consumption is too little is stuck with idle money. 'Flexibility' and 'liquidity' are obviously analogous concepts. There is, as well, a parallel development of this line of attack in the EV framework by R. Waud ('Net Outlay Uncertainty and Liquidity Preference as Behavior Toward Risk'), who claims

> It is shown that in the net-outlay uncertainty model that risk neutral investors, risk lovers, and plungers may all exhibit portfolio diversifying behavior *unlike* their implied behavior in the usual Tobin-type, mean-variance framework. [p. 499]

42.   E. Karni, 'The Transactions Demand for Cash: Incorporation of the Value of Time into the Inventory Approach', and 'The Value of Time and the Demand for Money'. In the latter paper Karni does, indeed, present direct empirical tests of equation (5.47). He expects

$$0.4 \leqslant \delta_{MW} \leqslant 0.9$$
$$\delta_{MT_w} = 0.4$$
$$\delta_{MPI} = 0.1$$
$$-0.5 \leqslant \delta_{Mi} \leqslant -0.4$$

the first on the basis of different values of S_x; that is, if $S_x = 1$, then there is no wage content to the cost of transactions and δ_{MW} is near 0.4. In fact, it comes out at or even above the upper limit. This test, however, is not of the form suggested in the text, here, and leaves me uneasy. In particular, it would seem that we are being encouraged to think of S_x and S_w as constants which may be represented by average values. In this event, all of the coefficients in equation (5.47) are known *a priori* and no empirical problem remains (try, for example, fitting a regression with the numbers above applied as restrictions). My suggestion, as in the text, is to use a 'variable coefficients' model to test this appealing hypothesis. Karni has also published a British test, along the same lines ('The Value of Time and the Demand for Money: Evidence from UK Time Series Data').

43.   J. Tobin, 'The Interest Elasticity of the Transactions Demand for Cash', pp. 241–2.

44.   A. Sastry ('The Effect of Credit on Transactions Demand for Cash') has extended the inventory model to deal with the case when credit is also available. He concludes (in a model that contained some errors: see the discussion in the *Journal of Finance*, December 1971) that (1) the demand for money is more interest-elastic when credit is available, and (2) a large firm will thereby have a larger interest elasticity than a small firm.

45.   As in C. Goodhart, *Money, Information and Uncertainty*, pp. 22–6.

46.   We find n^* first and then M^* follows, since all transactions are of equal size. The number of transactions is treated as an integer by Tobin; Baumol, it is clear, did not impose this restriction.

47.   E. L. Whalen, 'A Rationalization of the Precautionary Demand for Cash', p. 315.

48.   ibid., pp. 317–18.

49.   Recall, from Chapter 4, the argument by Weinrobe, that the negative interest elasticity of the demand for money is better established by the precautionary motive. Here we see that the two are pretty much on an equal footing in the inventory model, at least if you disregard the other *ad hoc* elements.

50.   V. Chitre, 'Wealth Effect on the Demand for Money'.

51.   This is basically a pure inventory model. Chitre shows that when equation (5.56) is maximised (M is the choice variable in this problem) and the individual is confronted with a change in wealth (W), then

1. an increase in W would actually lower the expected marginal return on holding money and hence provide a negative wealth effect (the direct effect);
2. but when the effect of wealth on expenditures (on PX) is included (as it should be) as well, this provides a positive influence.

In the same model, if the wealth-holder has a restricted line of credit, Chitre shows that this, too, tends to provide a positive wealth effect. M. L. Cropper, in a partly parallel paper ('A State-Preference Approach to the Precautionary Demand for Money'), shows that in a conventional portfolio environment – in which the investor must liquidate at short notice if a particular uncertain event occurs – if the chances of an enforced liquidation increase, so, too, will precautionary money balances.

52.   The paper by E. Karni and U. Ben-Zion ('The Utility of Money and the Transactions Demand for Cash'), referred to above, also has solutions similar to Chitre's. Thus, in a continuous-time model, if the individual continually adjusts his money balances between a minimum and a maximum, and money is an argument in the utility function, Ben-Zion and Karni obtain the following results:

1. the effect of the interest rate on minimum money balances is negative (but the value depends on the specification of the utility function);
2. the wealth effect on minimum balances works on the marginal utility of money (it declines with an increase in wealth); the concomitant increase in consumption will increase the effect of wealth on the minimum balance.

These are similar findings to those reported by – and discussed by – Chitre.

53.   M. Gray and M. Parkin, 'Portfolio Diversification as Optimal Precautionary Behaviour'. A paper by S. C. Tsiang ('The Precautionary Demand for Money: An Inventory-Theoretical Analysis') is also relevant here.

54.   A. Santomero ('A Model of the Demand for Money by Households') arrives at similar conclusions, although he is interested in the transactions demand for money:

It resulted in demand functions for each short term asset that were functions of rates of return and transactions costs of the asset in question and its adjacent assets only. [p. 100]

His model is inventory-theoretic (of a more specific sort). Santomero also notes that one should not aggregate currency and deposits since one makes different types of transactions with each of these two forms. Further, he notes that, if consumers can also hold stocks of commodities, then the transactions demand for money is thereby smaller.

55.　M. Parkin, R. Barrett and M. Gray, 'The Demand for Financial Assets by the Personal Sector of the U.K. Economy'.

56.　T. Saving, 'Transactions Costs and the Demand for Money'.

57.　ibid., p. 411.

58.　Saving, actually, has a much more general formulation in three directions:

1. He has $\bar{m}^i$, where $i = 1, \ldots, n$ is a series of other types of money. Actually, this is really necessary here, since the solution for only one variable is essentially trivial.
2. He has the consumer holding stocks of income and of consumer goods.
3. He imposes different storage costs on all three stocks (and on the different types of money).

59.　D. S. Dutton and W. P. Gramm, 'Transactions Costs, the Wage Rate, and the Demand for Money', p. 652.

60.　B. Motley, 'The Consumer's Demand for Money: A Neoclassical Approach'.

61.　This solution is done by analogy with the Jorgenson investment function. Thus equation (3.89), for the stock of consumer durables, is given by the Euler equation

$$\frac{\partial U}{\partial X(t)} - \frac{d}{dt}\frac{\partial U}{\partial \dot{X}}.$$

The choice for the stock of money is treated in the same way.

62.　B. Motley, 'The Consumer's Demand for Money: A Neoclassical Approach', p. 826.

63.　M. Nadiri, 'The Determinants of Real Cash Balances in the U.S. Total Manufacturing Sector'.

64.　T. Saving, 'Transactions Costs and the Firm's Demand for Money', p. 259.

65.　M. Miller and D. Orr, 'A Model of the Demand for Money by Firms'.

66.　ibid., pp. 415–16.

67.　E. Feige, *et al.* ('The Roles of Money in an Economy and the Optimum Quantity of Money') show for the utility function in which there is a single good that the inventory-theoretic model (cost-minimising) is equivalent to their utility-maximising approach. As M. Perlman ('The Roles of Money in an Economy and the Optimum Quantity of Money: Reply') notes, 'since factors of production are employed either in the production of that good, or in the transactions process, minimization of transactions costs and maximization of utility amount to the same thing' (p. 432). In our context, this establishes the generality of the Miller and Orr approach.

68.　M. Miller and D. Orr, 'The Demand for Money by Firms: Extension of Analytical Results'. In this paper it is argued that the correct interest rate for their model – which puts the cost of capital in a central role – is a long-term rate rather than a short-term rate. In this context it is well to remember the Price study (empirical) which found the opposite in practice.

69.　P. Frost, 'Banking Services, Minimum Cash Balances, and the Firm's Demand for Money'.

70.　γ_t is the transactions cost if the firm does not allow its deposits to vary. Thus the second term represents the adjustment on account of the variable balance.

71.　$D_{\mathrm{L}} = \bar{D} - \left(\dfrac{h+z}{3}\right)$, as above.

72.　U. Ben-Zion, 'The Cost of Capital and the Demand for Money by Firms'.

CHAPTER 6

The Term Structure of Interest Rates and the Demand for Money

6.1 Introduction

Economists interested in the demand for money have not made much use of the theory of the term structure of interest rates in developing explicit results for the former, and this is somewhat surprising for several reasons. In the first place, the main lines of the modern debate, between (1) expectations, (2) liquidity preference and (3) market segmentation, can be found in the basic theoretical work of monetary economics of (e.g.) I. Fisher, J. M. Keynes and J. R. Hicks, to mention only the best-known.[1] In the second place, as we have seen, the empirical work has shown, quite consistently, that one gets different results for differently termed interest rates in a wide variety of model specifications (of the demand for money). Finally, the problem of integrating a part of financial market theory into the mainstream of thinking on the role of money is a complicated and interesting one and, more to the point, one that monetary economists might well be able to use to improve the generality of their results.

In the pages that follow we will first attempt to present the debate over the term structure from Keynes and Hicks to the present, in such a way that it is clear both why and how the term-structure literature specialised in questions of only peripheral interest to the topic of the demand for money; then, we will consider how we can amend that traditional literature to deal with the case of money holding. We will begin our discussion with the development of the traditional Hicks–Lutz theory, develop briefly some material on the alternatives, and then consider the Keynesian formulation of the problem. The foregoing comprises the first (substantial) part of this chapter; but in line with the arguments of other chapters in this study, we will then turn to dynamic consumption and to portfolio models to generate

153

some further explicit conclusions for the demand for money. In these cases we will be able to establish some generalisations as to which interest rate – a long rate or a short rate – should work best in tests of the demand for money. Not surprisingly, the results depend on the formulation.

In particular, two sets of results are available. In the dynamic consumption framework, following the work of J. Stiglitz and J. Green,[2] we will show – in a problem set to cover three periods – that

1. the demand for third-period (or 'reservation') balances depends on both a long-term and a short-term rate, although which one is to dominate depends on which of these assets has more portfolio space; and
2. that the demand for first-period (or 'intermediate') balances must be aggregated with the demand for short-term bonds (as in Keynes) and, consequently, the appropriate interest rate for this aggregation is a long-term rate.

Some clarity can also be given to the traditional term-structure literature in this more general context. In the mean-variance framework, again in a three-period context, we find that, with respect to intermediate balances, a short-term rate always gives ambiguous results while the long-term rate generally produces the expected negative relationship. With regard to the important 'reservation' or third-period balances, the results are the same, except that one must first define the shape of the yield curve. In particular, when the yield curve is upsloping, so that the long-term rate is greater than the short-term rate, the interest rate effect on the demand for reservation balances is generally *positive*. Thus, on net, the mean-variance model establishes a firm preference for the long-term rate as the dominant rate for the demand for money, but also establishes that the shape of the yield curve is relevant to the result. Indeed, we will show that at least three rates – the long rate, the short rate, and an expected future rate – should be included in the demand for money, with the short rate, as an own rate, bearing a positive sign.

6.2 The expectations hypothesis and the demand for money [3]

While there are important precursors, it is convenient to begin our story with the work of J. Hicks in *Value and Capital*. Hicks, indeed, gave a peculiar twist to the subject of the term structure, which until that time was firmly in the mainstream of monetary thinking; this was in the interest, presumably, of being entirely clear about the unique aspects of the term structure problem. We can accept that rationale, it seems to me, now that more general treatments have placed his contribution in a richer context, but for some time there was a clear cost in divorcing the term structure problem from the demand for assets problem. Hicks began by assuming that one-period interest rates are determined in a general equilibrium framework in which either a long- or a short-term rate, but not both, are included; indeed, interest itself was justified in terms of the trouble (cost) of transactions:

> Under the conditions of our model, it must be the trouble of making transactions which explains the short rate of interest ... thus the imperfect 'moneyness' of those bills which are not money is due to their lack of general acceptability; it is this lack of general acceptability which causes the trouble of investing them, and causes them to stand at a discount. So far as our model economy is concerned, that is really all that needs to be said about the relation between money and interest. We have now seen how there comes to be a short rate of interest.[4]

Hicks, thus, regards the short-term interest rate as determined in the money market as the result of a trade-off between money and short-term securities. The characteristic of money that seems to provide a demand for it is its 'general acceptability', which is the result of one's being able to engage in economic activity with less 'trouble'. The interest rate on the nearest alternative to cash governs the use of this asset (along with, presumably, some scale variable, such as income or wealth). We then turn, following Hicks, to an analysis of what determines long-term interest rates.

Hicks begins his formulation of the problem of the term structure of interest rates by forming an analogy between spot and futures (forward) transactions and short- and long-term interest rates.

> A fundamental approach to the problem of interest suggests itself naturally, after the discussions of the preceding chapter. We have learnt to distinguish transactions according to the date at which they are due to be executed. Spot transactions are due to be executed currently – that is to say, in the current week in which they are drawn up. Forward transactions are due to be executed entirely at a future date – both sides of the bargain in the same future week. But there is no reason why the two sides of a bargain should be due to be executed at the same date. Thus we get a third type, loan transactions, which are such that only one side of the bargain is executed currently, the other being due to be executed at some future date, or perhaps a series of future dates. The essential characteristic of a loan transaction is that its execution is divided in time.[5]

A loan by Hicks's system, then, consists of two one-sided transactions in which a bond is exchanged for money and one or more forward transactions that 'undo' the loan arrangement. Indeed, while Hicks carefully distinguishes among (1) the money loan, (2) the spot transaction, and (3) the forward transaction, only (2) and (3) seem to emerge strongly in his theory of the term structure:

Looking at it this way, the rate of interest for loans of two weeks, running from our first Monday, is compounded out of the 'spot' rate of interest for loans of one week and the 'forward' rate of interest, also for one week loans, but for loans to be executed in the second week.[6]

This, the reader should note, is his analogy, and as such it contains a strong assumption, since it treats the 'spot' interest rate (often, indeed, taken to be the one-year interest rate) as analogous to the current price of (e.g.) coffee:

> it is possible to lend coffee for one year by selling coffee spot, lending the money proceeds, and covering the sale by a purchase on the forward market.[7]

If we dispensed with the analogy, we could frame the problem as that of disposing of commodities over various future periods, by using the bond market to effect the forward contract (long or short). The latter approach would treat the one-period interest rate as a forward rate, while in Hicks it is a spot rate; the terminology 'certainty equivalent' has come to describe the use of the one-period rate in this way, in the term-structure literature.

There are two aspects to the Hicksian term-structure theory – the expectations hypothesis, and the hypothesis of the liquidity premium. Hicks argues that calculated forward rates of interest, representing hypothetical 'futures' yields, are in fact determined by speculators. The forward rate is calculated as follows. Let the yield on an n-period bond, measured at time t, be described as R_{nt} in equation (6.1). Note that 'r' and 'R' will designate nominal interest rates 'or yields' throughout this chapter.

$$\text{price}_{nt} = \frac{C}{(1 + R_{nt})} + \ldots + \frac{C + F}{(1 + R_{nt})^n}. \tag{6.1}$$

Here C represents the coupon and F the face value of the bond. We can also suppose that there are a series of one-period forward rates such that an equivalent expression to equation (6.1) is given as equation (6.2):

$$\text{price}_{nt} = \frac{C}{(1 + r_{1t})} + \ldots + \frac{C + F}{(1 + r_{1t}) \ldots (1 + r_{nt})}. \tag{6.2}$$

Here the rate r_{nt} is assumed to apply only to the period between $n - 1$ and n; note, as well, that all of these rates are hypothetical (as was the yield, for that matter) and are calculated at time t. If, for convenience, we assume that $C = 0$ and $F = 1$ (or, as in Hicks, that all coupon payments are accumulated to the end of the contract), we can write out a series of results for a spectrum of differently dated securities (we do this by eliminating price between (6.1) and (6.2) to get the expression for the nth period yield). This produces equations (6.3):

$$1 + R_{1t} = 1 + r_{1t}$$

$$\qquad . \qquad \qquad . \qquad \qquad\qquad\qquad\qquad (6.3)$$

$$1 + R_{nt} = (1 + r_{1t}) \ldots (1 + r_{nt}).$$

Then, one can dig out the forward rates in equations (6.3) by directly comparing successive pairs of yields; this produces equation (6.4):

$$1 + r_{nt} = \frac{(1 + R_{nt})^n}{(1 + R_{n-1t})^{n-1}}. \qquad\qquad (6.4)$$

The hypothesis, then, is that these forward rates are, in fact, expected rates and are determined by speculative activity.

Hicks certainly recognised other than speculative behaviour and his formulation of the 'liquidity premium' hypothesis is a clear case in point. Hicks argued that, if no extra return is offered for long lending, most people would prefer to lend short. Since borrowers (presumably) have no such qualms, the forward market for loans has a 'constitutional weakness on one side, a weakness which offers an opportunity for speculation'.[8] Thus,

> [the] forward rate of interest for a particular future week ... is thus determined, like the future price of a commodity, at that level which just tempts a sufficient number of speculators to undertake the forward contract.[9]

That is, the actual forward rate exceeds the expected rate by a risk premium; one must pay people to gamble in the Hicksian casino. Furthermore, these premiums ought to rise with maturity, *ceteris paribus*. Equation (6.5) describes this situation.

$$_t r_{t+k} = E_t(R_{t+k}) + L_k \qquad 0 < L_1 < L_2 < \ldots . \qquad (6.5)$$

Attention should be directed to the '*ceteris paribus*' in the last paragraph, for the liquidity premium, while an appealing hypothesis, has not succumbed to direct empirical testing. For one thing, it is not generally correct to say that all people would prefer to lend short unless a special premium is offered, because it essentially depends on people's planned holding periods (in this case the length of time that they wish to commit their funds to the market). That is, individuals will have some configuration of planned receipts and expenditures which the long-term lending (or borrowing) exactly matches, in the ideal state. Then, to get them to depart from that state, some premium (to go either longer or, even, shorter) must be offered; there are many examples of such plans, but the Christmas or thrift clubs are a case in point. It is also possible that long-term securities are so desirable for an individual (or an institution) because their needs are so far in the future, that *no* appropriate security can be found; this is supposed to be the case of the life insurance company, for whom a 'solidity premium' would result.[10] Furthermore, while individuals might be thought to be risk-averse, it is conceivable that they are not or, that failing, that individuals perceive future consumption to be so desirable – and future earned income so uncertain – that they will pay a 'discount' (or 'solidity premium') to be able to hold a long-dated government bond. This perception comes from a problem in which the consumer maximises his expected utility over his lifetime.[11] Finally, and less relevantly, there are technical reasons why liquidity premiums might not be observed.[12]

6.2.1   *Lutz's restatement of the problem*

F. A. Lutz, in his paper on the term structure,[13] lays out quite carefully the assumptions needed to validate the expectations hypothesis, at least in its 'perfect' form. The assumptions are:

1. that there is certain and accurate forecasting in the market;
2. that there are no transactions costs;
3. that individuals have identical expectations;
4. that there is complete shiftability for lenders and for borrowers.

The last condition means that there are no restrictions on, and no prejudices against, say, holding ten one-year contracts covering the life of a loan of ten years or one ten-year contract (or any other combination of contracts), covering the same period. Lutz, then, deduces that:

1. holding period yields are equal;
2. the long-term rate can be conceived of as an average of future short-term rates;
3. the long-term rate can never fluctuate as widely as the short-term rate;
4. it is possible that the long-term rate may move temporarily contrari-wise to the short-term rate;
5. a rising yield curve indicates
   (a) that future interest rates are above the current one-period rate, and
   (b) that the long-term rate will rise later on.

Proposition 3 depends directly on Proposition 2; the influence of a given fluctuation in the short rate on the long rate is modified by the averaging of all future (expected) short rates which are assumed to be components of the long rate. Since these rates are accurately foreseen, the only adjustment needed for the long rate is the adjustment for the one rate dropped from the series and the one added at the other end. The short rate changes by the full amount, while the long rate changes by the contribution of the short to the average, and by the addition of the new rate at the end, also averaged. It is possible for this addition to be in a different direction and larger than the change in the short rate (as both are averaged) – hence Proposition 4. Proposition 5 also follows directly, since interest rates are determined by expectations and since expectations are accurate; that is, the events forecast in the yield structure inevitably come to pass (in the theory).

The speculator (if this emasculated personality could be so characterised) here is really anyone who is 'uncovered' in the bond market rather than a Keynesian 'plunger' who operates on his difference of opinion with the market. This definition has the awkward property, since forward rates are assumed to be determined by speculators, that it is hard to conceive of effective empirical tests. Evidence that forward rates predict badly is of no particular use – once we assume dominating speculation – since it only implies that speculators predicted badly, not that they do not determine interest rates. Even the finding of successful expectations-generating mechanisms is frustrated by the fact that more successful methods are always likely to be found (or at least to be hypothesised) and more reasonable ones to be hypothesised. One way out, as we will see, is the development of the alternative hypothesis – the segmentation or hedging hypothesis – although, once again, problems abound.

The theory just described is essentially vacuous if interpreted as an equilibrium theory; that is, there is no conceivable pattern of term-differentiated yields that it could not explain. Furthermore, conditions (1) to (3) ought to be relaxed if one wants to motivate money holding. That is, the absence of (1) and (3) were mentioned in Chapter 2, above, and the absence of (3) has been described as Keynes's rationale for the existence of a demand for money. The implication is, aside from interest rate risk associated with long contracts, that all bonds are equally (and perfectly) liquid in the expectations hypothesis. As we noted in Chapter 2, if one links money with the concept of liquidity, and liquidity with the term structure (at the short end), then money and long-term bonds are linked by means of the hypothesis of liquidity premiums (and by the proposition that long-term rates are determined by expectations about future short-term rates). But, since uncertainty and transactions costs (which provide a rationale for liquidity) are ruled out in the present case, one is (rather consistently, if you will recall the discussion of Hicks) also ruling money out of the problem.

Lutz also considers the rationale of the liquidity premium. In Hicks the liquidity premium arose because of a 'constitutional weakness' on one side of the market; in Lutz, it is made clear that this weakness has to do with uncertainty. Thus, even if all interest rates fluctuate to the same degree, the increasing haziness about long-term rates would suggest that a risk premium should be charged. But, as we noted above, uncertainty alone would not necessarily imply a monotonic liquidity premium (rising with term to maturity) since, if one's holding period is known for certain, no risk premium is required, no matter how fuzzy the view of interest rates before or after that maturity. So uncertainty also does not lead to unique conclusions about the risk premium without further assumptions about holding periods.

6.2.2   *Empirical tests of the expectations hypothesis*

There are two characteristics of the expectations hypothesis – as just described – which should be underscored at this point:

1. it is a non-monetary theory in the sense of not relying on frictions and uncertainties; and
2. it is irrefutable in a direct way.

We will return to the former concern below; with regard to the latter, we noted that, once we assume that interest rates are determined by expectations, we will be hard put to conceive of direct empirical tests. J. Conard gave this problem some considerable thought; observing that, while a perfect-foresight model could be tested directly – and in his opinion fails – a term structure model with uncertainty has some severe empirical problems:

> The problem of verification here arises from the impossibility of dogmatizing about what expectations are or have been at any time; without knowing these, disproof of the neoclassical theory is not possible [14]

The basic problem is that 'it is necessary in empirical work to specify how expectations are revised or formed'. Thus, one must always test a particular model which can then never claim to represent 'the' expectations hypothesis, but only a particular researcher's hypothesis; there are a lot of such models about. Of course, one must also account for differences in individual expectations and for the fact that expectations change over time (and even that the actual expectations-generating mechanism changes over time).

D. Meiselman, however, constructed an empirical test – of a direct nature – which seemed to get around the problems just raised.[15] He proposed a test, based on the earlier 'hyperinflation' and 'permanent income' models,[16] that utilised an 'error-learning' framework. Noting that forward rates are expected rates, by the expectations hypothesis, Meiselman suggested that revisions in forward rates (i.e., revisions in expectations) might normally be made in response to 'errors in prediction' of the spot interest rate (or, for that matter, of any target rate). Thus, if a rate had been expected to rise, and in fact fell, speculators (who, we assume, determine forward rates) would adjust their expectations downward, bringing the forward rate down as they also adjusted their portfolios in line with their new opinions. Formally, the actual equation he tested is given by equation (6.6):

$$_t r_{t+n} - _{t-1} r_{t+n} = a_n + b_n E_t + _t u_{t+n} \quad n = 1, \ldots, T \tag{6.6}$$

The pre-subscript here refers to the date at which the forward rate was observed. The E_t term, then, consists of the 'spot' rate for time t ($= _t R_{1t}$) minus the forward rate from the previous period ($= _{t-1} r_t$); in all of these formulas the post-subscript refers to the point in time to which the interest rate is assumed to refer. Thus, if one assumes that last period's forward rate ($= _{t-1} r_t$) referring to this period's spot rate ($= _t R_{1t}$) was the rate speculators expected to rule, then E_t is their error in prediction. *All* forward rates, Meiselman suggested, would be revised in response to the error in prediction of this interest rate; hence there would be n regression equations in (6.6).

Early tests on American and British data were often favourable,[17] but a host of problems emerged. While many of these problems are not directly relevant to the problem of the demand for money, it is just as well, since we will be enmeshed in models of price expectations in Chapter 7, to catalogue these problems now, since some of these will reappear in that discussion. Problems that need not detain us concern the measurement of hypothetical yield data,[18] the effect of tax laws on term-differentiated securities,[19] and the question of whether or not expectations 'horizons' are short or long.[20] This still leaves us with some severe problems, of a basic nature.

The main problem with the Meiselman formulation is that the attempt to separate the expectations hypothesis from its rivals is not all that convincing. A. Buse, for example, notes that

> the discriminatory power of the model with respect to alternative hypotheses is shown to be very low,

and, in particular, that

> such results are implied by any set of smoothed yield curves in which short-term interest rates have a greater variability than long-term rates.[21]

While it is a fact that short-term rates fluctuate more than long, it is also an economic fact which should be explained in the context of one's theory of the term structure of interest rates.[22] Buse, rather, suggests that

> To test the hypothesis that the Meiselman results are implied by any set of smoothed yield curves whose variance diminishes with maturity, the two sets of available data ... were ordered randomly, and the new orders were used to test the Meiselman model.[23]

The test employed was that of whether or not the regression coefficients and the coefficients of determination declined with the period to which the forward rate applied; when this was done, the random orderings were as convincing as the natural orderings.

Buse's procedure, which does not seem to depend on the greater variability of short yields as such, is certainly not a direct refutation. Earlier, indeed, it had been argued that Meiselman's model could not be effectively distinguished from a naive extrapolative model (itself referred to as the 'inertia' model) and this is about as much as one need say about its weakness to discriminate.[24] Further, there is something illogical about scrambling data, even when one's motives are scientific. In Meiselman's defence, too, it could be noted that in any event his estimating equation is based on the 'random walk' model; that is, a one-period forward rate, referring to time t, would be described as an unbiased random walk if

$$_t r_{t+1} = {}_{t-1} r_{t+1} + w_t \qquad (6.7)$$

where w_t is a random error with zero mean. Recognising Meiselman's dependent variable as $_t r_{t+1} - {}_{t-1} r_{t+1}$, we note that Meiselman successfully introduces an element (the error in prediction of the one-year rate) in addition to the random component. But in a general sense, Buse is correct in that a theory that attempts to explain a relatively small problem – while not correcting for a simultaneously occurring larger problem – is not going to be particularly plausible. That is, the real problem here is that changes in relative yields (i.e., term structure problems) are swamped by changes in the entire yield curve (i.e., demand for money problems) so that crude methods forecast about as well as (Meiselman's) sophisticated ones.

While direct tests of the expectations hypothesis – and, for that matter, indirect tests – abound, enough has been said here to permit us to move on into the topic of the demand for money, even though the environment is not a little hostile, as the pure theory of the term structure has been laid out. If we appreciate the difficulties that direct tests encounter, we can perhaps also appreciate that indirect tests, in other sectors of, for example, a macroeconomic model, might bear fruit. We will in the remainder of this section consider one such test, in the Hicksian framework; in the next section, two more models will be proposed, grafted, as it were, on to a Keynesian term structure theory.

Hicksian speculators can be conceived of, then, along the lines of the Meiselman 'error learning test'. Recalling the definition of the error of prediction above, we also recall that it contained the difference between an observed short period rate (R_1) and the previous forward rate, assumed to refer to (i.e., predict) that rate, but one period previously. Both of these rates are, of course, short-term rates; the link, then, is that all rates along the structure can be expected to adjust with this error, as Meiselman assumes (in equation 6.6). Let us, then, argue that the short-term rate is determined by (or largely influenced by) the authorities (perhaps in their conduct of monetary policy), while the long-term rate is determined by speculators, in the Hicksian fashion, responding to the errors in prediction of the authorities' effect on the one-year rate. Thus, if the authorities change the short rate downward, this will produce a negative 'error of prediction' of the one-year rate. This, under our assumptions, will generate the expectation that long-term rates will soon move down as well. Consequently, individuals will move out of money into long-term bonds (in anticipation of the price rise).[25] Indeed, this movement is important in explaining how the entire yield structure moves together. Equation (6.8), then, displays this hypothesis formally:

$$M_t = f(Y_t, r_t, E_t, M_{t-1}). \tag{6.8}$$

The expected sign on the E_t variable is positive.

6.4 Towards a Keynesian theory of the term structure

While the shifting nature of the debate over what Keynes said (and/or meant) makes summarisation of his views a trifle risky, because it leads us directly to the empirical results, it is worth while attempting to document the present consensus. Recalling that there are three elements to traditional term structure theory – expectations, the liquidity premium and segmentation (to be explained shortly) – we will describe here how the first two could be interpreted in the Keynesian framework. In Chapter 4 above, we actually offered a view of Keynes that was framed in the speculative mode (or, if you will, in terms of expectations). In that paradigm, it was argued that Keynes regarded the long-term rate as being determined by speculators who compared their disparate views as to what was a 'normal' rate of interest with actual market rates and revised their portfolios (of money and bonds) accordingly. Further, as with the Hicksian paradigm just discussed, short-term rates, in Keynes, are heavily influenced by the authorities who, presumably, deal in Treasury bills to further their short-run objectives. In Leijonhufvud's words:

> In Keynes' theory, on the other hand, the money-demand function depends not only upon income and the market rate of interest but also, and importantly, on a third variable, namely investor opinions with regard to the normal rate.[26]

Finally, investors' opinions about what is a normal rate (long rate, that is) are judged to be collectively inelastic, so that in the conduct of monetary policy the authorities must content themselves with having only short-term rates to control, their influence on long-term rates being hampered by the sticky interest rate expectations except, of course, in the long run.

There are several problems one immediately encounters in trying to bring Keynes's theory – as just described – into direct confrontation with the data. The first of these is that a long-run framework – in this view at least – tends to be one in which expectations and policy are merged. That is, in the long run (by Keynes) the authorities can and do influence expectations about what the normal rate is; indeed, it is part of Keynes's view that the authorities can and do persuade investors to adopt a normal rate that is not at the same time a market clearing rate, so long as they aggressively and consistently work on the short-term rate (which is, by assumption, at least partly under their control). The theories described in Chapter 4 under the Keynesian heading are generally long-run formulations; witness, again, a version of the Starleaf–Reimer equation, here given as equation (6.9):

$$M_t = a + b_1 Y_t + b_2 r_t + b_3 (r_t^e - r_t). \tag{6.9}$$

In the long run, we are asserting, we should observe some differences between the expected long-term rate and the actual long-term rate; but it is immediately obvious that this cannot be, for in the long run the long-term interest rate *is* the expected rate. This is not a dilemma, it should be clear, but it is basic to the testing of expectations hypotheses in general, as we have noted at several points in this chapter.

This being the case, one way out is to put down some explicit expectations-generating mechanism, of sound pedigree, and see how things come out. Thus, the error-learning mechanism, while not taken directly out of Keynes, can be interpreted in the Keynesian tradition. Starleaf and Reimer, in their turn, go for a 'permanent' type of measure for r_t^e; this is an appropriate strategy, but not with the long-run model, for the reasons given. For the term structure problem a short-run context is again appropriate. Not only is such a model in keeping with the short-run nature of Keynes's theory, but such an approach, because it permits an examination of the system in adjustment, also gives us a grip on Keynes's proposition that the authorities can tug at expectations, without instant success. Further, it can be argued that, instead of the term $(r_t^e - r_t)$, one might enter the difference between the long-term rate and the short-term rate here. Thus, it can be argued that in certain cases the short-term rate is dominated by the authorities, who change it by changing the discount rate (or by open market operations). The long-term rate, then, depends on expectations, but expectations which we could assume respond only slowly to changes in short-term rates. In any given quarter of the year, following a policy-induced change in the short-term rate (a rise, for instance), speculators will begin to revise upwards their expectations about what is a normal rate. We will observe a negative difference between r_L and r_s – because the adjustment is incomplete – being associated with a positive value of $M_t - M_{t-1}$ because speculators are likely to be moving into money from bonds in this event; thus the expected coefficient for the speculative proxy is negative in equation (6.10):[27]

$$M_t = f(Y_t, r_t, M_{t-1}, r_L - r_s).$$ (6.10)

We note that this is a joint hypothesis, as all such tests must be unless direct expectations data are available, the jointure here being between the general Keynesian paradigm adopted and the specific model of how expectations are formed.

The second element in the Keynesian theory of relevance to the term structure problem concerns the liquidity premium, the case for which we have already discussed. In Chapter 4 we also discussed the nonlinear test of the liquidity trap, conducted by Pifer and others, a literature that produced the general consensus that some evidence exists in favour of an asymptotic liquidity trap, but that the tests are possibly sensitive to assumptions about the functional form of the relationship. We now add another term, here, r_s/r_L, (to be explained in a moment), to produce equation (6.11):

$$M_t = \beta_1(r_L - r_{\min})^{\beta_2} Y_t^{\beta_3} \left(\frac{r_s}{r_L}\right)^{\beta_4} M_{t-1}^{\beta_5} + e_t.$$ (6.11)

The Keynesian theory, here again, combines two elements: that long-term interest rates are dominated by speculators, but that these speculators are generally risk-averse. Thus, the term $(r_L - r_{\min})$, where $r_{\min}$ is the lowest expected interest rate, represents the basic Keynesian expectations hypothesis. In a short-run context, if the actual long-term rate is close to the minimum interest rate expected, then we can presume that speculators are most likely to expect a fall in bond prices, whereas if $(r_L - r_{\min})$ is large, they will expect a rise. As the gap widens between the two, the probability of a rise is greater – consequently, they will (tend to) move into bonds and out of money. We expect, thusly, on the basis of this basic expectations hypothesis, a negative sign for β_4. So much for the expectations hypothesis.

In this discussion, then, a simple theory of the term structure of interest rates is employed in which expectations are measured by $r_{\min}$ and r_L represents the opportunity cost of holding money, both in the relation $r_L - r_{\min}$; these are influences on the demand for money. Since a basic term structure hypothesis is thereby included in the model, one could estimate the influence of the second element – the liquidity premium – by including the relationship r_s/r_L. Normally, then, we might expect this ratio to have some fixed value (say, 0.8); call this value V. Suppose, in fact, that r_s/r_L is actually less than V. In such an event, long-term rates are relatively favourable and investors will tend to move from short-term bonds (and from money) into long-term bonds. The influence of r_s/r_L on the demand for money would be positive, *a priori*.

This leaves us with a halfway literature, mostly empirical in nature – but not firmly either Keynesian or Neoclassical – in which what we might call

Monetary Theory and the Demand for Money

the 'explanatory power' of alternative interest rates is considered. While there are many prior contributions and scattered bits of information, Laidler's test is perhaps the first that adopted the technique of *ex post* rationalisation so common in this literature; thus

> It is possible to find a stable relationship between the demand for money and the rate of interest in terms of a test procedure similar to Friedman's (1959); the relevant rate is a short one; the interest elasticity of the demand-for-money function is probably in the range of -0.15 to -0.20; there is little evidence of the existence of the liquidity trap as part of the structure of a stable demand for money function.[28]

The model was the same as the Friedman model and covered the period 1892–1960. The short-term interest rate worked better, Laidler argued, because it was a better proxy for 'the' interest rate; if the long rate had worked better, it would have been a better proxy. Indeed, in a recent paper covering the same data. M. Khan actually does find in favour of a long-term rate.

This formal agnosticism, running contrary to both the Keynesian preference for a short rate and Keynes's preference for a long rate, has stimulated a considerable literature in this vein. Heller, for example,[29] tests the 'long run' function on postwar quarterly data for the United States and has also concluded that the short rate is more appropriate. On the same data, though, M. Hamburger, utilising a distributed lag model, finds in favour of a long-term rate.[30] My own early effort on (British) quarterly data finds no appreciable difference between the two.[31] On a Chow-type 'short-run' function, however, the long-term interest rate (the yield on the Consol) comes through much more strongly; this is especially true for the demand for narrow money. The explanation there was in some ways similar to that already suggested here; that is, the short rate is frequently not a good proxy for the market rate because of the pressure of monetary policy, while the long rate is free to show the opportunity cost and speculative influences that lead to the expected negative interest elasticity. As noted, in addition, the influence of expectations is better revealed in the short-run than in the long-run context. In contrast, S. Goldfeld uses the short-run model on postwar US quarterly data and finds in favour of a short-term rate (although, to be sure, his long-term rate is not that on government bonds).[32] Finally, one might mention again the British study of L. Price, which finds in favour of a short rate for business firms and a long rate for individuals.[33]

The results thus far seem to depend on the type of model chosen (long- or short-run), on the data tested (quarterly or annual), and even on the country for which the model is tested (United States or United Kingdom). Other results also make it clear that, whether one uses broad or narrow money (for example), the results might well be different. No generalisation is likely to fit

all of the studies, but one notes a tendency for broader measures to yield
slightly higher elasticities with shorter-term interest rates; see, for example,
the British study by G. Haache,[34] which is also not so sanguine about the
stability of the British demand for money in recent years.

6.5 An alternative to the speculative hypothesis

Partly for the record, but also partly to help pave the way for the more
general models presented in Sections 6.6 and 6.7 below, we will attempt here
a brief survey of the development of the segmentation or hedging hypothesis
in the term structure literature. While from the beginning hedging had often
been mentioned, it had not had a formal place in much of the literature,
mostly because it seemed to suggest the operation of (non-rational) rules of
thumb; these, in turn, are clearly difficult to capture in an optimising framework. While, as we shall see, the dynamic consumption framework is possibly especially hospitable in this context, we will in this section discuss the
early literature on the segmentation view.

As it turns out, there are plenty of precursors in the institutional literature
on financial markets, but the first major recent paper on the subject seems to
be that of J. Culbertson,[35] who makes use of the concept of the 'holding
period' to present the hypothesis. We have glossed over this important concept in our earlier discussion, since it is more easily explained in the context
of the dynamic consumption (or portfolio) framework; but from this point it
is essential to be clear about the various theorems constructed concerning
the holding period and its yield. An easy rationalisation is as follows. An
individual saving unit (or its agent) would form a plan of its ideal consumption stream and lay out its assets accordingly. Given a distaste for risk
(and no risk premiums) and positive transactions costs, as well as perfect
certainty (whether accurate or not), the unit would tend to align the actual
maturity of its assets with the expected maturity of its obligations (or planned needs). If its needs were uncertain for some reason, and if the unit were
risk-averse, it might even tend to hold assets shorter in maturity than its
expected obligations, planning to fill in the intervening period with an asset
of shorter term (or no term) which earns a certain return less (by a liquidity
premium) than that which could have been obtained by the unit otherwise.
But the essential point is that a distinct preference for matching asset
maturities with 'holding periods' will emerge.

Returning to Culbertson, we note that that author actually framed the
expectations hypothesis in terms of holding periods. In particular, since,

> as developed by John R. Hicks and Friedrich A. Lutz, the theory
> argues that the interest rate on a long-term debt tends to equal the

average of short-term rates expected over the duration of the long-
term debt . . .[36]

then 'holding period yields will be equal' for the average holding periods
observed in the market. This, to be sure, is Deduction 1, attributed above to
Lutz. Referring to the segmentation hypothesis as belonging more to practi-
cal men, Culbertson argues that the rate structure can be altered by open-
market operations differentiated by term-to-maturity and that this influence
of 'relative quantities' is the dominant factor determining the structure, with
expectations important 'mainly as a factor determining very short-run
movements in long-term rates'.[37] Culbertson puts his faith in four major
(essentially empirical) propositions:[38]

1. that, with regard to the liquidity difference between short- and long-
   term debt, 'short-term debt is more liquid than long-term debt';
2. that, while expectations are a factor, 'The behavior of most borrowers
   and lenders is not ordinarily governed by such expectations';
3. that there are substantial changes in the maturity structure of the
   supply of debt and this fact, coupled with the fact that demand is
   somewhat slow to respond, implies considerable segmentation effects;
4. that the difference in lending rates related to debt maturity is complicated, for example, by the size of the operation and, for that matter,
   by the size of the operator, so that prediction is extremely hazardous.

When he comes to look at the evidence, however, Culbertson fails to find
effective tests of his propositions. In particular, with regard to expectations,
Culbertson argues that the planning period for active speculators is obviously very short for two reasons:

1. because one can form more precise expectations about events in the
   near future; and
2. quite adequate fluctuations (that is, quite adequate enough for sizable
   gains) for short periods are averaged out (normalised) over longer
   periods of time.

The second point can be buttressed by noting that, not only does the financial press appear to think in these terms, but the relatively high leverage
available to bond markets makes life quite exciting at the short end of the
curve (for short periods of time). On the other hand, ordinary investors will
not plan for quick gains, and their conservative behaviour (he says) will
dominate in the market. This empirical proposition is further strengthened
by some allegations about how institutions will behave.

> The maintenance of a relatively constant portfolio structure in-
> sures the institution that its earnings will not turn out disastrously
> lower (or embarrassingly larger) than those of competitors.[39]

Culbertson, it would seem, is also pessimistic about the application of profit-maximising models to the portfolio behaviour of institutions.

To test for speculation, we look to the data to see 'the nature of the opportunities for successful speculation which were not taken.'[40] In particular, we look at holding period yields to see if one could have profited, but didn't. The holding period yield is here 'defined as that annual rate of return at which the discounted value of interest payments and the sale price of the debt is equal to the initial price'. (This is the definition of a yield, actually.) It is the rate of return for the holding period times the number of such (discounting) periods in the year. Thus, if we have dominance by speculators (and, perforce, a known market holding period equal to the planning period), we should observe equal holding period yields; that is, we should observe that 'holding period yields on debts of all maturities should be equal for any and all holding periods'. They aren't.

The most important flaw in this argument is the failure to distinguish between the *ex post* and the *ex ante* holding period when one turns to the data. It is the latter, the planned holding period, to which the theory refers; it is the consistency of plans that is relevant rather than the consistency of the results of the plans, even assuming perfect certainty. Culbertson notes all this, but yet observes that

> Study of the behavior of actual holding-period yields permits the drawing of some important conclusions about speculation in debt markets, for it indicates in clear terms the nature of the opportunities for successful speculation which were not taken. It indicates the extent to which speculation of the market was imperfect, because speculative activity was insufficient in scope or incorrect in form and did not succeed in bringing to equality the rates of return earned on different debts.[41]

Any test of this proposition, though, because it involves the assumption that the observed holding period was the same as the planned holding period, is basically a test of the proposition that forecasting models must be accurate. Until we know (or assume) how speculators arrive at their opinions, we cannot accuse them of failing to achieve profits, *ex post*. *Ex ante*, they *must* have perceived profits, or they are lunatics.

A second important strand of literature on segmentation has developed in recent years, usually attached to empirical results. J. Michaelsen, for example, who found some support for segmentation (and for expectations), argued that it was important, in formulating a hypothesis, to distinguish between the fixed liquidation date (as in the Hicks–Lutz theory) and the planning horizon, which never arrives. With regard to the latter,

> It would appear that most portfolios, and especially those of large institutional holders, have indeterminate rather than fixed

liquidation dates, their maturity composition remaining roughly constant over time or changing in response to forces other than the passage of time.[42]

For this he prescribes the mean-variance model (to be discussed below). B. Malkiel refers to the alternative view of the term structure as the 'hedging pressure' or 'institutional' hypothesis. His study is basically of an institutional nature with a good deal of discussion of how actual markets work; he concludes that

> The bond market is not segmented in any absolute manner. Utilizing aggregate data and the results of extensive interviews, we found that most bond investors substituted broadly among securities over wide ranges of the yield curve in accordance with their expectations ... [yet] strong maturity preferences are present in both sides of the market. A valid version of the segmentation hypothesis, then, asserts simply that many buyers and sellers must be paid differentiated premiums to induce them to move from their preferred maturities.[43]

This, one can recall, was part of our reason for putting the (variable) liquidity premium term (r_s/r_L) in the Keynesian demand for money function; it is also a generalisation of the rationale for the Hicks liquidity premium.

A growing literature has also attempted to construct 'efficient market' type models for the segmentation problem.[44] This is not the place to summarise such models, but it is worth mentioning that some further support for the segmentation view has been obtained in this context. Since, in these studies, the segmentation effect mainly fills the gap in the data left by the failure of the expectations model to be completely 'efficient', some room exists for other sorts of institutional behaviour. There have also been other attempts to integrate the two theories, most notable of which is that of Modigliani and Sutch.[45] In J. McCallum's words,

> This is characterized by a multiple horizon market and a willingness on the part of investors to acquire non-horizon instruments within a range called a habitat. It is argued that the existence of habitats gives the market a continuity which is not present in the segmentation theory.[46]

As we noted, this integration was also part of the Malkiel framework. McCallum further notes that, while the habitat (or an equivalent) might reasonably be supposed to have been proved, the multiple horizon has not. His own effort – just cited – indicates 'a market with distinct short and long horizon participants'.[47] Instead of following this debate, however, we will turn to some exact results in the dynamic consumption and mean-variance models, with regard to many of the issues just raised.

6.6 The demand for money in the dynamic consumption–term structure context

The rest of this chapter summarises the work of J. Bernstein and D. Fisher.

In this section we will consider an intertemporal demand-for-money problem in which we integrate the demand for money and the most general term structure solutions in the literature.[48] Basically, we will be constructing a dynamic consumption model, which, as noted above, extends the work of J. Stiglitz and J. Green, in order to come to grips formally with the choice of interest rate problem in the demand for money. What is proposed, in particular, is to mould a joint product around the dynamic consumption plan of the individual to see what the implications are for the traditional theory of the demand for money, particularly with regard to the appropriate interest rate to be employed as the *cross* interest rate in the demand for money and, most importantly, under what conditions it will be so employed. As we have noted, there are not many specific results of a theoretical nature, with those of Keynes (*a priori*) and the Keynesians (for a variety of reasons) standing out, but for different interest rates.

In the work that follows there will be provided a generalisation of the dynamic consumption–term structure models which will enable us to incorporate money-holding as an additional alternative to the individual faced with the problem of maximising his expected utility over a three-period horizon. Dividing money-holding into first- (and second-)period balances – which can be termed *intermediate* balances (M_1 and M_2) – and third-period balances – *reservation* balances (M_3) – one can show that

1. the dominant interest rate for the demand for reservation balances is either the long or the short rate, depending on the relative proportion of long- or short-term assets in the individual's portfolio; and
2. the dominant interest rate for intermediate balances is a long-term rate in view of the fact that intermediate balances must be aggregated with short-term assets in order to obtain a solution to the problem.

This last result provides a theoretical explanation of the aggregation of Keynes as described by Leijonhufvud – and discussed in Chapter 2 above. Finally, we will note that there are some policy implications in this work, particularly with regard to the influence of open-market operations on the demand for money, as this effect is influenced by the shape of the yield curve and by the relative proportion of long- and short-term securities in private portfolios.

Let us begin with the definition of the problem in terms of three separate constraints for the three periods (including two future periods) we require to have a meaningful analysis. Thus, let equation (6.12) describe the first period constraint and equations (6.13) the second and third period constraint, respectively.

$$C_1 + B_{s1} + B_{L1} + M_1 = W_1 \tag{6.12}$$

$$\left. \begin{array}{l} C_2 + B_{s2} + M_2 = W_2 + (1 + r_{s1})(B_{s1} + M_1) \\ C_3 + M_3 = W_3 + (1 + r_{s2})(B_{s2} + M_2) + (1 + R_{L1})B_{L1}. \end{array} \right\} \tag{6.13}$$

As it turns out, the solutions below depend critically on this set-up of the problem, so particular attention should be paid to the form of these equations. We postulate two bonds, a long bond (B_L) and a short bond (B_s); with holdings of money and bonds defined at the beginning of each period (1, 2, 3) and all future prices normalised (at unity), the three constraints represent a choice framework in which the individual can hold money or short bonds through period 1 and then reinvest (a percentage of) the proceeds in second-period bonds (B_{s2}) or he can hold long-term bonds – or, of course, he can do both in some proportion. Thus, on funds the individual holds in M_1 and B_{s1}, he will earn a return of r_{s1}, paid at the beginning of period 2 (note that money (M_1 and M_2) pays interest but that this interest rate is equal to r_{s1} by arbitrage (not by assumption)). At that point he can hold M_2 or B_{s2}, both paying interest of r_{s2} which he collects at the beginning of period 3. M_3, then, represents his reservation balance at the end of the programme, i.e., at the beginning of period 3. The alternative route is to hold B_{L1}, in which case R_{L1} – a yield covering the two periods – is the appropriate return, again collected at the beginning of period 3.

We may collapse equations (6.13) into one constraint, eliminating ($M_2 + B_{s2}$) in the process to get a single constraint, as in equation (6.14):

$$C_2 + \frac{C_3}{(1 + r_{s2})} + \frac{M_3}{(1 + r_{s2})} = W_2 + \frac{W_3}{(1 + r_{s2})} + \frac{(1 + R_{L1})}{(1 + r_{s2})}B_{L1}$$

$$+ (1 + r_{s1})(B_{s1} + M_1). \tag{6.14}$$

In this context it can be shown that (6.12) and (6.14) are the appropriate constraints, whether the holding period is one period or two, the latter being the assumption behind equations (6.13). The holding period I have in mind is the planned holding of the long-term bond. One should note, again, that the dichotomy between ($B_{s1} + M_1$) and B_{L1} is identical to that in Keynes (as described by Leijonhufvud), who aggregates all short-term assets. Short bonds and money, that is to say, are perfect substitutes (whether we are referring to the first-period sum or the second). We will return to these matters from time to time.

6.6.1 Second- and third-period equilibrium

The procedure followed in the important paper by J. Stiglitz was to solve a problem for the optimal consumption stream (C_1^*, C_2^*, C_3^*) in a deterministic framework and then to find the maximum expected utility for the same programme by picking the portfolio (either B_{s1}^* or B_{L1}^*). As J. Green pointed out, though, Stiglitz's consumers, since they are not assumed to maximise expected utility with bonds and first-period consumption in the same problem, are not in general equilibrium. He proposes the same two-stage iterative procedure, in which second- and third-period consumption are solved for deterministically in the first stage and then the optimal portfolio and C_1^* are found in a second stage. In the latter the consumer maximises expected utility when the stochastic variable is the future short-term interest rate (r_{s2}). This, too, becomes a variable in the demand for money. We will follow Green's approach here, but will also include money, as we have already noted.

Turning, then, to the first stage of the two-stage procedure, let us maximise equation (6.15) subject to equation (6.14), the second- and third-period constraint; here money is entered as an argument in the utility function, as in our earlier discussion in Chapter 3:

$$U(C_2, C_3, M_3). \tag{6.15}$$

The first-order conditions, then, for this problem are given as equations (6.16), where, for example, $U_2 = (\partial U/\partial C_2)$.

$$U_2 - \lambda = 0$$

$$U_3 - \frac{\lambda}{(1 + r_{s2})} = 0 \qquad U_M - \frac{\lambda}{(1 + r_{s2})} = 0$$

$$-C_2 - \frac{C_3}{(1 + r_{s2})} - \frac{M_3}{(1 + r_{s2})} + W_2 + \frac{W_3}{(1 + r_{s2})} + (1 + r_{s1})(B_{s1} + M_1)$$

$$+ \frac{(1 + R_{L1})}{1 + r_{s2}} B_{L1} = 0. \tag{6.16}$$

Immediately, we note a property of money-holding, that $U_M = U_3$, in equilibrium.

To generate the effects of the various variables on the demand for money, we will need to differentiate the first-order conditions for each variable separately. In this case it is interesting to calculate the effect of a change in r_{s2}, since this is a new variable in the context of the demand for money. This result is given by equation (6.17):

$$U_{M2}\frac{\partial C_2}{\partial r_{s2}} + U_{M3}\frac{\partial C_3}{\partial r_{s2}} + U_{MM}\frac{\partial M_3}{\partial r_{s2}} - \frac{\partial \lambda}{\partial r_{s2}(1 + r_{s2})} + \frac{\lambda}{(1 + r_{s2})^2} = 0. \tag{6.17}$$

After some manipulation we can obtain

$$\frac{\partial M_3}{\partial r_{s2}} = \frac{\lambda}{(1 + r_{s2})} \frac{D_{13}}{D} + \frac{1}{(1 + r_{s2})} [W_2 - C_2 + (1 + r_{s1})(B_{s1} + M_1)]\frac{D_{43}}{D} \quad (6.18)$$

where

$$D = \begin{Bmatrix} U_{22} & U_{23} & U_{2M} & -1 \\ U_{32} & U_{33} & U_{3M} & \dfrac{-1}{(1 + r_{s2})} \\ U_{M2} & U_{M3} & U_{MM} & \dfrac{-1}{(1 + r_{s2})} \\ -1 & \dfrac{-1}{(1 + r_{s2})} & \dfrac{-1}{(1 + r_{s2})} & 0 \end{Bmatrix}$$

and D_{13} is the appropriate minor. Unfortunately, (6.18) is not readily sign-able in this context (we will, though, return to the forward rate with more success at several points in the remainder of this chapter).

Turning to our other variables, we are able to generate the following comparative-statics results, directly:

$$\frac{\partial M_3}{\partial r_{s1}} = (B_{s1} + M_1)\frac{D_{43}}{D} \qquad \frac{\partial M_3}{\partial R_{L1}} = \frac{B_{L1}}{(1 + r_{s2})} \frac{D_{43}}{D}$$

$$\frac{\partial M_3}{\partial B_{s1}} = \frac{\partial M_3}{\partial M_1} = (1 + r_{s1})\frac{D_{43}}{D} \qquad \frac{\partial M_3}{\partial B_{L1}} = \frac{(1 + R_{L1})}{(1 + r_{s2})} \frac{D_{43}}{D} \qquad (6.19)$$

$$\frac{\partial M_3}{\partial M_2} = \frac{D_{43}}{D} \qquad \frac{\partial M_3}{\partial W_3} = \frac{D_{43}}{D} \frac{1}{(1 + r_{s2})}.$$

These results for the demand for reservation balances, then, would have the usual signs (negative for interest rates and positive for quantities and wealth variables) if the usual 'dominant diagonal' restrictions (see below for application of the dominant diagonal on the mean-variance model). We may readily compare the relative importance of the two interest rates on the demand for money (reservation balances) by calculating the following expression:

$$\frac{\partial M_3/\partial R_{L1}}{\partial M_3/\partial r_{s1}} = \frac{B_{L1}}{(B_{s1} + M_1)(1 + r_{s2})} \gtrless 1. \qquad (6.20)$$

Thus, clearly, the partial effect of the long rate will dominate the partial effect of the short rate if the consumer holds more of his wealth in long bonds than in short bonds and money (the latter modified by the renegotiation of funds invested in short assets in the second period) – subject, of course, to the consumer being either long or short in all of the securities.[49] Thus, for example, if the consumer holds positive quantities of all securities including money in period 1, then his relative response to the long-term rate will depend on the relative weight of long-term securities in his portfolio. This result follows from the dominance of the wealth effect through the constraint equation. Empirically, then, the relative dominance of long rates over short rates – or vice versa – is seen to depend on the composition of the portfolio. Thus one can, in actual circumstances, predict which rate will dominate in demand for money studies. For example, since business portfolios are generally 'shorter' than consumer portfolios, the short-term rate should affect the business demand for money relatively more. This, indeed, was noted in Chapter 4, in the case of the study by L. Price.

We may also calculate a term comparing the relative effects of changes in B_{s1} and B_{L1} on the demand for money; this is given as equation (6.21):

$$\frac{\partial M_3/\partial B_{L1}}{\partial M_3/\partial B_{s1}} = \frac{(1 + R_{L1})}{(1 + r_{s2})(1 + r_{s1})} \gtreqless 1. \tag{6.21}$$

Here, if each of the interest rates is positive, as we would of course expect, then the relative effects of B_{s1} and B_{L1} are seen to depend on the relation between the long rate and the product of the short rates. If one argues that $(1 + R_{L1}) = (1 + r_{s2})(1 + r_{s1})$ – i.e., if long- and short-term securities are perfect substitutes – then, of course, there is no difference between the relative effects of B_{L1} and B_{s1} on the demand for money. Otherwise, this relative influence depends on the shape of the yield curve.

We can gain another perspective on the implications of this approach by comparing the elasticities of the quantities with those of the interest rates (we must, of course, compare elasticities) on the demand for money. Defining δ_{BL} as the elasticity of the long-term bond on the demand for money, δ_{BS} as the elasticity of the short-term bond, γ_{RL} as the elasticity of the long-term interest rate on the demand for money and γ_{RS} as the elasticity of the short-term rate, we have the following, taken from the results in equation (6.19):

$$\frac{\delta_{BL}}{\gamma_{RL}} = \frac{1 + R_{L1}}{R_{L1}} > 1$$

$$\frac{\partial_{BS}}{\gamma_{RS}} = \frac{1 + r_{s1}}{r_{s1}} > 1. \tag{6.22}$$

In both cases, then, in so far as the interest rates and the bond holdings are positive, the quantity effect dominates the interest rate effect on the demand for money; *ceteris paribus*, then, open-market operations will be more decisive than relying on interest rate effects if we wish to control money holding.[50] The reason for this is that the wealth effect (from B_{s1}, B_{L1}) works on the total accumulated values of B_{s1} and B_{L1} while the interest rate effect (from r_{s1}, R_{L1}) works only on the new holdings of, say, B_{s1} at the end of the period. Finally, we note that if the long rate is greater than the short rate, then the relative short-rate effect – under the assumed conditions – dominates the relative long-rate effect (and conversely). That is, the relative advantage of working in short-term securities (and the disadvantage of working in short rates) – if a desired money stock target is used – is sharpened if (and when) the yield curve is upsloping. This, it might be argued, provides a rationale for the 'bills only' policy.[51] Further, one should note that a government funding operation (switch of short for long securities), *ceteris paribus*, by increasing the relative proportion of long to short debt in private portfolios, will tend to make open market operations relatively more effective in long-term securities, in terms of their effects on the demand for money. One might also compare policies across countries, *ceteris paribus*, arguing that a relative preference for operations in short debt would logically be associated with a relatively short-term debt (e.g., Canada compared with Britain).

We note, finally, that the discussion to this point has provided us with deterministic results for the optimal values of C_2, C_3 and M_3. These functions appear as equations (6.23), which we will be using in the next section. Note that the demand for money has three interest rates, all expected to increase residual balances when they rise.

$$C_2^* = H_{C2}[r_{s1}, r_{s2}, R_{L1}, (B_{s1} + M_1), B_{L1}, W_2, W_3]$$
$$C_3^* = H_{C3}[r_{s1}, r_{s2}, R_{L1}, (B_{s1} + M_1), B_{L1}, W_2, W_3]$$
$$M_3^* = H_{M3}[r_{s1}, r_{s2}, R_{L1}, (B_{s1} + M_1), B_{L1}, W_2, W_3]. \qquad (6.23)$$

These functions contain no surprises, but there is one matter not yet disposed of, and that concerns the intermediate period and its money balance (M_2). As things stand, we cannot solve for the demand for M_2 but only for the sum of $M_2 + B_{s2}$; furthermore, this demand is a residual (given H_{c2}) whose value actually depends on the length of the holding period for long-term bonds. Thus, equation (6.24) describes the residual demand when long-term bonds are held for two periods:

$$(B_{s2} + M_2)^* = W_2 + (1 + r_{s1})(B_{s1} + M_1) - H_{C2} \qquad (6.24)$$

while equation (6.25) describes the situation when the holding period for the long bond is only one period:

$$(B_{s2} + M_2)^* = W_2 + (1 + r_{s1})(B_{s1} + M_1) + \frac{(1 + R_{L1})}{(1 + r_{s2})}B_{L1} - H_{C2}. \qquad (6.25)$$

The second expression is unambiguously larger than the first (for $B_{L1} > 0$). This can be explained as the result of the addition to liquidity which results from the liquidation of long-term bonds after one period. This, as it turns out, is the only time when the holding period matters in this analysis.

6.6.2 *First-period equilibrium*

We turn finally to the solution for the first-period equilibrium. This case, of course, brings in uncertainty (about r_{s2}, the one-period rate from the first to the second future period) and is the most general problem discussed in this context. Note, especially, that this solution is worked on a very general utility function. Assume, then, that the consumer maximises (6.26) subject to equations (6.23) and (6.12) – as previously stated – by picking values of C_1 and the portfolio variables $(M_1 + B_{s1})$ and B_{L1}:

$$E[U(C_1, C_2, C_3, M_3)]. \tag{6.26}$$

This is equivalent – by application of our constraint and by our previous results – to maximising the following expression by choosing the optimal portfolio – $(M_1 + B_{s1})^*$ and B_{L1}^*.

$$E[U(W_1 - B_{s1} - M_1 - B_{L1}, H_{C2}, H_{C3}, H_{M3})]. \tag{6.27}$$

Here we note the presence, again, of the demands already derived for the second- and third-period optimal values. The first-order conditions in this case are given by equations (6.28):

$$E\left(-U_1 + U_2\frac{\partial H_{C2}}{\partial S_1} + U_3\frac{\partial H_{C3}}{\partial S_1} + U_M\frac{\partial H_{M3}}{\partial S_1}\right) = 0$$

$$E\left(-U_1 + U_2\frac{\partial H_{C2}}{\partial B_{L1}} + U_3\frac{\partial H_{C3}}{\partial B_{L1}} + U_M\frac{\partial H_{M3}}{\partial B_{L1}}\right) = 0 \tag{6.28}$$

where $S_1 = M_1 + B_{s1}$.

We may combine equations (6.28) to produce the following expression:

$$E\left[U_2\frac{\partial H_{C2}}{\partial B_{L1}}\left(\frac{\partial H_{C2}/\partial S_1}{\partial H_{C2}/\partial B_{L1}} - 1\right)\right] + E\left[U_3\frac{\partial H_{C3}}{\partial B_{L1}}\left(\frac{\partial H_{C3}/\partial S_1}{\partial H_{C3}/\partial B_{L1}} - 1\right)\right]$$

$$+ E\left[U_M\frac{\partial H_{M3}}{\partial B_{L1}}\left(\frac{\partial H_{M3}/\partial S_1}{\partial H_{M3}/\partial B_{L1}} - 1\right)\right] = 0 \tag{6.29}$$

Reference to the results in equations (6.19) enables us to write equation (6.29) as equation (6.30), then:

$$E\left\{\left(U_2\frac{\partial H_{C2}}{\partial B_{L1}} + U_3\frac{\partial H_{C3}}{\partial B_{L1}} + U_M\frac{\partial H_{M3}}{\partial B_{L1}}\right)\left[\frac{(1 + r_{s1})(1 + r_{s2})}{(1 + R_{L1})} - 1\right]\right\} = 0. \tag{6.30}$$

Then, again employing equations (6.19) and noting the relationships in equation (6.16), we may write the first bracketed term as

$$\lambda\frac{(1+R_{L1})}{(1+r_{s2})}\frac{D_{41}}{D} - \lambda\frac{(1+R_{L1})}{(1+r_{s2})(1+r_{s2})}\frac{D_{42}}{D} + \lambda\frac{(1+R_{L1})}{(1+r_{s2})(1+r_{s2})}\frac{D_{43}}{D}.$$

Further simplifications yield $U_{C3}(1+R_{L1})$ as the value of this expression, whence equation (6.30) is equivalent to the important result that

$$E\{U_{C3}[(1+r_{s1})(1+r_{s2}) - (1+R_{L1})]\} = 0. \tag{6.31}$$

Thus, if U_{C3} is constant, or if the household is risk neutral, then

$$(1+r_{s1})E(1+r_{s2}) = (1+R_{L1})$$

i.e., at equilibrium, the long-term rate is equal to the product of the expected short-term rates. This is obtained without explicit reference to an 'expectations hypothesis'. The implication, clearly, is that in a general model of consumer behaviour the special assumptions of the expectations hypothesis are unnecessary to establish that long rates are affected by expectations of future short-term rates.

We may conclude, then, by emphasising that in the first period (as in the second) it is necessary to combine money and short-term assets in order to achieve a solution. Thus for the demand for intermediate balances (plus short-term securities) the dominant interest rate is a long-term rate. This is the result of the fact that money and bonds are perfect substitutes – a change in the short-term rate merely causing a one-for-one shift within the aggregate – while a change in the cross rate (R_{L1}) induces a net change in that (aggregate) demand. We have not, of course, aggregated in an *ad hoc* fashion, but rather the aggregation naturally arises out of the general description of the consumption–portfolio choice process. In this case, the demand for M_3 is still dominated either by the long rate or the short rate, and it is only the less interesting 'intermediate' balances that have to be so treated. Variations in r_{s1} affect the quantity of money held, of course, but by the logic of the model used, this is merely a compositional effect. This, it would seem, provides the micro-foundations for the aggregation in monetary economics, which is consistent with the aggregation of Keynes. Finally, note that the expected sign for the short rate is positive (as an own rate) and for the long rate is negative (as a cross rate) on the demand for money.

6.7 Portfolio results for a term structure with money in it [52]

Again emphasising results obtained by J. Bernstein and D. Fisher [52], we may generate comparable results for the demand for money in a term structure context using mean-variance instead of dynamic consumption analysis. In this case the fundamental paper is that of G. Bierwag and M. Grove, although these authors did not include money in the problem.[53] As before, we need a three-period framework, and as before we will consider M_1, M_2 and M_3, where the last named will again appear in the utility function of the individual. To begin with, though, let us solve a problem without money in it, and derive the relevant results; we can later tack on money, provided the results established for the simpler case carry through (as they do) to the more complicated case.

6.7.1 A mean-variance term structure problem without money

Let us assume a single investor – with a fixed consumption plan – who has to allocate his fixed initial savings (S_1) between two securities, a long one (B_L) and a short one (B_s). In addition, let us assume that the wealth-holder has a horizon covering three periods in all (we are considering beginning of period wealth in each case) and can choose to hold the long-term security for one period or for two. Finally, we will incorporate this profile of a wealth-holder into the mean-variance model and assume that he maximises the expected utility of the first two moments of his projected income stream. As above, our first task is the construction of expressions for the mean and the variance – before we turn to the optimising problem and the results of comparative-statics experiments.

For our investor, the budget constraint for the first period is

$$B_{s1} + B_{L1} = \bar{S}_1 \tag{6.32}$$

where B_{s1} could, somewhat trivially, include money balances (paying an explicit interest rate equal, by arbitrage, to that on short-term bonds). Where we go from here depends on whether or not the wealth-holder has a two- or a one-period holding period. If he has the former (i.e., if he does not cash in whatever long-term bonds he holds until the third period), then his two additional constraints are given by equations (6.33):

$$B_{s2} = S_2 = B_{s1}(1 + r_{s1})$$
$$S_3 = B_{L1}(1 + R_{L1}) + B_{s2}(1 + r_{s2}) \tag{6.33}$$

where r_{s1} is the interest rate on a one-period (short-term) asset in the first period, r_{s2} is the one-period interest rate running over the second period, and R_{L1} is the interest rate (or, approximately, the yield) on the long-term asset (which, as noted, is assumed to be held until maturity, in this case). Defining $b_{s1} = B_{s1}/\bar{S}_1$ and $b_{L1} = B_{L1}/\bar{S}_1$, we can collapse (for fixed $\bar{S}_1$ defining initial wealth) the three constraints in the problem to equation (6.34):

$$S_3 = \bar{S}_1 \left[(1 - b_{s1})(1 + R_{L1}) + b_{s1}(1 + r_{s2})(1 + r_{s1}) \right]. \tag{6.34}$$

This expression, as it turns out, is also the appropriate constraint for a one-period holding period, so there is no difference in the results on account of a different perception of the holding period.

For the first of the two future periods the rate of return on the portfolio $(1 + R_{p1})$ is merely the ratio of S_2 to S_1 – a measure of the rate of growth of the portfolio; this, then, provides us with equation (6.35).

$$(1 + R_{p1}) = b_{s1}(1 + r_{s1}).\tag{6.35}$$

Similarly, for the second future period, we can compare the growth in wealth from the beginning of period 2 to the beginning of period 3:

$$(1 + R_{p2}) = \frac{S_3}{S_2} = \frac{b_{L1}(1 + R_{L1})}{b_{s1}(1 + r_{s1})} + (1 + r_{s2}).\tag{6.36}$$

Then, the yield for the entire portfolio $(1 + R_p)$ is given as the product of (6.35) and (6.36):

$$(1 + R_p) = (1 - b_{s1})(1 + R_{L1}) + b_{s1}(1 + r_{s1})(1 + r_{s2})\tag{6.37}$$

from which one can derive the following expression, clearly:

$$R_p = b_{s1}[(1 + r_{s1})(1 + r_{s2}) - (1 + R_{L1})] + R_{L1}.\tag{6.38}$$

The reader will note here the presence of an expression relating the long-term rate to the product of two short-term rates. Thus, if the long rate is equal to the product of the short rates, in which case long and short securities are perfect substitutes, then the rate of return on the portfolio (R_p) is equal to R_{L1}, whether long or short securities are held and without regard to holding period lengths. Such a strong condition, to be found for example in the work of Hicks,[54] is extremely unrealistic and precludes any effective analysis of the term structure problem or, as we shall see, of the demand-for-money problem. Finally, the expected value of the portfolio is given by equation (6.39):

$$E(R_p) = b_{s1}[(1 + r_{s1})(1 + E(r_{s2})) - (1 + R_{L1})] + R_{L1}.\tag{6.39}$$

Turning to the variance, since r_{s2} is the only stochastic variable, we can write

$$V(R_p) = \sigma^2(R_p) = E[b_{s1}(1 + r_{s1})(r_{s2} - E(r_{s2}))]^2 = \sigma^2 b^2_{s1}(1 + r_{s1})^2\tag{6.40}$$

where $\sigma^2 = E[r_{s2} - E(r_{s2})]^2 = V(r_{s2})$. This is a standard result, as above.

Our next step, then, is to assume a general utility function for our investor; this is given as equation (6.41), where $\partial \mathcal{U}/\partial E = \mathcal{U}_E > 0$:

$$u = \mathcal{U}[E(R_p), V(R_p)].\tag{6.41}$$

This function is maximised by choosing b_{s1}, the percentage of the investor's initial wealth in short-term securities; we will also assume that $\mathcal{U}$ is strictly concave in E and V and is homogeneous of degree $1 - \beta$ in the same arguments, with $\beta > 0$. We have defined the arguments of this function in equations (6.38) and (6.39); these, along with the implied assumption that the only stochastic variable in the problem, r_{s2}, is normally distributed, enables us to write the first-order condition as equation (6.42) and the second-order condition as (6.43), both in a separable form; note, especially, that

$$T = \{(1 + r_{s1})[1 + E(r_{s2})] - (1 + R_{L1})\}$$
$$S = [2\sigma^2 b_{s1}(1 + r_{s1})^2]$$

during the rest of this discussion.

$$\frac{\partial \mathscr{U}}{\partial b_{s1}} = \mathscr{U}_E T + \mathscr{U}_V S = 0 \qquad (6.42)$$

$$\frac{\partial \mathscr{U}}{\partial b_{s1}^2} = \mathscr{U}_{EE}T^2 + \mathscr{U}_{EV}TS + \mathscr{U}_{VE}ST + \mathscr{U}_{VV}S^2 + \mathscr{U}_V 2\sigma^2(1 + r_{s1})^2 < 0. \quad (6.43)$$

Turning, then, to our first-order condition, we seek firstly to establish some generalisations about the value of b_{s1}, the sole decision variable. It is clear from the forms of equations (6.42) and (6.43) that we must consider the portfolio problem here in three separate cases, depending on the relation between long rates and the product of expected short rates. Thus, if $T = 0$, then inspection of equation (6.42) tells us that either $\mathscr{U}_V = 0$ or $b_{s1} = 0$; $\mathscr{U}_V = 0$, of course, is an implication of the assumption of risk neutrality. This case is not particularly interesting, though.

Further, if $T > 0$, then the sign of $\mathscr{U}_V$ is equal to the negative of b_{s1}; if the inequality is reversed, the sign of $\mathscr{U}_V$ is the same as the sign of b_{s1}. Thus, if the product of the expected short rates is greater than the long-term rate – so that the first term in equation (6.42) is positive – then inspection of the first-order condition reveals, for example, that the wealth-holder will stay at his optimum by increasing his holdings of short-term bonds as the expected disutility from risk decreases (*ceteris paribus*). Conversely, if the product of the short rates is less than the long rate, then the wealth-holder will remain at the optimum by decreasing his holdings of short bonds as his expected marginal disutility from risk grows. Put another way, under alternative assumptions about $\mathscr{U}_V$, then Table 6.1 describes the wealth-holder's reactions at the optimum. Thus, as claimed, there are a number of cases, and an

Table 6.1 Short Bond Holdings under Alternative Specifications about the Term Structure and the Expected Marginal Utility of Risk.

	$\mathscr{U}_V = 0$	$\mathscr{U}_V > 0$	$\mathscr{U}_V < 0$
$T = 0$	unknown	$b_{s1} = 0$	$b_{s1} = 0$
$T > 0$	unknown	$b_{s1} < 0$	$b_{s1} > 0$
$T < 0$	unknown	$b_{s1} > 0$	$b_{s1} < 0$

interesting answer cannot be obtained only in the case in which the household displays no marginal interest in risk, in column (1). These are general results, not provided by Bierwag and Grove.

6.7.2   *The effect of a change in the long-term rate on the optimal portfolio*

To obtain results for the effect on the optimal portfolio of changes in the long-term rate, we differentiate equation (6.42). This directly produces equation (6.44):

$$\mathcal{U}_{EE}T\left(\frac{\partial b_{s1}}{\partial R_{L1}}T - b_{s1} + 1\right) + \mathcal{U}_{EV}TS\frac{\partial b_{s1}}{\partial R_{L1}} - \mathcal{U}_E + \mathcal{U}_{VE}S\left(\frac{\partial b_{s1}}{\partial R_{L1}}T - b_{s1} + 1\right)$$

$$+ \mathcal{U}_{VV}S^2\frac{\partial b_{s1}}{\partial R_{L1}} + \mathcal{U}_V 2\sigma^2(1 + r_{s1})^2\frac{\partial b_{s1}}{\partial R_{L1}} = 0. \quad (6.44)$$

This expression contains the second-order conditions (denoted here by A) given as equation (6.43) and thus may be rewritten as equation (6.45).

$$A\frac{\partial b_{s1}}{\partial R_{L1}} + \mathcal{U}_{EE}T(1 - b_{s1}) - \mathcal{U}_E + \mathcal{U}_{VE}S(1 - b_{s1}) = 0. \quad (6.45)$$

A, by assumption, is negative, and we can reorganise further the expression as equation (6.46), making use of the fact that

$$\mathcal{U}_{VE}S = \mathcal{U}_{VE}\left(\frac{\mathcal{U}_E}{\mathcal{U}_V}\right)T$$

from equation (6.42).

$$\frac{\partial b_{s1}^*}{\partial R_{L1}} = \left[\mathcal{U}_E - \left(\frac{\mathcal{U}_{EE}}{\mathcal{U}_E} - \frac{\mathcal{U}_{VE}}{\mathcal{U}_V}\right)\mathcal{U}_E T(1 - b_{s1})\right]\frac{1}{A}. \quad (6.46)$$

We have, consequently, established a general equation for the effect on the portfolio (i.e., on b_{s1}) of changes in the long-term rate. In this result we see that the conclusions depend on assumptions about the signs of (1) T, (2) $1 - b_{s1}$, and (3) $(\mathcal{U}_{EE}/\mathcal{U}_E) - (\mathcal{U}_{VE}/\mathcal{U}_V)$. With regard to the latter, 'dominant diagonal' assumptions on the utility function, described above, imply that

$$\frac{\mathcal{U}_{EE}}{\mathcal{U}_E} = \frac{\mathcal{U}_{VE}}{\mathcal{U}_V} = \begin{cases} <0 \text{ if } \mathcal{U}_V > 0 \\ >0 \text{ if } \mathcal{U}_V < 0 \end{cases} \quad (6.47)$$

That is, the value of this expression depends on the marginal utility of expected risk ($\mathcal{U}_V$).

A simple result obtains if $T = 0$, for in this case the effect of R_{L1} on b_{s1}^* is directly negative. Furthermore, in this case, the result holds whether the wealth-holder gets pleasure from risk ($\mathcal{U}_V > 0$) or is 'short' in either security.

The results for some more interesting cases are derived in Table 6.2 Thus, for $T > 0$, for example, we can establish that, if $b_{s1} > 1$ – when the wealth-holder is short in long-term securities – then Table 6.1 implies that $\mathcal{U}_V < 0$ and this, further, implies that $[(\mathcal{U}_{EE}/\mathcal{U}_E) - (\mathcal{U}_{VE}/\mathcal{U}_V)] > 0$. This establishes

Table 6.2 **Effect of a Change in the Long-Term Rate on Optimal Holdings of Short-Term Assets under Various Assumptions.**

	Position of wealth-holder			
	$b_{s1} > 1$	$b_{s1} = 1$	$0 < b_{s1} < 1$	$b_{s1} < 0$
$T > 0$	$\dfrac{\partial b_{s1}}{\partial R_{L1}} < \dfrac{\mathcal{U}_E}{A}$	$\dfrac{\partial b_{s1}}{\partial R_{L1}} = \dfrac{\mathcal{U}_E}{A}$	$\dfrac{\partial b_{s1}}{\partial R_{L1}} > \dfrac{\mathcal{U}_E}{A}$	$\dfrac{\partial b_{s1}}{\partial R_{L1}} < \dfrac{\mathcal{U}_E}{A}$
(sign)	(–)	(–)	(?)	(–)
$T < 0$	$\dfrac{\partial b_{s1}}{\partial R_{L1}} < \dfrac{\mathcal{U}_E}{A}$	$\dfrac{\partial b_{s1}}{\partial R_{L1}} = \dfrac{\mathcal{U}_E}{A}$	$\dfrac{\partial b_{s1}}{\partial R_{L1}} > \dfrac{\mathcal{U}_E}{A}$	$\dfrac{\partial b_{s1}}{\partial R_{L1}} < \dfrac{\mathcal{U}_E}{A}$
(sign)	(–)	(–)	(?)	(–)

that in this case a rise in the long-term rate will reduce the percentage of wealth the investor holds in short-term securities. Utilising the same approach, we can then show that, if the investor is short in long-term securities (column 1), holds no long-term securities (column 2) or is short in short-term securities (column 4), the expected effect of a rise in the long rate is a fall in the demand for short-term securities. Only in the case in which the investor has both longs and shorts in his portfolio (the normal case) is the effect ambiguous. These results hold regardless of our assumption about the relation between the long rate and the product of expected short rates. The mean-variance model, therefore, is shown to be rich in empirical implications for the individual case, although it turns out to be impossible to generalise in the one case in which an aggregate would be most satisfactory – the case in which both long-term and short-term securities are held. It is, of course, generally argued that a rise in long-term rates will lead to a shift towards a longer portfolio; this, we see, is not a completely general result, though, and it also establishes some ambiguity about the effect of the long-term rate on the demand for intermediate money balances.

6.7.3 *Other results*

With regard to the short-term interest rate, somewhat surprisingly, we are only able to establish a few signs for our portfolio problem, even with the homogeneity property of our utility function. This result is given as equation (6.48):

$$\frac{\partial b_{s1}}{\partial r_{s1}} = \left\{ - \mathcal{U}_E[1 + E(r_{s2})] - \mathcal{U}_V 4\sigma^2 b_{s1}(1 + r_{s1}) - \left(\frac{\mathcal{U}_{EE}}{\mathcal{U}_E} - \frac{\mathcal{U}_{VE}}{\mathcal{U}_V} \right) \mathcal{U}_E T \right.$$

$$\left. [1 + E(r_{s2})] - \left(\frac{\mathcal{U}_{VE}}{\mathcal{U}_E} - \frac{\mathcal{U}_{VV}}{\mathcal{U}_V} \right) \mathcal{U}_E T \sigma^2 b_{s1}^2 2(1 + r_{s1}) \right\} \frac{1}{A}. \quad (6.48)$$

The only case we can sign is the case when the product of the expected short rates is equal to the long-term rate ($T = 0$); in this case a rise in the short rate will increase the demand for short assets (and, presumably, interest-bearing money). Furthermore, and somewhat unexpectedly, a rise in the entire yield structure of an equal amount at both ends will not be neutral in its impact in this case. That is,

$$\frac{\partial b_{s1}}{\partial r_{s1}} + \frac{\partial b_{s1}}{\partial R_{L1}} = - \frac{\mathcal{U}_E}{A}[1 + E(r_{s2})] + \frac{\mathcal{U}_E}{A} = - \frac{1}{A}[\mathcal{U}_E E(r_{s2})] > 0 \quad (6.49)$$

recalling that $\partial b_{s1}/\partial R_{L1} < 0$ in this case. That is, a neutral shift in the yield curve, when $\mathcal{U}_V = 0$ or $b_{s1} = 0$ and the long-term rate is equal to the product of the expected short rates, produces a net rise in the holding of short-term securities. This arises because of the presence of $E(r_{s2})$ in equation (6.49); this term reflects the expectation for the stochastic variable, r_{s2}, and suggests that the wealth-holder's uncertainty about future one-period interest rates will induce net holdings of the more liquid asset in the event that all rates rise equally. That is, since his earnings rise unambiguously, he takes the opportunity to reduce his risk. But we are unable to establish any other signs.

There is an additional variable in this problem, $E(r_{s2})$, which will also have an effect on the optimal portfolio. The result here is given as equation (6.50):

$$\frac{\partial b_{s1}}{\partial E(r_{s2})} = \frac{1}{A} \left[- \mathcal{U}_E(1 + r_{s1}) - \left(\frac{\mathcal{U}_{EE}}{\mathcal{U}_E} - \frac{\mathcal{U}_{VE}}{\mathcal{U}_V} \right) \mathcal{U}_E T b_{s1}(1 + r_{s1}) \right]. \quad (6.50)$$

What one expects, clearly, is that a revision of one's expectations of the one-period rate to rule one period hence, *given* short and long rates, would unambiguously induce the investor to get into position to take advantage of his insight, whatever his portfolio position to begin with. This he would do by shifting from long-term to short-term securities if he revised his expectation upward. Indeed, reference to Table 6.1 establishes quite easily that this result obtains: in all cases the demand for short-term bonds responds positively to changes in expectations of future short-term rates.

6.7.4 *The optimal portfolio including money-holding*

Actually, we have already obtained some solutions for the demand-for-money problem in the preceding discussion. In particular, if we accept the aggregation of Keynes, as described by Leijonhufvud, in the case in which money held in either of the first two periods pays interest (defined to be r_{M1} and r_{M2}), then whatever we have said about the demand for short-term bonds for these two periods applies, as well, to the demand for money. These results are as follows.

1. The effect of a rise in the long-term rate is generally negative on the demand for money (plus short bonds) except in the important case in which both long- and short-term assets are held.
2. The effect of a rise in the expected short-term rate is unambiguously positive on the demand for money (plus short bonds). This is a new result and, indeed, could be tested.
3. The effect of a rise in the short-term rate is ambiguous in general on the demand for money (plus short bonds), but if it has any effect it will be a positive one as an 'own' rate.

But money has not been explicitly entered into the analysis, and no third period – or reservation – balances (M_3) have been discussed; we turn to a statement of the problem with money in it, although we will avoid generating further explicit results, except where necessary.

Firstly, let us define the individual's constraints for the three-period problem, as in equations (6.51), (6.52) and (6.53).

$$B_{s1} + M_1 + B_{L1} = \bar{S}_1 \tag{6.51}$$
$$B_{s2} + M_2 = (B_{s1} + M_1)(1 + r_{s1}) = S_2 \tag{6.52}$$
$$M_3 = (B_{s2} + M_2)(1 + r_{s2}) + B_{L1}(1 + R_{L1}) = S_3. \tag{6.53}$$

This, then, assumes a two-period holding period for the long-term bond. Note that the individual is presumed to begin with an initial wealth ($\bar{S}_1$), which he allocates to his three assets; that this wealth is augmented in period 2 by the interest earnings on bonds and money; and, finally, that this wealth is again augmented in period 3 by further interest earnings on the short-term assets (via $(1 + r_{s2})$) and by interest earnings on the long-term bond. Note, as well, that all of his final wealth is held in the form of money.

We may collapse equations (6.52) and (6.53) into a single constraint – and eliminate $(B_{s2} + M_2)$ – in which case our constraints are as follows ($b_{s1} = B_{s1}/S_1$, etc.):

$$b_{s1} + m_1 + b_{L1} = 1 \tag{6.54}$$
$$m_3 = (b_{s1} + m_1)[(1 + r_{s1})(1 + r_{s2}) - (1 + R_{L1})] + (1 + R_{L1}). \tag{6.55}$$

Firstly, we need the rate of return on the portfolio; since $(1 + R_{p1}) = S_2/S_1$ and $(1 + R_{p2}) = S_3/S_2$, we can obtain, directly,

$$R_p = (1 + R_{p1})(1 + R_{p2}) - 1 = (b_{s1} + m_1)[(1 + r_{s1})(1 + r_{s2}) - (1 + R_{L1})]$$
$$+ R_{L1} = M_3. \tag{6.56}$$

The variance, then, is given by equation (6.57); we assume, as well, that $E(r_{s2})$ is expected to be normally distributed:

$$V(R_p) = \sigma^2(R_p) = (b_{s1} + m_1)^2(1 + r_{s1})^2 E[r_{s2} - E(r_{s2})]^2$$
$$= \sigma^2(b_{s1} + m_1)^2(1 + r_{s1})^2. \tag{6.57}$$

Finally, define $G_1 = (b_{s1} + m_1)$, etc., for convenience, since we will be forced, as in the dynamic consumption framework, to analyse only the aggregation of short holdings.

Let us assume, for the stochastic part of the problem, that the consumer maximises his expected utility as defined in equation (6.58); here $m_3 = M_3/S_1$ is entered directly into the utility function and represents money-holding uniquely for fixed S_1 and $\mathcal{U}_E^* = E(\mathcal{U}_E)$, for example:

$$u = E\{\mathcal{U}[E(R_p), V(R_p), m_3]\} \qquad \mathcal{U}_E^* > 0, \mathcal{U}_V^* < 0, \mathcal{U}_M^* > 0. \tag{6.58}$$

The choice variables in our case are G_1 and m_3, but by application of the constraint equation for m_3 (equation 6.55) and by the definition of the mean and the variance, we may reduce the problem to that of maximising the following expression in G_1, σ^2, T and R_{L1}, where the last three are parameters:

$$\underset{\{G_1\}}{\text{Max } E}\left[\mathcal{U}\bigg(G_1\{(1 + r_{s1})[1 + E(r_{s2})] - (1 + R_{L1})\}\right.$$

$$\left. + R_{L1}, \sigma^2 G_1^2(1 + r_{s1})^2, G_1[(1 + r_{s1})(1 + r_{s2}) - (1 + R_{L1})] + (1 + R_{L1})\bigg)\right]. \tag{6.59}$$

We may obtain the first- order condition for this function directly as given by equation (6.60):

$$\frac{\partial \mathcal{U}^*}{\partial G_1} = \mathcal{U}_E^* T + \mathcal{U}_V^* S' + \mathcal{U}_M^*[(1 + r_{s1})(1 + r_{s2}) - (1 + R_{L1})] = 0. \tag{6.60}$$

Here T is as defined above, $S' = 2\sigma^2 G_1(1 + r_{s1})^2$ and $\mathcal{U}_E^* = E\mathcal{U}_E$; the additional element in this condition comes, of course, from third-period money holdings, which are assumed to impart utility, directly. Looking first at $\mathcal{U}_M^* = E\mathcal{U}_M$, we note that

$$E\mathcal{U}_M^*[(1 + r_{s1})(1 + r_{s2}) - (1 + R_{L1})] = E\mathcal{U}_M^* E[(1 + r_{s1})(1 + r_{s2})$$
$$- (1 + R_{L1})].$$

Since $\mathcal{U}_M^*$ and the term in square brackets are both stochastic and, by assumption, are distributed independently, we may carry the expectations operator inside the term in square brackets. When we do that, we obtain T, as defined above; this, in turn, enables us to write our first-order condition as equation (6.61):

$$\frac{\partial \mathcal{U}^*}{\partial G_1} = (\mathcal{U}_E^* + \mathcal{U}_M^*)T + \mathcal{U}_V^* S' = 0. \tag{6.61}$$

Note, about this result, that although m_3 is *finally* picked in a climate of certainty – when the wealth-holder arrives at the beginning of the third period – we are looking at his portfolio choices at the beginning of the first period. Thus, while from the point of view of third-period holdings of m_3 a non-stochastic formulation is evident, when the choice problem is that of picking first-period balances (G_1), plans for final wealth-holding (m_3) must reflect everything in the portfolio problem – rates of return, the variance, the stochastic expectation and most certainly, the utility from holding m_3. Even so, our demand for m_3 is derived after we obtain G_1^*.

As before, we could establish certain properties of our system, primarily for use in comparative-static experiments; but, since we will not solve these problems here, we will just look at the properties of the first-order condition. Of most interest, perhaps, are the measures of risk aversion (following Bierwag and Grove) and liquidity preference that one could derive here. The former is defined (by Bierwag and Grove) to be

$$\rho = -\frac{1}{2}\frac{\mathcal{U}_E^*}{\mathcal{U}_V^*}$$

which, when positive, indicates risk aversion ($\mathcal{U}_V^* > 0$). The latter is

$$\xi = -\frac{1}{2}\frac{\mathcal{U}_M^*}{\mathcal{U}_V^*}$$

and, when positive ($\mathcal{U}_V^* < 0$), indicates liquidity preference. This analysis, which as equation (6.62) indicates contains both measures, consequently separates risk aversion from liquidity preference in a manner not generally done in the literature. Indeed, as equation (6.62) also makes clear, both parameters reflect optimal portfolio choice:

$$G_1^* = (\rho + \xi)\frac{[(1 + r_{s1})(1 + E(r_{s2})) - (1 + R_{L1})]}{\sigma^2(1 + r_{s1})^2}$$

$$= (\rho + \xi)\frac{T}{\sigma^2(1 + r_{s1})^2}. \tag{6.62}$$

This is a considerable advantage gained by generalising to a term structure problem with money-holding; note that they affect optimal portfolios and therefore optimal money-holding in exactly the same way, although not with the same magnitude.

The demand for money in this problem, thus, is explicit in the analysis in three different ways:

1. G_1^* contains the aggregation of b_{s1}^* and m_1^*;
2. m_2^* is contained in the aggregation of $G_2^* (= b_{s2} + m_2)$, and is calculated from equation (6.52), as a residual;

188   *Monetary Theory and the Demand for Money*

3. we can calculate m_3^* from equation (6.55) directly as

$$m_3^* = G_1^*[(1 + r_{s1})(1 + r_{s2}) - (1 + R_{L1})] + (1 + R_{L1}). \qquad (6.63)$$

This is not, as it may seem, a trivial result, since the process of obtaining G_1^* involves m_3, as equation (6.62) makes clear.

We will not generate the comparative statics here, but we can report the following. Exactly the same results hold for the parameters R_{L1}, r_{1s} and $E(r_{s2})$ as before, with regard to the optimal value of G_{s1}. These are therefore properties of the demand for intermediate balances. With regard to the demand for final balances (m_3^*), we need merely insert G_1^* into equation (6.63). Thus, when the negative effect of R_{L1} on G_{s1}^* goes through – as it does in all but the cases when both securities are held in the portfolio – then, if the actual term structure is upsloping, so that the term in square brackets in equation (6.63) is negative, then, if the long-term rate rises, G_1^* will decline, and m_3^*, consequently, will increase. In the case when the yield curve is flat, $m_3^* = (1 + R_{L1})$ and again shows a positive influence, while in the case when the yield curve is downsloping (as, for example, at cyclical peaks), the traditional negative relation between money-holding and the long-term interest rate can be observed. This provides us with a theoretical reason for including a term like r_s/r_L in a demand for money function (as we reported above) if we wish to correctly capture the influence of the long-term rate. It also provides us with an explanation – if we think in the mean-variance framework – of why one might in particular cases obtain a weak result from the long-term rate on the demand for money – the yield curve might have changed its shape over the data period (as it frequently does).

We may argue the same way for r_{s1}, which produces an ambiguous effect on G_1^* and hence on m_3^*. Furthermore, as above, a neutral change in the term structure (when it is flat) produces a net increase in G_1^* and, consequently, affects m_3^*, subject to our reservations about the shape of the yield curve. Furthermore, as before, if $E(r_{s2})$ rises – that is, when the individual investor revises upward his forecast of the one-year rate one period hence – he will get into a position to profit from his insight by increasing his equilibrium holdings of short-term securities and money. He will do this because the alternative – holding a long-term bond until maturity – means he would bypass the renegotiated contract at the end of the first year (he must hold it two periods). With regard to his residual balances, m_3^*, however, it turns out that whether or not these will be increased depends on the shape of the yield curve. If the yield curve is downsloping, then equation (6.63) tells us that a shift from low-paying long-term bonds to short-term bonds will increase the overall return on the portfolio and m_3^* will increase (and vice versa). These might seem to be mechanical results, of course, but, as before, they require that we establish G_1^* as well as the shape of the actual yield curve. They depend, in a way, on the accuracy of expectations.

In this section, then, some new results for the demand for money were obtained. Most importantly, perhaps, the framing of the problem of the demand for money in a term structure context allowed us directly to model the influence of interest rate expectations on the demand for money. This is certainly a new result in the literature, and it is a definite result, given the shape of the yield curve. In addition, we can observe from equations (6.62) and (6.63) that changes in liquidity preference and risk preference also affect the situation, depending on the value of T, when we are discussing m_1, and on the shape of the actual yield curve when we are discussing m_3. We might, on net, make the prediction that the long-term rate will work better than the short-term rate on the demand for money (however formulated), so long as the restrictions implicit in the model are retained. Most importantly, one must identify the shape of the actual yield curve. This, then, suggests a factor that might impart some cyclical instability to the demand for money – and a factor that could be measured. Finally, and most importantly, the last two sections have produced arguments that three interest rates belong in the demand for money – a short or 'own' rate, an expected rate, and a long rate – and that the first two are expected to have a *positive* influence on intermediate money balances.

Footnotes

1. I. Fisher, *The Theory of Interest*; J. R. Hicks, *Value and Capital*; J. M. Keynes, *The General Theory*.
2. J. Stiglitz, 'A Consumption-Oriented Theory of the Demand for Financial Assets and the Term Structure of Interest Rates'; and J. Green, 'A Simple General Equilibrium Model of the Term Structure of Interest Rates'.
3. I have borrowed heavily from my paper, 'The Term Structure of Interest Rates' in Sections 6.2 and 6.4 of this chapter.
4. J. R. Hicks, *Value and Capital*, pp. 165–6.
5. ibid., p. 141.
6. ibid., p. 145.
7. ibid., p. 142.
8. ibid., pp. 146–7.
9. ibid., p. 147.
10. See, for example, comments in L. Wehrle, 'Life Insurance Investment: The Experience of Four Companies', and J. Conard, *The Behavior of Interest Rates*.
11. See C. Nelson, *The Term Structure of Interest Rates*, and J. McCulloch, 'An Estimate of the Liquidity Premium'.
12. It is worth pointing out that, while the calculation of the yield in equation (6.1) utilises only one security (in theory), that of the forward rate in equation (6.4) involves more than one. Thus, forward rates may differ systematically because the bonds concerned differ in coupon, face value, number of interest payments per year and, even, issue price. These problems have produced a literature: D. Fisher, 'The Structure of Interest Rates: A Comment'; B. Malkiel, *The Term Structure of Interest Rates*; A. Buse, 'Expectations, Prices, Coupons, and Yields'; J. McCulloch, 'Measuring the Term Structure of Interest Rates'; J. McCulloch, 'The Tax-Adjusted Yield Curve'; and R. Masera, *The Term Structure of Interest Rates*.
13. F. A. Lutz, 'The Structure of Interest Rates'.
14. J. Conard, *An Introduction to the Theory of Interest*, p. 354.
15. D. Meiselman, *The Term Structure of Interest Rates*.

16. P. Cagan, 'The Monetary Dynamics of Hyperinflation', and M. Friedman, *A Theory of the Consumption Function.*

17. D. Meiselman, *The Term Structure of Interest Rates*; D. Fisher, 'Expectations, the Term Structure of Interest Rates and Recent British Experience'. But see, for the British case, J. Grant, 'Meiselman on the Structure of Interest Rates', A. Buse, 'The Structure of Interest Rates and Recent British Experience: A Comment'; and the survey in J. Dodds and J. Ford, *Expectations, Uncertainty and the Term Structure of Interest Rates.*

18. These problems are discussed in the references in footnote 17 as well as by B. Malkiel, *The Term Structure of Interest Rates*; the earlier literature on the subject is described in D. Meiselman, *The Term Structure of Interest Rates*; R. Kessel, *The Cyclical Behavior of the Term Structure of Interest Rates*; and J. Conard, *An Introduction to the Theory of Interest* and *The Behavior of Interest Rates.*

19. See especially the literature cited in footnote 12 above.

20. The original paper here is that of J. Robinson ('The Rate of Interest'). J. Culbertson ('The Term Structure of Interest Rates'), whose work will be discussed below, also argued the case that actual participants in the securities markets tend to have short planning horizons. B. Malkiel (*The Term Structure of Interest Rates*) is also associated with this view. In a provocative paper, J. Wood ('Expectations and the Demand for Bonds') argued that, without the explicit assumption that all securities are held to maturity, the Hicks–Lutz models collapse to short-horizon models. Along the same lines, D. Luckett ('Multiperiod Expectations and the Term Structure of Interest Rates') demonstrated that the Meiselman model (supposedly a test of the long-horizon Hicks–Lutz model) and the Malkiel model (an explicitly short-horizon model) were both short-horizon models.

21. A. Buse, 'Interest Rates, the Meiselman Model, and Random Numbers', p. 49.

22. As done, for example, by B. Malkiel, *The Term Structure of Interest Rates.*

23. A. Buse, 'Interest Rates, the Meiselman Model, and Random Numbers', pp. 59–60.

24. R. Kessel, in *The Cyclical Behavior of the Term Structure of Interest Rates*, seems to have first discussed this problem at any length.

25. D. Fisher, 'The Speculative Demand for Money: An Empirical Test'. In this paper the expected sign was obtained, with some margin for error. It cannot be overemphasised, however, that this is a joint test, involving both the general perception of Hicks–Lutz and the specific perception of Meiselman. As well, a view of how short-term rates are determined is part of the paradigm. The discussion in the next section follows the same lines.

26. A. Leijonhufvud, *On Keynesian Economics and the Economics of Keynes*, p. 202.

27. In D. Fisher's 'The Speculative Demand for Money; an Empirical Test', the expected sign was achieved, but only marginally, on this test.

28. D. Laidler, 'The Rate of Interest and the Demand for Money', p. 544.

29. H. R. Heller, 'The Demand for Money: The Evidence from the Short-run Data', and M. Khan, 'The Stability of the Demand-for-Money Function in the United States, 1901–1965'.

30. M. Hamburger, 'The Demand for Money by Households, Money Substitutes, and Monetary Policy'. Hamburger notes that part of Heller's period includes 1947–51, a time in which US interest rates were pegged; his recalculation of the results destroys the difference between the interest rates noted by Heller.

31. D. Fisher, 'The Demand for Money in Britain: Quarterly Results'.

32. S. Goldfeld, 'The Demand for Money Revisited'.

33. L. Price, 'The Demand for Money in the United Kingdom: a Further Investigation'. Below, we will have occasion to recall this result when we discuss the dynamic consumption model.

34. G. Haache, 'The Demand for Money in the United Kingdom: Experience Since 1971'.

35. J. M. Culbertson, 'The Term Structure of Interest Rates'.

36. ibid., p. 487.

37. ibid., p. 489.

38. ibid., p. 490.

39. ibid., p. 499.

40. ibid., p. 500.

41. ibid.

42. J. Michaelsen, 'The Term Structure of Interest Rates and Holding-Period Yields on Government Securities', p. 461.

43. B. Malkiel, *The Term Structure of Interest Rates*, pp. 179–80.

44. Especially R. Roll, *The Behavior of Interest Rates*.

45. F. Modigliani and R. Sutch, 'Debt Management and the Term Structure of Interest Rates: An Empirical Analysis of Recent Experience'.

46. J. McCallum, 'The Expected Holding Period Return, Uncertainty, and the Term Structure of Interest Rates', p. 307.

47. ibid., p. 318.

48. This section contains part of the material in J. Bernstein and D. Fisher, 'Consumption, the Term Structure of Interest Rates, and the Demand for Money'. The basic papers this builds on are J. Stiglitz, 'A Consumption-Oriented Theory of the Demand for Financial Assets and the Term Structure of Interest Rates', and J. Green, 'A Simple General Equilibrium Theory of the Term Structure of Interest Rates'.

49. Note that these results, and those below, come directly from the constraint. This result, which implies that the wealth-holder is indifferent to the source of a change in his income or wealth, comes about, essentially, because the quantities of bonds were not inserted into the utility function (money was).

50. This statement is made subject to the qualification that we are showing relative effects. Thus, increases in the elasticities in question will increase the relative effectiveness of quantity changes compared with price changes, whatever their relative advantages.

51. The 'bills only' policy – that open-market operations should be conducted in the relatively broad short-term market – was popular in the early 1960s (R. Young and C. Yager, 'The Economics of "Bills Preferably" '). We are arguing that, from a theoretical point of view, this is a relatively correct strategy (if one has a money stock target) if the yield curve is upsloping (as it usually is). We have already illustrated a relative advantage to working in quantities.

52. J. Bernstein and D. Fisher, 'Optimal Portfolios and the Term Structure of Interest Rates', and J. Bernstein and D. Fisher, 'The Demand for Money and the Term Structure of Interest Rates: a Portfolio Approach'.

53. G. Bierwag and M. Grove, 'A Model of the Term Structure of Interest Rates'.

54. J. R. Hicks, *Value and Capital*.

CHAPTER 7

Inflation, Growth and the Demand for Money

7.1 Introduction

While problems of inflation – causes, consequences and cures, as they say – have dominated the recent monetary literature, a relatively small part of this same literature has investigated the relationship between the rate of change of prices and the demand for money. This is particularly noticeable in the theoretical literature. Part of this, no doubt, is the result of Monetarist influence on the debate: if inflation is caused (or significantly influenced) by the excess production of money – a proposition that is loosely consistent with a demand for money function that is homogeneous of degree 1 in all nominal variables – then one also might anticipate no important causal link between the rate of inflation (as the independent variable) and the demand for real balances, aside from secondary problems, such as the following:

1. money illusion effects,
2. non-neutral expectations effects, and
3. distribution effects.

These are, typically, not discussed in the literature. Secondly, while one can obviously enter the expected inflation rate as an *ad hoc* variable in the demand for money (and we will discuss such studies here), the most interesting theoretical literature here is that on 'money growth'. These studies, in turn, have concentrated on establishing stability properties or interesting correspondences with the static models and, partly as a consequence, have an unfulfilled empirical record of their own.

Of course, the traditional demand for money literature has looked into the relation between inflation and the demand for money, but not with much success, at least for developed countries. One exception is an empirical study by A. Shapiro on US data, and another is by J. Melitz, the latter on the French data.[1] Earlier, as Shapiro notes, Friedman and Schwartz expressed considerable pessimism as to the possibility of obtaining any results in the moderate inflation case (at least for the United States):

Failure has marked every attempt we know of to find a systematic relation between the quantity of money demanded in the United States and either the current rate of change in commodity prices or a weighted average of the past rates of change in prices, taken as an estimate of the rate of change expected to prevail in the future. Yet Cagan has found a close relation for other countries for periods marked by substantial price movements. The most plausible reason for the difference, in our view, is the small size of price changes in the United States except in wartime periods.[2]

Shapiro's model is really dynamic – and could be included in the discussion in Section 7.4 below, but it is worth pointing out here that his estimating equation is in a standard form – which we saw in Chapter 4 – which was tested by Shapiro for a second-degree Almon polynomial in all the independent variables; it appears as equation (7.1) here:

$$\Delta M_t = a + \sum_{i=0}^{n} b_i \Delta Y_{t-i} + \sum_{i=0}^{m} c_i \Delta r_{t-i} + \sum_{i=0}^{r} d_i \left(\frac{\Delta \dot{P}}{P}\right)_{t-i} \qquad (7.1)$$

Here r is a nominal short-term interest rate and $\dot{P}$ is dP/dt; the coefficient on the inflation term came out negative in his tests, as one might have expected on opportunity cost grounds. The money stock employed was narrow money, since time deposits proved not to have the expected effect, when they were taken as the dependent variable. This result, while clearly *ad hoc*, and involving some conflict between the nominal interest rate and the inflation rate, is important since it is a standard equation, tested in a standard way, as a comparison with the models in Chapter 4 (notably Laidler's) will verify;[3] the length of the lags, from smallest to longest, was $r < m < n$.

There is, though, one case that stands out – that of more rapid inflation – in which a role for the inflation rate has been shown to exist empirically; this literature has been written on 'hyperinflations' and on underdeveloped countries in which the 'inflationary tax' has been an instrument of fiscal policy. We will concentrate, through the first sections of this chapter, on this considerable literature – a literature based on work by I. Fisher and, in our generation, P. Cagan – before turning to the more theoretical work of the static and dynamic macroeconomic models in which the inflation rate (actual or expected) is a variable or in which an interesting role is played by the demand for money. In this connection, we will look at Friedman's recent models, in so far as they involve the demand for money, before briefly considering the Phillips Curve. Then, in the final section, we will take a quick turn through the studies of money-growth processes. When we discuss this topic we will usually be looking at the effect of various demand for money specifications on the results of theoretical and empirical exercises. This is, consequently, a peripheral literature for this study, which generally looks at the problem the other way around. Our discussion of these models, consequently, is not complete, but is, one hopes, at least representative.

7.2   Monetarist studies of the demand for money in the dynamic context

The relation between the nominal (i) and the real (r) interest rates now commonly employed in the textbook literature goes back at least to I. Fisher,[4] but its modern usage is perhaps clearest in Friedman's 'restatement' of the quantity theory as a theory of the demand for money. This function, which was employed in Chapter 4, is here assumed (with Friedman) to be homogeneous of degree 1 in P and Y:

$$M^d = f(P, i_b, r_e, \dot{P}/P; w, Y; u). \qquad \dot{P} = \frac{dP}{dt} \qquad (7.2)$$

The expected sign on the percentage rate of inflation, here measuring the opportunity cost of holding money in place of either equities or commodities, is negative, *a priori*; this brings us to an immediate complication, because the equity effect will not be equal to the commodity effect. That is, where P is the price level of commodities, it is obvious that whatever happens to commodity prices will be reflected in P, while equity prices – which reflect the market's anticipations about firms' profits (most likely) – may or may not respond fully to actual inflation. Friedman notes that if i_b and r_e (the returns on bonds and equities, respectively) change at the same rate, and all other nominal differences between bonds and equities are ignored, then equation (7.3) holds:

$$i_b = r_e + (\dot{P}/P)^e \qquad (7.3)$$

Friedman also provides an explanation, and a warning:

> that is, the 'money' interest rate is equal to the 'real' rate plus the percentage rate of change of prices. In application the rate of change of prices must be interpreted as an 'expected' rate of change and differences of opinion cannot be neglected, so we cannot expect [(7.3)] to hold; indeed, one of the most consistent features of inflation seems to be that it does not.[5]

P. Cagan's early paper on the subject – now a classic – begins with the manifesto that hyperinflations (inflations, arbitrarily, over 50 per cent per month) exhibit two important characteristics, both, we will see, important to the demand for money:

1. monetary events dominate real, providing isolation of the former; and
2. the quantity of real cash balances tends to decline in contrast to its behaviour in mild inflation (when it often rises).[6]

Cagan, then, assumes that all other assets are necessarily 'substitutes' for money (in the sense that a rise in their yield will reduce the demand for money); this is not correct, as a necessity, if more than one other asset is included explicitly in his demand function, but, of course, we have no real idea of the level of aggregation appropriate here. At any rate, the change in real cash balances is an interesting variable to look at under such conditions – conditions in which the financial institutions are under great pressure – if only because of the possibility that the demand for money could be unstable in this case.

Cagan's particular hypothesis is that changes in real cash balances in hyperinflation result from variations in the expected rate of change in prices.[7] That is, by increasing the yield on non-cash assets, we move along the (stable) demand function for real cash balances to a lower level. Recalling that Friedman's demand function was assumed to be homogeneous of degree 1 in P and Y, we now spell that out:

$$f(\lambda P, i_b, r_e, \dot{P}/P; w, \lambda Y; u) = \lambda f(P, i_b, r_e, \dot{P}/P; w, Y; u). \tag{7.4}$$

Then, letting $\lambda = 1/P$, we have Cagan's demand for real cash balances:

$$\frac{M}{P} = f[i_b, r_e, (\dot{P}/P)^e; w, Y/P; u]. \tag{7.5}$$

It is this demand function, where the expected rate of change of prices is included, whose properties under the condition of rapid inflation we will want to discuss. Cagan, in order to test the hypothesis that $(\dot{P}/P)$ dominates, makes two assumptions:

1. that desired real cash balances are equal to actual real cash balances at all times; and
2. that the expected rate of change of prices depends on the actual rate of change.

The former lets us read all observations as if they were on the demand curve and the latter leaves room for *ad hoc* price expectations-generating mechanisms.

Cagan proposes an error-learning model to deal with the expected rate of change of prices; thus,

> The expected rate of change of prices is revised per period of time in proportion to the difference between the actual rate of change in prices and the rate of change that was expected.[8]

In other words,

$$\left(\frac{dE}{dt}\right)_t = \beta(\dot{P}_t^a - \dot{P}_t^e) \qquad \text{where } \dot{P}_t^a = \left(\frac{d\log P}{dt}\right)_t. \tag{7.6}$$

β, then, is an adjustment parameter. Cagan measures $\dot{P}_t^e$ as a geometrically weighted average of past changes in the price level. The expression he uses is similar to Friedman's 'permanent income' measure as defined in Chapter 4;

we may describe this as 'permanent prices' and put it in the form of Friedman's equation here.

$$P_{\mathrm{p}}(T) = \beta \int_{-\infty}^{T} e^{(\beta-\alpha)(t-T)} P(t)\, dt. \tag{7.7}$$

This expression is then entered directly into his demand for money function (in which the interest rate and real income are dropped)[9] as its sole explanatory variable.

Cagan's results confirm that real cash balances over the data studied can be predicted from a model that uses past changes in prices as the sole explanatory variable; this was for seven hyperinflations. The model, which is the demand for money as things stand here, was judged to be stable as well. Among the qualitative discoveries about this function, the following stand out.

1. The lag in expectations tends to shorten (the elasticity of the demand for real balances with respect to the expected rate of price change tends to increase) as inflation rates get higher.

2. The total reaction to a change in prices depends on both the speed of adjustment and the elasticity of the adjustment function. This total reaction, in the study, varies from 0.54 for Hungary after World War II to 1.09 for Germany (after World War I). The condition for stability in this model is that this be less than 1.00. Since the value of 1.09 is one standard deviation from 0.92, Cagan can claim stability (of equilibrium) in his (demand-for-money) model.

Finally, we note that Cagan feels that increases in the quantity of money dominate the causal factors for these inflations. This latter conjecture is mentioned here because it has motivated much of the literature we will want to look at in the rest of this chapter.

R. Jacobs sets up Cagan's model as follows.[10] Let $m^{\mathrm{d}} = -\gamma - \alpha E$, where E is the expected rate of inflation. Let $dE/dt = \beta(\dot{P}/P - E)$ describe how expectations are revised. Let $dm/dt = \pi(m^{\mathrm{d}} - m)$ describe how actual real balances adjust to desired real balances (note that this relation was explicitly ignored in the description of the problem to this point); then we must explain $\dot{P}/P$, which we can do by the following 'forcing' equation:

$$\frac{\dot{P}}{P} = \frac{\dot{M}}{M} + \pi(m^{\mathrm{d}} - m). \tag{7.8}$$

Here actual inflation depends on the rate of production of nominal money and on the imbalance between desired and actual real balances (which is presumably eliminated in the commodity market). This, of course, partly endogenises the actual inflation rate (in contrast to Cagan's assumption) and implies that the Cagan estimating equation actually relates two mutually dependent variables *under his assumptions*. Jacobs suggests, instead, that we solve a proper reduced form in the exogenous variable, $\dot{M}/M$. When he does this, and re-estimates the adjustment parameters for Cagan's data, he obtains unstable inflation for Germany, Hungary and Greece. The explanation is that Cagan's model interprets all changes in the actual inflation rate as monetary-induced (and monetary-affecting), while in fact some changes were clearly not. In his system,

> real money balances are directly related to the driving force of the system, the rate of change of the money stock, and changes in the price level not described by the solution of the model ... will only degrade the quality of the fit.[11]

Jacobs also discusses models of R. Barro (see below) and M. Allais as suffering from similar defects.[12]

We mentioned above that this literature exists partly because an inflationary tax has been imposed in practice; this has produced a literature (for underdeveloped countries) which, as it turns out, involves the demand for money. The basic papers here are by M. Bailey, A. Marty and M. Friedman.[13] As D. Nichols points out,[14] both an increase in the demand for money and a reduction in its interest elasticity will increase the effect of the tax. The first is obvious and the second, depending as it does on the inability of money holders to avoid the tax, depends on

1. there being no close substitutes for money in domestic capital markets;
2. there being restrictions on domestic holdings of foreign currency; and
3. there being interest ceilings on private assets.

This, incidentally, is not as callous as it sounds, because, after all, the proposition is that a government with given real revenue needs (and only the money-creating machinery at its disposal) will not have to produce as much inflation in order to obtain its desired real tax revenues. This, aside from avoiding the disruptions of inflation, will quite possibly also make it easier for the government to achieve others of its objectives.

The Chicago School produced a second volume of studies on the rapid inflation problem; these studies were written in the early to mid-1960s using, roughly, the same methods just attributed to Cagan;[15] for continuity with what follows later, we will look at the Chilean problem analysed by J. Deaver.[16] As with Cagan, the problem is to analyse the demand for real cash balances; this time, however, a longer run of data is analysed than in Cagan's study (his figures went, at most, over thirty-six months), necessitating a look at real income as well; the period is 1932–55. We note that the rate of Chilean inflation was relatively high (compared with previous Chilean history) and that public resistance to the inflationary tax was relatively low.[17] Deaver also does a lot of work with expectations-generating mechanisms, but the equation of most interest here is given as equation (7.9):

$$\log\frac{M}{P} = b_0 + b_1 E + b_2\log\frac{Y}{P} + v. \tag{7.9}$$

E, as before, is the expected rate of inflation. Here Cagan's method was employed to proxy E. We have called E 'permanent prices'; Deaver also asks whether 'permanent income' dominates measured income in this rapid (but not hyper-) inflation case. But here he has his doubts:

> The investment market in Chile is not as well developed as in the United States, and is accessible to a smaller proportion of money holders. Moreover, the market for consumer durables is proportionally much smaller ... with choices so limited, the additional savings accumulated from transitory income may be kept in the form of cash. ...[18]

Thus Deaver anticipates that measured income – which includes the transitory component – may well dominate permanent income (from which the transitory component is removed) as an influence on the demand for money in an underdeveloped country. The following conclusions were reached, on the basis of his empirical tests.

1. The weighting pattern (via Cagan's method) on past inflation rates varied from four to nineteen years in length, but this was not related to the rapidity of the inflation (quicker inflation producing faster reactions) but to such things as political events. This, therefore, stands as evidence of instability of the demand for money in this case.

2. Measured real income elasticity was considerably less than unity; this coefficient, too, was unstable, ranging from 0.07 (at the same time that the longest lag was observed) to 0.63.

3. Permanent real income – unfortunately neither trend-adjusted nor with an estimated β coefficient – produced better fits in some periods and worse in others, but all but one estimate was below unity and notable instability was recorded.

Thus, while not the best possible test, this stands as evidence of instability of the demand for money – and evidence of a different set of arguments – at least on this test.

The study in the Meiselman volume by A. Diz analyses the same model, with the addition of the variance of the inflation rate, on the Argentinian data (their inflation was slightly less rapid than the Chilean inflation).[19] A better fit than the Chilean case was generally obtained, and the following additional comments can be made, in summary.

1. The variance term entered the calculations when inflation was more rapid. Diz comments:

> a greater variability may lead people to trust recently observed rates less and to look for more extensive evidence on which to base their expectations.[20]

One might also simply invoke the mean-variance theorems here.

2. The Cagan-style 'cost-elasticity' was somewhat higher than for the Chilean case.

3. The demand for currency responds to past inflation more rapidly than the demand for demand or savings and time deposits. This suggests some additional aggregation problems (as if there weren't enough) and a possible explanation for measured 'instability'.

4. Permanent income works generally quite well.

This work, consequently, establishes some further doubts about the simple models in the rapid inflation case.[21] We will return to the Chilean case below.[22]

7.3 The Fisher Effect

The 'Fisher Effect' that we have referred to in passing belongs to I. Fisher, of course, and it goes back to the 1898 *American Economic Review* paper, itself an attempt to deal with what Keynes was later to identify as the 'Gibson Paradox'. This latter arises, according to some economists writing in the Classical tradition, since the (by then) often noticed positive relationship between the price level and interest rates was not what one would expect in theory. In their theory, a higher interest rate would choke off business and produce deflation. One explanation that was given was Tooke's cost of production theory: being a cost, a higher interest rate would normally lead to a higher price in the short run, but if maintained would produce a fall in prices (in the long run) as credit arrangements were frustrated by the higher interest rates. To say the least, this equivocal theory has not been enthusiastically accepted, no doubt because the connection between a single price and the price level is hard to establish, and two 'schools of thought' have successfully explained the paradox. One of these can be referred to as a theory of the trade cycle, and Wicksell and Keynes are important here, and the other is the more technical 'Fisher Effect', which links the expected rate of inflation to the nominal interest rate.

The cycle models need not detain us for any considerable space here, although it is clear that a perception of the demand for money is involved, at least peripherally. Wicksell's explanation of the connection is prior, probably, although the version quoted here dates from 1936. Noting that the 'cost of production' school just described refers essentially to relative prices, Wicksell explains the relation between interest rates and the price level in the following terms.

> So a fall in the rate of interest, even though it is casual and temporary, will bring about a perfectly *definite* rise in prices. ... If the rate of interest remains at a low level [below the natural rate of interest] for a considerable period of time, the influence on prices must necessarily be cumulative.[23]

The converse also holds for a nominal rate of interest held above natural rate. Thus, if we observe a positive relation between prices and interest rates, it is only the result of chance: while the actual interest rate is below the (unobservable) natural rate (and is maintained there by the banks/monetary authorities), money is pumped into the system. As the actual rate rises (for whatever reason), the 'inflationary gap' persists for a time, although it steadily narrows until it disappears. Thus, for substantial time periods one would observe (substantial) periods in which prices and interest rates rise together (or fall together, to take the converse case). Not always, of course, but if monetary policy (or whatever causes the jump in the nominal interest rate) is generally characterised by sudden changes in the interest rate, and then maintained with only a gradual erosion until a new emergency produces another sudden change in the nominal rate, the data may well be dominated by this effect. The theory, that is to say, predicts no firm relationship unless institutional practice produces it.

Keynes's versions appear both in the *Treatise* and in the *General Theory*. In the *Treatise* he notes:

> For the extraordinary thing is that the 'Gibson Paradox' – as we may fairly call it – is one of the most completely established empirical facts within the whole field of quantitative economics, though theoretical economists have mostly ignored it.[24]

Keynes rejected the simple credit cycle explanation then in vogue – that an expansion of activity brings up both prices and interest rates – as inadequate since the correlation is long-run as much as it is short-run. Instead, he proposes a relation very like that just described as Wicksellian: the market rate of interest is sticky compared with the natural rate. Thus, sudden movements in the natural rate – to which the money rate must sooner or later adjust – set up substantial periods in which prices and interest rates move together, by the mechanism attributed to Wicksell. He mentions, among the institutional rigidities, regulations on usury.[25] In the *General Theory*, however, instead of the natural rate (supply = demand for money), we have the 'full employment rate':

It is evident, then, that the rate of interest is a highly psychological phenomenon. We shall find ... that it cannot be in equilibrium at a level below the rate which corresponds to full employment, because at such a level a state of true inflation will be produced, with the result that M_1 will absorb ever-increasing quantities of cash.[26]

Presumably, as the interest rate rises towards equilibrium, it is accompanied by price rises, the latter possibly diminishing in intensity as full employment is neared.

Irving Fisher's version, as noted, appeared first in 1898. He distinguished between the money rate of interest and the real rate of interest, as noted above.[27] Thus, if the money rate (the actual rate) is denoted by i, and if some rate of inflation is anticipated, then the real rate if interest is defined to be (approximately):

$$r = i - \frac{\dot{P}^e}{P} \qquad \dot{P} = \frac{dP}{dt} \qquad (7.10)$$

where, as with equation (7.3), the superscript 'e' designates an expectation. Thus, to Fisher, the relation between i and inflationary expectations is (given r) a positive one: a rise in anticipated inflation would tend to produce a rise in the money rate of interest, and conversely. Furthermore, any failure in the relationship (*ex post*) is accounted for either by the inaccuracy of expectations or, actually, by changes in r (see below). One would, of course, not observe the current rate of inflation being equal to the difference between the current money interest rate (i) and the current real interest rate (assuming that one had a suitable proxy for the latter), since the current inflation rate is only one of a number of guides to future (expected) inflation rates. Furthermore,

When the cost of living is not stable, the rate of interest takes the appreciation and depreciation into account to some extent, but only slightly and, in general, indirectly. That is, when prices are rising, the rate of interest tends to be high but not so high as it should be to compensate for the rise....[28]

Which leaves a nice empirical problem since a test would seem to depend on imperfect foresight, etc.

7.3.1   *Empirical studies of the Gibson Paradox and the Fisher Effect*

The direct studies of the Gibson Paradox in the literature – by D. Meiselman, P. Cagan and T. Sargent – have produced some scattered evidence on these competing hypotheses for the US data.[29] The Keynes–Wicksell natural rate hypothesis is generally dismissed out of hand, since it basically predicts no firm relationship between prices and interest rates unless institutional factors can be brought to bear. The Keynesian (or trade cycle) model is perfectly adequate for the cyclical paradox, but, as generally conceded, the paradox is also of a long-run nature, so those who want an explanation to cover all contingencies seem to end up with the Fisher Effect by default; on the other hand, the latter does not test easily, since both r and the expected rate of change of prices are unobservable in principle. Furthermore, the Fisher model posits a relation between the expected *change* in prices and interest rate rather than the *level* of prices and interest rate; the Gibson Paradox concerns the latter. In D. Meiselman's words,

> if people have perfect foresight, a stable rate of secular inflation will be associated with high interest rates and rising rates of inflation with rising interest rates, and similarly for declining prices. Thus, the Fisher hypothesis need not lead to the concurrent movement of levels of prices and yields. ... If, instead, the learning process is best approximated by weighted extrapolations of lagged price changes in which the current period is given a relatively large weight, interest rates and prices may move in the same direction.[30]

While the tests have generally produced implausibly long lags and (not independently) serial correlation, Sargent's work is unique in establishing the validity of Fisher's model, with generally short lags. So the empirical evidence on the Gibson Paradox seems to run in Fisher's favour, although the rejection of the alternatives is empirically casual.

Turning to the Fisher Effect itself, we note that there exists a considerable empirical literature, much of it devoted either to the correct measurement of inflationary expectations (via Cagan's mechanism, for example or, more rarely, the measurement of the real rate (by means of, for example, a simultaneous-equations system). As it turns out, given i, the nominal rate of interest, equation (7.10) – where the 'real rate' is not interpreted as the equity rate – permits us to solve our problem either by estimating the expected rate of change of prices or, alternatively, by estimating r. Given i, that is to say, one of the two is a residual, by definition. Thus we have two streams of literature to follow, although that on the estimation of r is not very large.

With regard to estimates of the expected rate of change of prices, the Cagan-style models, as noted, have tended to produce unbelievably long lags when applied to the problem of the Fisher effect, and there is, as well, evidence of instability in the lag. One contrasting approach has been to employ the well-known Livingston (US) data as a direct measure of expected inflation rates.[31] Thus W. Gibson used the data for tests of interest rates themselves, while S. Turnovsky and M. Wachter applied the data to the Phillips Curve problem.[32] The latter is not really relevant here, but the former is. Thus, for a series of US Government bond yields ranging from three months to ten years, the results of a test of equation (7.10) were well determined and showed that there was little evidence of any difference for different terms-to-maturity.[33] Furthermore, the lags were quite short (relatively), going up, at most, to six months, rather than to the much longer lags found using the distributed lag forms discussed earlier in this chapter. No direct test of stability was attempted in Gibson's paper, but there was some evidence of a shift of the function around 1965 (when inflation became more rapid). The Wachter–Turnovsky study made no mention of this latter possibility.[34]

Another set of problems with the Cagan–Friedman lag formulation is essentially econometric. In particular, the aggregation over time in their scheme could lead to overly long estimates of the lag, as the result of positive serial correlation in the residuals (as discussed in Chapter 4).[35] Furthermore, as noted already, there is the possibility of simultaneous-equations bias since there may well exist 'feedback' between prices and interest rates. This can be estimated, as is done by T. Sargent, for example,[36] and it can be bypassed, for example by estimating the real rate of interest directly (as well as, of course, using direct price expectations data, as already discussed). The clue to what to do here is contained in the following by T. Sargent:

> Only in the special case in which the LM curve is vertical, the IS curve is horizontal or the short-run Phillips curve is vertical ... does an increase in expected inflation produce an immediate equivalent jump in the nominal interest rate. These special sets of parameter values obviously impart a very monetarist or classical sort of behavior to the model.
>
> On this interpretation of Fisher's theory, all of the parameters influencing the slopes of the IS, LM, and Phillips curves are pertinent in evaluating its adequacy.[37]

This generalises the feedback problem and suggests either that a full model be constructed or, equivalently, that some sort of reduced form estimation be attempted. That, as it turns out, is the rationale for the 'rational expectations' approach.

Sargent, in particular, constructs a simple macro-model and then employs the 'rational expectations' mechanism to deal with the troublesome price expectations.[38] As it turns out, the model is aggregated above the demand function level so nothing of direct interest to the demand for money is available in this first exercise; but, at least, there is some evidence with regard to the Fisher Effect, and the 'rational approach' is of interest, as well. Rational expectations, to begin with, can be defined, somewhat mysteriously, by equation (7.11):

$$_{t+1}P_t^* = E_t[P_{t+1}]. \tag{7.11}$$

This, formally, says that all relevant (and available) information at t is employed in the formation of price expectations concerning $t + 1$; thus, most importantly, the effect of changes in the stock of money on the interest rate (the stock of money is one such relevant factor) would be felt through their effect on the conditional mathematical expectation on the right-hand side of equation (7.11).[39] Thus, in this scheme, changes in the money stock (presumably exogenous in origin) will affect the right-hand side of the equation; this will, as well, be influenced by all other relevant exogenous or predetermined data (including, of course, lags in the money stock). The rational expectations hypothesis is generally attributed to J. Muth;[40] a particularly efficient statement of the proposition is provided by J. Pesando:

> To be rational in the sense of ... Muth ... expectations must be generated by a reduced-form equation in the exogenous variables which actually generate the variable to be predicted.[41]

Thus, a geometric lag system of past prices may be rational, if no other variables seem to matter. Most researchers, though, believe that other current endogenous variables (the money stock, the rate of unemployment, etc.) matter, as well as other predetermined variables, in predicting prices.

7.3.2 *Anticipated inflation and the demand for money*

The preceding, by concentrating on the reduced form, keeps the structure of the model (and thus the demand for money) well in the background; but in further developments a more explicit role for the demand for money has been framed. For a first effort consider some work by Sargent and Wallace, who assume the following demand-for-money function, in which a future price level (P_{t+1}) appears and $M = \bar{M}$ (i.e., the money stock is constant:[42]

$$\log \frac{M}{P_t} = -\beta \log \frac{P_{t+1}}{P_t}. \tag{7.12}$$

This model, then, argues that the demand for money is a simple function of an expected rate of inflation (presumably under the assumption of perfect foresight). As it turns out, however, this simple model is consistent (when written as a difference equation in prices) with a variety of paths of the price level, some of which are unstable; we might judge this to be an undesirable property. Thus, following F. Black,[43] the solution of the difference equation in prices yields

$$\dot{P}_t = \left(1 + \frac{1}{\beta}\right)^t \dot{P}_0 \qquad \text{where } \dot{P}_t = \log \frac{P_{t+1}}{P_t} \tag{7.13}$$

which, for certain initial rates of inflation, will explode (up or down). Black
shows, though, that if the money stock is no longer constant (note that M
did not have a time subscript in equation (7.12)), a further lag is thereby
introduced, and for $\beta > 1$, stability is guaranteed. The demand-for-money
function, that is to say, is now *assumed* to be

$$\log \frac{M_t}{P_t} = -\beta \log \frac{P_{t+1}}{P_t} \qquad \beta > 1. \qquad (7.14)$$

Black, then, refers to $\beta > 1$ as the condition that the demand for money is
'sufficiently sensitive' to the rate of inflation (if it is not sufficiently sensitive,
adjustment is slower).[44] This, then, is a perfect foresight model with rational
expectations, which converges to a steady state with zero inflation (but by
different paths, depending on where one starts). The role of the demand for
money here is an assumed one, of course, and Black considers some further
variations along these lines:

1. the case when the demand for money depends on anticipated inflation
   for all other future periods (in addition to $t + 1$), in which case there is
   again no unique path (and, again, some chance of instability);
2. the case when uncertainty (a normal distribution) about future prices
   replaces the assumption about perfect foresight, in which case the path
   is again not unique (with even more chance of instability);
3. the case in which adaptive expectations replace rational expectations
   (only in special cases will the adaptive model be rational), in which case
   there is again no unique path towards equilibrium.

Note that in all these cases what jolts the system is an announced change in
monetary policy.

R. Mundell also offers us a look at the demand for money in the context
of inflationary expectations, following a path laid down by L. Metzler.[45]
Noting that anticipatory failures are not the only problem, he conjectures
that variations in the real rate of interest *itself* could produce the discrepan-
cies between the nominal rate and the sum of real rate and price expectations terms (as we have noted at several points in this discussion); this
involves the demand for money. Let us assume, with Mundell (and
Metzler),[46] that real investment depends on the real interest rate, that real
saving depends on real wealth, and that the demand for money depends on
the money interest rate and wealth. Mundell, then, in equation (7.15),
measured wealth as the discounted value of profits, where the real rate of
interest is used in the discounting of the perpetual stream of profits:

$$W = \frac{\pi}{r}. \qquad (7.15)$$

Thus, if the demand for money is assumed to be homogeneous of degree 1 in wealth, and if equation (7.16), a production function, holds –

$$\pi = c\left(\frac{Y}{P}\right) \tag{7.16}$$

– then our Fisherian demand for money is given by equation (7.17):

$$\frac{M^d}{P} = \frac{c(Y/P)}{r}f(i). \tag{7.17}$$

This, I submit, is an interesting function, depending as it does on both r and i, which does not appear elsewhere in the literature and, to my knowledge, has not been tested directly (although it could be considered to have been tested indirectly, by the tests of the Fisher Effect). Here, r affects the demand for money in the anticipated way and so does i, by assumption. When we substitute equation (7.10), for i, into equation (7.17), then we obtain, directly, the anticipated negative relation between the expected rate of inflation and the demand for money.

There is, as well, an interesting contribution to this literature by H. Grossman and A. Policano, in terms of an inventory-theoretic model of household behaviour; this was the most specific result I was able to locate in this context.[47] Breaking household balances into average working balances ($\bar{M}_w$) and average savings balances ($\bar{M}_v$), these authors assume that the first is used up on the purchase of commodity 1 (the average inventory of which is $\bar{G}_1$) while the second consists of money held for future purchases of commodity 2 (the average inventory of which is $\bar{G}_2$). The consumer, thus, picks his optimal frequency of purchases of the two goods ($= g_1^*$ and g_2^*) in a cost-minimising framework. Then, through the constraints, the optimal money holding in the two categories is given as

$$\bar{M}_w^* = \frac{X_1 T}{2S} - \bar{G}_1^*$$

$$\bar{M}_v^* = \bar{G}_2^* - \frac{X_2 T}{2S}. \tag{7.18}$$

Here $X_1/2$ is the average expenditure on good 1 and S is the frequency of receipts (T is the time period). The first of these expressions, then, argues that money holding is reduced by commodity purchases, while the second says that a rise in future desired purchases will stimulate money holding. In combination,

$$\bar{M}^* = \bar{M}_w^* + \bar{M}_v^* = \frac{(X_1 - X_2)T}{2S} - \bar{G}_1^* + \bar{G}_2^*. \tag{7.19}$$

Grossman and Policano also calculated $\bar{G}_1^*$ and $\bar{G}_2^*$ as

$$G_1^* = \left(\frac{\beta_1 X_1}{-2i_1}\right)^{1/2}$$

$$\bar{G}_2^* = \left[\frac{\beta_2 X_2}{2(2i_k - i_2)}\right]^{1/2} \tag{7.20}$$

where i_j ($j = 1,2, \ldots, k-1$) is the net nominal rate of return on the jth commodity (and is equal to the expected inflation rate ρ less the per unit storage cost) and i_k is the net nominal rate of return on earning assets (i.e., it is the nominal interest rate).

Interest rate and scale effects on money holding in this model are of the usual sort, but of special interest here is the effect of price expectations. Noting, first, that i_1 is negative as a result of the set-up of the model,[48] and assuming that $i_k > i_2$ (to give the household an incentive to economise on money holding), we have

$$\frac{\partial \bar{G}_1^*}{\partial \rho} = \frac{\bar{G}_1^*}{-2i_1} > 0$$

$$\frac{\partial \bar{G}_2^*}{\partial \rho} = -\frac{\bar{G}_2^*}{2(2i_k - i_2)} < 0 \tag{7.21}$$

whence $\partial \bar{M}^*/\partial \rho$ is clearly negative from equation (7.19). That is, in this model, if the consumer expects an increase in the rate of inflation he will increase his demand for present commodities (hence reducing his working balances) and reduce his demand for future commodities (reducing his need to stockpile money balances for future purchases). These are, as usual, exact results on account of the rigidity of the inventory-theoretic model.[49]

7.4   Some macroeconomic models and the role of the demand for money

The other side of the coin – as already pointed out – is the effect that different specifications of the demand for money have on the various macroeconomic models designed to deal (simultaneously) with the inflation problem. In this first section we will briefly consider some issues that involve the demand for money in the *IS–LM* framework; then, in Section 7.5, we will turn to the money-growth literature, and continue the line of attack started in Section 7.3. Two main areas seem to have been the focus of most of the static macro-work here: the models of nominal income determination generated around the Monetarist controversy, and the discussion of the Phillips

Curve, particularly in the Lipsey–Phillips tradition. We will consider these in turn, primarily for illustration.

To begin with, let us consider the 'basic *IS–LM* model' proposed by M. Friedman.[50] Friedman, in particular, argues that the main difference that emerges between Keynesians and Monetarists arises from a consideration of how they complete the basic *IS–LM* model which all (presumably) accept. This model has common equations given by equations (7.22):

$$\frac{C}{P} = f\left(\frac{Y}{P}, i\right) \tag{7.22a}$$

$$\frac{I}{P} = g(i) \tag{7.22b}$$

$$\frac{Y}{P} = \frac{C}{P} + \frac{I}{P} \tag{7.22c}$$

$$M^d = PL\left(\frac{Y}{P}, i\right) \tag{7.22d}$$

$$M^s = h(i) \tag{7.22e}$$

$$M^d = M^s. \tag{7.22f}$$

Friedman considers the demand-for-money equation as not in dispute; indeed, it is written here in the general version described in Chapter 4 and attributed to all schools of thought. What matters, says Friedman, is the method of completing the system, which has seven variables but only six equations in it; the choice, according to Friedman, is either equation (7.23) or (7.24):

$$P = P_0 \qquad \text{income-expenditure theory} \tag{7.23}$$

$$\frac{Y}{P} = y = y_0 \qquad \text{quantity theory} \tag{7.24}$$

The former represents the case of rigid prices, and the latter is a statement that the economy is operating at the full employment level of real income. Friedman quotes Keynes here, to justify equation (7.23):

> We are, as I have said, one equation short. Yet it might be a provisional assumption of a rigidity of money wages, rather than of real wages, which would bring our theory nearest to the facts.[51]

This leads, Friedman notes, to confrontations with the data which the Keynesian theory fails; further, the key differences between the Keynesian tradition and (by now) the Chicago tradition are:

1. that the Keynesians believe that a change in the quantity of money affects spending via the interest rate effect on spending, while

2. the Monetarists' view stresses direct wealth effects on portfolios (and then on final spending).

These are balance sheet adjustments which are, it seems, narrowly defined by the Keynesians and broadly defined by the Monetarists.[52]

While these results downgrade the role of the demand for money in the dispute, even Friedman acknowledges the possibility of adopting a different approach. Thus, in the second of the two 'model' papers by Friedman, he notes that one could complete the system by using equation (7.25):

$$M^d = Y\gamma(i). \tag{7.25}$$

Here Friedman relies on the empirical 'fact' that the demand for money has a unitary income elasticity; this, in effect, imposes a restriction on the solution (which has the effect of eliminating one variable). One might also use a dynamic relation like equation (7.26) to complete the system; in this case we involve the rate of inflation directly, as discussed by B. McCallum.[53]

$$\frac{dP}{dt} = \varphi(y - q). \tag{7.26}$$

Here y is actual real income and q is full employment real income, so $y - q$ is 'current excess demand'. In McCallum's empirical formulation, this appears as

$$\log P_t = \lambda\gamma(\log y_t - \log q_t) + (1 - \lambda)\log P_{t-1}. \tag{7.27}$$

McCallum is not interested in the demand for money as such; but in Friedman's version of the same model, it has a role. If the missing equation is taken as $Y = Py$, then a dynamic version of this equation can be written as equation (7.28):

$$\frac{d\log Y}{dt} = \frac{d\log P}{dt} + \frac{d\log y}{dt}. \tag{7.28}$$

Then, following the argument developed in Chapter 3 for the Patinkin dynamics, we can write two *ad hoc* adjustment equations for the two components of equation (7.28), appearing here as equations (7.29) and (7.30):

$$\frac{d\log P}{dt} = \left(\frac{d\log P}{dt}\right)^* + \alpha\left[\frac{d\log Y}{dt} - \left(\frac{d\log Y}{dt}\right)^*\right]$$
$$+ \gamma[\log y - (\log y)^*] \tag{7.29}$$

$$\frac{d\log y}{dt} = \left(\frac{d\log y}{dt}\right)^* + (1 - \alpha)\left[\frac{d\log Y}{dt} - \left(\frac{d\log Y}{dt}\right)^*\right]$$
$$- \gamma[\log y - (\log y)^*]. \tag{7.30}$$

Here the asterisk indicates an expected variable (for which equation (7.28) also holds). This system partitions the influences on prices and real income into real and nominal sources; furthermore, it is capable of illustrating Friedman's basic point that the important difference between the different perceptions of the system has to do with the adjustment process in the system. Thus, he argues, to a Keynesian, $\alpha = 0$ (there is no nominal source of disequilibrium) and $(d \log P/dt)^* = 0$, i.e., prices are expected to be rigid. This being the case, the system (7.28)–(7.30) collapses to equation (7.31):

$$\left(\frac{d \log y}{dt}\right)^* = \left(\frac{d \log Y}{dt}\right)^*. \tag{7.31}$$

Inflation, presumably, will be entirely unanticipated.

Friedman, as noted in Chapter 4, believes that the quantity theory of money – as a theory – is basically a theory of the demand for money; it is at its best, further, when the demand for money is a stable function of a few key variables. Thus, he argues, in the quantity world, $\alpha = 1$ and $\gamma = 0$. In words, the disturbance is entirely monetary ($\alpha = 1$) and prices adjust instantaneously ($\gamma = 0$). This being the case, equation (7.32), visibly different from (7.31), characterises the system:

$$\left(\frac{d \log P}{dt}\right)^* = \left(\frac{d \log Y}{dt}\right)^* - \left(\frac{d \log y}{dt}\right)^*. \tag{7.32}$$

The demand for money is relevant here because its stability (if such is the case) ensures that the inflationary pressure from a change in the supply of money is transmitted perfectly to the price level. Anything less than perfect stability would imply different values for γ and α. Thus Friedman could be interpreted as saying that the demand for money enters the simple Classical model, but not the simple Keynesian model, in the dynamic case.

Models such as those we have been discussing – with expected inflation rates – are treading closely on the Phillips Curve literature, although, again, the popular rational expectations approach to the Phillips Curve, because it focuses on the reduced form rather than the structure, is not of much help here. As well, the considerable strain of literature developed around (microeconomic) labour market theory is not relevant, as things stand. Even so, an interesting jointure exists, since one of the reasons why stable estimates of recent Phillips Curves are hard to come by could be that the role of money implicitly assumed in the models is itself unrealistic, especially in the rapid inflation case (when the demand for money might be unstable). The converse also has to be kept in mind. A place to locate this discussion is with the standard presentation of the Phillips Curve by R. Lipsey.[54] Putting aside the numerous *ad hoc* elements of a microeconomic nature common to this literature, we might follow Lipsey in one of his 'microeconomic' derivations, and extract a Phillips Curve from the following model:

$$L^s = a_0 + a_1 W \qquad\qquad a_1 > 0 \qquad\qquad (7.33a)$$
$$L^d = b_0 + b_1 W \qquad\qquad b_1 < 0 \qquad\qquad (7.33b)$$
$$\dot{W}/dt = \alpha(L^d - L^s) \qquad\qquad \alpha > 0 \qquad\qquad (7.33c)$$
$$UV = h \qquad\qquad\qquad\qquad\qquad (7.33d)$$
$$U = L^s - L \qquad\qquad\qquad\qquad (7.33e)$$
$$V = L^d - L \qquad\qquad\qquad\qquad (7.33f)$$
$$X = L^d - L^s. \qquad\qquad\qquad\qquad (7.33g)$$

Here V refers to vacancies and equation (7.33d), the only unusual relation, is an empirical 'fact' attributed to L. Dicks-Mireaux and J. Dow.[55] Combining the relevant relations produces an equation between the excess demand in the labour market (X) and unemployment in the form of a Phillips Curve:

$$X = \frac{h}{U} - U. \qquad\qquad (7.34)$$

Then, with $\dot{W}$ to represent disequilibrium in the labour market, a standard formulation is obtained.[56]

Transparently, in this derivation, the demand (or supply) of money is not involved, but all is not well, nevertheless, because (7.33c) cannot be taken as a general disequilibrium statement by itself (see the dynamics in Chapter 3); that is, we might more generally write equation (7.35) rather than (7.33c):

$$\frac{dW}{dt} = \alpha_1(L^d - L^s) + \alpha_2(M^s - M^d) + \alpha_3(B^s - B^d) \qquad (7.35)$$

as well as providing adjustment equations for di/dt and dP/dt; we might also include a commodity market disequilibrium. This, then, gives us a clue as to why estimates of the Phillips Curve might produce unstable results. The time path of the wage rate will tend to reflect disequilibrium in the money and commodity markets as well as the labour market.[57] Thus, in the rapid inflation case – a case known to involve potential instability in the demand for money – the simple models may well prove to be unreliable without inclusion of structural parameters from the other markets involved in the disequilibrium. These structural parameters, once general disequilibrium is admitted, will come from either the demand or supply curves depending on whether one is 'above' or 'below' equilibrium. Finally, we should note that an equation for dP/dt and di/dt also exists in the general case and include (in the general case) labour market disequilibrium in their specifications. In general, estimates of the demand for money in inflationary conditions have generally not been so comprehensive and certainly have not included the structure of other markets. A clear implication is that much of the evidence alleging instability of the demand for money (and, for that matter, of the Phillips Curve) may be the result of mis-specification which increases with the rate of inflation. We turn, then, to more self-consciously dynamic formulations.

7.5   Growth and the demand for money [58]

Standard Neoclassical growth theory has produced a considerable literature on how to incorporate money into the various models, but the results have been far from satisfying. A major part of the problem is that growth models tend to produce conclusions about equilibrium growth rates, and in this context much of the disequilibrium flavour of the Keynes-versus-the-Classics debate that figures so prominently in the rest of the literature is lost. Suppose, for example, that the only money in the system is a commodity money (e.g., gold); then the following propositions are valid:

> There could only be higher money prices if the real cost of obtaining gold were lowered. There is an equilibrium quantity of money, and an equilibrium growth rate of the money supply, equal to the growth rate of everything else.[59]

But a commodity money economy is far from that which we are interested in and, for a pure credit money economy (for the moment accepting the fiat money of the central government as a credit arrangement, as discussed in Chapters 2 and 3),

> We find ... that there is no price equation to determine the value of money in terms of goods and services. It is impossible to determine the equilibrium price-level, as before, from the price side. On the quantity side we have to reinterpret the quantity equation, going into detail about the supplies and demands, from the individual entities, from which they are derived.[60]

Which, patently, brings the various formulations of the demand for money into the problem.

Let us begin, then, with Friedman. As with the adjustment models described in Section 7.4, Friedman argues that two important empirical generalisations buttress money-growth theory:

1. the nominal amount of money is determined by conditions of supply; and
2. the real amount of money is determined by conditions of demand.

Thus, if money grew at the rate of μ, so that

$$M(t) = M_0 e^{\mu t} \qquad (7.36)$$

then, assuming no distribution effects, if individuals attempt to keep their real balances unchanged, the path of equilibrium prices is given as

$$P(t) = P_0 e^{\mu t} \tag{7.37}$$

and, since $Y = Py$ for fixed y, the path of income is given by

$$Y(t) = (Y_0 + \mu M_0)e^{\mu t}. \tag{7.38}$$

This, then, is exactly the same result that we argued held for the commodity money economy of Hicks, and provides the explanation. Friedman also shows that inflation brings welfare losses and deflation welfare gains – this arises because of distortions in individuals' consumption patterns brought about as (with real money balances in their utility functions) they attempt to avoid the inflationary tax. With money costing no resources to produce,

> Our final rule for the optimum quantity of money is that it will be attained by a rate of price deflation that makes the nominal rate of interest equal to zero.[61]

Again, as this view is empirically justified by Friedman, the stable demand for money is necessary for the conclusions to hold.[62]

A more formal statement of the Neoclassical money-growth model at this point will serve to illustrate its conclusions and to provide an effective standard of comparison for the Keynes–Wicksell-type models. To begin with the difference:

> The essential features of Keynes–Wicksell ... monetary growth models ... are the specification of an independent investment function and the assumption that prices change only in response to excess demand in the goods market. In neoclassical monetary growth models, by contrast, there is no independent investment function and all markets are continuously in equilibrium.[63]

This, of course, is a distinction we have already emphasised. Thus, for the Neoclassical model, assume that the *per capita* demand for real balances is given by equation (3.39), in which the arguments are the *per capita* capital stock and the expected rate of inflation:

$$\left(\frac{M}{PN}\right)^d = L\left[\frac{K}{N}, \left(\frac{\dot{P}}{P}\right)^e\right]. \tag{7.39}$$

If the money market is always in equilibrium $\left(m = \dfrac{M}{PN} = \left(\dfrac{M}{PN}\right)^d\right)$, then the actual rate of inflation is given by equation (7.40):

$$\frac{\dot{P}}{P} = \mu - n - \frac{1}{m}\left[L_1 \frac{d(K/N)}{dt} + L_2 \frac{d(\dot{P}/P)^e}{dt}\right]. \tag{740}$$

μ here is the rate of expansion of the nominal money supply, and n is the rate of population growth.[64] In the steady state, with inelastic expectations,

$$\frac{\dot{P}}{P} = \mu - n$$

and the parameters (L_1 and L_2) of the demand for money do not enter into the determination of the inflation rate; but off this steady state they do. This judgement was verbalised earlier in this section.[65]

J. Stein originally built his description of the Keynes–Wicksell model on Patinkin's short-run dynamic model as described in Chapter 3. In particular, Stein proposed equation (7.41) to explain price changes.

$$\frac{d \log P}{dt} = \lambda \left(\frac{I}{K} - \frac{S}{K} \right). \tag{7.41}$$

This model, which has the characteristic described by S. Fisher, has an undesirable property, as well:

> It is apparent that there cannot be inflation without excess demand if equation [7.41] determines the rate of inflation, and thus a steady state with inflation requires persistent excess demand.[66]

This is undesirable because it implies that individuals will be perpetually unable to achieve their optimal utility, even though their expectations are correct. Stein's early papers do not present a resolution of this problem, but in his book (1971) he carefully works out the case when equation (7.41) is replaced with equation (7.42):

$$\frac{d \log P}{dt} = \left(\frac{d \log P}{dt} \right)^* + \lambda \left(\frac{I}{K} - \frac{S}{K} \right). \tag{7.42}$$

This, one might note, is similar to equation (7.29), of Friedman; note that the description of inflation here is different from that in the derived relation for the Neoclassical model in equation (7.40)

Returning to the topic of the demand for money, let us note the following direct results. The demand for money in the Neoclassical model is explicitly given by equation (7.39) and has the *a priori* properties that

$$L_1 > 0$$
$$L_2 < 0.$$

It is in *per capita* terms. On the other hand, if we adopt the Keynes–Wicksell model, then the demand for real balances per unit of capital is given by equation (7.43):

$$\left(\frac{M}{P} \right)^d = L \left[y(x) + \frac{\pi}{\lambda}, \, r(s) + \rho^*, \, i, \, \theta v \right]. \tag{7.43}$$

Here $v = M/PK$ and θ is the result of a portfolio constraint – it is the ratio of net claims of the private sector upon the public sector per dollar of money (ρ is an inflation rate). In this case, we obtain the following results for the demand for money:

$$L_1 > 0 \qquad\qquad L_2 < 0$$
$$L_3 < 0 \qquad 1 > L_4\theta > 0.$$

These results are conventional, of course, with the addition of two results for the inflation rate: expected inflation reduces the demand for money, and actual inflation, embodied in the result L_1, increases it. The expectation of inflation, incidentally, is by the private sector and not by the auctioneer here. S. Fisher also presents a synthesised model which has the same properties as the Keynes–Wicksell model, establishing the formal similarity of the two approaches. This similarity is generally the result of having a common structure, although, to be sure, the demand for money is *assumed* in the Neoclassical model (and the inflation rate derived), while the Keynes–Wicksell model approaches the problem the other way round, beginning with a description of inflation.

Finally, we return to the long-run–short-run demand for money problem – raised by G. Chow and discussed at length in Chapter 4 – but in the growth context; this material is drawn from a paper by J.-M. Grandmont.[67] Grandmont proposes that the short-run demand for nominal money be written as

$$\log M^d(t) = \log A + a \log M(t-1)$$
$$+ b \log P(t) + c \log\left[1 + \left(\frac{\dot{P}}{P}\right)^e\right] + e \log y(t)$$
$$+ f \log\left[1 + \left(\frac{\dot{y}}{y}\right)^e\right] + h \log i(t). \quad (7.44)$$

Here he expects $a, b, e > 0$, $h < 0$ and $a + b = 1$ (absence of money illusion) but has no *a priori* view for c or f. When measured by distributed lags, the two expected variables could easily be called 'permanent prices' and 'permanent real income'. Thus, f might be expected to be positive on the grounds of expecting larger and more frequent expenditures in the (near) future, but could be negative if we reduce our current money balances in anticipation of a future 'cash flow', both being induced by a larger expected income. Similarly, if we expect the rate of inflation to accelerate, we may begin our liquidation of money balances now. This reduces to the Chow short-run model of Chapter 4, for $c = f = 0$.

We may assume that the nominal interest rate is constant and that income and prices grow steadily. In that case it is reasonable to put the actual rates into equation (7.44) in place of $(\dot{y}/y)^e$ and $(\dot{P}/P)^e$; one might also argue that the path of the demand for money is the same as the path for actual money, $M(t) = M^d(t)$, although both sets of assumptions leave one a little hard pressed to explain inflation itself. Equation (7.44) also defines the time path for the money stock, and Grandmont shows that for $0 < a < 1$ an initial value $M^*(o)$ equal to

$$\log M^*(o) = \frac{1}{1-a}\left\{\log A + \left[c - \frac{ab}{(1-a)}\right]\log\left(1 + \frac{\dot{P}}{P}\right)\right.$$

$$\left. + \left[f - \frac{ae}{1-a}\right]\log\left(1 + \frac{\dot{y}}{y}\right)\right\} + \frac{1}{1-a}[b\log P^*(o)$$

$$+ e\log y^*(o) + h\log i^*] \quad (7.45)$$

will tend to grow along the same path. This equation, for $0 = t$, gives the long-run demand directly, under the above assumptions. In a general form, this is

$$M^*(t) = H[P^*(t), y^*(t), i^*, (\dot{P}/P), (\dot{y}/y)] \quad (7.46)$$

which, for specific values of $P^*(t)$, $y^*(t)$ and i^*, yields the testable equation (7.47):[68]

$$\log M^*(t) = \log A + b\log P(t) - ab\log\left(1 + \frac{\dot{P}}{P}\right) + e\log y(t)$$

$$+ ae\log\frac{\dot{y}}{y} + h\log i(t). \quad (7.47)$$

This expression is equivalent to the Chow long-run demand for money if

1. $(\dot{P}/P)$ and $(\dot{Y}/Y)$ are both zero, or
2. $a = 0$

and establishes the generality of the Grandmont model, although, to be sure, the interest rate mechanism in the Grandmont model is not particularly adventuresome. Grandmont also performs some tests on the French data which suggest that indeed $a + b = 1$ and $c = 0$ hold for the French case; the latter result was not the case in the Melitz paper, which was mentioned above.[69]

Footnotes

1. A. Shapiro, 'Inflation, Lags, and the Demand for Money'; J. Melitz, 'Inflationary Expectations and the French Demand for Money, 1959–70'.
2. M. Friedman and A. Schwartz, *A Monetary History of the United States*, p. 657. The wartime studies he is referring to are M. Friedman, 'Prices, Income, and Monetary Change in

Three Wartime Periods', and E. Lerner, 'Inflation in the Confederacy, 1861–65'. Also worth mentioning is a paper by R. Roll, 'Interest Rates and Price Expectations During the Civil War'. Roll argues that bond prices in the North were sensitive (in the early years of the war) to swings in the fortunes of the northern armies; since the war was financed mainly by deficit financing, it is clear that prices reflected these same expectations as well.

3. The Melitz study considers the expected rate of inflation (measured by a distributed lag) as an alternative to a measure of the nominal interest rate (itself measured as the average bond yield, centred at six to eight years in maturity). Inflation outperforms the interest rate in an economy in which inflation does not exceed seven per cent per year. Melitz notes, and worries about, the rapid growth of the money stock in France during the period (as much as eighteen per cent per year). But for his broader measures of money, the fits are quite good. He published his data, for those who might be interested in comparisons (see also the study by J.-M. Grandmont, 'On the Short-Run and Long-Run Demand for Money' for more French data, a derivation of Equation (7.1), and an empirical contradiction).

4. I. Fisher, 'Appreciation and Interest', and *The Theory of Interest*. This is discussed in more detail below.

5. M. Friedman, 'The Quantity Theory of Money: A Restatement', p. 9.

6. In a companion study, E. Lerner ('Inflation in the Confederacy, 1861–65') found M/P falling during the Civil War for the Confederacy, even though prices 'only' rose ten per cent a month, on average. Much of this, though, was after the first quarter of 1863, when M/P stood at ninety per cent of the prewar figure. Lerner offers an *ad hoc* explanation of what happened to the Confederacy after that time.

7. P. Cagan, 'The Monetary Dynamics of Hyper-Inflation'.

8. ibid., p. 37.

9. Cagan drops the interest rate because 'the fact that a stable-valued money does not pay interest means little in time of hyperinflation' (pp. 52–3); he drops real income because the fluctuations in real income are much smaller than the fluctuations in real cash balances. One might add that the lack of monthly (or quarterly, for that matter) data on real income is a factor, as well. Only in the final stages of the hyperinflation, says Cagan, does an appreciable effect from real income seem to matter. Incidentally, Cagan excludes many observations – which do not fit his hypothesis well – taken from the ends of the hyperinflations for three of the seven cases studied. As noted below, this model is 'non-rational' in that the actual rate of inflation will be above or below (depending on whether inflation is declining or accelerating) the expected rate of inflation.

10. R. Jacobs, 'A Difficulty with Monetarist Models of Hyperinflation'.

11. ibid., p. 343.

12. R. Barro, 'Inflation, the Payments Period, and the Demand for Money'; M. Allais, 'A Restatement of the Quantity Theory of Money'.

13. M. Bailey, 'The Welfare Cost of Inflationary Finance'; A. Marty, 'Growth and the Welfare Cost of Inflationary Finance'; and M. Friedman, 'Government Revenue from Inflation'.

14. D. Nichols, 'Some Principles of Inflationary Finance'.

15. D. Meiselman, *Varieties of Monetary Experience*. Two of the studies are not discussed in this section, although they are relevant to the topic of this book. The study of Canada by G. Macesich ('Supply and Demand for Money in Canada') is in the tradition of the studies of Chapter 4. The study of South Korea and Brazil by C. Campbell ('The Velocity of Money and the Rate of Inflation: Recent Experiences in South Korea and Brazil') is of the basic Friedman model interpreted, with the assumption that it is homogeneous of degree 1 in Y, as a velocity equation. He finds, for Brazil, that increases in real income were leading to the absorption of some of the 'inflationary tax' by increasing the demand for real balances. For South Korea, results were less clear, possibly because the South Korean government seems to have flirted with price stability for parts of the period studied.

16. J. Deaver, 'The Chilean Inflation and the Demand for Money'.

17. The money supply rose by 12,000 per cent, P by 12,850 per cent and velocity by seventy per cent, over the period.

18. J. Deaver, 'The Chilean Inflation and the Demand for Money', p. 32.

19. A. Diz, 'Money and Prices in Argentina, 1935–1962'.

20. ibid., p. 101.

21.   Diz's study was completed in 1966. The idea for the use of the variance of inflation (and, as Diz does, for the use of past rates of change of the money stock to explain prices) may well belong to another Chicago/Chile study by A. Harberger ('The Dynamics of Inflation in Chile'), although the latter's context was not explicitly the demand-for-money problem. On the latter point, in the demand for money model of D. Dutton ('The Demand for Money and the Price Level') the following function, basically that of Diz, is analysed:

$$\log\left(\frac{M}{NP}\right)_t = \gamma - \alpha E_t + \eta \log\left(\frac{Y}{N}\right)_t$$

where N is population and $\Delta E_t = \beta(\Delta \log P_{t-1} - E_{t-1})$. The resulting second-order difference equation in $\log P_t$ provides the following conclusions:

1. stability in the Cagan model requires that $\alpha\beta < 1$; and
2. 'only in the case where $\alpha\beta < \sqrt{(1-\beta)^2}$, however, is the price level a convergent monotonic function of the money supply' (p. 1169).

This, then raises the possibility that rapid oscillations can occur in the inflation series calling into question any analysis of the stability of the demand for money (pro or con) when a simple geometric lag (or a mis-specified model) is employed. This applies, says Dutton, to Diz, Deaver and Cagan in some actual cases.

22.   In a recent paper ('The Dynamics of Inflation in Latin America') R. Vogel, somewhat surprisingly, found that the same Monetarist model fits well across sixteen Latin-American countries. The model is

$$\left(\frac{\dot{P}}{P}\right)_t = \alpha + \beta_1\left(\frac{\dot{M}}{M}\right)_t + \beta_2\left(\frac{\dot{M}}{M}\right)_{t-1} - (1-\beta_3)\left(\frac{\dot{Y}}{Y}\right)_t + \beta_4\left[\left(\frac{\dot{P}}{P}\right)_{t-1} - \left(\frac{\dot{P}}{P}\right)_{t-2}\right] + \gamma_t$$

and it just failed to pass an F-test. As we commented (and will discuss further below), there is a problem here because of a contemporaneous endogenous variable (the rate of change of income) and because of the lagged dependent variable. Further, there are potential non-Monetarist influences operating on all the variables but the money stock (by assumption), so this can hardly be taken to be a solely Monetarist model – it just has money in it (see E. Sheehey, 'The Dynamics of Inflation in Latin America: Comment').

23.   K. Wicksell, *Interest and Prices*, pp. 94–5.

24.   J. Keynes, *A Treatise on Money*, Vol. 2, p. 198.

25.   We should note here that the trade cycle theory of the *General Theory* (or the *Treatise*) is perfectly adequate to deal with the short-run Gibson Paradox. Keynes realised this and also realised that the long-run relationship needed to be explained. The Paradox thus persists for the long run, and for that he proposed the Wicksellian model.

26.   J. Keynes, *The General Theory*, p. 198.

27.   The real rate is not to be confused with the natural rate of Wicksell – Wicksell's natural rate equates savings and investment (without inflation).

28.   I. Fisher, *The Theory of Interest*, p. 43.

29.   D. Meiselman, 'Bond Yields and the Price Level: The Gibson Paradox Regained'; P. Cagan, *Determinants and Effects of Changes in the Stock of Money*, 1875–1960; T. Sargent, 'Interest Rates and Prices in the Long Run: A Study of the Gibson Paradox'.

30.   D. Meiselman, 'Bond Yields and the Price Level: The Gibson Paradox Regained', pp. 120–1.

31.   Joseph Livingston is a nationally syndicated columnist; his expected price data are of the cost of living, as judged by business economists. There are other data in the series as well.

32.   W. Gibson, 'Interest Rates and Inflationary Expectations: New Evidence', and S. Turnovsky and M. Wachter, 'A Test of the "Expectations Hypothesis" Using Directly Observed Wage and Price Expectations'.

33.   Gibson's equation is $i = a_0 + a_1(\dot{P}/P)^e$. There is some further work on this 'term structure' problem. In particular, J. Carr and L. Smith ('Money Supply, Interest Rates and the Yield Curve') note that, while 'unexpected monetary changes have a significant but temporary impact on real interest rates, with the greatest impact occurring on the short end of the market',

nevertheless, 'the term structure for real interest rates resembles closely the term structure for nominal rates' (p. 593).

34.   J. Pesando ('A Note on the Rationality of the Livingston Price Expectations') argues that the Livingston data are not rational in the sense defined below, and may not (therefore) represent market opinion. There is, as well, a study of the German hyperinflation by J. Frenkel ('The Forward Exchange Rate, Expectations and the Demand for Money: the German Hyperinflation'), which uses 'interest parity' theory to derive inflationary expectations. But since this was only seen by this author as a working paper, it would not do to discuss it further here.

35.   We noted this problem in Chapter 4, in a different context. See T. Cargill and R. Meyer, 'Interest Rates and Prices since 1950', and V. Corbo, *Inflation in Developing Countries*. In the former, correction produced the conclusions that the lags were short and that there was evidence of instability in the US data, centred around 1960.

36.   T. Sargent, 'Interest Rates and Prices in the Long Run: A Study of the Gibson Paradox'.

37.   T. Sargent, 'Rational Expectations, the Real Rate of Interest, and the Natural Rate of Unemployment', p. 430.

38.   The reason for using a rational model is one's belief that monitoring only the past behaviour of prices is insufficient – that other variables matter. Examples of important studies using other than just the past behaviour of prices are those by F. Modigliani and R. Shiller ('Inflation, Rational Expectations, and the Term Structure of Interest Rates') and J. Rutledge, *A Monetarist Model of Inflationary Expectations*.

39.   R. Roll ('Rational Response to the Money Supply') puts a paradox as follows. Consumers, obviously, use the past behaviour of the money stock to predict money stocks and (hence) prices in the future. Thus,

> By the very act of making decisions on the basis of anticipated money stocks, however, consumers decrease the empirical connection between future changes in money and the current price of goods. . . . [an] analogy to a perfect stock market can be made: a firm whose earnings have grown period after period will not find its common stock changing in price after the next earnings increase unless these earnings deviate from the anticipated. [pp. 587–8]

We are reminded here of comments made in Chapters 4 and 6 about the difficulty of capturing (empirically) interest rate expectation effects when interest rates are assumed to be (or are) determined by expectations. There is a study by J. Rutledge (*A Monetarist Model of Inflationary Expectations*) which argues that the correct way to model expectations is to assume that they are costly to assemble and to solve an optimising problem in which overall objectives (e.g., a consumption plan) are constrained by this cost (and others). This is by analogy with business forecasting.

40.   J. Muth, 'Rational Expectations and the Theory of Price Movements'.

41.   J. Pesando, 'A Note on the Rationality of the Livingston Price Expectations', p. 850.

42.   T. Sargent and N. Wallace, 'The Stability of Models of Money and Growth with Perfect Foresight'.

43.   F. Black, 'Uniqueness of the Price Level in Monetary Growth Models with Rational Expectations'.

44.   The solution is $y_t = a_1 \lambda_1^t + a_2 \lambda_2^t$ where y_t is the time path of inflation,

$$\lambda_{1,2} = \left(\frac{1}{2}\beta\right)\left[(1 - \beta) \pm \sqrt{(1 + 2\beta + \beta^2 - 4k\beta)}\right]$$

and

$$k = \left(\log \frac{M_{t-1}}{M_t}\right) \Big/ \left(\frac{P_t}{P_{t+1}}\right) > 1.$$

45.   R. Mundell, *Monetary Theory*; L. Metzler, 'Wealth, Saving, and the Rate of Interest'.

46.   As described in E. Karni, 'Inflation and the Real Interest Rate: a Long Term Analysis'.

47.   H. Grossman and A. Policano, 'Money Balances, Commodity Inventories, and Inflationary Expectations'.

48.   The motive for holding working balances in this model is that receipts occur less frequently than purchases of commodity 1. If, as it turns out, $i_1 > 0$, then optimal purchases will

be less frequent than income receipts, and the model collapses. Purchases of G_2 are less frequent than income receipts.

49.   There is an earlier paper by R. Barro along similar lines ('Inflation, the Payments Period, and the Demand for Money'). Barro analyses a transactions costs model for employers and employees, in which both agents choose whether to hold a rapidly depreciating currency or an alternative (and safer) asset which is relatively costly to acquire. When fit on the Cagan data (not for Greece and Russia) the fits are good and support the (exact) *a priori* expectations for the coefficients of the model. R. Jacobs (A Difficulty with Monetarist Models of Hyperinflation') points out that Barro's model relates two mutually dependent variables; when it is re-specified in terms of the rate of change of the nominal money stock, the results are not at all impressive.

50.   M. Friedman, 'A Theoretical Framework for Monetary Analysis' and 'A Monetary Theory of Nominal Income'. See also M. Friedman, 'Comments on the Critics' and the papers by the critics: K. Brunner and A. Meltzer ('Friedman's Monetary Theory'), J. Tobin ('Friedman's Theoretical Framework') and P. Davidson ('A Keynesian View of Friedman's Theoretical Framework for Monetary Analysis'). These papers are notable for the sense of ritual that they convey.

51.   J. M. Keynes, *The General Theory*, p. 276.

52.   For example, see the surveys written by Y. Park ('Some Current Issues on the Transmission Process of Monetary Policy') and E. Foster ('Costs and Benefits of Inflation').

53.   B. McCallum, 'Friedman's Missing Equation: Another Approach'.

54.   R. Lipsey, 'The Micro Theory of the Phillips Curve Reconsidered: A Reply to Holmes and Smyth'.

55.   L. Dicks-Mireaux and J. C. Dow, 'The Determinants of Wage Inflation: United Kingdom, 1946–56'.

56.   As W. Branson points out, to go the one step further and link the rate of change of prices to unemployment, one must assume that the functional distribution of income is constant. In actual fact this is somewhat implausible and it is more likely not only that the variance is significant, but also that it is sensitive to inflation (by cost-push, after all) and to disturbances originating in other markets. This suggests, as the text argues, that equation (7.33c) is incomplete.

57.   In the case of Lipsey we could argue that the money market clears itself and that the capital stock is fixed so that a direct relation exists between the commodity and labour markets. Lipsey describes his conception as 'non-Walrasian'; an interpretation can be given as follows. Suppose commodity (with fixed capital stock), money, and bond market equilibrium curves can be drawn in the style of Patinkin as

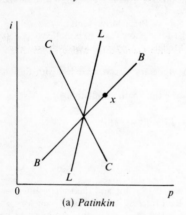
(a) *Patinkin*

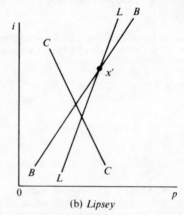
(b) *Lipsey*

Thus, in the Walrasian world of (a), as attributed to Patinkin, it is impossible to conceive of being off the CC curve and not also off at least one other curve – consider point x. That is the point made above in the text. Of course, if we are willing to scrap our three-sector model, or even to abandon an overall solution, we can draw case (b). Here point x' illustrates the Lipsey situation, where all but one market is in equilibrium; this, then, is non-Walrasian, in the sense of not having an overall solution, as drawn.

58. This section was drawn up from the literature cited, but the reader might well consult a paper by R. Dornbusch and J. Frenkel ('Inflation and Growth') for an effective survey of the entire literature.

59. J. Hicks, *Capital and Growth*, p. 280. This, roughly, is how Friedman and Schwartz (*A Monetary History of the United States*) and Cagan (*Determinants and Effects of Changes in the Stock of Money*) explain the most important variations in pre-Federal Reserve American inflation rates – i.e., as induced by changes in the supply of gold (as well as its cost of production) primarily as the result of major discoveries of that period. A stable demand for money obviously assists in this dynamic context.

60. J. Hicks, *Capital and Growth*, p. 281.

61. M. Friedman, 'The Optimum Quantity of Money', p. 34.

62. Friedman's model is in the Neoclassical tradition, although its avoidance of explicit structural relationships in favour of empirical generalisations makes it somewhat unique in that literature. This latter judgement is also the theme of the review of Friedman's book on the *Optimum Quantity of Money* by F. Hahn ('Professor Friedman's Views on Money').

63. S. Fisher, 'Keynes–Wicksell and Neoclassical Models of Money and Growth', p. 880.

64. This work follows the paper by S. Fischer (ibid.). The distinction and much of the analysis is that of J. Stein, 'Neoclassical and Keynes–Wicksell Monetary Growth Models', for example.

65. Following a paper by J. Frenkel and C. Rodriquez ('Wealth Effects and the Dynamics of Inflation') we note that wealth effects are also relevant here. In their discussion, an increase in the money stock actually generates an increased capital stock (this is in contrast to a paper by M. Sidrauski, 'Inflation and Economic Growth'). Their framework is Neoclassical.

66. S. Fisher, 'Keynes–Wicksell and Neoclassical Models of Money and Growth'. p. 880. The later version, as well as the definitive discussion of this literature, appears in J. Stein, *Money and Capacity Growth*.

67. J.-M. Grandmont, 'On the Short-Run and Long-Run Demand for Money'.

68. $i^*(t) = i^*$, and $P^*(t)$ and $Y^*(t)$ are given by

$$P^*(t) = P^*(0)\left(1 + \frac{\dot{P}}{P}\right)^t$$

and

$$Y^*(t) = Y^*(0)\left(1 + \frac{\dot{Y}}{Y}\right)^t.$$

These can be estimated as 'permanent variables'.

69. J. Melitz, 'Inflationary Expectations and the French Demand for Money, 1959–70'.

APPENDIX A

Household Behaviour and the Demand for Money

A.1 General introduction

The primary purpose of this appendix is to develop the dominant elements that have been instrumental in forming the present atemporal-certainty theory of the demand for money by households. The literature pertaining to the micro-foundations of monetary theory occupies a central place in the history of economic theory; yet there is no single source where a complete mathematical survey exists. The principal task of this appendix then is to present such a survey.

A second, but by no means trivial, purpose is to extend and generalise the various models, so as to make it perfectly clear how the many important contributions can be evaluated. Indeed, we believe that this work reveals the inherent interconnections between the different theories. Once the work has been placed in its context, and the similarities and differences exploited, it is then possible to be quite precise as to the differences one might anticipate with regard to the empirical implications of these theories. Consequently, we have chosen to emphasise the ability of the micro-models to generate empirical behavioural restrictions. In this respect, we are following the tradition of the barter theory of individual behaviour, as exemplified in the work of Samuelson.[1] Moreover, to integrate the barter and monetary analyses, it seems appropriate to make the overriding issue with each of the monetary models its ability to produce all or any of the restrictions from barter theory and, if not (or if they differ, for that matter), to explain why the restrictions fail to hold. As will be seen, an effective comparison is thereby established.

An individual undertaking economic transactions is characterised by a budget constraint(s) and a relationship depicting his preferences. Micro-monetary theory has accepted this framework and has concentrated on the appropriate inclusion of money balances either in the constraints or in the utility function (or both). We begin with the simplest forms in which the decision to hold money appears as an appendage to be determined after the individual has formulated the other aspects of his plan, as is the case of the

222

Classical theories, as interpreted by contemporary authors such as Lloyd, Brunner and Marschak.[2] We next proceed to the Neoclassical framework, where money enters the utility function in a like manner to any other commodity. Indeed, one may state that the distinction between the Classical and Neoclassical themes is that in the latter money generates utility, while in the former it does not. A criticism of the basic Neoclassical approach centres around this difference, since it is felt that money thereby loses its distinct role, which it must occupy in realistic decision processes. To alleviate this criticism, Clower and others (although retaining money in the preference relation) return to the Classical view of distinguishing money from other commodities by the manner in which it constrains the feasible transactions an individual may undertake.[3]

A.2   The Lloyd Classical model

A.2.1   *Equilibrium*

C. Lloyd develops a model wherein individuals hold money, not because they want to, but because they must.[4] This implies that money balances do not affect the desires or preferences of the individual, but only the behavioural constraints.

Let us define the utility function (representing preferences) as

$$u = U(x_1, \ldots, x_n) \tag{A1}$$

where u is utility, U is the utility function and x_i is the quantity demanded of the ith real commodity (not including the money commodity). We assume, as is usual, that the utility function is twice continuously differentiable, and strictly quasi-concave with $U_i \geqslant 0$ (not all zero).[5] The individual then maximises equation (A1) with respect to the demands and subject to the budget constraint given as equation (A2):

$$\Sigma_{i=1}^n p_i x_i + M = Y + \bar{M}. \tag{A2}$$

Here p_i is the fixed positive finite money price of the ith real commodity, M is the quantity of money demanded, and $Y(\geqslant 0)$ and $\bar{M}(\geqslant 0)$ (not both zero) are the fixed nominal values of income and the money endowment, respectively.

The money requirement constraint is given by

$$M = \kappa \Sigma_{i=1}^n p_i x_i \tag{A3}$$

where $\kappa > 0$ is a fixed constant. Equations (A1) and (A3) then formalise the idea that the household demands money because it must (as long as the value of expenditure is positive), since M is not entered directly into the utility function and since κ is positive. This model has been characterised as one in which the individual faces its own quantity equation.

The programme for the individual is to

$$\underset{(x_1, \ldots, x_n, M)}{\text{Max.} \quad U(x_1, \ldots, x_n)}$$

subject to

$$\Sigma_{i=1}^n p_i x_i + M = Y + \bar{M} \tag{A4}$$
$$M = \kappa \Sigma_{i=1}^n p_i x_i.$$

The solution to the system (A4) is recursive in nature. The individual first determines $x_1, \ldots, x_n$ given $p_1, \ldots, p_n$, Y, $\bar{M}$ and U and then, with κ and with $x_1, \ldots, x_n$ predetermined, it determines M. We can combine (A2) and (A3) as

$$(1 + \kappa) \Sigma_{i=1}^n p_i x_i = Y + \bar{M} \tag{A5}$$

and so the Lagrangean of the system is

$$\mathcal{L} = U(x_1, \ldots, x_n) - \lambda[(1 + \kappa) \Sigma_{i=1}^n p_i x_i - Y - \bar{M}]$$

and the first-order conditions are [6]

$$U_i - \lambda(1 + \kappa)p_i = 0 \qquad\qquad i = 1, \ldots, n \tag{A6}$$
$$-(1 + \kappa)\Sigma_{i=1}^n p_i x_i + Y + \bar{M} = 0.$$

From equation set (A6) we can determine $x_1, \ldots, x_n$ and λ and then with $x_1, \ldots, x_n$ we can substitute into (A3) to derive M. Hence, the demand functions can be written out as equations (A7):

$$x_i = h_i(p_i, \ldots, Y, \bar{M}) \tag{A7}$$
$$M = \kappa \Sigma_{i=1}^n p_i h_i(p_i, \ldots, p_n, Y, \bar{M}) = h_M(p_1, \ldots, p_n, Y, \bar{M}).$$

A.2.2   *Comparative equilibria results*

We now proceed to generate results for the Neoclassical restrictions. The homogeneity property of the demand functions is easily established, and the result is not unexpected. If all the prices, income and money endowment change in the same proportion, then the utility function is not affected and the new value of the constraint is given as (where α is the percentage change)

$$\alpha(1 + \kappa)\Sigma_{i=1}^n p_i x_i = \alpha(Y + \bar{M}).$$

These facts establish that the real commodity demand functions (h_i for $i = 1, \ldots, n$) are homogeneous of degree 0 in prices, income and the money endowment. Further, this implies that the right-hand side of equation (A3) is now $\alpha \kappa p_i x_i$ and thus the new demand for money balances is $\alpha M = \alpha h_M(p_1, \ldots, p_n, Y, \bar{M})$. This function, that is to say, is homogeneous of degree 1 in money prices, income and the money endowment.

To determine the effects of a change in p_k, Y and $\bar{M}$ upon the demand functions we must differentiate equations (A6) and (A3), the latter because of the two-tier nature of the problem, as described below. This yields [7]

$$\begin{bmatrix} \mathbf{U}'' & -(1+\kappa)\mathbf{p} \\ -(1+\kappa)\mathbf{p}^T & 0 \end{bmatrix} \begin{bmatrix} \dfrac{\partial \mathbf{x}}{\partial \mu} \\[2mm] \dfrac{\partial \lambda}{\partial \mu} \end{bmatrix} = \begin{bmatrix} \mathbf{0}_n \\ -1 \end{bmatrix} \qquad (A8)$$

$$\frac{\partial x_i}{\partial \mu} = -\frac{D_{n+1\,i}}{D} \qquad i = 1, \ldots, n \,[8] \qquad (A9)$$

$$\mu = Y, \bar{M}.$$

Furthermore, since $M = \kappa \Sigma_{i=1}^n p_i x_i = \kappa(Y + \bar{M} - M)$ from the budget constraint, then we can write $M = [\kappa/(1+\kappa)](Y + \bar{M})$; therefore,

$$\frac{\partial M}{\partial \mu} = \frac{\kappa}{(1+\kappa)} > 0 \qquad \mu = Y, \bar{M}. \qquad (A10)$$

As a consequence, the second Neoclassical restriction is satisfied. In other words, the marginal propensity to demand any commodity is the same irrespective of the source of the change in income (with prices constant).

The substitution effect is

$$\lambda(1+\kappa)\frac{D_{ki}}{D} = \frac{\partial x_i}{\partial p_k} + (1+\kappa)x_k\frac{D_{n+1\,i}}{D}; \qquad i, k = 1, \ldots, n$$

then, defining the left side of this expression as S_{ik} and using equation (A9),

$$S_{ik} = \frac{\partial x_i}{\partial p_k} + x_k\frac{\partial x_i}{\partial Y} + \kappa x_k\frac{\partial x_i}{\partial \bar{M}}. \qquad i, k = 1, \ldots, n \qquad (A11)$$

Therefore, the substitution effect (S_{ik}) is composed of the price effect $(\partial x_i/\partial p_k)$, the income effect $[x_k(\partial s_i/\partial Y)]$, and the money endowment (or real balance) effect $[\kappa\kappa_k(\partial x_i/\partial \bar{M})]$. Finally, we note that $\partial M/\partial p_k = 0$ and thus the demand for money is invariant with respect to a change in any money price.

The third Neoclassical restriction, namely that the substitution effects are symmetric, likewise holds in this model, since $\mathbf{U}''$ is symmetric (so that $D_{ij} = D_{ji}$) and therefore

$$S_{ij} = \lambda(1+\kappa)\frac{D_{ij}}{D} = \lambda(1+\kappa)\frac{D_{ji}}{D} = S_{ji}.$$

Proceeding, we can establish a fourth restriction (see Samuelson).[9] That is, from the second-order conditions, and from the fact that each substitution effect consists of a single ratio of the co-factor to the determinant of the matrix in (A8) multiplied by a positive number, we can prove that the matrix of substitution effects is negative semi-definite; furthermore, $S_{ii} < 0$, for $i = 1, \ldots, n$, for our fifth restriction.

The sixth restriction, that $\Sigma_{j=1}^{n} p_j S_{ij} = 0$, follows directly from the homogeneity property of the real demand functions. Moreover, by the nature of the demand-for-money function, we can also prove the seventh restriction by means of equation (A7). Thus, from (A7),

$$\frac{\partial M}{\partial p_j} = \kappa\left(x_j + \Sigma_{i=1}^{n} p_i \frac{\partial x_i}{\partial p_j}\right).$$

Then, using equation (A11), we have

$$\frac{\partial M}{\partial p_j} = \kappa\left[x_j + \Sigma_{i=1}^{n} p_i\left(S_{ij} - x_j \frac{\partial x_i}{\partial Y} - \kappa x_j \frac{\partial x_i}{\partial \overline{M}}\right)\right]$$

and, from the budget constraint,

$$\frac{\partial M}{\partial p_j} = \kappa x_j + \kappa\Sigma_{i=1}^{n} p_i S_{ij} + \kappa x_j\left(\frac{\partial M}{\partial Y} - 1\right) + \kappa^2 x_j\left(\frac{\partial M}{\partial \overline{M}} - 1\right).$$

Then from equation (A10)

$$\frac{\partial M}{\partial p_j} = \kappa\Sigma_{i=1}^{n} p_i S_{ij} + \kappa x_j \frac{\kappa}{(1 + \kappa)} - \kappa^2 x_j\left(\frac{\kappa}{(1 + \kappa)} - 1\right)$$

and, since $\partial M/\partial p_j = 0$, then

$$\frac{\partial M}{\partial p_j} = \kappa\Sigma_{i=1}^{n} p_i S_{ij} = 0,$$

which implies that $\Sigma_{i=1}^{n} p_i S_{ii} = 0$ because $\kappa > 0$, or $\Sigma_{j=1}^{n} p_j S_{ji} = 0$.

Finally, from $S_{ij} = S_{ji}$ we have $\Sigma_{j=1}^{n} p_j S_{ij} = 0$. Therefore, in this basic Classical model the complete list of Neoclassical restrictions is obtained.

A.3 A generalised Marschak–Brunner Classical model[10]

A.3.1 *Equilibrium*

Suppose that, instead of the individual having a fixed nominal income, he is now endowed with quantities of the n real commodities so that[11]

$$\bar{x} = (\bar{x}_1 \ldots \bar{x}_n)^T \geqslant 0.$$

In this case nominal income is now the sum of the value of the commodity endowments. In addition, we can generalise the money requirements constraint to be

$$M = F(p_1, \ldots, p_n, x_1, \ldots, x_n, \bar{x}_1, \ldots, \bar{x}_n, \bar{M}) \qquad (A12)$$

where F is twice continuously differentiable, homogeneous of degree 1 in prices and money endowment, strictly quasi-convex, and $F(p_1, \ldots, p_n, 0, \ldots, 0, \bar{x}_1, \ldots, \bar{x}_n, \bar{M}) = 0$, with $F_i > 0$ for $i = 1, \ldots, n$ of the commodities.[12]

The individual's programme is to maximise utility equation (A1) subject to equations (A2) and (A12). The first-order conditions are

$$U_i - \lambda(p_i + F_i) = 0 \qquad\qquad i = 1, \ldots, n \qquad (A13)$$

$$-\sum_{i=1}^{n} p_i(x_i - \bar{x}_i) - F(\mathbf{p}, \mathbf{x}, \bar{\mathbf{x}}, \bar{M}) + \bar{M} = 0.$$

From equations (A13) we can derive the demand functions for the n real commodities and money as

$$x_i = h_i(p_1, \ldots, p_n, \bar{x}_1, \ldots, \bar{x}_n, \bar{M}) \qquad i = 1, \ldots, n \qquad (A14)$$

$$M = h_M(p_1, \ldots, p_n, h_1, \ldots, h_n, \bar{x}_1, \ldots, \bar{x}_n, \bar{M}).$$

From equations (A13) we observe that the rate of commodity substitution, U_i/U_j, is not, as in the previous model, equal to the relative prices, p_i/p_j; instead, it is equal to the ratio of money prices and each price, p_k, is modified by the term F_k. F_k is the increase in the demand for money needed to replenish the endowment bundle utilised in the planned increase in the demand for the ith real commodity. Therefore $p_i + F_i$ is the 'marginal demand cost' to the individual of an increase in the quantity x_i. Thus, the rate of commodity substitution between commodity i and commodity j is equal to the ratio of marginal demand costs for i and j.

A.3.2 *Comparative equilibria results*

If all prices and the money endowment change in the same proportion, then $U_i/U_j = (p_i + F_i)/(p_j + F_j)$ both before and after the change; this result obtains because U is not affected and because F is homogeneous of degree 1 in prices and the money endowment. This also means that the budget constraint is not affected by the change in the exogenous variables. Consequently, h_i for $i = 1, \ldots, n$ is homogeneous of degree 0 in $\mathbf{p}$, $\bar{\mathbf{x}}$ and $\bar{M}$, and h_M is homogeneous of degree 1 in the same variables.

If there is a change in the endowment of the kth real commodity, then

$$
\begin{bmatrix}
\mathbf{U}'' - \lambda \mathbf{F}_\mathbf{x}'' & -(p + \mathbf{F}_\mathbf{x}') \\
\\
-(p + \mathbf{F}_\mathbf{x}')^T & 0
\end{bmatrix}
\begin{bmatrix}
\dfrac{\partial \mathbf{x}}{\partial \bar{x}_k} \\
\\
\dfrac{\partial \lambda}{\partial \bar{x}_k}
\end{bmatrix}
=
\begin{bmatrix}
\lambda \dfrac{\partial \mathbf{F}_\mathbf{x}'}{\partial \bar{x}_k} \\
\\
-p_k + \dfrac{\partial F}{\partial x_k}
\end{bmatrix}
\tag{A15}
$$

and so

$$
\frac{\partial x_i}{\partial \bar{x}_k} = \lambda \Sigma_{j=1}^n \frac{\partial F_j}{\partial \bar{x}_k} \frac{D_{ji}}{D} + \left(\frac{\partial F}{d\bar{x}_k} - p_k\right) \frac{D_{n+1\,i}}{D}
\tag{A16}
$$

$$
\frac{\partial M}{\partial \bar{x}_k} = \frac{\partial F}{\partial \bar{x}_k}. \qquad\qquad i, k = 1, \ldots, n
$$

The change in the kth real commodity endowment has three effects on the real demands. First there is the effect on the budget constraint, which is $-p_k(D_{n+1\,i}/D)$; second there is the direct effect on the money demand function, $(\partial F/\partial \bar{x}_k)(D_{n+1\,i}/D)$; finally, there is the indirect effect on the money demand function. Notice that if $\bar{M}$ changes then we must replace $(\partial F/\partial \bar{x}_k)$ with $(\partial F/\partial \bar{M})$ and replace p_k with 1 in equation (A16). This implies that, unless changes in any endowment affect F in an identical manner, in terms of first derivatives and second-order cross derivatives, then the marginal propensity to demand varies with the different sources of the change in income (with prices constant).

Because of the characteristics of this model, the symmetry of cross-substitution effects and the negativeness of the own-substitution effects (as well as the other Neoclassical restrictions depending on these properties in some way) do not hold. These conclusions can be derived from the fact that

$$
du = \Sigma_{i=1}^n U_i dx_i = \lambda \Sigma_{i=1}^n (p_i + F_i)\, dx_i = 0,
$$

and from the budget constraint,

$$
-\Sigma_{i=1}^n p_i dx_i - \Sigma_{i=1}^n F_i dx_i + \left(p_k - \frac{\partial F}{\partial \bar{x}_k}\right) d\bar{x}_k + \left(\bar{x}_k - x_k - \frac{\partial F}{\partial p_k}\right) dp_k = 0.
$$

Upon solving, we have

$$
\frac{\partial \bar{x}_k}{\partial p_k} = \frac{\dfrac{\partial F}{\partial p_k} + x_k - \bar{x}_k}{\dfrac{\partial F}{\partial \bar{x}_k} - p_k}.
\tag{A17}
$$

Next, utilising equation (A14) we obtain

$$
\left.\frac{\partial x_i}{\partial p_k}\right|_{u=\bar{u}} = \frac{\partial x_i}{\partial p_k} + \frac{\partial x_i}{\partial \bar{x}_k} \frac{\partial \bar{x}_k}{\partial p_k}
\tag{A18}
$$

and, in the same fashion as we derived $\partial x_i / \partial \bar{x}_k$, we obtain

$$\frac{\partial x_i}{\partial p_k} = \lambda \frac{D_{ki}}{D} + \lambda \Sigma_{j=1}^n \frac{\partial F_j}{\partial p_k} \frac{D_{ji}}{D} + \left(x_k + \frac{\partial F}{\partial p_k} - \bar{x}_k \right) \frac{D_{n+1i}}{D}. \quad i, k = 1, \ldots, n$$

(A19)

Substituting (A17) and (A19) into (A18) we find that

$$\left. \frac{\partial x_i}{\partial p_k} \right|_{u=\bar{u}} = \lambda \frac{D_{ki}}{D} + \lambda \Sigma_{j=1}^n \left(\frac{\partial F_j}{\partial p_k} + \frac{\partial F_j}{\partial \bar{x}_k} \right) \frac{D_{ji}}{D}.$$

(A20)

Now, by definition, S_{ik} is given by the right side of equation (A20) and it is obvious that $S_{ik} \neq S_{ki}$ because, in general, the term under the summation sign in (A20) is not 0. $S_{ii} \nless 0$ because (A20) contains the off-diagonal elements D_{ji}/D and this implies that the matrix of substitution effects is not negative semi-definite. Finally, it follows directly from the homogeneity property that $\Sigma_{j=1}^n p_j S_{ij} = 0$ and since $S_{ij} \neq S_{ji}$ we also *cannot* claim the added restriction that $\Sigma_{j=1}^n p_j S_{ji} = 0$.

At this point, having considered two versions of different degrees of generality of the Classical model, we turn to the analysis of the models developed in the Neoclassical style, where households not only *must* but also *desire* to hold money.

A.4 The Samuelson–Patinkin model

A.4.1 *Equilibrium*

In his work on monetary theory, P. Samuelson has continually espoused the view that money cannot properly be treated like any other commodity.[13] This belief led him to include not only money balances in the utility function but also all money prices; indeed, if we were to eliminate prices as objects of utility, with a budget constraint such as that exhibited as equation (A2), we would derive results that show money to be no different from any other commodity. Thus, to capture the effect desired – that money provides utility not for its own sake but for what it can buy – along with money there must appear the commodity prices – suitably defined in terms of the money commodity itself. We can write this utility function as equation (A21).[14]

$$u = U(x_1, \ldots, x_n, M, p_1, \ldots, p_n).$$

(A21)

Even so, this function does not capture the essential property of money as an intermediate (in exchange). That is, we must impose a homogeneity condition on the utility function; this, usually, is that U is homogeneous of degree 0 in the money prices and money itself.

Once we impose a homogeneity condition when prices enter the utility function, it also becomes necessary to specify whether these prices are money prices or prices defined in terms of some fictitious unit of account (i.e., absolute or nominal prices). For example, if $U(x_1, \ldots, x_n\, Mq_M, q_1, \ldots, q_n)$ is homogeneous of degree 0 in the absolute prices, which are denoted by the letter q, and q_M is the absolute price of money, then we can divide all prices by q_M (where $q_i/q_M = p_i$) and arrive at a form identical to (A21). Yet (A21) is homogeneous of degree 0 in money and the money prices, while the function defined with absolute prices does not have this property but rather is homogeneous of degree 0 in the absolute prices. Furthermore, the fact that the homogeneity conditions assumed in the two utility functions are different, even though their domains are identical, has important implications for the homogeneity property of the resulting demand functions that emanate from the two models. This discussion should inspire a certain amount of carefulness on this subject.

It should also be mentioned, at this juncture, that a special case of (A21) is $u = U(x_1, \ldots, x_n, M, P)$ where P is a money price index of $p_1, \ldots, p_n$; here, with the homogeneity condition, we get $u = U(x_1, \ldots, x_n, M/P)$. This means that all the results derived by D. Patinkin with respect to the individual's demand-for-money function can be viewed as a highly important special case of the work of Samuelson.[15] It is for this reason that we deal with the more general Neoclassical model.

A variant of the Samuelson–Patinkin model may be formulated as follows:

$$\text{Max.} \qquad U(x_1, \ldots, x_n, M, p_1, \ldots, p_n) \tag{A22}$$
$$(x_1, \ldots, x_n, M)$$

subject to

$$\Sigma_{i=1}^n p_i (x_i - \bar{x}_i) + M - \bar{M} = 0.$$

The first-order conditions, then, are of the following form:

$$U_i - \lambda p_i = 0 \qquad i = 1, \ldots, n$$
$$U_M - \lambda = 0 \tag{A23}$$
$$\Sigma_{i-1}^n p_i(x_i - \bar{x}_i) + M - \bar{M} = 0.$$

From equations (A23) we can solve for the demand functions:

$$x_i = h_i(p_1, \ldots, p_n, \bar{x}_1, \ldots, \bar{x}_n, \bar{M}) \qquad i = 1, \ldots, n \tag{A24}$$
$$M = h_M(p_1, \ldots, p_n, \bar{x}_1, \ldots, \bar{x}_n, \bar{M}).$$

Notice from equations (A23) that we have the rate of substitution of any real commodity for money equal to the money price of that commodity. This condition reflects the unit of account role of money in the analysis (i.e., that the money price of money is unity.)

A.4.2 *Comparative equilibria results*

For a change in the endowment of any commodity we may compute that

$$
\begin{bmatrix} \mathbf{U}'' & -\mathbf{p} \\ -\mathbf{p}^T & 0 \end{bmatrix} \begin{bmatrix} \dfrac{\partial \mathbf{x}}{\partial} \\[6pt] \dfrac{\partial M}{\partial \mu} \\[6pt] \dfrac{\partial \lambda}{\partial \mu} \end{bmatrix} = \begin{bmatrix} \mathbf{0}_{n+1} \\[12pt] -\delta \end{bmatrix}
\tag{A25}
$$

and so

$$
\frac{\partial x_i}{\partial \mu} = -\delta \frac{D_{n+2i}}{D} \qquad\qquad i = 1, \ldots, n
\tag{A26}
$$

$$
\frac{\partial M}{\partial \mu} = -\delta \frac{D_{n+2n+1}}{D}. \qquad \delta = \begin{cases} p_i \text{ when } \mu = \bar{x}_i \\ 1 \text{ when } \mu = \bar{M} \end{cases} \quad i = 1, \ldots, n.
$$

$$
\mu = \bar{x}_1, \ldots, \bar{x}_n, \bar{M}
$$

Therefore, we obtain the first Neoclassical restriction which states that the change in demand for any commodity is the same regardless of the source of the change in income, when prices are held constant. Also, as claimed earlier, we may write the demand functions as D. Patinkin does: $x_i = h_i(p_1, \ldots, p_n, \Sigma_{i=1}^n p_i \bar{x}_i + \bar{M})$, for $i = 1, \ldots, n$ and $M = h_M(p_1, \ldots, p_n, \Sigma_{i=1}^n p_i \bar{x}_i + \bar{M})$.

The price effects in the modified Samuelson model are:

$$
\frac{\partial x_i}{\partial p_k} = \frac{\lambda D_{ki}}{D} - \Sigma_{j=1}^n \frac{\partial U_j}{\partial p_k} \frac{D_{ji}}{D} - \frac{\partial U_M}{\partial p_k} \frac{D_{jn+1}}{D} + (x_k - \bar{x}_k) \frac{D_{n+2i}}{D}
\tag{A27}
$$

$$
\frac{\partial M}{\partial p_k} = \frac{\lambda D_{kn+1}}{D} - \Sigma_{j=1}^n \frac{\partial U_j}{\partial p_k} \frac{D_{jn+1}}{D} - \frac{\partial U_M}{\partial p_k} \frac{D_{jn+1}}{D}
$$

$$
+ (x_k - \bar{x}_k) \frac{D_{n+2n+1}}{D} \qquad i,k = 1, \ldots, n
$$

Obviously, the right side of equations (A27) may be analysed by means of substitution and income effects. To obtain the substitution effect, take the total differential of (A21), when p_k changes and set $du = 0$,

$$
\Sigma_{i=1}^n U_i dx_i + U_M dM + \frac{\partial U}{\partial p_k} dp_k = 0.
$$

From the first-order conditions we have

$$\lambda\left(\Sigma_{i=1}^{n}\, p_i dx_i + dM\right) + \frac{\partial U}{dp_k}\, \partial p_k = 0. \tag{A28}$$

Next, the differential equation for the budget constraint, when the individual is compensated with the endowment $\bar{x}_k$, is

$$-\Sigma_{i=1}^{n}\, p_i dx_i + (\bar{x}_k - x_k)\, dp_k - dM + p_k d\bar{x}_k = 0. \tag{A29}$$

Utilising the demand functions (A24), we can write equations (A28) and (A29) as,

$$\lambda \Sigma_{i=1}^{n} p_i \left(\frac{\partial h_i}{\partial p_k} + \frac{\partial h_i}{\partial \bar{x}_k}\frac{\partial \bar{x}_k}{\partial p_k}\right) + \left(\frac{\partial h_M}{\partial p_k} + \frac{\partial h_M}{\partial \bar{x}_k}\frac{\partial \bar{x}_k}{\partial p_k}\right) + \frac{\partial U}{\partial p_k} = 0$$

$$\tag{A30}$$

$$-\Sigma_{i=1}^{n} p_i \left(\frac{\partial h_i}{\partial p_k} + \frac{\partial h_i}{\partial \bar{x}_k}\frac{\partial \bar{x}_k}{\partial p_k}\right) - \left(\frac{\partial h_M}{\partial p_k} + \frac{\partial h_M}{\partial \bar{x}_k}\frac{\partial \bar{x}_k}{\partial p_k}\right) + (\bar{x}_k - x_k) + \frac{\partial \bar{x}_k}{\partial p_k} p_k = 0.$$

Hence, with equation (A30) we find that,

$$\frac{\partial \bar{x}_k}{\partial p_k} = \left[-\left(\frac{\partial U}{\partial p_k}\Big/\lambda\right) + x_k - \bar{x}_k\right](p_k)^{-1}. \tag{A31}$$

This implies that, with (A26) and (A27),

$$\left.\frac{\partial x_i}{\partial p_k}\right|_{u=\bar{u}} = \frac{\partial x_i}{\partial p_k} + \frac{\partial x_i}{\partial \bar{x}_k}\frac{\partial \bar{x}_k}{\partial p_k}$$

$$\left.\frac{\partial x_i}{\partial p_k}\right|_{u=\bar{u}} = \lambda \frac{D_{ki}}{D} - \Sigma_{j=1}^{n} \frac{\partial U_j}{\partial p_k}\frac{D_{ji}}{D} - \frac{\partial U_M}{\partial p_k}\frac{D_{jn+1}}{D} + \frac{\partial U}{\partial p_k}\frac{D_{n+2i}}{\lambda D}.$$

Since

$$\left.\frac{\partial x_i}{\partial p_k}\right|_{\bar{u}} = S_{ik},$$

we may define

$$S_{ik} = \mathscr{S}_{ik} - \frac{\partial U}{\partial p_k}\frac{D_{n+2i}}{\lambda D}$$

and call S_{ik} the net substitution effect between commodity i and price k. From the computation of S_{ik} we find that the own-substitution effects are not negative and so the matrix of substitution effects is not negative semi-definite.

By the homogeneity condition imposed on utility, we deduce that

$$\Sigma_{i=1}^{n} \frac{\partial U}{\partial p_i} p_i + U_M M = 0. \tag{A32}$$

Then, differentiating equation (A25) with respect to x_j $(j = 1, \ldots, n)$

$$\Sigma_{i=1}^{n} \frac{\partial U_j}{\partial p_i} p_i + U_{Mj} M = 0 \qquad j = 1, \ldots, n \tag{A33}$$

and, with respect to M,

$$\Sigma_{i=1}^{n} \frac{\partial U_M}{\partial p_i} p_i + U_{MM} M = -U_M. \tag{A34}$$

Hence, by equation (A25) the assumption of homogeneity of degree 0 in money prices and money implies that the marginal utility of any real commodity is homogeneous of degree 0 in the same variables (from A26) and that the marginal utility of money, defined in equation (A27), is homogeneous of degree -1 in these same variables. This means that $U_j/U_j = \alpha p_i/\alpha p_j$ and $U_i/\alpha^{-1} U_M = \alpha p_i$ where α is the proportional change in the prices and $\bar{M}$, and thus the rates of commodity substitution are identical to those in equation (A23). Further, the budget constraint is now

$$\alpha \Sigma_{i=1}^{n} p_i (x_i - \bar{x}_i) + M - \alpha \bar{M} = 0.$$

Thus, if M is homogeneous of degree 1 in the money prices and money endowment, then the real commodity demands are homogeneous of degree 0.
   To prove the homogeneity of M define

$$Y = \Sigma_{i=1}^{n} p_i \bar{x}_i + \bar{M}$$

so that

$$M = h_M(p_1, \ldots, p_n, Y),$$

where

$$\frac{\partial M}{\partial Y} = -\frac{D_{n+2n+1}}{D},$$

as in equation (A26). Now consider

$$A = \Sigma_{i=1}^{n} \frac{\partial M}{\partial p_i} p_i + \frac{\partial M}{\partial Y} \bar{M}.$$

We want to show that $A = M$. Using (A26) and (A27), A becomes

$$A = \frac{1}{D}\left(\lambda \Sigma_{i=1}^{n} p_i D_{in+1} - \Sigma_{i=1}^{n} \Sigma_{j=1}^{n} p_i D_{jn+1} - \Sigma_{i=1}^{n} p_i \frac{\partial U_M}{\partial p_i} D_{n+1n+1} \right.$$

$$\left. + \Sigma_{i=1}^{n} (x_i - \bar{x}_i) p_i D_{n+2n+1} - \bar{M} D_{n+2n+1} \right). \tag{A35}$$

For the term $\lambda \Sigma_{i=1}^n p_i D_{in+1}$ we have, by expanding D around alien co-factors, that

$$-\Sigma_{i=1}^n p_i D_{in+1} - D_{n+1n+1} = 0;$$

so

$$\lambda \Sigma_{i=1}^n p_i D_{in+1} = -\lambda\, D_{n+1n+1}. \qquad (A36)$$

Next,

$$\Sigma_{i=1}^n \Sigma_{j=1}^n p_i \frac{\partial U_j}{\partial p_i} D_{jn+1} = \Sigma_{j=1}^n D_{jn+1} \left(\Sigma_{i=1}^n p_i \frac{\partial U_j}{\partial p_i} \right)$$

and, from equation (A33),

$$\Sigma_{i=1}^n p_i \frac{\partial U_j}{\partial p_i} = -MU_{jM}.$$

Also,

$$D = \Sigma_{j=1}^n U_{jM} D_{jn+1} + U_{MM} D_{n+1n+1} - D_{n+2n+1},$$

and consequently

$$-M\, \Sigma_{j=1}^n U_{jM} D_{jn+1} = -MD + MU_{MM} D_{n+1n+1} - MD_{n+2n+1}.$$

Hence,

$$\Sigma_{i=1}^n \Sigma_{j=1}^n p_i \frac{\partial U_j}{\partial p_i} D_{jn+1} = -MD + MU_{MM} D_{n+1n+1} - MD_{n+2n+1}. \quad (A37)$$

In addition, from equation (A34) we have

$$\Sigma_{i=1}^n p_i \frac{\partial U_M}{\partial p_i} D_{n+1n+1} = (-\lambda - U_{MM}M) D_{n+1n+1}. \qquad (A38)$$

Now, substituting (A36), (A37) and (A38) into (A35), and recalling the budget constraint, we have

$$A = \frac{1}{D} \left(-\lambda D_{n+1n+1} + MD - MU_{MM} D_{n+1n+1} + MD_{n+2n+1} + \lambda D_{n+1n+1} \right.$$

$$\left. + U_{MM} MD_{n+1n+1} - MD_{n+2n+1} \right). \qquad (A39)$$

Therefore $A = M$, which implies that h_M is homogeneous of degree 1 in the money prices and the money endowment and h_i, for $i = 1, \ldots, n$, is homogeneous of degree 0 in the same variables.

Recently, R. Dusansky and P. Kalman proved that, if the marginal utility of real commodities is homogeneous of degree k in money prices and M and if the marginal utility of money is homogeneous of degree $k - 1$ in the prices and M, then the demand functions have the same homogeneity property as in this model.[16] One can see that their condition is a straightforward generalisation of the Samuelson–Patinkin assumption when one views the Dusansky–Kalman condition in terms of the utility function and not the marginal utilities. The latter condition is that U must be homogeneous of degree k in $p_1, \ldots, p_n$ and M (rather than as above, homogeneous of degree 0 in the same variables). Even so, taking their lead, the most general assumption is that U must be homothetic with respect to $p_1, \ldots, p_n$ and M.

The homogeneity property leads naturally to the restriction that $\Sigma_{j=1}^n p_i S_{ij} = 0$ because from the homogeneity of h_i,

$$0 = \Sigma_{j=1}^n \frac{\partial x_i}{\partial p_j} p_j + \frac{\partial x_i}{\partial \bar{M}} \bar{M}$$

and, using equations (A26), (A27) and the definition of S_{ij}, we can obtain the desired result. However, since $S_{ij} \neq S_{ji}$, in general we do not have the property that $\Sigma_{j=1}^n p_j S_{ji} = 0$.

A.5 The Lloyd–Morishima Neoclassical model [17]

The Samuelson–Patinkin model, because of its structural generality, admits few of the Neoclassical restrictions. This conclusion, itself not surprising, has lent respectability to the argument that monetary demand theory contributes virtually nothing to the description of household behaviour. Were one to accept this view, then one could, as well, argue that the effort to develop this theory has been wasted; one should, in fact, study the empirical relationships without reliance on theoretical restrictions, since, in effect, almost all findings will be consistent with the theory. These, however, are mistaken impressions which stem from the tacit acceptance of the specific form of the utility function representing individual preferences that was used above, and appeared as equation (A21). We will develop an alternative.

To begin with, while we argued that equation (A21) captured the essence of a monetary economy, we did not also point out that this function treats all of the arguments with an even hand. In particular, the consumer reacts *directly* to changes in any of the demands and prices in the domain of U according to its preferences. Moreover, this reaction initiates changes in the quantities of each commodity demanded, which in turn alters the absolute and relative contribution of the various variables to the level of preference satisfaction. This sweeping adjustment is an extremely unrealistic mode of behaviour and it is more realistic to argue that consumers do not react in such a complete manner but actually lump together commodities exhibiting similar characteristics. More precisely, individuals may be assumed to group classes of commodities in various ways, and the values of these 'independent' classes will then determine the degree of preference satisfaction. This independence can be worded thusly: if the quantity of a variable in one category changes, then it does not alter the absolute contribution to utility of any other class. Even more specifically, if $x_1, \ldots, x_l$ and $x_{l+1}, \ldots, x_n$ are the two classes, then changes in x_i with $i = 1, \ldots, l$ do not affect the indifference relations between $x_{l+1}, \ldots, x_n$.

Suppose that our consumer classifies real commodities into one group and the financial variables $(M, p_1, \ldots, p_n)$ into the other, so that changes in $M, p_1, \ldots, p_n$ do not affect the indifference relations of $x_1, \ldots, x_n$. This categorisation further elucidates the 'indirect' role of the financial variables in utility, and implies that the utility function is written as

$$u = U[\varphi(x_1, \ldots, x_n), M, p_1, \ldots, p_n] \tag{A40}$$

where $[\partial(\varphi_i/\varphi_j)/\partial v] = 0$ for $v = M, p_1, \ldots, p_n$. The function φ is referred to as the *branch* or *proper* utility function and equation (A40) is called a Sono weakly separable utility function.[18] If U, given by equation (A40), is homothetic with respect to $M, p_1, \ldots, p_n$, then the utility function is also homothetically weakly separable. It seems that equation (A40) captures the complete essence of money being useful not for itself but for what it can purchase. Firstly, money balances and money prices are in the domain and U is appropriately homothetic. In addition, if we view φ as the branch utility function, then the financial variables do not 'directly' affect the branch function (e.g., $\varphi_M = 0$), but only 'indirectly' affect it (e.g., $U_{\varphi M} \neq 0$). In this framework U may be viewed as the 'composite' utility function. Thus, it is natural to ask whether or not equation (A40) implies the reinstatement of the Neoclassical restrictions, and we turn to that literature.

A.5.1 *Equilibrium*

M. Morishima and C. Lloyd tackled the problem concerning the existence of the Neoclassical restrictions with a homothetically weakly separable utility function, as defined by equation (A40).[19] Although each author focused on different aspects and used different methods of proof, one may generalise their arguments along the following lines. Let us assume the utility function

$$u = U[\varphi(x_1, \ldots, x_n), M, p_1, \ldots, p_n] \tag{A41}$$

where U is homothetic with respect to $M, p_1, \ldots, p_n$ (with the usual regularity conditions); $U_\varphi > 0$; and $\varphi_i > 0$ and not all zero for $i = 1, \ldots, n$. The budget constraint is given by

$$\Sigma_{i=1}^n p_i(x_i - \bar{x}_i) + M - \bar{M} = 0. \tag{A42}$$

In this problem, the individual selects $x_1, \ldots, x_n$ and M by maximising (A41) subject to (A42). This leads to the following first-order conditions:

$$U_\varphi \varphi_i - \lambda p_i = 0 \qquad\qquad i = 1, \ldots, n$$
$$U_M - \lambda \quad\quad = 0 \tag{A43}$$
$$-\Sigma_{i=1}^n p_i(x_i - \bar{x}_i) - M + \bar{M} = 0.$$

These conditions reflect the fact that $(\varphi_i/\varphi_j) = (p_i/p_j)$ for $i, j = 1, \ldots, n$ and so the rates of commodity substitution for the real commodities are independent of the financial variables and equal to the relative prices. Also, $(U_\varphi \varphi_i/U_M) = p_i$ for $i = 1, \ldots, n$ which means that the rate of substitution between any real commodity i and money is not independent of the financial variables and is equal to the money price of i.

The form of the real demand functions implied by equation (A43) may be derived from an alternative programme. If the consumer maximises $\varphi(x_1, \ldots, x_n)$ subject to (A42) and to the constraint that $M = M^0$ where M^0 is the optimal demand determined from (A43), then this is an equivalent formulation. That is, maximise $\varphi(x_1, \ldots, x_n)$ subject to $\Sigma_{i=1}^n p_i x_i = E$ where

$$E = \Sigma_{i=1}^n p_i \bar{x}_i + \bar{M} - M^0. \tag{A44}$$

In this case the first-order conditions for this sub-programme are

$$\varphi_i - \gamma p_i = 0 \qquad\qquad i = 1, \ldots, n \tag{A45}$$
$$-\Sigma_{i=1}^n p_i(x_i - \bar{x}_i) + M^0 - \bar{M} = 0$$

where $\gamma = \lambda U_\varphi^{-1}$. Since $(\varphi_i/\varphi_j) = (p_i/p_j)$ for $i, j = 1, \ldots, n$; since M^0 is consistent with equations (A43) and (A45); and since the budget constraint is the same, then the real demands derived from (A45) are identical to those implied by (A43). Hence,

$$x_i = h_i(p_1, \ldots, p_n, \bar{x}_1, \ldots, x_n, \bar{M}) = H_i(p_1, \ldots, p_n, E) \ i = 1, \ldots, n$$
$$M = h_M(p_1, \ldots, p_n, \bar{x}_1, \ldots, \bar{x}_n, \bar{M}). \tag{A46}$$

It is important to realise though that we are not stating that the real demands are determined independently of money balances, but only that the influence of M enters through the income term and not through the price terms.

A.5.2   Comparative equilibria results

Because of the assumption of weak separability, we find that equation system (A27), which depicts the effect of a change in p_k on the demands, should be modified. Totally differentiating (A45) yields [20]

$$
\begin{bmatrix} \boldsymbol{\varphi}'' & -\mathbf{p} \\ (-\mathbf{p})^T & 0 \end{bmatrix}
\begin{bmatrix} \dfrac{\partial \mathbf{x}}{\partial p_k} \\[2ex] \dfrac{\partial \gamma}{\partial p_k} \end{bmatrix}
=
\begin{bmatrix} \mathbf{0}_{k-1} \\ \gamma \\ \mathbf{0}_{n-k} \\ (x_k - \bar{x}_k) \end{bmatrix}
+
\begin{bmatrix} \\[6ex] \dfrac{\partial h_M}{\partial p_k} \end{bmatrix}
\tag{A47}
$$

Therefore, the price effects are

$$
\frac{\partial x_i}{\partial p_k} = \gamma \frac{\mathscr{D}_{ki}}{\mathscr{D}} + (x_k - \bar{x})\frac{\mathscr{D}_{n+1i}}{\mathscr{D}} + \frac{\partial h_M}{\partial P_k}\frac{\mathscr{D}_{n+1i}}{\mathscr{D}}
$$

$$
i, k = 1, \ldots, n \tag{A48}
$$

where $\mathscr{D}$ is the determinant of the matrix on the left side of (A47) and $\mathscr{D}_{ji}$ for $i, j = 1, \ldots, n + 1$ are the appropriate co-factors. As opposed to (A27), however, the substitution effect is now given simply as

$$
S_{ik} = \gamma \frac{\mathscr{D}_{ki}}{\mathscr{D}} = \lambda U_\varphi^{-1}\frac{\mathscr{D}_{ki}}{\mathscr{D}};
$$

furthermore, there is a direct income effect, $(x_k - \bar{x}_k)\,(\mathscr{D}_{n+1i}/\mathscr{D})$, and an indirect income effect, $(\partial h_M/\partial p_k)(\mathscr{D}_{n+1i}/\mathscr{D})$. Clearly, as was stated earlier, the effect of money balances on the real demands when a price changes surfaces through the income component; indeed, the last term in the vector on the right side of (A47) is

$$
\frac{\partial E}{\partial p_k} = -\left[(x_k - \bar{x}_k) + \frac{\partial h_M}{\partial p_k}\right].
$$

These results imply that along with the restrictions derived in the modified Samuelson–Patinkin model we now obtain the remaining restrictions for the real demands. The substitution effects are symmetric, that is,

$$
\lambda U_\varphi^{-1}\frac{\mathscr{D}_{ki}}{\mathscr{D}} = \lambda U_\varphi^{-1}\frac{\mathscr{D}_{ik}}{\mathscr{D}}
$$

the own-substitution effects are negative $\lambda U_\varphi^{-1}(\mathscr{D}_{ii}/\mathscr{D}) < 0$ (so that the matrix of substitution effects is negative semi-definite); and finally, $\Sigma_{j=1}^{i} p_j S_{ji} = 0$. It must be emphasised that the indirect income effect is not the same as a 'real balance effect' although, to be sure, it does show the existence of an interdependence between the real commodities and money balances in this model.

A.6 The Clower–Lloyd Neoclassical model

A.6.1 *Equilibrium*

The previous model recognises that the homothetically weakly separable utility function provides an excellent formalisation of the notion that an individual's preference for money is based on what money can buy. There is, however, another characteristic, and that is that a consumer who plans to purchase an amount of some commodity must simultaneously plan to sell an appropriate quantity of money in exchange. R. Clower, and later C. Lloyd, P. Kalman, R. Dusansky and B. Wickström, have pointed out that the traditional budget constraint suggests transactions that are consistent with a barter economy, in that *any* commodity may be used as a medium of exchange.[21] Thus, to limit the number of commodities that are utilised as means of payment, it is argued, one must impose restrictions on the budget constraint. These restrictions must be such as to assign a central role to money (as the sole means of exchange) so that money is involved in each exchange.

Accordingly, we set up the problem so that the consumer has an initial specification in which real commodities are divided into two groups: those that are net demands ($x_i - \bar{x}_i > 0$) and those that are net supplies ($x_i - \bar{x}_i < 0$). We assume, then, that $i = 1, \ldots, l$ are net demands and that $i = l + 1, \ldots, n$ are net supplies. The individual must supply money for the net demand and demand money for the net supplies. This implies that there are two budget constraints, viz., an expenditure constraint and an income constraint, as exhibited in the following two equations:

$$\Sigma_{i=1}^{l} \, p_i(x_i - \bar{x}_i) + M - \bar{M} = 0 \qquad (A49)$$

$$\Sigma_{i=l+1}^{n} \, p_i(x_i - \bar{x}_i) + m = 0. \qquad (A50)$$

Here (A49), written in terms of net demands, is the expenditures constraint, and (A50) is the income constraint. We must also, then, notice that there are two demands for money in this problem. We may refer to M as the reservation demand and to m as the transactions demand; there is, further, no reason for these two demands to be identical. One result is that this structure provides a theoretical justification for distinct demand-for-money functions characterised along the lines of their roles in the exchange process. The different demand functions arise out of the nature of the preferences and constraints of the individual and not from the *ad hoc* specification of a separable money demand function such as that commonly employed in the macroeconomic literature – in which certain variables (notably income) determine the transactions position and certain other variables (notably the interest rate) determine the reservation position.

The existence of transactions and reservation balances entails necessary changes in the utility function of the Lloyd–Morishima model. Utility is now defined by

$$u = U[\varphi(x_1, \ldots, x_n), M, m, p_1, \ldots, p_n] \qquad (A51)$$

where U has the usual properties and $U_m > 0$. Equation (A51), clearly, is consistent with the ideas we have been developing here with respect to the interaction of real and financial variables, in a general way, and the role of money, in a particular way, since we have grouped M and m with the money prices.

Before proceeding to specify the first-order conditions of this programme, we rewrite the expenditure constraint (A49) as

$$\Sigma_{i=1}^n p_i(x_i - \bar{x}_i) + M + m - \bar{M} = 0 \qquad (A52)$$

where, now, equations (A49) and (A50) are equivalent to (A52) and (A50); we do this for convenience. The individual then maximises (A51) subject to (A52) and (A50). The appropriate Lagrangean is

$$\mathscr{L} = U[\varphi(x_1, \ldots, x_n)M, m, p_1, \ldots p_n] - \lambda_1[\Sigma_{i=1}^n p_i(x_i - \bar{x}_i) + M + m$$
$$- \bar{M}] - \lambda_2[\Sigma_{i=l+1}^n p_i(x_i - \bar{x}_i) + m] \quad (A53)$$

and the first-order conditions are

$$\begin{aligned} U_\varphi \varphi_i - \lambda_1 p_i &= 0 & i &= 1, \ldots, l \\ U_\varphi \varphi_i - (\lambda_1 + \lambda_2)p_i &= 0 & i &= l+1, \ldots, n \end{aligned}$$
$$U_M - \lambda_1 = 0, \quad U_m - (\lambda_1 + \lambda_2) = 0 \qquad (A54)$$
$$-\Sigma_{i=1}^n p_i(x_i - \bar{x}_i) - M - m + \bar{M} = 0, \quad -\Sigma_{i=l+1}^n p_i(x_i - \bar{x}_i) - m = 0.$$

By the manner in which we have transformed the expenditure constraint, we may observe a definite relationship between the marginal utilities of the reservation and transactions balances. We find that

$$U_M + \lambda_2 = U_m \qquad (A55)$$

and so the Lagrangean multiplier associated with the income constraint determines the differential between the marginal utilities of M and m. Thus, if $\lambda_2 = 0$ at the optimum, then, at the margin, the transactions and reservation demands are perfect substitutes.[22]

Finally, equations (A54) – along with the fact that the utility function is weakly separable – may be solved to yield

$$\begin{aligned} x_i &= h_i(p_1, \ldots, p_n, E_1, E_2) & i &= 1, \ldots, n \\ M &= h_M(p_1, \ldots, p_n, \bar{x}_1, \ldots, \bar{x}_n, \bar{M}) \\ m &= h_m(p_1, \ldots, p_n, \bar{x}_1, \ldots, \bar{x}_n, \bar{M}) \end{aligned} \qquad (A56)$$

where
$$E_1 = \Sigma_{i=1}^n p_i \bar{x}_i + M - M^0 - m^0;$$
$$E_2 = \Sigma_{i=l+1}^n p_i \bar{x}_i - m^0;$$

and M^0 and m^0 are, respectively, the optimal reservation and transactions demands. These results establish that the Neoclassical restriction referring to the effects of changes in the different sources of income on demand is satisfied in the Clower–Lloyd model.

A.6.2 Comparative equilibria results

From equation system (A54) we find that when $\bar{x}_k$ changes, for $k = l + 1, \ldots, n$, then [23]

$$
\begin{bmatrix} U'' & -p & -q \\ (-p)^T & 0 & 0 \\ (-q)^T & 0 & 0 \end{bmatrix}
\begin{bmatrix} \dfrac{\partial x}{\partial \bar{x}_k} \\[1ex] \dfrac{\partial M}{\partial \bar{x}_k} \\[1ex] \dfrac{\partial m}{\partial \bar{x}_k} \\[1ex] \dfrac{\partial \lambda_1}{\partial \bar{x}_k} \\[1ex] \dfrac{\partial \lambda_2}{\partial \bar{x}_k} \end{bmatrix}
=
\begin{bmatrix} \mathbf{0}_{n+2} \\[1ex] -p_k \\[1ex] -p_k \end{bmatrix}
\qquad (A57)
$$

where $p = p_1 \ldots p_n 1\ 1)^T$ and $q = (0 \ldots 0\ p_{l+1} \ldots p_n\ 0\ 1)^T$. As a consequence,

$$\frac{\partial x_i}{\partial \bar{x}_k} = -p_k \left(\frac{D_{n+3i} + D_{n+4i}}{D} \right) \qquad i = 1, \ldots, n.$$

$$\frac{\partial M}{\partial \bar{x}_k} = -p_k \left(\frac{D_{n+3n+1} + D_{n+4n+1}}{D} \right)$$

$$\frac{\partial m}{\partial \bar{x}_k} = -p_k \left(\frac{D_{n+3n+2} + D_{n+4n+2}}{D} \right). \qquad (A58)$$

If $k = 1, \ldots, l$ then the term $-p_k(D_{n+4s}/D)$ for $s = 1, \ldots, n + 2$ would not appear and if $\bar{M}$ changed, then not only would $-p_k(D_{n+4s}/D)$ not appear, but, in addition, the price term would be unity.

The price effects are easily derived in light of the computations from the Samuelson–Patinkin model. For a change in p_k, $k = l + 1, \ldots, n$,

$$\frac{\partial x_i}{\partial p_k} = (\lambda_1 + \lambda_2) \frac{D_{ki}}{D} - \Sigma_{j=1}^n \frac{\partial U_j}{\partial p_k} \frac{D_{ji}}{D} - \Sigma_{j=l+1}^n \frac{\partial U_j}{\partial p_k} \frac{D_{ji}}{D} - \frac{\partial U_M}{\partial p_k} \frac{D_{n+1i}}{D}$$

$$- \frac{\partial U_m}{\partial p_k} \frac{D_{n+2i}}{D} + (x_k - \bar{x}_k) \left(\frac{D_{n+3i} + D_{n+4i}}{D} \right). \qquad i = 1, \ldots, n \quad (A59)$$

For $\partial M/\partial p_k$ replace i with $n + 1$ and for $\partial m/\partial p_k$ replace i with $n + 2$. If $k = 1, \ldots l$, then λ^2 and D_{n+4s} vanish from the price effect equation. But our story is not yet complete, since we have not made use of the separability assumption. As in Section A.5, we know that h_i for $i = 1, \ldots, n$ in equation (A56) is derived from

$$
\begin{aligned}
&\varphi_i - \gamma_1 p_i = 0 &&i = 1, \ldots, l \\
&\varphi_i - (\gamma_1 + \gamma_2)p_i = 0 &&i = l + 1, \ldots, n \qquad\text{(A60)} \\
&-\Sigma_{i=1}^n p_i(x_i - \bar{x}_i) - M^0 - m^0 + \bar{M} = 0, \quad -\Sigma_{j=i+1}^n p_i(x_i - \bar{x}_i) - m^0 = 0.
\end{aligned}
$$

Equation set (A60) implies that (A59) is transformed using

$$
\begin{bmatrix} \varphi'' & -\mathbf{p} & -\mathbf{q} \\ (-\mathbf{p})^{\mathrm{T}} & 0 & 0 \\ (-\mathbf{q})^{\mathrm{T}} & 0 & 0 \end{bmatrix} \begin{bmatrix} \dfrac{\partial \mathbf{x}}{\partial p_k} \\[2ex] \dfrac{\partial \gamma_1}{\partial p_k} \\[2ex] \dfrac{\partial \gamma_2}{\partial p_k} \end{bmatrix} = \begin{bmatrix} \mathbf{0}_{k-1} \\ \gamma_1 + \gamma_2 \\ \mathbf{0}_{n-k} \\ (x_k - \bar{x}_k) + \dfrac{\partial M}{\partial p_k} + \dfrac{\partial m}{\partial p_k} \\[2ex] (x_k - \bar{x}_k) + \dfrac{\partial m}{\partial p_k} \end{bmatrix} \qquad\text{(A61)}
$$

where $\mathbf{p} = (p_1 \ldots p_n)^T$ and $\mathbf{q} = (0 \ldots 0\ p_{l+1} \ldots p_n)^T$. Thus

$$
\begin{aligned}
\frac{\partial x_i}{\partial p_k} = (\gamma_1 + \gamma_2)\frac{\mathscr{D}_{ki}}{\mathscr{D}} &+ (x_k - \bar{x}_k)\left(\frac{\mathscr{D}_{n+1i} + \mathscr{D}_{n+2i}}{\mathscr{D}}\right) + \frac{\partial M}{\partial p_k}\frac{\mathscr{D}_{n+1i}}{\mathscr{D}} \\
&+ \frac{\partial m}{\partial p_k}\left(\frac{\mathscr{D}_{n+1i} + \mathscr{D}_{n+2i}}{\mathscr{D}}\right) \qquad i = 1, \ldots, n.
\end{aligned} \qquad\text{(A62)}
$$

If $k = 1, \ldots, l$ then γ_2 and $(x_k - \bar{x}_k)(\mathscr{D}_{n+2i}/\mathscr{D})$ vanish from equation (A62). Therefore, the price effect of the real demands is comprised of a substitution effect

$$
(\gamma_1 + \gamma_2)\frac{\mathscr{D}_{ki}}{\mathscr{D}} = (\lambda_1 + \lambda_2)U_\varphi^{-1}\frac{\mathscr{D}_{ki}}{\mathscr{D}}(k = l, \ldots n);
$$

a direct income effect

$$
(x_k - \bar{x}_k)\left(\frac{\mathscr{D}_{n+1i} + \mathscr{D}_{n+2i}}{\mathscr{D}}\right);
$$

an indirect income effect from the reservations balances

$$
\frac{\partial M}{\partial p_k}\frac{\mathscr{D}_{n+1i}}{\mathscr{D}};
$$

and an indirect effect from transactions balances –

$$\frac{\partial m}{\partial p_k}\left(\frac{\mathcal{D}_{n+1i}}{\mathcal{D}} + \frac{\mathcal{D}_{n+2i}}{\mathcal{D}}\right).$$

Hence, since $\mathcal{D}$ is symmetric, then $\mathcal{D}_{ik} = \mathcal{D}_{ki}$ and so for the net demands, $i, k = 1, \ldots, l$; it follows that

$$S_{ik} = \lambda_1 U_\varphi^{-1}\frac{\mathcal{D}_{ki}}{\mathcal{D}} = \lambda_1 U_\varphi^{-1}\frac{\mathcal{D}_{ik}}{\mathcal{D}} = S_{ki}$$

and the net supplies, $i, k = l + 1, \ldots, n$ yield

$$S_{ik} = (\lambda_1 + \lambda_2)U_\varphi^{-1}\frac{\mathcal{D}_{ki}}{\mathcal{D}} = (\lambda_1 + \lambda_2)U_\varphi^{-1}\frac{\mathcal{D}_{ik}}{\mathcal{D}} = S_{ki}.$$

Therefore, there is a modified symmetry condition that holds for each class of commodities. If the symmetry condition is to extend across net demands and net supplies, i.e. for $i = 1, \ldots l$ and $k = l + 1, \ldots, n$, then λ_2 must equal zero at the optimum, which further implies that transactions and reservations balances have to be perfect substitutes at the margin.

An interesting question immediately arises. Is there a way to construct an empirical test of the proposition that $\lambda_2 = 0$? There is. From Equations (A56) and (A62) for $i = l + 1, \ldots, n$ and $k = 1, \ldots, l$, we have

$$\lambda_1 U_\varphi^{-1} = \frac{\partial x_i}{\partial p_k} + x_k\frac{\partial x_i}{\partial E_1} \qquad\qquad i = l+1, \ldots, n$$

$$(\lambda_1 + \lambda_2)U_\varphi^{-1} = \frac{\partial x_k}{\partial p_i} + x_k\left(\frac{\partial x_k}{\partial E_1} + \frac{\partial x_k}{\partial E_2}\right). \qquad k = 1, \ldots, l. \qquad \text{(A63)}$$

From the definitions of E_1 and E_2 and since

$$\frac{\partial x_i}{\partial \bar{x}_i} = \frac{\partial x_i}{\partial E_1}\frac{\partial E_1}{\partial \bar{x}_k}, \frac{\partial x_k}{d\bar{x}_i} = \frac{\partial x_k}{\partial E_1}\frac{\partial E_1}{d\bar{x}_i} + \frac{\partial x_k}{\partial E_2}\frac{\partial E_2}{\partial \bar{x}_i}$$

and

$$\frac{\partial x_k}{\partial \bar{x}_1} = \frac{\partial x_k}{\partial E_1}\frac{\partial E_1}{\partial \bar{x}_k},$$

then

$$\frac{\partial x_i}{\partial E_1} = \frac{\partial x_i}{\partial \bar{x}_k}\left(p_k - \frac{\partial M}{\partial \bar{x}_k} - \frac{\partial m}{\partial \bar{x}_k}\right)^{-1}$$

$$\frac{\partial x_k}{\partial E_1} = \frac{\partial x_k}{\partial \bar{x}_k}\left(p_k - \frac{\partial M}{\partial \bar{x}_k} - \frac{\partial m}{\partial \bar{x}_k}\right)^{-1} \qquad\qquad \text{(A64)}$$

$$\frac{\partial x_k}{\partial E_2} = \left[\frac{\partial x_k}{\partial \bar{x}_i} - \frac{\partial x_k}{\partial \bar{x}_k}\left(p_i - \frac{\partial M}{\partial \bar{x}_i} - \frac{\partial m}{\partial \bar{x}_i}\right)\left(p_k - \frac{\partial M}{\partial \bar{x}_k} - \frac{\partial m}{\partial \bar{x}_k}\right)^{-1}\right]\left(p_i - \frac{\partial m}{\partial \bar{x}_i}\right)^{-1}.$$

Equation set (A64) then, implies that

$$\frac{\lambda_1}{\lambda_1 + \lambda_2} = \frac{\dfrac{\partial x_i}{\partial p_k} + x_k\left[\dfrac{\partial x_i}{\partial \bar{x}_k}\left(p_k - \dfrac{\partial M}{\partial \bar{x}_k} - \dfrac{\partial m}{\partial \bar{x}_k}\right)^{-1}\right]}{\dfrac{\partial x_k}{\partial p_i} + x_i\left[\dfrac{\partial x_k}{\partial \bar{x}_i}\left(p_i - \dfrac{\partial m}{\partial \bar{x}_i}\right)^{-1} + \dfrac{\partial x_k}{\partial \bar{x}_k}\left(p_k - \dfrac{\partial M}{\partial \bar{x}_k} - \dfrac{\partial m}{\partial \bar{x}_k}\right)^{-1}\dfrac{\partial M}{\partial \bar{x}_i}\right]}$$

$$i = l + 1, \ldots, n; k = 1 \ldots, l. \qquad \text{(A65)}$$

Therefore, because the right side of equation (A65) contains only observables, if it is equal to 1, then it must follow that $\lambda_2 = 0$.

Continuing with the Neoclassical restrictions, the matrix of substitution effects is negative semi-definite and $(\lambda_1 U_\varphi^{-1})(\mathscr{D}_{ii}/\mathscr{D}) < 0$ or $[(\lambda_1 + \lambda_2)U_\varphi^{-1}]$ $(\mathscr{D}_{ii}/\mathscr{D}) < 0$; that is, the own-substitution effects are negative irrespective of whether the commodity is in net demand or net supply. The homogeneity condition, which states that the real demands are homogeneous of degree 0 in the money prices and $\bar{M}$ and that the transactions and reservation balances are homogeneous of degree 1 in the same variables, follows from the homotheticity assumption on the utility function.[24] However, regardless of whether or not utility is homothetic, the demand for real commodities is homogeneous of degree 0 in money prices, E_1 and E_2. This is clear since the rate of commodity substitution of the branch utility function for each of the net demands and net supplies is equal to their relative prices before and after the change in the prices, E_1 and E_2 (recall that φ is independent of the financial variables). This, further, implies that the equivalence of the two homogeneity conditions on h_i for $i = 1, \ldots, n$ occurs when the utility function is homothetic in the financial variables.

By the Laplace expansion of a determinant,

$$-\Sigma_{j=1}^n p_j \frac{\mathscr{D}_{js}}{\mathscr{D}} = \begin{cases} 1 & \text{if } s = n + 1 \\ 0 \end{cases}$$

$$-\Sigma_{j=l+1}^n p_j \frac{\mathscr{D}_{js}}{\mathscr{D}} = \begin{cases} 1 & \text{if } s = n + 2 \\ 0 \end{cases}.$$

This leads us to the conclusion that

$$\lambda_1 U_\varphi^{-1}\Sigma_{j=1}^n p_j \frac{\mathscr{D}_{ji}}{\mathscr{D}} + \lambda_2 U_\varphi^{-1}\Sigma_{j=l+1}^n p_j \frac{\mathscr{D}_{ji}}{\mathscr{D}} = 0$$

$$i = 1, \ldots, n \qquad \text{(A66)}$$

and thus

$$\Sigma_{j=1}^n p_j S_{ij} = 0 = \Sigma_{j=1}^n p_j S_{ji}.$$

Notice that the last restriction is satisfied although $S_{ij} \neq S_{ji}$ if i is a net demand (net supply) and j is a net supply (net demand) unless $\lambda_2 = 0$, since all we need is that the sum $(\Sigma_{j=1}^n p_j S_{ji})$ equals 0. Thus the complete symmetry of the substitution effects is a sufficient but not necessary condition for the last Neoclassical restriction; this establishes the complete list of restrictions for this modified Clower–Lloyd model.

It appears, then, that when time and uncertainty are not explicitly taken into account and when the only costs of transactions are the prices of the commodities themselves, then this model is a good representation of the behaviour of an individual in a monetary economy.

Footnotes

1. P. A. Samuelson, *The Foundations of Economic Analysis* and 'What Classical Monetary Theory Really Was'.

2. C. Lloyd, 'Two Classical Monetary Models'; K. Brunner, 'Inconsistency and Indeterminacy in Classical Economics'; and J. Marschak, 'The Rationale of the Demand for Money and of "Money Illusion"'.

3. R. W. Clower, 'A Reconsideration of the Microfoundations of Monetary Theory'; R. Dusansky and P. J. Kalman, 'The Foundations of Money Illusion in a Neoclassical Micro-Monetary Model'; P. J. Kalman, R. Dusansky and B. Wickström, 'On the Major Slutsky Properties When Money is the Sole Medium of Exchange'.

4. C. Lloyd, 'Two Classical Monetary Models'.

5. $U_i = \partial U / \partial x_i$ is the marginal utility of the ith real commodity.

6. The second-order conditions are fulfilled because of the strict quasi-concavity of U and the linearity of the constraints. We assume an interior solution throughout.

7. U'' is the matrix of second-order partial derivatives of the utility function, $\mathbf{p} = (p_1 \ldots p_n)^T$ is the column vector of prices, T denotes transpose, $\partial x / \partial \mu$ is the column vector $[(\partial x_1 / \partial \mu) \ldots (\partial x_n / \partial \mu)]^T$ and 0_n is an n-dimensional column vector of zeros.

8. D is the determinant of the matrix in equation system (8) and D_{ij} for $i, u = 1, \ldots, n + 1$ is the appropriate co-factor of the ith row and jth column.

9. P. Samuelson, *The Foundations of Economic Analysis*.

10. J. Marschak, 'The Rationale of the Demand for Money and of Money Illusion', and K. Brunner, 'Inconsistency and Indeterminacy in Classical Economics'.

11. $\bar{x} \geq 0$ means $x_i \geq 0$ for $i = 1, \ldots, n$ and not all $\bar{x}_i = 0$ for $i = 1, \ldots, n$.

12. $\partial F / \partial x_i = F_i$ and $\mathbf{x} = (x_i, \ldots, x_n)^T$.

13. P. A. Samuelson, *Foundations of Economic Analysis* and 'What Classical Monetary Theory Really Was'.

14. The utility function also has the other assumptions which were imposed in the Lloyd model.

15. D. Patinkin, *Money, Interest, and Prices*.

16. R. Dusansky and P. J. Kalman, 'The Foundations of Money Illusion in a Neoclassical Micro-Monetary Model'.

17. C. Lloyd, 'Preferences, Separability, and the Patinkin Model', and M. Morishima, 'Consumer Behaviour and Liquidity Preference'.

18. M. Sono, 'The Effect of Price Changes on the Demand and Supply of Separable Goods'.

19.   M. Morishima, 'Consumer Behaviour and Liquidity Preference', and C. Lloyd, 'Preferences, Separability, and the Patinkin Model'.

20. φ'' is defined in a similar manner to U'' and the γ in the vector on the right side of Equation (A47) is the kth element.

21.   R. Clower, 'A Reconsideration of the Microfoundations of Monetary Theory'; P. J. Kalman, R. Dusansky, and B. Wickström, 'On the Major Slutsky Properties when Money is the Sole Medium of Exchange'; and C. Lloyd, 'The Microfoundations of Monetary Theory: Comment'.

22.   The double constraints are not necessarily consistent with the transactions rules of a monetary economy. Suppose that it is possible for

$$\Sigma_{i=1}^{n} p_i(x_i - \bar{x}_i) + M + m - \bar{M} \leqslant 0,$$
$$\Sigma_{i=l+1}^{n} p_i(x_i - \bar{x}_i) + m \leqslant 0$$

and $\bar{M} = 0$. These modified constraints mean, with $\bar{M} = 0$, that the income constraint must be satisfied as an inequality (which, incidentally, yields $\lambda_2 = 0$, which implies that $\bar{M}$ and m are perfect substitutes). Consequently the consumer's net supply of real commodities exceeds his transactions demand. The proceeds of this excess are devoted to the net demand of real commodities and the reservation demand for money. Hence we see that non-money commodities are exchanged for each other and the rules we established for a monetary economy are violated. What is happening here is that, not only must we have two budget constraints, but also the possible signs of these constraints must not allow an excess of the real commodity net supply to be used for demanding other non-money commodities. Naturally, equality constraints do away with such problems.

23. U'' is the Hessian of the homothetically separable utility function.

24.   The proof is similar to the one set out in the Samuelson model.

The Demand for
Money by the Firm

B.1 Introduction

It is rather surprising, when one regards the theoretical literature on the corporate demand for money, to find that the interest on this topic, generated by micro-monetary economists has arisen only quite recently. This is especially interesting in view of the long and important history shared by the barter theories of the consumer and producer, on the one hand, and the monetary theory of the consumer, on the other.[1] Indeed, as late as 1972, J. R. Moroney could assert, 'I would suggest that the theory of money has not yet been satisfactorily integrated with the pure theory of production'.[2] One can observe, then, that this under-development of micro-monetary economics is such that, when products, factors of production and technology are introduced, money generally vanishes from the scene.

It is not difficult to see the reasons why the introduction of money into production theory requires a special effort. Most generally, in basic Neoclassical theory, the firm has a technology,[3] while the household has preferences. Thus, while money can appear in the preference function of a consumer, money does not affect the technology of a firm. This obviously means that money cannot be viewed as a factor of production. In the words of Gabor and Pearce, 'It seems clear to us that there is an essential difference between money and any other factor. Production could conceivably be carried on without money.'[4] Moroney says, 'It seems justifiable to conclude that money should not be viewed as a factor of production';[5] finally, from Thomas Saving, 'Significantly, I think, money balances are not treated directly as a factor of production.'[6] The problem, then, is the following: without a corporate preference function and without making money a factor of production, how can money meaningfully enter the decision process of the firm (in ways other than just by affecting costs)? To put the matter succinctly, what are the benefits of holding money to the firm?

The answer to this question lies in the realisation that, although money is not a factor of production, it is 'productive'. Its productiveness, though, lies not in its technological facets, but with regard to the transactions mechanisms by which the firm operates. That is to say, the benefits of holding money arise out of its ability to reduce the costs associated with the transactions that the firm undertakes in carrying out production operations. The solution to this question was found by Gabor and Pearce in 1958, and again by Thomas Saving in 1972;[7] indeed, although these studies are framed in different terms, the thrust of their arguments is essentially the same. Further, one can demonstrate that the Saving work is a very important generalisation of the Gabor–Pearce paper. This generalisation is due to the adoption of complex transaction cost functions complementary to production cost functions. In studying the corporate demand for money literature, we can view the so-called inventory models of Baumol, Fisher and Miller and Orr as specific transactions costs models with specific exchange relationships.[8] The Lange, Gabor–Pearce and Vickers models can then be thought of as specific transaction cost models with *general* exchange relationships;[9] and, finally, the Saving and Dutton–Gramm–McDonald papers, as *general* transactions cost models with *general* exchange relationships.[10]

B.2   The Baumol–Fisher–Tobin model

B.2.1   *Equilibrium*

The model that we present in this section is basically an extension of the one developed in S. Fisher, which builds on the inventory approach followed by Baumol and by Miller and Orr.[11] Assume that the firm has a production function represented by equation (B1):

$$y = f(K, L_p) \tag{B1}$$

where y is output, K is capital services, L_p is labour services used in production, and f is the production function, itself assumed to be twice continuously differentiable and strictly concave with positive marginal products.

The firm uses another form of labour for carrying out transactions, so that

$$L_p + L_T = \text{L} \tag{B2}$$

where L_T is labour services needed for transactions and L is total labour, The relationship between L_T and the number of transactions is given by

$$n = \beta L_T \tag{B3}$$

where n is the number of transactions and $1/\beta$ is the average quantity of labour services used for transactions and β is a fixed positive constant.[12] Fisher also assumes that, in this case, the average holdings of money balances are related to the flow of net operating revenues (i.e. revenues minus production costs) divided by the number of transactions, so that

$$\bar{M} = \frac{R}{n} \tag{B4}$$

where R is net operating revenues, and $\bar{M}$ is average money balances. This means that, using (B4) and (B3), we have $\bar{M} = R(\beta L_T)^{-1}$. Therefore, combining (B1)–(B4), we obtain

$$y = f\left[K, L - \left(\frac{\bar{M}}{R}\right)^{-1}\right]. \tag{B5}$$

This equation shows us that, although money appears in the function, it is not as a factor of production. Money balances enter (B5) because of the specific institutionalisation of the transactions process by means of equations (B3) and (B4).

The costs associated with the operations of the firm are classified as production costs, inventory costs and exchange costs. The production costs are $w_l L_p + w_k K$, where w_l is the factor price of labour and w_k is the factor price of capital. The exchange costs are $w_l L_T$ and the inventory costs are $w_m \bar{M}/R$, where $w_m > 0$.[13]

The programme confronting the firm is to maximise profits by selecting K, L and $\bar{M}/R$, where profits are defined as

$$\Pi = pf\left[K, L - \left(\beta\frac{\bar{M}}{R}\right)^{-1}\right] - w_l L - w_k K - w_m \frac{\bar{M}}{R} \tag{B6}$$

and p is the product price. The first-order conditions for an interior solution are denoted by

$$\frac{\partial \Pi}{\partial K} = pf_1 - w_k = 0$$

$$\frac{\partial \Pi}{\partial L} = pf_2 - w_l = 0 \tag{B7}$$

$$\frac{\partial \Pi}{\partial\left(\frac{\bar{M}}{R}\right)} = \beta^{-1}pf_2\left(\frac{\bar{M}}{R}\right)^{-2} - w_m = 0$$

where f_1 is the marginal product of capital and f_2 is the marginal product of labour used in production. The optimality conditions show us that the marginal product of average money balances deflated by revenues is equal to the average cost of money holding (w_m). From equation set (B7) we can solve for K, L, $\bar{M}/R$; with this solution we can substitute into (B4) and (B3) to get L_T (which determines n); then, with L and L_T we can determine L_p. Finally, given L_p

and K, we get y and so also net operating revenues. Thus, from the equation

$$\bar{M} = R\sqrt{\left(\frac{w_l}{\beta w_m}\right)} \tag{B8}$$

which is derived from the second and third equations of (B7), we can determine the optimal quantity of average money balances.

A natural question immediately arises – how does the optimal decision alter when bonds are introduced into the problem? We can assume, in the same spirit as equation (B4), that

$$p_b\bar{B} = \frac{R}{n}(n-1) \tag{B9}$$

where $\bar{B}$ is the average holding of bonds and p_b is the price of bonds. In this event we are essentially saying that the firm converts revenues earned from operations into money and bonds in the proportions given by (B4) and (B9), since combining equations (B4) and (B9) yields the result that $p_b\bar{B} + \bar{M} = R$. Because of the way in which bonds enter the model, we can solve for either $\bar{M}/R$ or $\bar{B}/R$ from the first-order conditions, but not for both simultaneously. The bonds we are discussing are ones that are part of the assets of the firm and so the revenues generated by the bonds in any period are $p_b\bar{B}r_b$, where r_b is the rate of interest.

By recalling equations (B9) and (B4) and defining $i_b = r_bR$, we can write the profits function of the firm as

$$\Pi = pf\left[K, L - \left(\beta\frac{\bar{M}}{R}\right)^{-1}\right] - w_lL - w_kK - (w_m + i_b)\frac{\bar{M}}{R} + i_b. \tag{B10}$$

Maximising profits with respect to capital, labour and $\bar{M}/R$ yields (for an interior solution) the same equations as in (B7) with the modification that now,

$$\frac{\partial\Pi}{\partial\left(\frac{\bar{M}}{R}\right)} = \beta^{-1}pf_2\left(\frac{\bar{M}}{R}\right)^{-2} - (w_m + i_b) = 0 \tag{B11}$$

where w_m is the average inventory cost of money (in order to be able to carry out the transactions) adjusted in this case to consider the forgone interest on bonds which money-holding entails. From the first two equations of (B7) and (B11) we can determine K, L and $\bar{M}/R$. Then we can solve for L_T, n, L_p and y. Then, from y and p, which yield net operating revenues, we get bond and money holdings from equations (B12):

$$\bar{M} = R\sqrt{\left[\frac{w_l}{\beta(w_m + i_b)}\right]}$$

$$\bar{B} = \frac{R}{p_b}\left\{1 - \sqrt{\left[\frac{w_l}{\beta(w_m + i_b)}\right]}\right\} \tag{B12}$$

B.2.2   *Comparative equilibrium*

If the price of the product increases, we may ask what the effect is on capital, labour and $\bar{M}/R = \bar{m}$. Differentiating the first-order conditions with respect to p yields

$$\begin{bmatrix} pf_{11} & pf_{12} & pf_{12}\beta_{\bar{m}}^2 \\ pf_{21} & pf_{22} & pf_{22}\beta_{\bar{m}}^2 \\ pf_{21} & pf_{22} & p\bar{m}^{-1}(f_{22}\bar{m} - 2f_2) \end{bmatrix} \begin{bmatrix} \dfrac{\partial K}{\partial p} \\ \dfrac{\partial L}{\partial p} \\ \dfrac{\partial \bar{m}}{\partial p} \end{bmatrix} = \begin{bmatrix} -f_1 \\ -f_2 \\ -f_2 \end{bmatrix}. \tag{B13}$$

$\partial \bar{m}/\partial p$ is directly zero, of course, and we may arrive at the signs for the other variables as follows. First,

$$\frac{\partial K}{\partial p} = f_2 \frac{f_2 2p^2 \bar{m}^{-1}}{f_1 D} \left(\frac{f_{22}}{f_2} - \frac{f_{12}}{f_1} \right)$$

where $D = -2p^3 \bar{m}^{-1} f_2 (f_{11}f_{22} - f_{12}^2) < 0$ by the strict concavity of f. This establishes that, if

$$\left(\frac{f_{22}}{f_2} - \frac{f_{12}}{f_1} \right) < 0$$

which is true when the production function is homogeneous of degree 1 (or, more generally, homothetic), then $\partial K/\partial p > 0$. Similarly,

$$\frac{\partial L}{\partial p} = f_2 \frac{f_2 2p^2 \bar{m}^{-1}}{f_1 D} \left(\frac{f_{11}}{f_1} - \frac{f_{21}}{f_2} \right) > 0$$

if f is homogeneous of degree 1. Thus an increase in p exerts the standard effect on the factors of production but does not affect $\bar{m}$. Moreover, since $p_b \bar{b} + \bar{m} = 1$, where $\bar{b} = \bar{B}/R$, and $\partial \bar{m}/\partial R = 0$, then $\partial \bar{b}/\partial p = 0$, $\partial L_p/\partial p = \partial L/\partial p$, and $\partial L_T/\partial p = 0$. In this model changes in the price of output only trigger effects on the variables that directly affect the production process and their associated costs.

If the average inventory cost of money (w_m) increases, then we find that

$$\frac{\partial \bar{m}}{\partial w_m} = \frac{p^2}{D}(f_{11}f_{22} - f_{12}^2) < 0$$

$$\frac{\partial K}{\partial w_m} = 0$$

$$\frac{\partial L}{\partial w_m} = \frac{p^2}{\beta D \bar{m}^2}(f_{11}f_{22} - f_{12}^2) > 0.$$

These results tell us that an increase in the average cost on money will

decrease the average holdings of money per net operating revenues, will
have no effect on capital and will increase the demand for labour. In ad-
dition, because $\partial \bar{m} / \partial w_m < 0$ then $\partial \bar{b} / \partial w_m > 0$ and $\partial L_T / \partial w_m > 0$. Thus, the
holdings of money balances and the labour demand for transactions pur-
poses may be viewed as substitutes in the exchange process. The firm decreases its holdings of money and uses more labour for the purpose of
purchasing bonds, as the average cost of money increases. Moreover, given
the definition of D, we can rewrite $\partial \bar{m} / \partial w_m$ and $\partial L / \partial w_m$ as

$$\frac{\partial \bar{m}}{\partial w_m} = - \frac{\bar{m}}{2 w_l} \qquad \frac{\partial L}{\partial w_m} = \frac{1}{2 w_l \beta \bar{m}}$$

whence we see that a simple relationship obtains between these two effects,

$$\frac{\partial L}{\partial w_m} = \frac{- \partial \bar{m}}{\partial w_m} \bigg/ \beta m^2,$$

on account of the dual role of labour in this model. Therefore, from the
relationship of L, L_p and $\bar{m}$, we see that when w_m changes there is no effect
on L_p. The result may be computed from the fact that $L_p = L - (\beta \bar{m})^{-1}$ and
from the relationship between $\partial L / \partial w_m$ and $\partial \bar{m} / \partial w_m$. This implies that, not
only is $\partial L_T / \partial w_m > 0$, but also

$$\frac{\partial L_T}{\partial w_m} = \frac{\partial L}{\partial w_m}.$$

Turning to the effect of a change in i_b, we note that the results are identical
to those obtained when w_m changes because of the manner in which i_b enters
the first-order conditions. These derivations show us that we can view
capital and labour as independent commodities with respect to the transactions process, although they can be complements or substitutes in the production process. This is on account of the fact that the firm utilises labour in
two distinct ways (for transactions and for production), while it utilises capital only for production.

Finally, we consider the results if the factor prices of capital and labour
are changed; in this event we obtained (for w_k)

$$\frac{\partial \bar{m}}{\partial w_k} = 0$$

$$\frac{\partial K}{\partial w_k} = - \frac{2 p^2 \bar{m}^{-1} f_2 f_{22}}{D} < 0$$

$$\frac{\partial L}{\partial w_k} = \frac{2 p^2 \bar{m}^{-1} d_2 f_{21}}{D}.$$

Here the sign of $\partial L / \partial w_k$ actually depends on the complementarity or substitutability of capital and labour in production. Also, here, the effects on L_T,

$\bar{b}$ are zero, while we find that $(\partial L_p/\partial w_k) = (\partial L/\partial w_k)$. So changes in the factor price of capital do not elicit any responses in the exchange process, but only influences factor requirements.

For w_l we obtain

$$\frac{+\bar{m}}{\partial w_l} = -\frac{p^2}{D}(f_{11}f_{22} - f_{12}^2) > 0$$

$$\frac{\partial K}{\partial w_l} = \frac{2p^2\bar{m}^{-1}f_2f_{12}}{D}$$

$$\frac{\partial L}{\partial w_l} = [p^2(f_{11}f_{22} - f_{12}^2)/\beta\bar{m}^2 - 2p^2\bar{m}^{-1}f_2f_{11}]\frac{1}{D} < 0.$$

Again we find that $\bar{m}$ and L interact through the transactions process, while L and K interact through the production mechanism. Indeed, there are fundamental differences arising from the changes in the different factor prices; where the price of money initiates changes only in the control variable of the exchange process, the price of capital influences the production decisions, and finally the price of labour exerts effects on both the exchange and production relations. The latter point is clearly established from the fact that $\partial L/\partial w_l$ can be broken into

$$\frac{\partial L_T}{\partial w_l} = p^2(f_{11}f_{22} - f_{12}^2)/\beta\bar{m}^2 D < 0$$

$$\frac{\partial L_p}{\partial w_l} = 2p^2f_2f_{11}/\bar{m}D < 0,$$

where an increase in the price of labour decreases the demand for both types of labour services. One can further state that $\bar{m}$ and L_T are substitutes in the transactions process, according to the signs of $(\partial\bar{m}/\partial w_l) = (-\partial m/\partial w_m)$, and $(\partial L_T/\partial w_l) = (-\partial L/\partial w_m)$.

B.3 The Lange–Gabor–Pearce model

B.3.1 *Equilibrium*

The material presented in this section is based on the analyses from studies by Lange, Gabor and Pearce, Vickers and Turnovsky.[14] Although these works are framed in different terms from the 'inventory' models, we can view the analysis of this part of the appendix as a generalisation of Section B.2 above. This generalisation manifests itself around equations (B3), and (B4) of the Baumol–Fisher–Tobin model, which can be summarised by

$$\bar{M} = R(\beta L_T)^{-1}$$

or

$$\bar{M} = [pf(K, L) - w_lL - w_kK](\beta L_T)^{-1}.$$

The above equations relate the holdings of average money balances in a very specific manner to capital and labour (used for production and transactions purposes). Indeed, given prices, and if we do not distinguish between labour used in production and labour used in exchange (i.e., if there is not a fixed coefficient relationship between the two types of labour), we can write

$$\bar{M} = g(K, L), \tag{B14}$$

where (B14) is an obvious generalisation of the inventory model. We may refer to g as a money requirements function which is twice continuously differentiable and strictly convex. We can view money as depending on prices, but since prices are exogenous there is little need to complicate matters by defining prices to be in the domain of g. Naturally, though, comparative equilibrium exercises will be influenced by what actually appears in the left side of equation (B14).

In this model we have a production function given by

$$y = f(K, L). \tag{B15}$$

Thus profits are now given by

$$\Pi = pf(K, L) - w_k K - w_l L = w_m \bar{M} \tag{B16}$$

where w_m is the average cost of holding money balances. The firm maximises profits subject to the money requirements function, and so the Lagrangean is,

$$\mathscr{L} = pf(K, L) - w_k K - w_l L - w_m \bar{M} - \lambda[g(K, L) - \bar{M}].$$

The first-order conditions for an interior solution are as follows;

$$\frac{\partial \mathscr{L}}{\partial K} = pf_1 - w_k - \lambda g_1 = 0$$

$$\frac{\partial \mathscr{L}}{\partial L} = pf_2 - w_l - \lambda g_2 = 0 \tag{B17}$$

$$\frac{\partial \mathscr{L}}{\partial \bar{M}} = -w_m + \lambda = 0$$

$$\frac{\partial \mathscr{L}}{\partial \lambda} = -g(K, L) + \bar{M} = 0.$$

We can immediately observe that $\lambda = w_m$ and so λ is the marginal (and average) cost of money. In addition, because λ is equal to a positive number, this implies that, even if we interpreted (B14) as a money requirements constraint with $\bar{M} \geqslant g(K, L)$, then at the optimum, with positive holdings of money, $\bar{M}$ must equal and not exceed its requirements. The firm, then, never plans to hold money in quantities above that which is required for carrying out operations. The remaining equations of (B17) tell us that the value of the marginal product for a factor must equal the marginal production cost of that factor plus the marginal transactions cost associated with that particular input. In other words, $pf_1 = w_k + w_m g_1$ and $pf_2 = w_l + w_m g_2$. The system denoted by equation set (B17) may be solved in a recursive fashion. Trivially, $w_m = \lambda$; then, given the prices, the first two equations of (B17) can be solved for capital and labour. With this solution we can then substitute into the money requirements function and determine $\bar{M}$.

The introduction of bonds is a relatively straightforward matter. The money requirements function now also depends on the quantity of bonds, so that the Lagrangean becomes

$$\mathcal{L} = pf(K, L) - w_k K - w_l L - w_m \bar{M} + rp_b \bar{B} - \lambda[g(K, L, \bar{B}) - \bar{M}] \tag{B18}$$

Note that these bonds are part of the assets of the firm since $\bar{B} > 0$. The optimality conditions from (B17) are applicable, with the appropriate modifications on the $\partial L/\partial \gamma = 0$ equation and with the addition of an equation for bonds.

$$\frac{\partial \mathcal{L}}{\partial \bar{B}} = rp_b - \lambda g_3 = 0 \tag{B19}$$

Since $\lambda = w_m$, then $rp_b = w_m g_3$ or $rp_b/w_m = g_3$; that is, the marginal revenue from bonds divided by the marginal inventory cost of money equals the marginal transactions costs incurred in purchasing bonds.

B.3.2 Comparative equilibrium

Suppose we ask the same kinds of questions that were posed in Section B.2.2? Firstly, what are the effects of an increase in the price of output? Substituting $\lambda = w_m$ into the first two equations of (B17) and (B19) and differentiating these three equations with respect to p yields the following system:

$$\begin{bmatrix} pf_{11} - w_m g_{11} & pf_{12} - w_m g_{12} & -w_m g_{13} \\ pf_{21} - w_m g_{21} & pf_{22} - w_m g_{22} & -w_m g_{23} \\ -w_m g_{31} & -w_m g_{32} & -w_m g_{33} \end{bmatrix} \begin{bmatrix} \dfrac{\partial K}{\partial p} \\ \dfrac{\partial L}{\partial p} \\ \dfrac{\partial \bar{B}}{\partial p} \end{bmatrix} = \begin{bmatrix} -f_1 \\ -f_2 \\ 0 \end{bmatrix} \tag{B20}$$

Thus,

$$\frac{\partial K}{\partial p} = w_m g_{22} f_1 f_2 (pf_{22}/f_2 - pf_{12}/f_1)/D - w_m^2 [(g_{33} g_{22} - g_{32}^2) f_1$$

$$- (g_{33} g_{12} - g_{32} g_{13}) f_2]/D. \tag{B21}$$

If f is homothetic then the term in the first round brackets is negative; D, which is the determinant of the matrix from the left side of (B20), is negative by the second-order conditions; and, finally, the term in the second round brackets is positive by the strict convexity of g. Thus a sufficient condition for $\partial K/\partial p$ to be positive is that

$$g_{33}g_{12} - g_{32}g_{13} \leqq 0, \tag{B22}$$

which implies that bonds must have a stronger impact on g_1/g_3 relative to the impact of labour on that ratio. The ratio, of course, shows the rate of substitution of capital for bonds needed in order to retain the same level of money balances. Next,

$$\frac{\partial L}{\partial p} = w_m g_{33} f_1 f_2 (p f_{11}/f_1 - p f_{21}/f_2)/D$$

$$- w_m^2 [(g_{33}g_{11} - g_{31}^2) f_1 - (g_{33}g_{12} - g_{32}g_{13}) f_2]/D \tag{B23}$$

and again (B22) is a sufficient condition for $\partial L/\partial p > 0$.

$$\frac{\partial \bar{B}}{\partial p} = -f[w_m g_{31}(p f_{22} - w_m g_{22}) - w_m g_{32}(p f_{21} - w_m g_{21})]/D$$

$$+ f_2 [w_m g_{31}(p f_{12} - w_m g_{12}) - w_m g_{32}(p f_{11} - w_m g_{11})]/D. \tag{B24}$$

The sign of the right side of (B24) is ambiguous because of the presence of the interaction of bonds with capital and labour in the transaction process. The fact that the sign of $\partial \bar{B}/\partial p$ cannot be determined implies that the sign of $\partial \bar{M}/\partial p$ cannot be determined. However if $\bar{B}$ did not enter the money requirements function or if g was strongly separable between K and L on the one hand and $\bar{B}$ on the other, then $\partial K/\partial p > 0$, $\partial L/\partial p > 0$, $\partial \bar{B}/\partial p = 0$ and so $\partial \bar{M}/\partial p > 0$ if g_1, g_2 are positive and $\partial M/\partial p < 0$ if g_1, g_2 are negative. The firm's ability to produce more output as p increases must arise from increases in capital and labour and thus creates a need for a greater amount of money balances if the increased factor demands lead to larger money requirements.

The effects of an increase in the factor price of capital on the control variables are given by

$$\frac{\partial K}{\partial w_k} = \frac{1}{D}[w_m^2(g_{33}g_{22} - g_{32}^2) - w_m g_{33} p f_{22}] < 0 \tag{B25}$$

$$\frac{\partial L}{\partial w_k} = \frac{1}{D}[w_m g_{33} p f_{21} - w_m^2(g_{33}g_{21} - g_{23}g_{31})], \tag{B26}$$

where by (B22) the term in the round brackets is non-positive and so if $f_{21} > 0$ then $\partial L/\partial w_k < 0$.

$$\frac{\partial \bar{B}}{\partial w_k} = \frac{1}{D}[w_m g_{31}(p f_{22} - w_m g_{22}) - w_m g_{32}(p f_{21} - w_m g_{21})] \tag{B27}$$

and the sign of $\partial \bar{B}/\partial w_k$ is ambiguous unless we sign the cross partial derivatives. If the inputs and average bond holdings are separable in the requirements function then the right side of (B27) is zero. Again because of the ambiguities of $\partial \bar{B}/\partial w_k$ and of $\partial L/\partial w_k$ we cannot determine the sign of $\partial \bar{M}/\partial w_k$. Obviously, because of the similar fashion in which capital and labour influence the transactions process, we expect similar conclusions from the effects of an increase in w_l.

$$\frac{\partial K}{\partial w_l} = \frac{1}{D}[w_m g_{33} pf_{12} - w_m^2(g_{33}g_{12} - g_{32}g_{13})] \tag{B28}$$

$$\frac{\partial L}{\partial w_l} = \frac{1}{D}[w_m^2(g_{33}g_{11} - g_{31}^2) - w_m g_{33} pf_{11}] < 0 \tag{B29}$$

$$\frac{\partial \bar{B}}{\partial w_l} = \frac{1}{D}[w_m g_{32}(pf_{11} - w_m g_{11}) - w_m g_{31}(pf_{12} - w_m g_{12})] \tag{B30}$$

Finally an increase in the price of bonds yields the following equations

$$\frac{\partial K}{\partial p_b} = -\frac{r}{D}[(w_m^2 g_{23}g_{12} - w_m g_{23} pf_{12} + w_m g_{13}f_{22}p - w_m^2 g_{13}g_{22})] \tag{B31}$$

$$\frac{\partial L}{\partial p_b} = -\frac{r}{D}[(w_m^2 g_{11}g_{23} - w_m g_{23} pf_{11} + w_m g_{13}f_{21}p - w_m^2 g_{13}g_{21})] \tag{B32}$$

$$\frac{\partial \bar{B}}{\partial p_b} = -\frac{r}{D}[p^2(f_{11}f_{22} - f_{12}^2) + w_m^2(g_{11}g_{22} - g_{12}^2)$$

$$- pf_{22}w_m g_{11} - w_m g_{22} pf_{11} + 2w_m g_{12} pf_{21}] > 0. \tag{B33}$$

An increase in the price of bonds increases the value of the firm's bond-holdings and so also increases its revenues and planned demand for bonds. The term inside the square bracket on the right side of (B33) is positive from the fact that $f(K, L) - g(K, L, \bar{B})$ is a strictly concave function. We should note that an increase in the rate of interest will yield the same results as (B31), (B32) and (B33) except that r is replaced by p_b in these equations.

B.4 The Saving model

B.4.1 *Equilibrium*

Probably the most general statement concerning the corporate demand for money was developed by Thomas Saving and then later modified by Dutton, Gramm and McDonald.[15] We will specify a framework that is a modified version of the original Saving paper; we will do this in the context of developing the manner in which the Lange–Gabor–Pearce model is related to the Saving framework.

We will retain the production function denoted as (B15), but instead of writing a money requirements function, we will specify a transactions cost function,

$$c_t = T_c(K, L, \bar{M}, \bar{B}), \tag{B34}$$

where the transactions cost function can be thought of as being derived from a programme where, given the quantities of capital, labour, money, bonds and output (which depends on capital and labour), one must find the minimum costs associated with carrying out the exchange processes. The transactions cost function is twice continuously differentiable and strictly convex.

To compare the previous model with Saving's let us rewrite equation (B34) in implicit form as

$$\mathcal{T}(K, L, \bar{M}, \bar{B}, c_T) = 0. \tag{B35}$$

Then, with the appropriate measure of transactions costs – so that they are measured in units of the inputs – and if the conditions of the implicit function theorem are satisfied, we can write

$$\bar{M} = g(K, L, \bar{B}),$$

which is the money requirements function from the previous model.

The planning problem for the firm is to maximise (B36) with respect to K, L, $\bar{M}$ and $\bar{B}$:

$$\Pi = pf(K, L) - w_k K - w_l L - w_m \bar{M} + r_b p_b \bar{B} - T(K, L, \bar{M}, \bar{B}). \tag{B36}$$

The first-order solutions for an interior solution are:

$$\frac{\partial \Pi}{\partial K} = pf_1 - w_k - T_1 = 0$$

$$\frac{\partial \Pi}{\partial L} = pf_2 - w_l - T_2 = 0 \tag{B38}$$

$$\frac{\partial \Pi}{\partial \bar{M}} = -w_m - T_3 = 0$$

$$\frac{\partial \Pi}{\partial \bar{B}} = r_b p_b - T_4 = 0.$$

Therefore, from equation set (B38) at the optimum $T_3 = \partial T/\partial \bar{M} < 0$, and $T_4 = \partial T/\partial \bar{B} > 0$; that is, an increase in money balances decreases transactions costs, while increases in bond-holdings (and also by assumption capital and labour) increase transactions costs. Hence we find that money is a commodity that is cost-saving with regards to the exchange networks.

B.4.2 *Comparative equilibrium*

Let us, then, investigate the changes in the equilibrium position when the different exogenous variables are altered and, for simplicity, when bonds do not enter the problem. Firstly, the effects of an increase in the product price are found from the following system:

$$
\begin{bmatrix}
pf_{11} - T_{11} & pf_{12} - T_{12} & -T_{13} \\
pf_{21} - T_{21} & pf_{22} - T_{22} & -T_{23} \\
-T_{13} & -T_{23} & -T_{33}
\end{bmatrix}
\begin{bmatrix}
\dfrac{\partial K}{\partial p} \\[4pt]
\dfrac{\partial L}{\partial p} \\[4pt]
\dfrac{\partial \bar{M}}{\partial p}
\end{bmatrix}
=
\begin{bmatrix}
-f_1 \\
-f_2 \\
0
\end{bmatrix}
\qquad \text{(B39)}
$$

$$
\frac{\partial K}{\partial p} = T_{33}f_1 f_2(pf_{22}/f_2 - pf_{12}/f_1)/D
$$
$$
-f_1(T_{33}T_{22} - T_{23}^2)/D + f_2(T_{33}T_{12} - T_{13}T_{23})/D, \qquad \text{(B40)}
$$

where $D < 0$ is the determinant of the matrix on the left side of (B39). Here, if

$$
T_{33}T_{12} - T_{32}T_{13} \leqslant 0 \qquad \text{(B41)}
$$

then $\partial K/\partial p > 0$. Notice the similarity between condition (B22) and (B41) in establishing the result that an increase in the output price leads to an increase in the demand for capital; thus

$$
\frac{\partial L}{\partial p} = T_{33}f_1 f_2(pf_{22}/f_2 - pf_{12}/f_1)/D
$$
$$
- f_1(T_{33}T_{22} - T_{23}^2)/D + f_2(T_{33}T_{12} - T_{13}T_{23})/D, \qquad \text{(B42)}
$$

again by (B41) and, by the assumed concavity, convexity and homogeneity assumptions, the right side of (B42) is positive. Furthermore,

$$
\frac{\partial \bar{M}}{\partial p} = f_1[(pf_{21} - T_{21})T_{23} + (pf_{22} - T_{22})T_{13}]/D
$$
$$
-f_2[pf_{11} - T_{11})T_{23} + (pf_{12} - T_{12})T_{13}]/D, \qquad \text{(B43)}
$$

the right side of which cannot be signed.

An increase in w_k leads to

$$
\frac{\partial K}{\partial w_k} = -[pf_{22}T_{33} + T_{22}T_{33} - T_{32}^2]/D < 0 \qquad \text{(B44)}
$$

since $D < 0$ by the second-order conditions, $f_{ii} < 0$ by the strict concavity of

f, $T_{ii} > 0$ by the strict convexity of T. On the other hand, when we calculate,

$$\frac{\partial L}{\partial w_k} = [T_{33}pf_{21} - (T_{33}T_{12} - T_{13}T_{23})]/D \tag{B45}$$

$$\frac{\partial \bar{M}}{\partial w_k} = [T_{31}(pf_{22} - T_{22}) - T_{32}(pf_{21} - T_{21})]/D \tag{B46}$$

the results are ambiguous. Indeed, we can only establish 'own' effects as opposed to 'cross' effects when the prices of capital, labour and money change, as can be seen from

$$\frac{\partial K}{\partial w_l} = [T_{33}pf_{12} - (T_{33}T_{12} - T_{32}T_{13})]/D, \tag{B47}$$

$$\frac{\partial L}{\partial w_l} = [(T_{33}T_{11} - T_{31}^2) - T_{33}pf_{11}]/D < 0, \tag{B48}$$

and

$$\frac{\partial \bar{M}}{\partial w_l} = [T_{32}(pf_{11} - T_{11}) - T_{31}(pf_{12} - T_{12})]/D. \tag{B49}$$

Thus, for a change in the price of money,

$$\frac{\partial K}{\partial w_m} = (T_{23}T_{12} - T_{23}pf_{12} + T_{13}f_{22}p - T_{13}T_{22})/D, \tag{B50}$$

$$\frac{\partial L}{\partial w_m} = -(T_{11}T_{23} - T_{23}pf_{11} + T_{13}f_{21}p - T_{13}T_{21})/D, \tag{B51}$$

and

$$\frac{\partial \bar{M}}{\partial w_m} = [p^2(f_{11}f_{22} - f_{12}^2) + (T_{11}T_{22} - T_{12}^2)$$
$$- pf_{22}T_{11} - T_{22}pf_{11} + 2T_{12}pf_{21}]/D > 0. \tag{B52}$$

In conclusion, we may note that the Saving model is the most general one in this series, with the two other models being important, but nevertheless special cases. In addition we have shown how each of the frameworks is related through the various institutional arrangements of the transactions process; money in no case was considered as a direct factor of production.

Footnotes

1. The micro-foundations of the monetary theory of the individual was the topic of Appendix A.
2. J. R. Moroney, 'The Current State of Money and Production Theory', p. 335.
3. This technology may or may not be changing.

4. A. Gabor and I. Pearce, 'The Place of Money Capital in the Theory of Production', pp. 540–1.

5. J. R. Moroney, 'The Current State of Money and Production Theory', p. 341.

6. T. Saving, 'Transactions Costs and the Firm's Demand for Money', p. 346.

7. A. Gabor and I. Pearce, 'The Place of Money Capital in the Theory of Production' and T. Saving, 'Transactions Costs and the Firm's Demand for Money'.

8. W. Baumol, 'The Transactions Demand for Cash: An Inventory Theoretic Approach'; S. Fisher, 'Money and the Production Function'; and M. Miller and D. Orr, 'A Model of the Demand for Money by Firms'.

9. O. Lange, 'The Place of Interest in the Theory of Production'; A. Gabor and I. Pearce, 'The Place of Money Capital in the Theory of Production'; and D. Vickers, *The Theory of the Firm: Production, Capital, and Finance*.

10. T. Saving, 'Transactions Costs and the Firm's Demand for Money' and D. Dutton, W. Gramm and J. McDonald, 'Transactions Costs, the Wage Rate, and the Firm's Demand for Money'.

11. S. Fisher, 'Money and the Production Function'; W. Baumol, 'The Transactions Demand for Cash: An Inventory Theoretic Approach'; and M. Miller and D. Orr, 'A Model of the Demand for Money by Firms'.

12. By including $\beta \neq 1$ we have a more realistic way of circumventing the dimension problem associated with equation (B3).

13. We should observe that for the optimal M to be greater than zero given $\beta > 0$, $R > 0$, $w_l > 0$, then $w_m > 0$ so that if $\bar{M}$ earns interest, the costs associated with holding money must exceed the associated revenues. In addition since $L_T = n/p$, then $w_l L_T = w_l(n/\beta)$ and so the average cost per transaction is w_l/β.

14. O. Lange, 'The Place of Interest in the Theory of Production'; A. Gabor and I. Pearce, 'The Place of Money Capital in the Theory of Production'; D. Vickers, *The Theory of the Firm: Production, Capital, and Finance*; D. Vickers, 'The Cost of Capital and the Structure of the Firm'; and S. Turnovsky, 'Financial Structure and the Theory of Production'.

15. T. Saving, 'Transactions Costs and the Firm's Demand for Money' and D. Dutton, W. Gramm and J. McDonald, 'Transactions Costs, the Wage Rate, and the Firm's Demand for Money'.

Bibliography

Ahmad, S. 'Transactions Demand for Money and the Quantity Theory' McMaster University Working Paper #75–04 (April 1975).

Allais, M. 'A Restatement of the Quantity Theory of Money' *American Economic Review* (December 1966).

Almon, S. 'The Distributed Lag between Capital Appropriations and Expenditures' *Econometrica* (January 1965).

Ando, A. and F. Modigliani 'The Relative Stability of Monetary Velocity and the Investment Multiplier' *American Economic Review* (September 1965).

Arrow, K. *Essays in the Theory of Risk-Bearing* (Chicago: Markham, 1971).

Artis, M. and M. Lewis 'The Demand for Money in the United Kingdom, 1963–1973' *Manchester School* (June 1976).

Bailey, M. 'The Welfare Cost of Inflationary Finance' *Journal of Political Economy* (April 1956).

Bank of England 'Competition and Credit Control' articles from the *Quarterly Bulletin*, Vol. 11 (1971).

Barrett, C. and A. Walters 'The Stability of Keynesian and Monetary Multipliers in the United Kingdom' *Review of Economics and Statistics* (November 1966).

Barro, R. 'Inflation, the Payments Period, and the Demand for Money' *Journal of Political Economy* (December 1970).

—— and H. Grossman 'A General Disequilibrium Model of Income and Employment' *American Economic Review* (March 1971).

Baumol, W. J. 'The Transactions Demand for Cash: An Inventory-Theoretic Approach' *Quarterly Journal of Economics* (November 1952).

Becker, W. E. Jr. 'Determinants of the United States Currency–Demand Deposit Ratio' *Journal of Finance* (March 1975).

Benassey, J. 'Neo-Keynesian Disequilibrium Theory in a Monetary Economy' *Review of Economic Studies* (October 1975).

Ben-Zion, U. 'The Cost of Capital and the Demand for Money by Firms' *Journal of Money, Credit, and Banking* (May 1974).

Berglas, E. and A. Razin 'Preferences, Separability and the Patinkin Model: A Comment' *Journal of Political Economy* (January/February 1974).

Bernstein, J. and D. Fisher 'Consumption, the Term Structure of Interest Rates, and the Demand for Money' Concordia University Working Paper (1976).

—— —— 'Weak Separability and Household Behavior in a Monetary Economy' Concordia University Working Paper (1976).

—— —— 'Optimal Portfolios and the Term Structure of Interest Rates' Concordia University Working Paper (1977).

—— —— 'The Demand for Money and the Term Structure of Interest Rates: A Portfolio Approach' mimeo (1977).

Bierwag, G. and M. Grove 'A Model of the Term Structure of Interest Rates' *Review of Economics and Statistics* (February 1967).

Black, F. 'Uniqueness of the Price Level in Monetary Growth Models with Rational Expectations' *Journal of Economic Theory* (January 1974).

Blume, M. E. and I. Friend 'The Asset Structure of Individual Portfolios and Some Implications for Utility Functions' *Journal of Finance* (May 1975).

Borch, K. 'The Rationale of the Mean-Standard Deviation Analysis: Comment' *American Economic Review* (June 1974).

Branson, W. *Macroeconomic Theory and Policy* (New York: Harper and Row, 1972).

Breslaw, J. and D. Fisher 'The Non-Linear Estimate of the Liquidity Trap: British Estimates of a Reformulated Model' Concordia University Working Paper (1976).

Bronfenbrenner, M. and T. Mayer 'Liquidity Functions in the American Economy' *Econometrica* (October 1960).

Brown, A. J. 'Interest, Prices and the Demand Schedule for Idle Money' *Oxford Economic Papers* (May 1939).

Brunner, K. 'Inconsistency and Indeterminacy in Classical Economics' *Econometrica* (April 1951).

—— 'A Survey of Selected Issues in Monetary Theory' *Schweizerische Zeitschrift für Volkswirtschaft und Statistik* (No. 1, 1971).

—— and A. H. Meltzer 'Predicting Velocity: Implications for Theory and Policy' *Journal of Finance* (May 1963).

—— —— 'Economics of Scale in Cash Balances Reconsidered' *Quarterly Journal of Economics* (August 1967).

—— —— 'Liquidity Traps for Money, Bank Credit, and Interest Rates' *Journal of Political Economy* (January/February 1968).

—— —— 'The Uses of Money: Money in the Theory of an Exchange Economy' *American Economic Review* (December 1971).

—— —— 'Friedman's Monetary Theory' *Journal of Political Economy* (September/October 1972).

—— —— 'Money, Debt, and Economic Activity', *Journal of Political Economy* (September/October 1972).

Buchanan, J. M. 'An Outside Economist's Defence of Pesek and Saving' *Journal of Economic Literature* (September 1969).

Buse, A. 'Interest Rates, the Meiselman Model, and Random Numbers' *Journal of Political Economy* (February 1967).

—— 'The Structure of Interest Rates and Recent British Experience: A Comment' *Economica* (August 1967).

—— 'Expectations, Prices, Coupons, and Yields' *Journal of Finance* (September 1970).

Cagan, P. *Determinants and Effects of Changes in the Stock of Money, 1875–1960* (New York: Columbia University Press, 1965).

—— 'The Monetary Dynamics of Hyper-Inflation' in M. Friedman (ed.) *Studies in the Quantity Theory of Money* (Chicago: University Press, 1956).

Campbell, C. 'The Velocity of Money and the Rate of Inflation: Recent Experiences in South Korea and Brazil' in D. Meiselman (ed.) *Varieties of Monetary Experience* (Chicago: University Press, 1970).

Cargill, T. and R. Meyer 'Interest Rates and Prices Since 1950' *International Economic Review* (June 1974).

Carr, J. and L. Smith 'Money Supply, Interest Rates, and the Yield Curve' *Journal of Money, Credit, and Banking* (August 1970).

Cass, D. and J. E. Stiglitz 'Risk Aversion and Wealth Effects on Portfolios with Many Assets' *Review of Economic Studies* (July 1972).

Chetty, V. K. 'On Measuring the Nearness of Near-Moneys' *American Economic Review* (June 1969).

—— 'On Measuring the Nearness of Near-Moneys: Reply' *American Economic Review* (March 1972).

Chitre, V. 'Wealth Effect on the Demand for Money' *Journal of Political Economy* (June 1975).

Chow, G. 'Tests of Equality Between Sets of Coefficients in Two Linear Regressions' (July 1960).

—— 'On the Long-run and Short-run Demand for Money' *Journal of Political Economy* (April 1966).

Clark, C. 'The Demand for Money and the Choice of a Permanent Income Estimate' *Journal of Money, Credit, and Banking* (August 1973).

Classen, E.-M. 'On the Indirect Productivity of Money' *Journal of Political Economy* (April 1975).

Clinton, K. 'The Demand for Money in Canada, 1955–70: Some Single-Equation Estimates and Stability Tests' *Canadian Journal of Economics* (February 1973).

Clower, R. 'Classical Monetary Theory Revisited' *Economica* (May 1963).

—— 'The Keynesian Counter-Revolution: A Theoretical Appraisal' in F. Hahn, F. Brechling (eds.) *The Theory of Interest* (London: Macmillan, 1965).

—— 'A Reconsideration of the Microfoundations of Monetary Theory' *Western Economic Journal* (December 1967).

—— 'The Anatomy of Monetary Theory' *American Economic Review* (February 1977).

—— and J. G. Riley 'The Foundations of Money Illusion in a Neoclassical Micro-Monetary Model: Comment' *American Economic Review* (March 1976).

Conard, J. *An Introduction to the Theory of Interest* (Berkeley: University of California Press, 1959).

—— *The Behavior of Interest Rates* (New York: Columbia University Press, 1966).

Conlisk, J. 'Cross Country Inflation Evidence of the Moneyness of Time Deposits' *Economic Record* (June 1970).

Corbo, V. *Inflation in Developing Countries* (Amsterdam: North-Holland, 1974).

Courchene, T. and H. Shapiro 'The Demand for Money: A Note from the Time Series' *Journal of Political Economy* (October 1964).

Cramer, J. *Empirical Econometrics* (Amsterdam: North-Holland, 1969).

Cropper, M. L. 'A State-Preference Approach to the Precautionary Demand for Money' *American Economic Review* (June 1976).

Culbertson, J. M. 'The Term Structure of Interest Rates' *Quarterly Journal of Economics* (November 1957).

Davidson, P. 'Money and the Real World' *Economic Journal* (March 1972).

—— 'A Keynesian View of Friedman's Theoretical Framework for Monetary Analysis' *Journal of Political Economy* (September/October 1972).

—— *Money and the Real World* (London: Macmillan, 1973).

Davis, R. and J. Guttentag 'Are Compensating Balances Irrational?' *Journal of Finance* (March 1962).

Deaver, J. 'The Chilean Inflation and the Demand for Money' in D. Meiselman (ed.) *Varieties of Monetary Experience* (Chicago: University Press, 1970).

Debreu, G. *Theory of Value* (New York: John Wiley, 1959).

deLeeuw, F. 'The Demand for Money – Speed of Adjustment, Interest Rates, and Wealth' Board of Governors of the Federal Reserve System *Staff Economic Studies* (1965).

DePrano, M. and T. Mayer 'Tests of the Relative Importance of Autonomous Expenditure and Money' *American Economic Review* (September 1965).

Dicks-Mireaux, L. and J. C. Dow 'The Determinants of Wage Inflation: United Kingdom, 1946–56' *Journal of the Royal Statistical Society* (1959).

Dickson, H. and D. R. Starleaf 'Polynomial Distributed Lag Structures in the Demand Function for Money' *Journal of Finance* (December 1972).

Diz, A. 'Money and Prices in Argentina, 1935–1962' in D. Meiselman (ed.) *Varieties of Monetary Experience* (Chicago: University Press, 1970).

Dodds, J. and J. Ford *Expectations, Uncertainty and the Term Structure of Interest Rates* (London: Martin Robertson, 1974).

Dornbusch, R. and J. Frenkel 'Inflation and Growth' *Journal of Money, Credit, and Banking* (February 1973).

Dusansky, R. and P. J. Kalman 'The Real Balance Effect and the Traditional Theory of Consumer Behavior: A Reconciliation' *Journal of Economic Theory* (December 1972); 'Erratum' *Journal of Economic Theory* (February 1973).

—— —— 'The Foundations of Money Illusion in a Neoclassical Micro-Monetary Model' *American Economic Review* (March 1974); 'Errata' *American Economic Review* (December 1974).

—— —— 'The Foundations of Money Illusion in a Neoclassical Micro-Monetary Model: Reply' *American Economic Review* (March 1976).

Dutton, D. S. 'The Demand for Money and the Price Level' *Journal of Political Economy* (September/October 1971).
—— and W. P. Gramm 'Transactions Costs, the Wage Rate, and the Demand for Money' *American Economic Review* (September 1973).
—— —— and J. McDonald 'Transactions Costs, the Wage Rate, and the Firm's Demand for Money' mimeo, University of Iowa (April 1974).
Eisner, R. 'Another Look at Liquidity Preference' *Econometrica* (July 1963).
—— 'Non-Linear Estimates of the Liquidity Trap' *Econometrica* (September 1971).
Fand, D. I. 'Some Implications of Money Supply Analysis' *American Economic Review* (May 1967).
Feige, E. L. *The Demand for Liquid Assets* (Englewood Cliffs, New Jersey: Prentice-Hall, 1964).
—— and M. Parkin 'The Optimal Quantity of Money, Bonds, Commodity Inventories, and Capital' *American Economic Review* (June 1971).
—— —— R. Avery, and C. Stones 'The Roles of Money in an Economy and the Optimum Quantity of Money' *Economica* (November 1973).
—— and P. Swamy 'A Random Coefficient Model of the Demand for Liquid Assets' *Journal of Money, Credit, and Banking* (May 1974).
——'Alternative Temporal Cross-Section Specifications of the Demand for Demand Deposits' in H. Johnson and A. Nobay (eds.) *Issues in Monetary Economics* (Oxford: University Press, 1974).
Fisher, D. 'The Structure of Interest Rates: A Comment' *Economica* (November 1964).
—— 'Expectations, the Term Structure of Interest Rates and Recent British Experience' *Economica* (August 1966).
—— 'The Demand for Money in Britain: Quarterly Results, 1951–1967' *Manchester School* (December 1968).
—— 'Real Balances and the Demand for Money' *Journal of Political Economy* (November/December 1970).
—— 'The Speculative Demand for Money: An Empirical Test' *Economica* (May 1973).
—— 'Wealth Adjustment Effects in a Macroeconomic Model' in M. Parkin and A. Nobay (eds.) *Contemporary Issues in Economics* (Manchester: University Press, 1975).
—— 'The Term Structure of Interest Rates' in R. Thorn (ed.) *Monetary Theory and Policy* (2nd edn.) (New York: Praeger, 1976).
Fisher, I. 'Appreciation and Interest' *American Economic Review* (1898).
—— *The Purchasing Power of Money* (New York: Augustus M. Kelley, 1963).
—— *The Theory of Interest* (New York: Augustus M. Kelley, 1965).
Fisher, S. 'Keynes-Wicksell and Neoclassical Models of Money and Growth' *American Economic Review* (December 1972).
—— 'Money and the Production Function' *Economic Inquiry* (December 1974).
Foster, E. 'Costs and Benefits of Inflation' *Studies in Monetary Economics* (Federal Reserve Bank of Minneapolis, 1972).
Frenkel, J. 'The Forward Exchange Rate, Expectations, and the Demand for Money: the German Hyperinflation' University of Chicago mimeo (1976).
—— and C. Rodriquez 'Wealth Effects and the Dynamics of Inflation' *Journal of Money, Credit, and Banking* (May 1975).
Freund, R. J. 'The Introduction of Risk into a Programming Model' *Econometrica* (July 1956).
Friedman, M. 'Prices, Income, and Monetary Change in Three Wartime Periods' *American Economic Review* (May 1952).
——'The Quantity Theory of Money: A Restatement' in M. Friedman (ed.) *Studies in the Quantity Theory of Money* (Chicago: University Press, 1956).
—— *A Theory of the Consumption Function* (Princeton: University Press, 1957).
—— *A Program for Monetary Stability* (New York: Fordham University Press, 1960).
—— 'Post-War Trends in Monetary Theory and Policy' *National Banking Review* (September 1964).
—— 'Interest Rates and the Demand for Money' *The Journal of Law and Economics* (October 1966).

—— 'The Optimum Quantity of Money' in M. Friedman *The Optimum Quantity of Money and Other Essays* (Chicago: Aldine, 1969).

—— 'The Demand for Money: Some Theoretical and Empirical Results' in M. Friedman *The Optimum Quantity of Money and Other Essays* (Chicago: Aldine, 1969).

—— *The Optimum Quantity of Money and Other Essays* (Chicago: Aldine, 1969).

—— 'The Monetary Studies of the National Bureau' in M. Friedman *The Optimum Quantity of Money and Other Essays* (Chicago: Aldine, 1969).

—— 'A Theoretical Framework for Monetary Analysis' *Journal of Political Economy* (March/April 1970).

—— 'A Monetary Theory of Nominal Income' *Journal of Political Economy* (March/April 1971).

—— 'Government Revenue from Inflation' *Journal of Political Economy* (July 1971).

—— 'Comments on the Critics' *Journal of Political Economy* (September/October 1972).

—— and W. Heller, *Monetary Versus Fiscal Policy* (New York: Norton, 1969).

—— and D. Meiselman 'The Relative Stability of Monetary Velocity and the Investment Multiplier in the United States, 1897–1958' in E. C. Brown *et al.*, *Stabilization Policies* (Englewood Cliffs, New Jersey: Prentice-Hall, 1963).

—— and A. J. Schwartz, *A Monetary History of the United States*, 1867–1960 (New York: Columbia University Press, 1963).

—— —— *Monetary Statistics of the United States* (New York: Columbia University Press, 1970).

Frost, P. 'Banking Services, Minimum Cash Balances, and the Firm's Demand for Money' *Journal of Finance* (December 1970).

Gabor, A. and I. Pearce 'The Place of Money Capital in the Theory of Production' *Quarterly Journal of Economics* (November 1958).

Gandolfi, A. E. 'Stability of the Demand for Money During the Great Contraction 1929–1933' *Journal of Political Economy* (September/October 1974).

—— and J. Lothian 'The Demand for Money from the Great Depression to the Present' *American Economic Review* (May 1976).

Geary, P. T. and M. Morishima 'Demand and Supply under Separability' in M. Morishima, *et al.*, *Theory of Demand, Real and Monetary* (Oxford: University Press, 1973).

Gibson, W. 'Demand and Supply Functions for Money in the United States: Theory and Measurement' *Econometrica* (March 1972).

—— 'Interest Rates and Inflationary Expectations: New Evidence' *American Economic Review* (December 1972).

—— 'Demand and Supply Functions for Money: A Comment' *Econometrica* (March 1976).

Goldfeld, S. 'The Demand for Money Revisited' *Brookings Papers on Economic Activity* (No. 3, 1973).

Goldman, S. M. 'Flexibility and the Demand for Money' *Journal of Economic Theory* (October 1974).

Goodhart, C. *Money, Information and Uncertainty* (London: Macmillan, 1975).

—— and A. Crockett 'The Importance of Money' *Bank of England Quarterly Bulletin* (June 1970).

Grandmont, J.-M. 'On the Short-Run and Long-Run Demand for Money' *European Economic Review* (No. 4, 1973).

—— and G. Laroque 'The Liquidity Trap' *Econometrica* (January 1976).

—— —— 'On Temporary Keynesian Equilibria' *Review of Economic Studies* (February 1976).

Grant, J. 'Meiselman on the Structure of Interest Rates' *Economica* (February 1964).

Gray, M. and M. Parkin 'Portfolio Diversification as Optimal Precautionary Behaviour' in M. Morishima, *et al.*, *Theory of Demand, Real and Monetary* (Oxford: University Press, 1973).

Green, H. *Aggregation in Economic Analysis* (Princeton: University Press, 1964).

Green, J. 'A Simple General Equilibrium Model of the Term Structure of Interest Rates' Harvard Institute of Economic Research, Discussion Paper (March 1971).

—— 'Temporal General Equilibrium in a Sequential Trading Model with Spot and Futures Transactions' *Econometrica* (November 1973).

Griliches, Z. 'A Note on Serial Correlation Bias in Estimates of Distributed Lags' *Econometrica* (January 1961).

Grossman, H. 'Money, Interest, and Prices in Market Disequilibrium' *Journal of Political Economy* (September/October 1971).
—— 'The Nature of Quantities in Market Disequilibrium' *American Economic Review* (June 1974).
—— and A. Policano 'Money Balances, Commodity Inventories, and Inflationary Expectations' *Journal of Political Economy* (December 1975).
Gurley, J. and E. Shaw *Money in a Theory of Finance* (Washington: Brookings Institution, 1960).
Haache, G. 'The Demand for Money in the United Kingdom: Experience Since 1971' *Bank of England Quarterly Bulletin* (September 1974).
Hahn, F. 'Professor Friedman's Views on Money' *Economica* (February 1971).
—— 'Equilibrium with Transactions Costs' *Econometrica* (May 1971).
—— 'On Transactions Costs, Inessential Sequence Economies and Money' *Review of Economic Studies* (October 1973).
Hamburger, M. 'The Demand for Money by Households, Money Substitutes, and Monetary Policy' *Journal of Political Economy* (December 1966).
Hammond, B. *Money and Politics in America* (Princeton: University Press, 1957).
Harberger, A. 'The Dynamics of Inflation in Chile' in *Measurements in Economics: Studies in Mathematical Economics in Memory of Yehuda Grunfeld* (Palo Alto: Stanford University Press, 1963).
Harris, S. (ed.) *The New Economics* (New York: Alfred A. Knopf, 1947).
Hart, O. 'A Proof of the Impossibility of Obtaining General Wealth Comparative Statics Properties in Portfolio Theory' Princeton University (mimeo) (1974).
Heller, H. R. 'The Demand for Money: The Evidence from the Short-run Data' *Quarterly Journal of Economics* (May 1965).
Henderson, J. and R. Quandt *Microeconomic Theory* (2nd edn.) (New York: McGraw-Hill, 1971).
Hicks, J. R. 'Mr. Keynes and the "Classics"; A Suggested Interpretation' *Econometrica* (July 1937).
—— *Value and Capital* (Oxford: University Press, 1946).
—— *Capital and Growth* (Oxford: University Press, 1965).
—— *Critical Essays in Monetary Theory* (Oxford: University Press, 1967).
Hulett, D. 'More on an Empirical Definition of Money: Note' *American Economic Review* (June 1971).
Hynes, J. 'On the Theory of Real Balance Effects' *Journal of Money, Credit, and Banking* (February 1974).
Jacobs, R. L. 'Estimating the Long-Run Demand for Money from Time-Series Data' *Journal of Political Economy* (November/December 1974).
—— 'A Difficulty with Monetarist Models of Hyperinflation' *Economic Inquiry* (December 1975).
Jensen, M. (ed.) *Studies in the Theory of Capital Markets* (New York: Praeger, 1972).
Johnson, H. G. 'Monetary Theory and Policy' *American Economic Review* (June 1962).
—— 'Recent Developments in Monetary Theory – a Commentary' in D. Croome and H. G. Johnson (eds.) *Money in Britain, 1959–1969* (Oxford: University Press, 1970).
—— 'Keynes' General Theory: Revolution or War of Independence' *Canadian Journal of Economics* (November 1976).
Johnston, J. *Econometric Methods* (2nd edn.) (New York: McGraw–Hill, 1972).
Kalman, P. J., R. Dusansky and B. Wickström 'On the Major Slutsky Properties When Money is the Sole Medium of Exchange' *International Economic Review* (October 1974).
Karni, E. 'Inflation and the Real Interest Rate: a Long Term Analysis' *Journal of Political Economy* (March/April 1972).
—— 'The Transactions Demand for Cash: Incorporation of the Value of Time into the Inventory Approach' *Journal of Political Economy* (September/October, 1973).
—— 'The Value of Time and the Demand for Money' *Journal of Money, Credit, and Banking* (February 1974).

—— 'The Value of Time and the Demand for Money: Evidence from UK Time Series Data' *Australian Economic Papers* (December 1975).

—— and U. Ben-Zion 'The Utility of Money and the Transactions Demand for Cash' *Canadian Journal of Economics* (February 1976).

Kaufman, G. 'The Demand for Currency' Board of Governors of the Federal Reserve System, *Staff Economic Studies* (January 1966).

Keran, M. 'Selecting a Monetary Indicator – Evidence from the United States and Other Developed Countries' *Federal Reserve Bank of St. Louis Review* (September 1970).

Kessel, R. *The Cyclical Behavior of the Term Structure of Interest Rates* (New York: Columbia University Press, 1965).

Keynes, J. M. 'The Ex-Ante Theory of the Rate of Interest' *Economic Journal* (June 1937).

—— *A Treatise on Money* (2 volumes) (London: Macmillan, 1958 (1930)).

—— *The General Theory of Employment, Interest and Money* (New York: Harcourt, Brace, 1936).

Khan, M. 'The Stability of the Demand-for-Money Function in the United States, 1901–1965' *Journal of Political Economy* (November/December 1974).

Khusro, A. 'An Interpretation of Liquidity Preference' *Yorkshire Bulletin of Economic and Social Research* (January 1952).

Klein, B. 'Competitive Interest Payments on Bank Deposits and the Long-run Demand for Money' *American Economic Review* (December 1974).

Klein, L. R. *Economic Fluctuations in the United States: 1921–1941* (New York: John Wiley, 1950).

Konstas, P. and M. Khouja 'The Keynesian Demand-for-Money Function: Another Look and Some Additional Evidence' *Journal of Money, Credit, and Banking* (November 1969).

Laffer, A. 'Trade Credit and the Money Market' *Journal of Political Economy* (March/April 1970).

Laidler, D. 'Some Evidence on the Demand for Money' *Journal of Political Economy* (February 1966).

—— 'The Rate of Interest and the Demand for Money' *Journal of Political Economy* (December 1966).

—— 'The Definition of Money: Theoretical and Empirical Problems' *Journal of Money, Credit, and Banking* (August 1969).

—— *The Demand for Money: Theories and Evidence* (Scranton, Pennsylvania: International Textbook Company, 1969).

—— and M. Parkin 'The Demand for Money in the United Kingdom, 1956–1967: Preliminary Results' *Manchester School* (September 1970).

Lancaster, K. 'A New Approach to Consumer Theory' *Journal of Political Economy* (April 1966).

—— *Mathematical Economics* (New York: Macmillan, 1968).

Lange, O. 'The Place of Interest in the Theory of Production' *Review of Economic Studies* (June 1936).

—— 'Say's Law: A Restatement and Criticism' in O. Lange, *et al., Studies in Mathematical Economics and Econometrics* (Chicago: University Press, 1942).

Laumas G. 'The Degree of Moneyness of Savings Deposits' *American Economic Review* (June 1968).

—— and P. Laumas 'The Definition of Money and the Relative Importance of Autonomous Expenditures and Money' *Metroeconomica* (April 1970).

Lee, T. H. 'Substitutability of Non-Bank Intermediary Liabilities for Money: The Empirical Evidence' *Journal of Finance* (September 1966).

—— 'On Measuring the Nearness of Near-Moneys: Comment' *American Economic Review* (March 1972).

Leijonhufvud, A. *On Keynesian Economics and the Economics of Keynes* (New York: Oxford University Press, 1968).

Lerner, E. 'Inflation in the Confederacy, 1861–65' in M. Friedman (ed.) *Studies in the Quantity Theory of Money* (Chicago: University Press, 1956).

Lipsey, R. 'The Micro Theory of the Phillips Curve Reconsidered: A Reply to Holmes and Smyth' *Economica* (February 1974).

Lloyd, C. 'The Real Balance Effect and the Slutsky Equation' *Journal of Political Economy* (June 1964).

—— 'On the Real Balance Effect: A Reply' *Oxford Economic Papers* (March 1966).

—— 'Two Classical Monetary Models' in J. Wolfe (ed.) *Value, Capital and Growth* (Edinburgh: University Press, 1968).

—— 'Preferences, Separability, and the Patinkin Model' *Journal of Political Economy* (May/June 1971).

—— 'The Microfoundations of Monetary Theory: Comment' *Western Economic Journal* (September 1971).

Luckett, D. 'Multiperiod Expectations and the Term Structure of Interest Rates' *Quarterly Journal of Economics* (May 1967).

Lutz, F. A. 'The Structure of Interest Rates' *Quarterly Journal of Economics* (November 1940).

McCall, J. J. 'Differences Between the Personal Demand for Money and the Business Demand for Money' *Journal of Political Economy* (August 1960).

McCallum, B. 'Friedman's Missing Equation: Another Approach' *Manchester School* (September 1973).

McCallum, J. 'Expected Holding Period Return, Uncertainty, and the Term Structure of Interest Rates' *Journal of Finance* (May 1975).

McCulloch, J. 'Measuring the Term Structure of Interest Rates' *Journal of Business* (January 1971).

—— 'An Estimate of the Liquidity Premium' *Journal of Political Economy* (January 1975).

—— 'The Tax-Adjusted Yield Curve' *Journal of Finance* (June 1975).

Macesich, G. 'Supply and Demand for Money in Canada' in D. Meiselman (ed.) *Varieties of Monetary Experience* (Chicago: University Press, 1970).

Maddala, G. S. and R. C. Vogel 'The Demand for Money: A Cross-Section Study of Business Firms: Comment' *Quarterly Journal of Economics* (February 1965).

Malkiel, B. *The Term Structure of Interest Rates* (Princeton: University Press, 1966).

Markowitz, H. 'Portfolio Selection' *Journal of Finance* (March 1952).

—— *Portfolio Selection* (New York: John Wiley, 1959).

Marschak, J. 'The Rationale of the Demand for Money and of Money Illusion' *Metroeconomica* (August 1950).

Marty, A. 'Growth and the Welfare Cost of Inflationary Finance' *Journal of Political Economy* (February 1967).

Masera, R. *The Term Structure of Interest Rates* (Oxford: Clarendon Press, 1972).

Meigs, A. J. *Free Reserves and the Money Supply* (Chicago: University Press, 1962).

Meinich, P. 'Money Illusion and the Real Balance Effect' *Statskonomisk Tidsskrift* (January 1964).

—— 'Lloyd and the Real Balance Effect' *Oxford Economic Papers* (November 1964).

Meiselman, D. *The Term Structure of Interest Rates* (Englewood Cliffs, New Jersey: Prentice-Hall, 1962).

—— 'Bond Yields and the Price Level: The Gibson Paradox Regained' in D. Carson (ed.) *Banking and Monetary Studies* (Homewood, Illinois: Richard D. Irwin, 1963).

—— (ed.) *Varieties of Monetary Experience* (Chicago: University Press, 1970).

Melitz, J. 'Inflationary Expectations and the French Demand for Money, 1959–70' *Manchester School* (March 1976).

Meltzer, A. H. 'The Demand for Money: The Evidence From the Time Series' *Journal of Political Economy* (June 1963).

—— 'Yet Another Look at the Low Level Liquidity Trap' *Econometrica* (July 1963).

—— 'The Demand for Money: A Cross-Section Study of Business Firms' *Quarterly Journal of Economics* (August 1963).

Metzler, L. 'Wealth, Saving and the Rate of Interest' *Journal of Political Economy* (April 1951).

Meyer, L. 'Wealth Effects and the Effectiveness of Monetary and Fiscal Policy' *Journal of Money, Credit, and Banking* (November 1974).

—— 'Alternative Definitions of the Money Stock and the Demand for Money' *Federal Reserve Bank of New York Monthly Review* (October 1976).

Meyer, P. A. and J. A. Neri 'A Keynes–Friedman Money Demand Function' *American Economic Review* (September 1975).

Michaelsen, J. 'The Term Structure of Interest Rates and Holding Period Yields on Government Securities' *Journal of Finance* (September 1965).

Miller, M. and D. Orr 'A Model of the Demand for Money by Firms' *Quarterly Journal of Economics* (August 1966).

—— —— 'The Demand for Money by Firms: Extension of Analytic Results' *Journal of Finance* (December 1968).

Mills, T. 'Sensitivity and Stability of the UK Demand for Money Function, 1963–1974' Warwick Discussion Paper (November 1975).

Modigliani, F. and M. Miller 'The Cost of Capital, Corporation Finance, and the Theory of Investment' *American Economic Review* (June 1958).

Modigliani, F. and R. Shiller 'Inflation, Rational Expectations, and the Term Structure of Interest Rates' *Economica* (February 1973).

—— and R. Sutch 'Debt Management and the Term Structure of Interest Rates: An Empirical Analysis of Recent Experience' *Journal of Political Economy* (August 1967).

Morishima, M. 'Consumer Behavior and Liquidity Preference' in M. Morishima *et al.*, *Theory of Demand, Real and Monetary* (Oxford: University Press, 1973).

Morgan, E. V. 'The Essential Qualities of Money' *Manchester School* (September 1969).

Moroney, J. 'The Current State of Money and Production Theory' *American Economic Review* (May 1972).

—— and B. Wilbratte 'Money and Money Substitutes' *Journal of Money, Credit, and Banking* (May 1976).

Motley, B. 'The Consumer's Demand for Money: A Neoclassical Approach' *Journal of Political Economy* (September/October 1969).

Mundell, R. *Monetary Theory* (Pacific Palisades: Goodyear, 1971).

Muth, J. 'Rational Expectations and the Theory of Price Movements' *Econometrica* (July 1961).

Nadiri, M. 'The Determinants of Real Cash Balances in the US Total Manufacturing Sector' *Quarterly Journal of Economics* (May 1969).

Näslund, B. 'Some Effects of Taxes on Risk-Taking' *Review of Economic Studies* (July 1968).

Nelson, C. *The Term Structure of Interest Rates* (New York: Basic Books, 1972).

Newlyn, W. T. *Theory of Money* (2nd edn.) (Oxford: Clarendon Press, 1971).

—— 'The Essential Qualities of Money: A Note' *Manchester School* (December 1972).

Nichols, D. 'Some Principles of Inflationary Finance' *Journal of Political Economy* (March/April 1974).

Niehans, J. 'Money in a Static Theory of Optimal Payment Arrangements' *Journal of Money, Credit, and Banking* (November 1969).

Orr, D. 'A Note on the Uselessness of Transactions Demand Models' *Journal of Finance* (December 1974).

Ostroy, J. 'The Informational Efficiency of Monetary Exchange' *American Economic Review* (September 1973).

Park, Y. 'Some Current Issues on the Transmission Process of Monetary Policy' IMF *Staff Papers* (March 1972).

Parkin, M. 'Discount House Portfolio and Debt Selection' *Review of Economic Studies* (October 1970).

——, R. Barrett and M. Gray 'The Demand for Financial Assets by the Personal Sector of the UK Economy' Proceedings of the London Business School Conference on *Modelling the UK Economy* (June 1972).

——, M. R. Gray and R. J. Barrett 'The Portfolio Behaviour of Commercial Banks' in D. Heathfield and K. Hilton (eds.) *The Econometric Model of the United Kingdom* (London: Macmillan, 1970).

Patinkin, D. *Money, Interest, and Prices* (2nd edn.) (New York: Harper and Row, 1965).

—— 'Money and Wealth: A Review Article' *Journal of Economic Literature* (December 1969).

Perlman, M. 'The Roles of Money in an Economy and the Optimum Quantity of Money: Reply' *Economica* (November 1973).

Pesando, J. 'A Note on the Rationality of the Livingston Price Expectations' *Journal of Political Economy* (August 1975).

Pesek, B. and T. Saving *Money, Wealth, and Economic Theory* (New York: Macmillan, 1967).

Pierce, D. and D. Shaw *Monetary Economics* (London: Butterworth, 1974).

Pifer, H. 'A Non-Linear Maximum Likelihood Estimate of the Liquidity Trap' *Econometrica* (April 1969).

Pigou, A. 'Economic Progress in a Stable Environment' *Economica* (August 1947).

—— *The Veil of Money* (London: Macmillan, 1949).

Poole, W. and E. Kornbluth 'The Friedman–Meiselman CMC Paper: New Evidence on an Old Controversy' *American Economic Review* (December 1973).

Prais, Z. 'Real Money Balances as a Variable in the Production Function: Comment' *Journal of Money, Credit, and Banking* (November 1975).

Price, L. 'The Demand for Money in the United Kingdom: A Further Investigation' *Bank of England Quarterly Bulletin* (March 1972).

Radcliffe Report of the Committee on the Workings of the Monetary System (London: HMSO, August 1959).

Robinson, J. 'The Rate of Interest' *Econometrica* (April 1951).

Roll, R. *The Behavior of Interest Rates* (New York: Basic Books, 1970).

—— 'Interest Rates and Price Expectations During the Civil War' *Journal of Economic History* (June 1972).

—— 'Rational Response to the Money Supply' *Journal of Political Economy* (May/June 1974).

Rutledge, J. *A Monetarist Model of Inflationary Expectations* (Lexington, Massachusetts: D. C. Heath, 1974).

Samuelson, P. A. *The Foundations of Economic Analysis* (Cambridge, Massachusetts: Harvard University Press, 1945).

—— 'What Classical Monetary Theory Really Was' *Canadian Journal of Economics* (February 1968).

—— 'The Fundamental Approximation Theorem of Portfolio Analysis in Terms of Means, Variances, and Higher Moments' *Review of Economic Studies* (October 1970).

Santomero, A. 'A Model of the Demand for Money by Households' *Journal of Finance* (March 1974).

—— 'On the Role of Transactions Costs and the Rates of Return on the Demand Deposit Decision' Federal Reserve Bank of Philadelphia Research Papers (October 1975).

Sargent, T. 'Interest Rates and Prices in the Long Run: A Study of the Gibson Paradox' *Journal of Money, Credit, and Banking* (February 1973).

—— 'Rational Expectations, the Real Rate of Interest, and the Natural Rate of Unemployment' *Brookings Papers on Economic Activity* (No. 3, 1973).

—— and N. Wallace 'The Stability of Models of Money and Growth with Perfect Foresight' *Econometrica* (November 1973).

Sastry, A. 'The Effect of Credit on Transactions Demand for Cash' *Journal of Finance* (September 1970).

Saving, T. 'Outside Money, Inside Money, and the Real Balance Effect' *Journal of Money, Credit, and Banking* (February 1970).

—— 'Transactions Costs and the Demand for Money' *American Economic Review* (June 1971).

—— 'Transactions Costs and the Firm's Demand for Money' *Journal of Money, Credit, and Banking* (May 1972).

Selden, R. T. 'Monetary Velocity in the United States' in M. Friedman (ed.) *Studies in the Quantity Theory of Money* (Chicago: University Press, 1956).

—— 'The Post-War Rise in the Velocity of Money – A Sectoral Analysis' *Journal of Finance* (December 1961).

Shackle, G. *Uncertainty in Economics* (Cambridge: University Press, 1955).

Shapiro, A. A. 'Inflation, Lags, and the Demand for Money' *International Economic Review* (February 1973).

Sheehey, E. 'The Dynamics of Inflation in Latin America: Comment' *American Economic Review* (September 1976).

Shell, K. 'Selected Elementary Topics in the Theory of Economic Decision-Making Under Uncertainty' in B. Szegö and K. Shell *Mathematical Methods in Investment and Finance* (Amsterdam: North-Holland, 1972).

Sidrauski, M. 'Inflation and Economic Growth' *Journal of Political Economy* (December 1967).

Sinai, A. and H. Stokes 'Real Money Balances: An Omitted Variable from the Production Function?' *Review of Economics and Statistics* (August 1972).

Slovin, M. and M. Sushka 'The Structural Shift in the Demand for Money,' *Journal of Finance* (June 1975).

Smith, W. L. 'On Some Current Issues in Monetary Economics: An Interpretation' *Journal of Economic Literature* (September 1970).

Sono, M. 'The Effect of Price Changes on the Demand and Supply of Separable Goods' *International Economic Review* (September 1961).

Spitzer, J. 'The Demand for Money, the Liquidity Trap, and Functional Form' *International Economic Review* (February 1976).

Sprenkle, C. 'The Uselessness of Transactions Demand Models' *Journal of Finance* (December 1969).

—— 'On the Observed Transactions Demand for Money' *Manchester School* (September 1972).

Starleaf, D. R. and R. Reimer 'The Keynesian Demand Function for Money: Some Statistical Tests' *Journal of Finance* (March 1967).

Starrett, D. 'Inefficiency and the Demand for "Money" in a Sequence Economy' *Review of Economic Studies* (October 1973).

Stein, J. 'Neoclassical and Keynes–Wicksell Monetary Growth Models' *Journal of Money, Credit, and Banking* (May 1969).

—— *Money and Capacity Growth* (New York: Columbia University Press, 1971).

Steindl, F. 'Money and Bonds as Giffen Goods' *Manchester School* (December 1973).

Stiglitz, J. 'A Consumption-Oriented Theory of the Demand for Financial Assets and the Term Structure of Interest Rates' *Review of Economic Studies* (October 1967).

Tanner, J. 'The Indicators of Monetary Policy: An Evaluation of Five' *Banco Nazionale del Lavoro, Quarterly Review* (December 1972).

Teigen, R. 'Demand and Supply Functions for Money: Another Look at Theory and Measurement' *Econometrica* (March 1976).

—— 'Demand and Supply Functions in the United States: Some Structural Estimates' *Econometrica* (October 1964).

Thomas, J. J. 'Some Aggregative Problems in the Estimation of Partial Adjustment Models of the Demand for Money' *Recherches Economiques de Louvain* (June 1975).

Thompson, E. 'Intertemporal Utility Functions and the Long Run Consumption Function' *Econometrica* (April 1967).

Timberlake, R. and J. Fortson 'Time Deposits in the Definition of Money' *American Economic Review* (March 1967).

Tobin, J. 'Liquidity Preference and Monetary Policy' *Review of Economics and Statistics* (May 1947).

—— 'The Interest Elasticity of the Transactions Demand for Cash' *Review of Economics and Statistics* (August 1956).

—— 'Liquidity Preference as Behaviour Towards Risk' *Review of Economic Studies* (February 1958).

—— 'Money, Capital, and Other Stores of Value' *American Economic Review* (May 1961).

—— 'The Theory of Portfolio Selection' in F. Hahn and F. Brechling (eds.) *The Theory of Interest Rates* (London: Macmillan, 1965).

—— 'Friedman's Theoretical Framework' *Journal of Political Economy* (September/October 1972).

Tooke, T. *A History of Prices* 6 vols. (New York: Adelphi, 1836–57).

Tsiang, S. C. 'The Precautionary Demand for Money: An Inventory-Theoretical Analysis' *Journal of Political Economy* (January/February 1969).

—— 'The Rationale of the Mean-Standard Deviation Analysis, Skewness Preference, and the Demand for Money' *American Economic Review* (June 1972).

Tucker, D. 'Macroeconomic Models and the Demand for Money Under Market Disequilibrium' *Journal of Money, Credit, and Banking* (February 1971).

Tullock, G. 'Competing Monies' *Journal of Money, Credit, and Banking* (November 1975).

Turnovsky, S. 'Financial Structure and the Theory of Production' *Journal of Finance* (December 1970).

—— and M. Wachter 'A Test of the "Expectations Hypothesis" Using Directly Observed Wage and Price Expectations' *Review of Economics and Statistics* (February 1972).

Ulph, A. and D. Ulph 'Transactions Costs in General Equilibrium Theory' *Economica* (November 1975).

Van Doorn, J. *Disequilibrium Economics* (London: Macmillan, 1975).

Vickers, D. *The Theory of the Firm: Production, Capital, and Finance* (New York; McGraw-Hill, 1968).

—— 'The Cost of Capital and the Structure of the Firm' *Journal of Finance* (March 1970).

Vogel, R. 'The Dynamics of Inflation in Latin America' *American Economic Review* (March 1974).

Walters, A. 'Monetary Multipliers in the U.K., 1880–1962' *Oxford Economic Papers* (November 1966).

—— 'The Radcliffe Report – Ten Years After. A Survey of Empirical Evidence' in D. Croome and H. Johnson (eds.) *Money in Britain, 1959–1969* (Oxford: University Press, 1970).

—— and N. Kavanagh 'The Demand for Money in the United Kingdom, 1877–1961: Some Preliminary Findings' *Oxford Institute of Statistics Bulletin* (May 1966).

Waud, R. 'Net Outlay Uncertainty and Liquidity Preference as Behavior Toward Risk' *Journal of Money, Credit, and Banking* (November 1975).

Wehrle, L. 'Life Insurance Investment: the Experience of Four Companies' in J. Tobin and D. Hester (eds.) *Studies in Portfolio Behavior* (New York: John Wiley, 1967).

Weinrobe, M. 'A Simple Model of the Precautionary Demand for Money' *Southern Economic Journal* (July 1972).

—— 'The Demand for Money by Six Non-Bank Financial Intermediaries' *Western Economic Journal* (June 1973).

Whalen, E. L. 'A Cross-Section Study of Business Demand for Cash' *Journal of Finance* (September 1965).

—— 'A Rationalization of the Precautionary Demand for Cash' *Quarterly Journal of Economics* (May 1966).

White, K. 'Estimation of the Liquidity Trap with a Generalized Functional Form' *Econometrica* (January 1972).

—— 'The Effect of Bank Credit Cards on the Household Transactions Demand for Money' *Journal of Money, Credit, and Banking* (February 1976).

Wicksell, K. *Interest and Prices* (New York: Augustus M. Kelley, 1965).

Wicksteed, P. *The Common Sense of Political Economy* (revised edn.) Vol. 1 (London: Routledge and Kegan Paul, 1933).

Wood, J. 'Expectations and the Demand for Bonds' *American Economic Review* (September 1969).

Yeager, L. B. 'Essential Properties of the Medium of Exchange' *Kyklos* (No. 1, 1968).

Young, R. and C. Yager, 'The Economics of "Bills Preferably"' *Quarterly Journal of Economics* (August 1960).

Zellner, A. D. Huang and L. Chau 'Further Analysis of the Short-run Consumption Function' *Econometrica* (July 1965).

Index